Saturday's Child

10/2/05

Dear Theresa,
So nice to have
met you. I wish you
the very best.
Ernestine L. Martin

Saturday's Child

BY ERNESTINE L. MARTIN

CHAPEL HILL
PRESS, INC.

ISBN Number 1-880849-67-4
Library of Congress Catalog Number 2003109703

Printed in the United States of America
08 07 06 05 04   10 9 8 7 6 5 4 3 2

Dedication

TO MY GRANDCHILDREN One of the most important lessons in life is to learn to be your own person. Have courage, strength, and belief in yourself. Don't be afraid to live in the real world. Whatever you do, don't expect life to be like the fairy-tales we read to you during your childhood. Life is generally not "and they lived happily ever after." Few are that fortunate. Don't wear blinders to cover what you don't want to see. Never allow your pride to become so important that you will not admit you're wrong when you are. Never use stubbornness or meanness as a weapon. Don't be afraid to wander beyond your little circle of family and friends. You will find it fascinating, rewarding, and yes, at times, even disappointing. It's a big world out there! Go out and enjoy it, and try to leave a little of yourself behind for the next generation to enjoy.

Rewarding as living can be, however, life will have its disappointments as well. Learn to walk away from them without bitterness and then move on. Regardless, it will open your eyes to how others think, feel, and live. It will instill within you a better understanding of the world that encircles your life. At the same time, it opens your mind even more, allowing more choices in your actions and thoughts. The rewards are tremendous. Treat everyone the way you would want them to treat you. Honesty is still the best policy. Have and show compassion to those less fortunate than you, not pity. They don't want that. To be handicapped in any way, physically or mentally, can make life more difficult than it is already. Never forget: *There, but for the grace of God, go I.*

As I sit here writing this dedication to each of you, I hope that my memoirs will help you in some little way as you travel down the road of life. Don't let your success in life be based on just monetary wealth: it will mean little unless you use it wisely. Most of my life was built around fear, a lack of will to exercise my own strength, and the inability to become my own person. Through God's help, I overcame each one. It took years, filled with tears, and a courage that I never knew I had until I stood up and faced myself. I have lived long enough to know that no one is perfect. We all have faults. Give life your best shot. You only go around once, so make sure you don't waste it. Today, when I look back on where I came from, the trials and tribulations throughout most of my life and my ability to survive them, it gives me a good feeling about myself. After having gone through it all, I found a person I really like: me (also known as "Buddy" or "Grandma"). Make the most of each day. You never know if it will be your last.

May your lives never be a disappointment to you, and remember, only you can create the person you want to be. I know that I have given you a little more food for thought, but each of you has had a good upbringing, and this, all by itself, makes me proud to be your grandmother. I leave each of you with this one thought: my little angel and I will always be with you, looking over your shoulder and knowing when you need a little help, a little push.

My life stories, set down here to the best of my memory, are not meant to offend anyone. They are my impressions and opinions of the events and times that made up my life. Other people I speak of within the many pages of *Saturday's Child* may feel offended by my words, but they are as entitled to their opinions as I am to mine. The bits and pieces of each of my stories are based on the truth as I saw it, as I lived it, and as I remembered it, considering my age.

Contents

THE BEGINNING xiii

MY BIRTHPLACE, MY HOME 1

   Knollcroft 1

   My Family: New Jersey 2

MY CHILDHOOD 7

   Mandy, My Beloved Mammy 7

   Eula's Story 10

   Polly, Our Parrot 15

   My First Job 17

   My Best Friend, Eunice, and Her Family 19

   My Playhouse 23

   Quarantine Signs 24

   Grammar School 24

   The Famous Knollcroft Dogs 25

   Circus Time 31

   Vendors of the 1930s 34

   Grandfather Ritter's Death 36

"The Martians Are Coming!" 38

1930s–1940s: Favorite Ice Cream Stores 40

"Those Girls" 41

The Cherry, Mulberry, and Chestnut Trees 43

My Sixth Grade Teacher, Miss Cowan 45

"The Old Ladies" 46

Fourth of July 49

Visiting Grandparents in North Carolina 50

Visiting Family in Brunswick, Georgia 73

The Ride that Made Me Claustrophobic 76

The Gypsies 79

The Elliott Street Gang 83

April Fools' Day 93

Craig's Bobsled 94

Ice Skating 95

Walt's "Old Jug" Car and Sidecar Cycle 96

"Monopoly" and Swimming 96

Archie's Road Stand 97

Unusual Characters in Our Neighborhood 99

    Old Man Beech and His Wife 99

    Old Dickie Hunt 100

    Old Mrs. Gordon and Her Daughter, Edna 102

The Hoboes, Tramps, and the CCC Camps 103

Spunky and the Wedding Cake 104

Halloween 107

Wine Making and Wine Tasting 110

Old-Fashioned Fun 112

Explosion at Hercules Powder Company 117

World War II 118

My Sister, Florence 130

My Younger Sister, Pauline 137

My Buddy, Sid 138

My Job at Western Union 150

Events Leading Up to Graduation Day 152

Obtaining My Driver's License 154

Preparing for High School Graduation and College 155

High School Graduation 157

Greenbrier Junior College 158

Katherine Gibbs Business School 168

Meeting and Dating Pepper Martin 171

OUR WEDDING, AUGUST 21, 1948 175

Our Honeymoon 179

MARRIAGE 185

Our First Child, Paul J. Martin 186

My Guardian Angel 189

Go for the House 193

The Deaths of My Grandparents 193

The Silent Treatment 194

Our Third Child, Kevin Timothy Ferris Martin 197

Winning a Car: My 1956 Red Four-Door Plymouth 198

Promises and Demands of the Catholic Church 200

Pepper's Side of the Family 202

Pauline and Her Family 207

1960s through 1980s 213

My Many Jobs 217

Our Fourth Child, Brian Francis Martin 221

Typical Holiday Dinner with the Family 226

On Strike 228

A Bump on the Tracks 231

Our Trips to Brunswick, Jacksonville, and Kingsley Lake 233

Mother's Flirtatious Moments 239

The Belly Dancers 242

Selena' Party 247

Paul and Debbie's Wedding 248

Crystal Palace, My Fifteen Minutes of Fame 248

Pilfering Petals 249

Our Performance on the Amtrak Train 251

Mother's Move to Brunswick, Georgia 253

Savannah's Bridge 254

The Blessing of the Shrimp Boats 255

Kevin, Brunswick Police Officer 256

Arrival of Family and Friend 257

A Moonlight Cruise 257

Kevin and Mindy's Wedding 260

Cumberland Island 263

My Banishment from the Ritter Family 265

Our Four Grandchildren 270

Travis' Story 273

Kelsey's Story 276

Our Trip to Ireland 277

Pepper's Illness, Fairleigh Dickinson University/EPOP Group 288

Writing Fiction and Poetry 292

Pepper's Death 297

MY LIFE AS A WIDOW 299

My Trip to Italy 300

My Trip to Spain and Portugal 309

76th Infantry Division's Last Tour 312

SEPTEMBER 11, 2001 318

A Visit to Brian's House 322

Seven Layers of Love and How It Continued to Grow 324

Cape May with Kevin and Mindy 334

Pauline's Death 336

My Mother's Death 337

Going Forward 339

Until Next Time 341

Appendix A: Knollcroft Kennels Champions 343

Appendix B: "The Martians Are Coming!"—Recipe 346

Appendix C: Visiting Family in Brunswick, Georgia—Recipe ... 348

Appendix D: On Strike—Recipe 350

Appendix E: Our Trips to Brunswick, Jacksonville,

    and Kingsley Lake—Recipe 352

Appendix F: A Moonlight Cruise—Recipe 354

Appendix G: Our Four Grandchildren—Recipes 356

Appendix H: Fiction and Poetry 363

    Reflections 363

    Generations: Walking Down the Path of Life 375

    Nature at Work 376

    A Day on the Beach 378

Appendix I: A Visit to Brian's House—Recipes 381

Appendix J: Seven Layers of Love and

    How It Continued to Grow—Recipe 384

Appendix K: Cape May with Kevin and Mindy—Recipe ... 386

The Beginning

My story begins long before I was born, before my mother and father met and became man and wife. It is the story of two families. The Ritter family lived in Morristown, New Jersey, and enjoyed a comfortable, financially secure lifestyle. However, they allowed pleasures to rule over their faith. The Whorton family came from a small settlement in the lowlands of North Carolina's Craven/Pamlico county area. Life was a constant struggle with unending hardships. Nothing came easy. Their life was wrapped around work, family, faith, and prayer.

For me, my family began after my grandmother, Florence A. Ritter, died in 1922. During the early years of their marriage, my grandparents had three children, but my dad was the only surviving child. His brother and sister died at young ages. After that, Grandmother doted on Dad's every whim including, at the age of eight, his wanting and receiving a pet goat and a small cart. Her affections and love created not one, but two spoiled men.

Following her death, my grandfather, John Thomas Ritter, and my father, Paul Marvin Ritter, found themselves alone, lost, and without the love Grandmother had given them so freely. For the first time, they had to depend on each other for everything. Their faith in God was never as strong as Grandmother's. She was considered the most prominent and valued member of the First Baptist Church, both socially and financially.

Grandfather and Dad had faith, but it was on their terms. Going to church did not take away their pain. After services, they left feeling more sorrowful than when they entered the church. They turned to sports and other pleasures, hoping that these would ease them through their grief. Closeness began to bring this father and son together and, eventually, it grew into a lasting love.

When Dad was a young man, Grandfather taught him the ways of the world and how to survive the many ups and downs of life. He became a man who was determined to enjoy his life to the fullest. Dad was an expert in handling and shooting pistols and rifles. Being a skilled hunter, he traveled in many remote places throughout our country where game was exciting to hunt. He loved fishing alone most of the time and in an area where serenity prevailed, which left him with a peaceful feeling. Even though Dad was not a religious man, he appreciated and respected the many gifts God put upon this earth for man to enjoy.

For a few years, Dad operated a small retail business, but this type of work gave him little satisfaction. Morristown was in the midst of a building boom during the late 1800s and early 1900s. Dad went into construction work and eventually opened his own roofing business around 1921.

Grandmother and Grandfather Ritter (the only picture I have of my grandmother).

I knew little of Grandfather Ritter's roots, as he never spoke of his family except to say that he was of German background. Grandmother's family included two brothers, their wives, and children. All three families visited frequently. Uncle Bill and Uncle Dave Stillwell, and Grandmother's dear friend, Auntie Young, helped the Ritter men overcome their grief by giving them their support and love. Serenity slowly came back into their lives. After many

My father with his goat and cart.

months, love and laughter began to fill the emptiness within Knollcroft, their home in Morristown.

The Whorton side of my family lived entirely different lives from those of the Ritter family. The Whorton family roots in the United States probably go back to a man named Phillipp Wharton, who, at age fourteen, left England for the New World as a passenger aboard the ship *Truelove*. The *Truelove*, under the command of Robert Dennis, cleared Gravesend on or about June 10, 1635, bound for Bermuda. After stopping there, the *Truelove* set sail for Virginia, finally arriving in Yarmouth Port sometime during 1636. Phillipp Wharton's presumed descendants moved to what is now North Carolina in the early 1700s, where they established a small settlement near a waterway named Broad Creek, which empties into the Neuse River. They were among the first settlers of English descent within this area. Around 1750, they named the settlement Whortonsville.

My father as a young boy with his younger cousin, Sheldon Scoble.

*My father showing his day's catch of fish during his
stay at my grandparents' home in Whortonsville.*

Dad cleaning pheasants he shot while hunting in the fields surrounding Whortonsville.

My Aunt Affie said that Grandfather's mother, Charlotte Phipps, is believed to have been related to the Phipps family, which owned a lot of property around Edenton, North Carolina. During the 1940s, the Phipps family donated 2,700 acres of land on Cape Hatteras to the government; this land became part of the Cape Hatteras National Seashore when it was established in 1953.

Religion was the basis for the union of my grandparents, Fred Silverthorn Whorton and his wife, Louvenia Ernestine. Ten children resulted from their marriage. Family was important, since Grandfather had many brothers and sisters. As the families grew, they bought sections of farmland to produce food for their tables, as well as an income. They used the inlets, rivers, and bays for fishing to supply food and added income as well. Life was not easy in the lowlands, but it fulfilled the body and soul of each inhabitant.. Their entire lives were built on sharing, caring, and loving each other. Their lives resembled the motion of a seesaw. No matter how little they had, dignity walked with them. Money was hard to come by, let alone keep. They were country folk who carried God in their hearts and a hand, outstretched, always ready to help a friend, stranger, or member of the family. Grandmother had two, much older half-sisters who had moved out of the area, traveling as far off as Texas and two half-brothers who continued to live within the settlement. Looking back, I can see why my heart belonged to these plain, unpretentious folk.

Grandfather Ritter and my dad would vacation down in Pamlico County, where they did a great deal of hunting and fishing. During the early 1900s along the Carolina coastline and inlets, many homes were used as boarding houses for the well-to-do sportsmen from other states and areas. Times were hard for people in the lowlands, and families began to open their homes to these men. My maternal grandmother and grandfather opened their home as a boarding house. The Whortonsville area was known for its excellent hunting and fishing and attracted many Yankee sportsmen throughout the four seasons. It maintained an officially recognized post office, a general store, a church, and a graveyard.

Mother and her three sisters helped manage the home when the sportsmen would come. Mother met my father in 1922. She was sixteen years old.

Grandfather Whorton in the late 1930s.   *Grandmother Whorton in the late 1930s.*

The family's four girls—Leonia, Lillie, Areta (my mother), and Affie—had little time to stand before the mirror and admire their youthful features. Beauty was not to be their enjoyment. They were denied the thrill of experiencing zest and gusto in their lives. Schooling and chores at home were considered two of their three top priorities. The other priority involved their strict Baptist upbringing. Mother and her sisters had no say-so when it came to their lives. They had little choice because their religious background restricted them in many areas. Their recreation consisted mainly of church-related social functions and chaperoned affairs.

Mother was thin with a small frame. She had a radiant complexion, which she credited to Grandmother's well-balanced meals. The table always held several different vegetables. Mother had soft green eyes and lovely brown, bobbed hair. The moment my father saw her beautiful smile, he fell in love.

From that time on, the Whorton's boarding home became my dad's favorite lodging. Several years went by and each goodbye became harder. He was in love and found the separation and distance unbearable. During this same period, Granddaddy Ritter met and fell in love with my mother's widowed Aunt Love. She also lived in the same small community with her children. Eventually, they married as well.

Slowly, hunting took a back seat for both men. When Mother was nineteen years old, Dad asked her to marry him. They notified the circuit judge that they wanted to get married and needed his services. Due to the hard times, big weddings were unknown in Pamlico County. The circuit judge only came around at certain times of the month. Therefore, in order to get married, they had to go up to Bayboro, which held the territorial jail and courtroom. They brought Preacher Woodard with them so he could perform the ceremony along with the circuit judge, who took care of the legal papers. These preparations made it possible for them to leave immediately for the North as husband and wife.

Mother as a small girl sitting on shelf in her family's general store. Note her clothing, shoes, and what I believe are two pickle barrels, typical of the old general stores of yesteryear.

The old Whorton family truck/car, which seldom ran, and several of my cousins.

*Grandmother, Aunt Affie, and Granddaddy
standing in the yard of their farmhouse. Note
mule and the wheel of one of the family's wagons.*

My Birthplace, My Home

KNOLLCROFT   Knollcroft was the name of our beautiful home; a home that sat nestled neatly on a small hill. It was my birthplace, my security. When I was a child, Knollcroft represented a mystical strength that I loved and welcomed; it was always there for me, protecting me from all the unknowns that lay just beyond its manicured lawns.

Like a coin, however, Knollcroft had another side, a side known only to its occupants, the ugly side outsiders never knew existed. Knollcroft was also my tormentor, my prison. It failed to protect me from the hatred and greed that festered and grew so deeply over the years among those living inside its strong walls. It was here, lingering and smoldering, where the complexities and entanglements of my family began. It was here at Knollcroft on February 16, 1929, that I made my entrance into the world in the form of a small, frail newborn.

I was born on a gloomy, rainy Saturday morning and immediately became known as Mother's Saturday's child. Years later, I learned that this name came from the old Scottish nursery rhyme describing bairns (the Scottish word for "child") born on each of the seven days of the week. The oldest description of Saturday's child simply states, that he or she "has far to go." Another, more recent version states that Saturday's child "works hard for its living." As I look back, both versions carried more truth than fiction. No matter which version I use, Saturday's child has had a long road to travel, as well as a life filled with hard work. Nothing has ever come easy! A painful existence became a way of life, right from the beginning. I was a small, frail

A view of the front section of my home, Knollcroft.

infant, given the name Lavenia Ernestine Ritter, the middle child of a well-to-do family.

At an early age, I began to live in a constant state of uncertainty as well as fear of people, fear of not living up to expectations, and fear of life beyond Knollcroft's picture-perfect lawns. These feelings remained deeply embedded within me for decades, haunting me, coloring my every thought and action, controlling my very existence. My struggle to survive forced me to look beyond the reflection I saw every time I looked in my mirror. This is my story, the story of an insignificant person who worked hard to survive many difficulties as she traveled down the road of life and, finally, found peace and satisfaction in her own being.

MY FAMILY: NEW JERSEY I always felt that my father was special, one of a kind. From the time I was a small child, he was my Prince Charming, my hero. However, as the years passed, I began to see his other side, the side that took me decades to understand, accept, and learn to live around. All he ever wanted was a son. I became his substitute for that.

Mother, on the other hand, was different. Her thoughts and actions were never her own. Her entire life was based on other people's thoughts, actions, beliefs, and lifestyles. She reminded me of a puppet whose moods, thoughts, and words of each moment were determined by the puppeteer who manipulated the strings that controlled each and every aspect of her life.

Florence was my older sister. As is often the case with a firstborn child, she never had to compete with anyone or share anything until I was born. Suddenly, she found herself no longer the main attraction. As young as she was, I believe that this classic sibling rivalry changed Florence's personality, making her, at least from my point of view, manipulative, clever, and, worst of all, cruel. Born in 1926, she was the strongest in mind and body of us three girls. I feared her most of all.

Mother and Dad.

Pauline, my younger sister, was born during 1934. Like me, her life was plagued with all kinds of insecurities. Unlike me, she was the spoiled one, the favorite child, the baby.

Most times, I felt as if I lived with two different fathers, as I never knew what to expect. Dad amazed me. Regardless, I loved him! I felt safe when I was near him. As a small child, I relished his excitement, unpredictability, and demanding ways, which kept him aloof, yet gentle and kind when it was necessary. Even though Dad was not a religious man, he appreciated and respected the many gifts God put upon this earth for man to enjoy.

I cherish the few pictures I have of him. I treasure one in particular, which shows Dad driving his pet goat harnessed to a small cart, which I mentioned earlier. He carried that same mischievous look his entire life. Dad knew exactly what he wanted and never stopped until he obtained his desires, goals, or whatever.

Mother; my older sister, Florence; and me.

He made the decisions. He was king of his castle, right up to his death. We were his jesters, his wards, his property.

As a child, I remember my father's rough appearance and unpolished manners. Even though he owned the business, he was a roofer. He was one of the guys, all of whom wore the same type of clothing: tarry pants, pants that had holes in the knees, as well as holes in the seat. Mother was constantly sewing patches on every pair of pants he wore.

Mother, me, Dad, and Florence.

However, when he wasn't in his roofing clothes, he enjoyed being well dressed, yet comfortable and sporty looking. He was not a sophisticated man. I always found it funny whenever he tried to put on a manly air, because it never seemed to fit him. However, this pretense depended on the company he was with or the event he was attending.

Because Dad became bald at an early age, his shapely head always appeared well polished, giving his appearance a more masculine look. As Dad aged, his resemblance to the actor Telly Savalas was astonishing. His eyes were wide, soft green in color, set in a full face. A hint of laughter seemed to lurk within his smile. His masculinity was never questioned.

Dad loved being the center of attention and gained this by being a storyteller. Every time he would tell a story, it would never be the same. He entertained everyone with his great imagination and fascinating tales. His stories were similar to the great fish stories, which only became bigger and better over time. The truth was always lost early in the story once he captivated

his audience. However, he could end a story when one least expected it. Many were left with only confused looks as he would either leave or change the subject to something totally different. He was a complicated man.

As I had mentioned earlier, Dad and Granddaddy Ritter were similar in personality. They were both difficult to understand but Dad knew how to smile. That was one of the more pleasant differences. However, shortly after Dad married Mother in July 1925, Granddaddy and Aunt Love also married. The Ritter men never separated, and Knollcroft became the home for both families.

Pauline, my kid sister, about three years old.

Aunt Love was a petite lady. Graying, bobbed hair encircled her gentle face. When Grandfather and Aunt Love stood together, they looked like Mutt and Jeff, a funny looking couple. He was tall, and she was very small. Aunt Love was a great help to my mother in many ways. Her presence made it possible for Mother to enjoy a greater freedom within the social circles of Morris County.

Hubert came north with Aunt Love. He was her youngest child by her first husband, Raymond Whorton, my grandfather Whorton's brother. Hubert was like the older brother we never had, and as young girls, we loved him. His bedroom was on the third floor of Knollcroft. To

Aunt Love.

5

go up into this area of the house was always a thrill, especially when Hubert gave his permission. A section of rooms, also on the third floor, was considered the attic. It was here, amongst the old trunks of clothing and accessories, that we allowed our imaginations to run rampant.

Hubert, holding two of Daddy's field-trial pups.

Affie, my mother's younger sister, came north during the early 1930s and attended nursing school. She stayed with our family on weekends. After graduating, she married Clarence Dawley. They had a daughter, Diane, and made their home in Bloomfield, which was approximately fifteen miles from our home. This completes the outline of my immediate family in New Jersey.

Affie was a petite and gentle, loving person. Like my mother, she had her own beauty. Her face was round and delicate with high cheekbones, which appeared more pronounced whenever she smiled. She had bluish-gray eyes and short, bobbed, brown hair. Even as Affie aged, she never lost her loveliness. Long after her death in November 1995, she remains close and dear within my heart and memory. She was my mentor, my best friend.

My childhood relationship with my aunt was not that close. I resented her for many years because of my claustrophobia. (A story later in this book will explain my problem.) She was my aunt, and I was her niece, and that was it! As the years went by, she had a tremendous influence on me. She became my confidante and advisor, my mentor, and more of a sister than an aunt. She helped me to understand and care for family, even when we knew the contempt that existed among its individual members.

My Childhood

MANDY, MY BELOVED MAMMY   Her name was Amanda "Mandy" Squire, our beloved mammy! During the early thirties, Mandy came to live with us. She was born and raised in Whortonsville, North Carolina, just across the creek from Grandmother's home. Poor times invaded these coastal lowlands, not just for the Blacks but for the white people as well. The entire community depended, as I have said, on the out-of-state sportsmen who came into the area for hunting and fishing. It was the Squire men who became their guides, taking them through treacherous waterways and unfamiliar hunting grounds.

The sportsmen stayed in the various boarding houses throughout the county during the sporting seasons. Mandy's family worked for my grandparents in their general store, at their cotton gin, on their farm, as well as in their home when the hunters and fishermen boarded there. Over the years, my father and grandfather developed a lasting friendship with the Squire family.

During one of my father's hunting trips, he asked Mandy if she would like to come north and live and work as a member of his family. Dad had heard of Mandy's tragedy involving her child (which I will describe presently) and felt the move would be good for her. She accepted the invitation without hesitation. Mother and Aunt Love were thrilled when Mandy arrived. In no time at all, we became guests in "her" home. She took over completely. Her love of family and sense of belonging were all she needed.

I fell in love with Mandy the moment she stepped through the front door. Her huge arms flew open to embrace each one of us. Mandy's warmth

was immediately felt. She was laughing, crying, and hollering, all at the same time. She mesmerized me, as I had never seen anybody do that. She pressed me against her oversized body. I felt her warmth, strength, and love. Instantly, Mandy became "my" family.

I will never forget how Mandy's heavy body would lumber around the kitchen. It fascinated me as her frame completely overpowered the stove, hiding the range as if it had never existed. Mandy's flesh would almost lay over it as she bent down to remove a pan of biscuits from the oven. Her large and bountiful frame would cruise slowly throughout the multitude of rooms. Her feather duster barely touched the assorted pieces of furniture, sweeping up the dust balls as they slid from one small area to another. When she would remove the rugs to the backyard for their weekly beating, the neighborhood kids and I would gather to watch her. What a wallop she had! We would all cringe while thanking the good Lord it was the rugs getting beaten and not us.

Mandy worked hard around our home, keeping it fresh and clean. If she weren't cleaning, she would be cooking up some sort of Southern dish, filling our kitchen with delightful aromas. No potpourri of today could ever match the scents Mandy would achieve with her many mixtures of spices. Mandy had her own strange odors as well. The cheap perfumes with which she doused herself so freely and the strong and heavy powders that she applied to her oversized body created an unspeakable aroma. Pauline would often run up behind her, saying, "Mandy, you 'tink!" At that, Mandy would smile and, quickly, add, "Lordy, child, get yo'self from under my feet." Mandy's ritual would begin. She would pull Pauline into the thickness of her body, giving her a bear-like hug and a gentle love-tap on her small behind to send her on her way.

We never saw Mandy's hair, as it was always covered with some kind of kerchief. It seemed exotic to us, since we knew of no one else who ever wore a headpiece like hers. Our questions were always left unanswered, even when we tried to coax or bribe her to reveal this tantalizing secret. She would smile, give us pat on our heads and send us on our way. Nary a single strand was exposed! Never a clue to what really existed under it! She enjoyed keeping us

wondering, guessing, and watching for one lock of hair to slip out from under her kerchief.

Was it black like the rest of her? Could it be a brilliant red or yellow? If it were silver or white, Mandy might be afraid she looked like a witch or something weird and figured it was better to keep it covered. God forbid! Maybe Mandy had no hair at all and kept that secret concealed so we wouldn't laugh at her! All of these things would go through my mind as I stared at her mysterious headpiece. I could feel the guilt of my thoughts seep through my small frame while the taunter refused to cooperate.

This piece of cloth appeared glued as it never moved regardless of the job she was doing. No matter how hard I tried to unravel this mystery, Mandy never revealed her secret. Her eyes were large and dark, but always seemed to sparkle and glow with warmth. She had a large mouth with beautiful white teeth and a smile that only expressed complete tenderness. How they glistened against the blackness of her skin! The colors of our skins never interfered with the love that our family shared with Mandy.

My sister, Florence, was the only one who refused to show any caring toward Mandy. She treated her in a rather standoffish way, almost as if she thought she was better than Mandy. I would dash into Mandy's arms for her hugs, but Florence never did. She always stood back and acted like she was surveying the situation. She would walk away, saying nothing. Florence may have thought she was too old for all that affection; after all, she was nearly three years older than I.

Mandy came to live with us a year before my younger sister was born. I was her favorite up to that time, and then my little world began to collapse around me. Pauline arrived. I watched as Mother doted over the new arrival. I wasn't allowed in the room. Her words to me were "You almost killed me! Get out!" I watched from the other side of the door as Florence was allowed to touch and hold Pauline. At an early age, rejection had entered into my life, leaving me with a pain that I could not understand. Mandy was completely caught up in her work. She was now helping Mother with the baby.

Mother's anger toward me continued. She seemed to want nothing to do with me. She couldn't look at me without reminding me of how difficult my

birth had been and how I almost killed her when I was born. I walked about the house wondering what she meant. Her few kisses and hugs stopped completely, leaving me puzzled. She found fault in everything I said or did. She often referred to me as looking like some poor white-trash child from Whortonsville. I didn't know what she meant, but it didn't sound very nice, and it made me feel sad. My very existence seemed to irritate her. I was constantly being told what a disappointment I was to her, nothing like Florence. We were always being compared, and I, of course, was never what Mother expected or wanted.

By the time I was ready for kindergarten, I had become a very shy child. This infuriated Mother even more. Her only words were, "What is wrong with you?" and "You don't act like any of the little girls in your classroom!" I felt like an old toy being discarded. I was only a child, but once again, I felt Mother neither wanted nor loved me. The thought, "I almost killed her," would not leave me, nor did I understand its meaning.

Mandy adored Pauline, as she reminded her of her own young but deceased daughter, Eula. When Mandy would occasionally speak of her, tears would obscure the sparkling eyes to which we were so accustomed. Before my grandfather Ritter died, I was innocent and unacquainted with the finality of death, its meaning, grief and sorrow, and the flesh that became so cold and unbending. For some reason, I could feel Mandy's pain and her terrible suffering, even though I didn't understand death. Finally, the day came when Mandy told Florence and me of her tragedy.

EULA'S STORY It was a warm summer day, some years before, when Mrs. Lupton, one of the ladies for whom Mandy worked, needed some special supplies from Bayboro. She asked Mandy to take the small two-wheeled cart instead of the large wagon. Mrs. Lupton felt the smaller cart would be easier for both Mandy and the mule to handle.

Mandy got little Eula and headed toward the area where the mule was standing. As Mandy was hitching the mule to the cart, she spotted several bees flying just above the animal's head. Mandy quickly put Eula in the cart

and then began to swat the bees. To Mandy's horror, they became more aggressive, stinging the mule's neck, head, and eyes. The mule went berserk. Mandy tried to calm him, but his uncontrollable behavior knocked her to the ground. Her large, heavy body moved faster than a bolt of lightning as she tried to avoid the constantly moving iron-shod hoofs of the animal. She felt one hoof after another strike and tear at her frame. She knew she was bleeding badly. She rolled quickly to get out from under them. The upheaval of the dirt and dust from the sandy soil only added more confusion to the scene. It appeared to lift above the confrontation only to fall quickly and mix into the pools of blood. A slick and slippery area was now underfoot and added more difficulty to Mandy's attempts to escape.

Little Eula was sitting in the cart when this battle began. Her screams of fright only made Mandy fight harder. She had to calm the mule! No matter what she did, nothing was working! Mandy had become as berserk as the mule. With all the confusion, Eula tumbled out of the cart. The crazed mule began stomping on her small body. Mandy fought to get to her. By now, Mandy's bloody body was caked with dirt. She pounded him with her fists constantly, trying to push him to the ground with all the weight of her immense body. She could not stop him. The mule would not drop. Exhausted, Mandy managed to stand her ground. Her eyes became fixed upon the scene in disbelief. She struggled, watching her child's small body, which now resembled a limp, lifeless, battered rag doll. The cart continued smashing down on Eula as the animal kicked and jumped.

As she told Florence and me the terrible story, Mandy paused as she tried to restrain her emotions, but her voice, by now, conveyed all her unleashed pain, all the anger of those few horrific moments. I found myself immobilized by such horror. I wanted to cry out for her. I wanted to comfort her and put my small arms around her, but my body was motionless. The story frightened me, as I never saw or heard of something so terrible. All I could think of was "My poor, dear, ol' Mandy." My eyes filled with tears. Florence, in spite of her usual reserve with Mandy, was trying to hold back her own tears.

Neither of us said a word as Mandy continued. With her own bleeding and torn hands, Mandy fought to control the mule by yanking on the bit, pushing

rearward as he kicked, brayed, and bit at her forceful body. Finally, with the help of a whip, she managed to calm him just long enough to get to her child.

We saw terror once again return to Mandy's eyes. They seemed to be protruding out of their sockets, and tears were streaming down her cheeks. I tried to stop her from going on, but it was impossible. She couldn't hear me. Her cry was too loud. Finally, Mandy stopped, until she regained enough composure to continue her story.

Mandy gazed down on the small body that had been her little girl. Her flesh was badly torn. Screaming and wailing, she snatched up the crumpled, mutilated body, ran to the house, and laid it, ever so gently, on the edge of the porch. Eula was now safe. Mandy turned, still shrieking, and lunged toward the now-placid animal. With a huge board in hand, she battered the mule until he dropped dead. She returned to her child, rocking and cradling it in her arms, lying protectively over it until family came to her aid.

Mandy cried bitterly. I found myself crying with her, hugging her, and wanting only to comfort her in my childish way. It was my first experience of feeling someone's tragic pain and grief. I was bewildered by my own feelings. I was just a child who found herself experiencing feelings beyond her young years! I noticed stains from earlier tears were still lingering on my sister's cheeks as she ran out of the room after Mandy finished her story. She never said a word. Our eyes remained red and swollen for the remainder of that day. We never asked or mentioned anything more about little Eula. We knew the agonizing pain Mandy carried in her heart every day of her life.

That night as I lay in my bed, I found it very difficult to sleep. That terrible scene kept appearing before my eyes. I wanted to hide. I crept further under the blanket, trying desperately to forget Eula's crumpled body, only to find that the darkness frightened me even more. I cried, but no one heard me. My body began to shake. I felt cold as my thoughts continued to return to the tragic scene. I felt my eyes filling with tears. "Little children should never suffer like that," I whispered. My heart ached for little Eula, but I also felt a fear of not knowing what unknown terror I might find myself facing tomorrow. Suddenly, I heard myself praying, "Dear God, please don't let this ever happen to me!" I kept repeating those words over and over until I fell asleep.

The next morning, I awoke to a beautiful sunny day. However, the torments of that night still showed clearly on my face. It took many days before I was able to put that tragic scene to rest. Nothing that horrific could ever be forgotten and, sadly, it never was.

I was amazed at Mandy's ability to love so easily while living with so much pain. She became my silent heroine and my very first mentor. Unfortunately, she never knew of these feelings because I failed to tell her of my devotion and love. Years later, I realized how much I had learned from this gentle and loving woman.

No matter what Pauline said to Mandy, whether it was about her strange and peculiar odors, a complaint about one of us, or just baby talk, Mandy would slap her huge thighs, bellow a deep belly laugh, pick her up, and, hug her tightly. We would hear Pauline give a little gasp for breath. Mandy would smile and, slowly, release her. How I wished I were Pauline at those moments, just to be picked up and hugged like that! God, I wanted my mother to be as free with her love towards me as Mandy was with Pauline.

A simple, spontaneous hug may have taken away those strange feelings I could not explain. Mother hugged Florence and Pauline! The anger I felt so much of the time over her total lack of affection and interest in me was gnawing at my gut. No matter what I did, I could not come up to my mother's expectations of me. But I couldn't do anything about it. I didn't know how, and I was afraid of everything that had to do with my miserable relationship with her.

My father, on the other hand, was always the happiest when he was able to play his children against one another. He would shower Florence with love and totally neglect me or vice versa. He often remarked that he had given Florence his mother's name, and therefore, she was most important to him.

Mother had graced me with Grandmother Whorton's given name. Therefore, as he often remarked, he looked differently upon me. From that time on, I was a Whorton rather than a Ritter in both of their eyes. As silly as it sounds, throughout my childhood, Mother delighted in my father's silent rejection of me because of my name.

When Pauline was born, Mother insisted that this baby was going to be named after Dad. To my father's delight, his youngest child was named

*Pauli*ne. She would be special in his eyes! Mother was so right and proud of her conniving decision. Pauline was his favorite child right up to his death.

Dad was able to have a relationship with me even though he felt as he did. He told me that he loved Grandmother Whorton, even though she was a rebel. After all, we were Yankees. Mother's family were poor white Southerners who could not be compared to the financial status of the Ritter family. When I was a child, that statement never bothered me because it really meant nothing. All I knew was how much I adored him. He was completely unpredictable and a total individual. We never knew where we stood with him, but when he showed us attention, it was the greatest. He either gave too much or he gave nothing. From moment to moment, he could be as different as day is to night.

Mandy was my security blanket. I could always run to her. She knew how to wipe away those tears of anguish or pain from an unexpected injury or from an aching heart. She could make everything all right with just a hug, a smile, or one of her just-baked goodies. We knew that when she gave us one of her special treats, she was giving us a small part of herself. Mandy never stopped working, always devoted to each of us, but Pauline got the special hugs. She was the baby!

Mandy returned to North Carolina when I was about twelve years old. Several of her children and their families were still living around Pamlico County, and like most people when we're separated from family, she was eager to return to them after being away for so many years. Mandy died several years later and was buried in the local colored Baptist church cemetery alongside her little Eula.

Just a note of interest: The picture portraying Aunt Jemima on the packaging of Pancake Mix from the early 1900s (and through a multitude of decades) always reminded me of my beloved Mandy. What even surprised me more was the fact that the actress who portrayed Aunt Jemima during the 1950s was also named Ernestine. Ethel Ernestine Harper, after working as a schoolteacher in the South for twelve years, came north in 1936 to embark on a career as a singer and actress, and eventually lived and died in Morristown. I found this

woman's story fascinating because of her tremendous determination to believe in herself and her convictions about the things that affected people's lives.

POLLY, OUR PARROT   Polly, our beautiful yellow and green parrot, was a remarkable bird. We had her for at least twelve years, as she was one of the first things I remembered as a child. Mother kept Polly caged most of the time or as often as she could. Unfortunately, this bird learned how to pick the latch and quickly found the pleasures of freedom by departing through any open window or door. Polly always seemed to be two steps ahead of Mother.

The neighborhood kept her busy and contented. She knew where she lived, always returning home after she stirred up enough trouble amongst the neighbors. She usually perched in Mrs. Hazen's apple tree, which was across the street from our house. There she would sit by the hour and wait for the neighborhood women to start calling their children to come home. Mrs. Vito, in particular, would stand on her upstairs porch and call her two sons, Anthony and Rudolph.

Polly seemed to favor Mrs. Vito over the other women: she would immediately start the same call as Mrs. Vito, "Anthony! Rudolph! Come home!" "Anthony! Rudolph! Come home!" Then, Polly would add her own comment, "Come home, damn it." As Mrs. Vito's voice became louder, Polly would make a stronger squawk. It seemed as if they were trying to outdo each other. Matters only worsened when Polly began adding one curse word after another. Mrs. Vito would become enraged because she felt the neighborhood children were imitating her. She would scream out all kinds of threats to that other voice, since she never knew whether it was Polly, the neighborhood women, or the kids on the block. Mrs. Vito would go to each neighbor's house, expressing her anger and contempt for the neighborhood children.

Even though Mrs. Vito had come from Italy many years ago, she never bothered to learn to speak much English. However, that never stopped her from screaming. The madder she got, the thicker her accent became. Few knew what she was spilling out, but everyone felt it was a lot of curse words. This behavior of Mrs. Vito lasted as long as we had Polly. It was an intolerable

situation. The neighbors often remarked that Mrs. Vito and Polly's antics kept them well entertained.

Polly's favorite person was Dad. Dad spent hours teaching this clever parrot how to speak. Before long, Polly knew every possible curse word and was sounding more and more like Dad. Every time Reverend Hoorseman would come to the house for a visit, Polly would delight in addressing him, "Hello! How the hell are you?" We all knew where Polly had learned that phrase. It was Dad's doing, although he never acknowledged such folly. Oh, how she loved to talk, and once started, Polly would not stop for anyone.

Polly managed to keep our house in a constant uproar. She knew exactly when to upset Mother: on the day when the good reverend would arrive for his weekly visit and afternoon tea! Polly was impossible to cage, as she seemed to sense the reverend's visit. The moment the doorbell rang, Mother would open the door and usher the good reverend into the formal living room. Out of nowhere, would come a squawking welcome, "Hello! How the hell are you?" It was downhill all the way after that. The more Polly greeted Reverend Hoorseman, the more vile her dialogue became. Polly now forgot the few refined words that Dad had taught her. This bird was in big trouble with Mother as she squawked up a storm!

The good reverend would try to help Mother get Polly back into her cage. He somehow managed to look like a very concerned person who just wanted to assist Mother in her search for this master imitator. However, during one particular visit, he forgot himself when he coldly announced, "Jesus, if that damn bird was mine, I'd kill him! Areta, shut him up for Christ's sake!" He continued, sounding more and more like Paul and Polly, "How in the hell can you allow this? Paul is a son of a bitch! Jesus Christ!" Mother was shocked—one might even say "devastated." She had never heard this honorable man who served the Lord talk so horribly. The good reverend suddenly realized what he had done and found himself speechless. What could he say? Endless apologies became their entire conversation. The visit was ruined. Upon Polly's capture, Mother removed her to another location, only to have this aggressor's squawking voice continue. It penetrated throughout the entire house.

This rivalry between Polly and the good reverend lasted for many years. Reverend Hoorseman was always happy when he heard that his antagonist was flying about the neighborhood rather than waiting to squawk out every profanity she knew at him. This great parrot loved to perform. She always managed to do it her way!

One day, Polly unfortunately wandered into the coal bin on the day coal was being delivered. Apparently she failed to get out in time and was crushed by the coal as it came down the coal shoot. We called and searched throughout the neighborhood but she was nowhere to be found. The house suddenly seemed very quiet. No more squawking, cursing, imitating whomever. Poor Polly! One month later, as Dad was shoveling coal to go into the furnace, he found our beloved Polly. The memory of her comes alive whenever I see a parrot similar in color to our dear Polly.

MY FIRST JOB   I began to learn how to develop good work habits at the early age of six, thanks to my mother. She volunteered me to help Auntie Young with her house chores. After Grandmother died, Auntie Young stayed very close to my father and grandfather. The three of them became like family, thus creating "Auntie Young."

Many years later, when I thought of my first job, I had to honestly give Mother some of the credit. She taught me how to work without any praise at all. "One is expected to do only their best without expecting any flattery," was her usual comment; "Constant compliments are not healthy. You know whether you did a good job or not," was another. As young as I was, these stern remarks were hurtful.

I was the only one of my sisters who worked before the age of nineteen. Mother never made those remarks to Florence or Pauline, simply because they never worked! As a youngster and later, as a teenager, when I worked in the Western Union office, I resented Mother's lack of interest, concern, or pride in any of the jobs that I obtained. She constantly reminded me that I was an embarrassment to the Ritter family for working. "How dare you make your father and me look as if we need our children to help out financially!" she would scream angrily and shake that damn finger at me until I hoped it would fall off.

Mother's denouncement of me was becoming an everyday occurrence, and I found myself trying to please her more and more. Finally, I gave up. I didn't know how to react to her constant harangue. By now, I had become a terribly introverted child within the walls of Knollcroft.

About an hour of each of my Saturday mornings was spent down at Auntie Young's home. I was expected to dust her furniture and to wipe up any dust balls that were lying about on her wooden floors. She was unable to bend down or get on her knees. She lived just a short distance from our home, which made it possible for me to walk there. I was fascinated with her home and all of its old and strange contents.

When I arrived, I would always check behind the front door just to make sure no one was hiding there. It was as if I had just entered a home from the past. There was no electricity, which made the rooms dark and gloomy. Everything was old, including Auntie Young. In one corner of Auntie Young's living room was her piano. My job included keeping those ivory keys slick and shiny. Not a trace of dust or dirt was to be found or felt when Auntie Young decided to play her favorite songs. She would carefully lay back the piano cover to expose the creamy-white keys and then settle herself on the piano stool. She always acted as if she were giving a performance, even though I was the only other person in the house.

She touched the keys so gently, then proudly let her fingers dance up and down the keyboard. She created marvelous sounds and rhythms. I would stop, turn my head as if I were giving my approval—only for a minute though, just to let her know I was listening and enjoying every note. What a performance! Auntie Young became oblivious to my presence. She was completely absorbed in her music. A smile would make its way across her wrinkled face. She loved to entertain me by playing her favorite church music. Occasionally, she would play one of the more popular songs of the day as I hummed along. Auntie Young was very nice to me. The entire atmosphere made me feel warm and happy. I never felt like it was a job.

I remember one particular lamp that sat on one of her small tables. It was the first lamp I ever saw that had to be lit with a match. I had to handle it very carefully because it was an oil lamp with a Tiffany shade. That, in itself,

meant nothing to me except that I knew I had better not break it or I would be in big trouble with everyone. I shook every time I got near it. This lamp, when lit, gave off a glow that would give the entire room the warm and enchanting aura of a period long gone. Whenever I remarked about its beauty, Auntie Young always said, "It's the lampshade that does it!" She taught me to appreciate the value of her precious items. Even now, I can't help but wonder whatever happened to that lamp and its rare and unusual shade.

Auntie Young always prepared a snack for me after I had finished my job. She would serve me hot chocolate from one of her lovely English chocolate pots. She would set one of her delicate chocolate cups and saucers, filled with hot, frothy chocolate, in front of me. However, the biggest thrill would come when she would appear with a tray of either cookies or small cakes just for me.

Auntie Young made me feel important, and I loved it. The dignity she showed when playing hostess as we shared cocoa, tea, and cake made me feel as if I were royalty. While I waited for Auntie Young to make the cocoa and tea, my favorite fantasy kept me entertained.

I imagined myself to be a queen who was sitting at a lovely gold-trimmed table, waiting for her tea and cakes. The queen would be dressed in one of her fanciest outfits, laden with jewels, and on her head would be a beautiful, but top-heavy crown. The queen was regal looking and waiting for the arrival of her handsome knight. He was going to sweep her up and take her off with him. My dream world, for only those few minutes, always left me with pleasant thoughts. When Auntie Young returned with her goodies, I would tuck my imaginary character away until another special time. I walked home, wrapped in the warmth of tranquility. I looked forward to my Saturday mornings at Auntie Young's as her little housekeeper.

MY BEST FRIEND, EUNICE, AND HER FAMILY My first and best friend was Eunice Daily. We spent our entire childhoods sharing everything. Our home was like a magnet for Eunice, since there was always something going on. To this day, she still says that our home was magic to her. Eunice always felt that my father was the perfect role model as a father. She considered

her father an old man. Mr. Daily, who had retired from United States Shipping Lines, was always at home when we were still kids. Mrs. Daily often remarked that my father was "a diamond in the rough" as well as "one of a kind." It took many years before I could appreciate this compliment. I felt proud when I understood the full meaning of it. Dad was my "diamond in the rough."

Mrs. Daily was a lovely, gracious, and outgoing woman. She loved music and wanted Eunice to play an instrument. At first, Eunice played the violin, but that only lasted a short time. Mrs. Daily invested in a harp, and Eunice

Eunice Daily, my best friend, with cat.

learned to play it beautifully. She played in many local recitals and performances. In order to get the harp to the area where a recital was being held, Mrs. Daily had to buy a car with a back seat large enough to hold the harp. She was determined that such a car existed and began her unusual search.

Everybody thought she was acting ridiculously, but she found what she needed after months of looking. Mrs. Daily found a large, old Packard with a back seat wide enough to hold the harp without damaging it. Her problem was solved. From that time on, Eunice never missed a recital. I loved to hear the sounds that came from such a beautiful musical instrument. I was learning the clarinet, but not with the same enthusiasm. My clarinet had a harsh sound when compared to the soft sounds of the harp. Regardless, the two of us became the entertainment for our mothers' social afternoon teas.

Mrs. Daily was actively involved in the Eastern Star organization. I believe it was connected with the Freemasons. Mother became interested and had the necessary qualifications to become a member. She and Mrs. Daily became officers throughout their many years with this group of ladies.

It was considered one of the more prestigious organizations in the area and an honor to be a member. Mother loved the organization's social events, which happened about four times a year. It was dress up time, which meant long evening gowns and all the frills that went with them. These two ladies shared one social function after another and kept their friendship for decades. Mrs. Daily lived to be 107 years old.

My father and mother admired Mr. Daily because he was an intelligent and interesting person. He was very serious minded and didn't have much of a sense of humor. According to Dad, Mr. Daily came alive when he joined Dad and the other neighborhood men at one of the local bars. This group was never happy until they had Mr. Daily singing, laughing, joking, and staggering home. He never refused to join them. Mrs. Daily often said, "He was the first one out the door!" Mother wanted to pop Dad more than once when this happened because she always knew Dad had instigated it. The group went on deep-sea-fishing trips several times during the year. Lasting friendships developed among this group of men, even though they all had different personalities.

Eunice and I learned to swim together at the Morristown YMCA, which was located on Washington Street at that time. We were members and enjoyed our time there. We were required to buy or rent their black or gray tank-type bathing suit, since no other suit was allowed in the pool. Our membership entitled us to use the gym and the bowling alley as well.

The only picture I have of Eunice with her mother, Mrs. Daily.

THE DAILY RECORD, MORRISTOWN, N. J., SATURDAY, MARCH 18, 1933.

Turning 'Em Away Yet At YMCA Circus

Matinee And Evening Performances Today Will End Fine Exhibition

The big "Y" gymnasium was packed and several hundred turned away last night long before Director Bob Coutts signaled for the start of the Grand Parade of the Community Circus at 8 o'clock.

Record crowds are expected at the two performances today, the matinee at 2 o'clock for which the admission fee for children under 12 has been reduced to 15 cents and the evening performance at 8 o'clock.

Four wonderful special attractions are on the program for tonight only (1) The famous Scotch Band of Montclair which made such a hit last year will be here again with their bag pipes and resplendent uniforms.

(2) William Morley, well known local son of Scotland, will play the pipes for Jimmy Downey in a special jig act.

(3) Two members of the University of Pennsylvania wrestling team, William Decker, of Morris Plains, and Charles Moore, of Plainfield, will give an exhibition of wrestling, in time 135 pound class.

The Newark Turnverein Squad of 12 marvelous gymnastics will also tonight put on a special exhibition of star acts.

The show last night had all the snap and finish of a professional performance. Thrilled by the big crowd, even the smallest performers went through their parts with a dash that won continuous applause, while the more mature members of the various acts outdid themselves with a wonderful display of art, beauty and skill. The clofns were funnier than ever, have new tricks for each performance.

Unstinted praise is being showered on all the performers who are so gladly giving their services and on the directors, Robert Coutts and Associate Ray Prideaux; T. H. Wis, General Chairman; R. H. McLeod, of the "Props"; Dr. J. H. Samuel, chairman of the Parade; D. F. Williamson, chairman of the Tickets; E. W. Thompson, Chairman of the Ushers; C. S. Carrell, Treasurer in charge of ticket booths, and their Associates.

The Concessions did a big business in the Y. M. C. A. lobby, under the Chairmanship of Mrs. T. H. Wis, assisted by a number of representative women's organizade, cakes, balloons, hot-dogs, tions. Ice cream, peanuts, lemonhamburgers, crackerjacks, etc., were on sale throughout the evening.

A second street parade, in response to great demand, was staged this afternoon at one o'clock.

Wall Street at a Glance

(By Associated Press)

	Yesterday's Close	Today's 1:30
Adams Exp	5¼	5
Am Can	59⅜	59⅝
Am Fgn Pow	6	6
Am T & T	103¾	102⅝
Anaconda	7⅜	7½
Auburn	37½	37½
B & O	11¼	11⅜
Beth St	14⅜	13⅞
Case (J.I.)	47⅜	47¼
Chrysler	10⅜	10⅝
Col Gas	12⅛	12⅝
Cons Gas	49	49
Cont Can	43⅝	44
Elec P & L	5½	5⅜
Gen El	14⅝	14⅝
Gen Foods	26¾	26½
Gen Motors	13⅜	12⅞
Int T & T	7⅛	7
Kennecott	10⅛	10
Mont Ward	13⅞	13½
Nat Bisc	39	39½
N Y Cent	19⅞	20
Packard	2⅝	2⅝
Penn RR	18⅛	18⅜
Pub Ser NJ	41½	42⅜
Radio	4⅝	4½
Sears Roeb	19⅞	19⅜
Socony Vac	6¾	6¾
South Pac	16⅜	16⅝
St Brands	16⅞	17⅛
St Oil Cal	23¾	23¾
St. Oil NJ	26¼	26¼
Texas	13⅝	13½
Unit Corp	7¼	7
Unit Gas Imp	17⅜	16¾
U S Rubber	4½	4⅜
U S Steel	30½	30¼
Util Pow & Lt	3⅝	3¼
West & Mfg	27	26⅝

Call Money 4%

Newspaper article about the YMCA Circus, 1933.

The YMCA's gym was the location where many circuses were held for a number of years. We would sit upstairs in the balcony and look down wide-eyed upon the many acts. No matter how exciting it was, it never came up to the real excitement of the circus that, just a few years earlier, had ridden in on the rails and paraded up to the circus grounds.

Eunice and I attended Camp Washington, located on Schooley's Mountain, for a week during several summers. That was enough. Two weeks was much too long for being confined and ordered about. It was extremely organized. Once we entered our teen years, neither of us went to camp.

We walked to and from school together including going home for lunch. There was no busing. It was a one-mile walk each way. However, we made it fun by walking and balancing ourselves on the retaining walls in front of the many homes we had to pass. Our mothers were always busy fixing our lunches while they listened to their favorite radio programs. Aunt Jenny's stories, Helen Trent, and Stella Dallas were just a few of the popular daily radio shows presented during the noon hour, five days a week. Our mothers never missed these programs. It was their special time, and we were taught to respect this by being quiet. In time, we found ourselves just as eager to hear the next episode as they.

MY PLAYHOUSE   One day, as we walked in the direction of the dog kennels, my father told me that he had a surprise for me. "Where are we going, Daddy?" I asked. He didn't answer. He just looked down on me and smiled. My thoughts turned inward. My Prince Charming was by my side and that was all that mattered. I was happy. The next thing I knew, we stopped in front of the small building that was his office for Knollcroft Kennels. I remembered how quietly he told me that he no longer needed this space. He was in the process of combining both offices within our home.

As my father spoke, I found myself trying to understand what he was actually saying. In disbelief, I realized that he was turning Knollcroft's office over to me to use as a playhouse, my very own playhouse. I was dumbfounded as he handed me the key with orders to unlock the door. Excitedly, I followed his command. The door opened. Wide-eyed, I stared into the open room. I never expected such a wonderful gift. It was my very own playhouse!

Enchanted at the thought of having something I could call my own, I ran and told Mother. She became enraged at my announcement. "How dare your father do this without consulting with me first! Give me the key," Mother shouted as she snatched it out of my hand. "I have already told the other girls that they could use it as their playhouse." I could feel tears streaming down my cheeks. Again, feelings of being unwanted by Mother tore at my stomach.

QUARANTINE SIGNS When one of us came down with measles, mumps, chicken pox, or any other contagious disease, our doctor had to notify the local board of health and they would come to the home and post a quarantine sign on the front door. The sign had to remain intact until the quarantine period was over. No one was allowed to come in if they had not had the disease. This method of quarantine helped the towns to control many contagious diseases. However, over time, they learned through research that the incubation period was prior to the manifestation of physical symptoms (usually seven to twenty-one days before physical symptoms, depending on the disease). Chicken pox was the one disease to which this did not always apply. The practice of posting the notification on the door was finally stopped by the mid 1940s. Our front door sported the quarantine sign many times during my childhood. It always made the entire household feel as if one of us had the plague.

GRAMMAR SCHOOL Alexander Hamilton School was considered new when I started kindergarten in September 1933. I was almost five years old. There were approximately thirty-one children in my class. Many of these children eventually graduated from high school with me. A few, however, had dropped out of school for one reason or another by the time they reached the eighth grade. Education was not considered the top priority for many students at this time. Several boys had to drop out of school and find jobs to help support their families, because the Depression imposed hardships on many.

Miss Kronenberg was my teacher. I was far from being one of her favorite students. She was constantly complaining to Mother about me. She felt I was not like the other little girls in her class.

Alexander Hamilton School, Second Grade, October 11, 1935. I still recognize many of my class-mates. Front row (l–r): Carol Squire, Lloyd Jacobs, Jeannie Monahan, Cynthia Husk, Charlie Mahoney, Jean Angerbauer, Danny Morrison, me, and [?]. Middle row (l–r): Anson Beckwith, [?], Raymond Smith, [?], Ernest Carter, Dorothy Mays, Ralph Stiles, and Bertha Korn. Back row (l–r): Ivan Metszer, Sylvia Krauss, [?], Ernest Santangelo, Thomas Jackson, Norman Kelly, and Robert Rynearson.

Mother always apologized for my behavior. What had I done? I couldn't understand it. As soon as Mother got me home, she would become her usual critical self. This happened, time and time again. Finally, one day, Dad told Mother to stop—he had heard enough. He went to school and had it out with Miss Kronenberg. Dad had dated her several times, long ago, so they knew each other "*well*" according to Dad. That was it. She never found fault with me again. Once again, Dad became my Prince Charming, my hero.

THE FAMOUS KNOLLCROFT DOGS   Dad was well known throughout the dog world because he raised champion English setters and pointers. His dogs carried the name "Knollcroft." When Dad traveled the dog-show circuit, his setters won "Best of Show" many times over. His travels included most of the northeast. The Morris and Essex Dog Show was held in

The Show · 1935

Panorama of the Morris and Essex Kennel Club Show at Geralda Farms, 1935.

Madison, New Jersey, and during the 1930s and 1940s, it was considered as prestigious as the Westminster Dog Show, held in Madison Square Garden, is today. Dad always returned home with many ribbons and beautiful sterling silver trophies. Every year new pieces of silver would be added to the already accumulated keepsakes.

At first, Mother was impressed with the many celebrities and the high-society crowd who attended these shows. However, that did not last long. Mother quickly realized that it was also a drinking crowd that patronized these affairs. Thereafter, she found it very hard to accept them, regardless of their social status. She was proud of Dad and his expertise in breeding and training these beautiful show dogs, but it was difficult for her to be a part of it. The only time she ever showed any real interest was when she cleaned and polished the lovely silver pieces that he would bring home. In the beginning, she tried to enjoy it as much as Dad, but she became totally disillusioned by it all.

It became almost comical, as well as sad, to watch mother create a theatrical production out of her concerns over Dad's drinking. She would have the entire family, except Pauline who was considered too young to watch Mother's unusual performances, gather in the formal living room. Then Mother would leave the room, only to return wearing an old Prohibition-era dress. A feathery scarf flowed from around her neck. A band around her short, bobbed hair was useless, but to her, it was part of the outfit and act. She would enter the room as if she were trying to glide across the floor with

DAILY RECORD 5/26/1934

Sealyham Terrier Best Dog In Largest Show Held At Giralda Farms

5-26-34

Nearly 15,000 People View 2,900 Dogs At Annual Exhibit Of Morris And Essex Kennel Club Held At Giralda Farms, Madison, On Saturday -- Weather No Handicap

MADISON—Occasional showers and unseasonably co¹d weather could not damper the ardor of dog lovers as the Giralda Farms of Mrs. Marcellus Hartley Dodge proved the setting for America's largest dog show on Saturday. The eighth annual string of the Morris and Essex Kennel Club show on the big polo field on Loantaka Way drew close to 2,900 individual entries as many specialty shows were combined with the regular events while fully 15,000 people viewed the exhibit.

Perfectly handled in every detail, the Morris and Essex Club exhibit drew more entries than even the three day Westminster Kennel Club show in New York and it attracted fanciers from every section of the country and Canada, including the heads of many kennel organizations.

It was the first time in the eight seasons that the weather was bad and generally it has ranged to the other extreme of very hot. Saturday topcoats were comfortable and many of the dogs had either special blankets or else were wrapped in auto robes, their master's coats or towels. All of the animals were benched in big tents but the judging went on in the open. A large tent was provided for this but the rain was never heavy enough to drive the officials to cover.

Capturing the highest honor of the show was Gunside Babs of Holybourne, a Sealyham imported from England only a month ago and downed by S. Y. Froelich, of New York. George S. Thomas picked the white-haired terrier over an Irish setter, Russian wolfhound, Great Dane, Pomeranian and bulldog in the final event.

Mrs. Dodge, hostess for the day, did not show her own champions but many principal awards came to other Morris Countians.

Mrs. Paul Moore's Champion

Great Hearth Laddie Playboy, a Dalmatian, was placed fourth in matian Class n which Rocksisticus Kennels of Mendham had the winner dogs and best of winner in Rocksisticus Richard.

In Salukis, the winner dogs, best of winners and beat ' breed was Mazagam Dhole, owned by George McKay Schieffelin of Gladstone, while the winner, bitches, was Peggy or Allenfot, shown by Mrs. S. Y. L'Hommedieu, of Sand Spring road. Kelso Kennels, of Bernardsville, had the best of breeed in Ch. Maxke of Kelso and winner, bitches in Belgic of Kelso in the Schipperkes division.

Another leading prize went to Mrs. Moore when Veta of Wooley was proclaimed vinner, bitches, in Golden Retrievers.

Many others from this vicinity, some showing for the first time and others who have the habit of only exhibiting at this show, were winners of lesser prizes but a goodly number of the ribbons and plates came to Morris County.

Mrs. Dodge, President of the Kennel Club and Mr. Dodge was chairman of the show committee. They were assisted by Raymond Patterson and A. McClure Haily, secretary and show manager respectively of Giralda Farms.

The exhibitors from Morris County and immediate vicinity with the type of dogs they showed included:

A. Albright, 3rd and Lois Albright, Chatham, Scottich terrier; Armistice Kennels, Hanover, Irish setters and German Shepherd Dogs; Mrs. M. Ethel Ash, Towaco,

Smooth Dachshund; Eric G. W. Barradale, Milington, beagle; John G. Bates, Morristown, Wire foxterriers and pointer; Mrs. F. A. Blazier, Green Village, Boston terrier; Mrs. Herman Bokes, Par Hills, Welsh terriers; Robert Braithwaite, Florham Park, Shetland sheepdog; Mrs. Hazel Bright, Whippany, English setters; Miss Elizabeth C. Bringley, Morristown, Irish setters; Mrs. E. B. C. Buckley, Far Hills, papillons; Mrs. Ella L. Bulger, Habor, Chow Chows; Mrs. William Childs, Bernardsville, Schipperkes; H. Cork, Hanover, German Shepherd.

Mrs. W. E. Crabtree, Chatham, Foxterrier, Scottish terrier, dachshund; Mrs. John H. Benison, Jr., Convent, French poodle; Arthur B. DeWitt, Millington, German shepherd; Miss Edna Dickinson, Chatham, Chow chow; Doreborn Kennels, Millington, German Shepherd; Cyrle F. dos Passos, Mendham, pointer; Jack Duffy, Madison, fox terrier; Mrs. Mable Farr, Madison, wire foxterrier, collie; Thomas Farrell, Convent, cocker spaniel; Richard Ferreanlo, Hanover, Irish setter; G. W. Fiske, Madison(airedale terriers, Cairn terrier;

Mrs. Halsey Fiske, Bernardsville, pekingese, cocker spaniels; F. J. Frank, Madison, bloodhound; Mrs. F. J. Frank, Madison, Chesapeake Bys; A. L. Frederick, Millington, German shepherd; Mrs. Richard Gambrill, Peapack, sealyhams; Mics Gertruce S. Hall, Morristown, bedlington terriers; Frank Haskell, Far Hills, English springer spaniel; Harry Hiler, Denville, pointer; Miss Hildra R. Hutchinson and William J. Hutchinson, Mendham, Clumber spaniels; Charles Jagger, Denville, Irish setter; Kelso Kennels, Bernardsville, Schipperkes.

John McGregor Little, Mountain Arlington, Irish setters; Harry L. Livsey, Madison, fox terrier; Miss Cornelia R. Lum, Chatham, Irish terriers John Markenzie, Convent, wire fox terrier; J. R. MacQueen, Far Hills, Labrador retriever; Evelyn G. Malcolm, Irish terrier; M. E. Marsh, Madison, kuvasz; Carroll F. Masiry, Morristown, Irish setter; Mrs. W. S. Mears, Chatham, Chow chow; Charles M. Newcombe, Far Hills, cocker spaniel; Mrs. Charles M. Newcombe, Sahal; Adolph Henry Nies, Morristown, Irish setter; Anna and John Papr, Mt. Lakes, English setters; Mr. and Mrs. R. A. Parkhurst, Hanover, Irish setters, fox terriers, Scottish terrier; Harry L. Parks, Morris Plains, beagles.

C. M. Peer, Denville, English setter; Mrs. Perkins, Hanover, German shepherd; Mrs. George M. Pinney, Morristown, German Shepherd; Mrs. George B. Post, jr., Bernardsville, Cairn terrier; Mrs. Harry S. Quinn, Madison, fox terrier; Mrs. J. Rose Quinn, Madison, Scottish terrier; Paul M Ritter, Morristown, English setters; Mrs. William Roache, Hanover, German shepherd.

Ron set Kennels, Madison, German shepherd; Mrs. David O. Ross, Morristown, Irish setter; Mr. and Mrs. Charles Scribner, Far Hills, Cairn terriers; Mr. and Mrs. Karl P. M' Greenmen, Montville, German pointers; Mrs. L. J. Sheridan.

Newspaper description of the Morris and Essex Kennel Club Show, 1934; my father is mentioned at the bottom of the far-right column.

both arms stretched out. She wore a pair of high heels that made her wobble. These were Mother's most ridiculous moments. Whatever possessed her to act so foolish over something so serious? Dad put up with her amusing antics but always got back at her by bringing some kind of liquor with him. His sterling silver flask was never out of sight, and this only made matters worse.

To this day, as I look back, it makes no sense. The first time Mother performed, we thought she had gone crazy. We had all we could do not to fall in the floor laughing. With great pride, Mother would announce to the family that her strict Southern Baptist upbringing was against drinking and fast living. She would not allow her family to be caught up in the evils of drink. She would go on and on until she became too exhausted to continue. None of us dared to move until she discharged us with words such as "Don't walk with the devil cause he'll take you to hell," and then finalized her act with a prayer. No one dared say a word or look at Mother as we hurried out of the room. Life in the household returned to its usual complexities and confusions. We considered it normal. We knew nothing else.

As small children, we usually left the room in a daze, not knowing what to say for fear of what might happen next. My father continued his nightly drinking parties, regardless of Mother's feelings. Naturally, more and more arguments occurred each time he would come home. His drinking usually lasted about ten days, and then he would stop. We never knew when he would start up again. However, his drinking never interfered with him training, grooming, and showing his English setters.

Recently, through the help of the English Setter Association of America, Inc., the secretary, Mrs. Dawn S. Ronyak, was kind enough to contact the association's historian, Carl Sillman, who immediately became interested in my request for any information regarding my dad and the champion English setters he bred at Knollcroft Kennels.

Carl sent me an e-mail informing me that he was familiar with my dad's kennel and was only too happy to help me in locating the information I was seeking. Within twenty-four hours, Carl had sent me a list of five English setter champions from Dad's kennel, including their AKC registration numbers and the dates when the dogs won their AKC championships:

Knollcroft Prince, A-56009, November 1936

Knollcroft White Flash, A-85176, November 1937

Knollcroft Bess, A-56100, June 1938

Knollcroft Chief, A-85174, July 1938

Knollcroft Nancy Lou, A-174058, September 1943

(For more details, please see Appendix A.)

This news from Carl was exciting as well as informative because I had no documentation of any records, ribbons, or trophies on my father's many dogs. To this day, I can still see Dad's huge ribbon book. It consisted of white, blue, yellow, and red ribbons, each representing the class in which one of Knollcroft's dogs won. Dad was proud of each ribbon regardless of how his dog placed in the ring. Each one represented all of his hard work. Unfortunately, they must have been thrown out, as were all of Dad's important documents. I have a small sterling silver cocktail shaker that mother had given me many years ago. Dad received this trophy—R.S. Andrews Trophy, Winners Bitch—for one of his bitches at the Kennel Club of Buffalo. However, it does not give the year or the name of the bitch.

Dad also kept a ledger on different medications for diseases common among dogs. He created a medication formula that actually worked to cure a serious viral disease known as distemper. Back in the 1930s, distemper was usually fatal once a dog came down with it. I often spoke to Dr. Ferris about my dad's medical book. One day, Dad allowed Dr. Ferris to look over his many formulas, and she immediately became intrigued. She was also a lover of dogs and knew the dangers of many of the diseases Dad wrote about, including his medical formula for each one. This book was another of his prized possessions. I often wonder what happened to it.

Dad on a hunting trip.

Carl is in the process of generating a list of champion English setters bred by Dad. Apparently, Knollcroft White Flash went Best of Opposite to the great Ch. Daro of Maridor at the 1940 English Setter

Association Annual Specialty. This gentleman spent many hours searching in the English Setter Archives in order for me to bring back a time in the dog world when the Ritter name was highly respected. Knollcroft Kennels was and still is a name to be proud of. Thanks to this kind man, I have been able to show the legacy my father left for his family. It had nothing to do with money. It was his determination, love of the English setter breed, self-pride, and the ability to create perfection in his show dogs and field-trial pointers. The Knollcroft Kennels was named after our home, Knollcroft. My son, Kevin, has the unusual jagged wooden sign with gold lettering saying "Knollcroft." This sign was about five feet long and two feet wide, and it always hung over the front porch of our home.

Kylie Myers was one of Dad's professional trainers and groomers. He excelled as a handler, once he and Dad's dog entered and paraded around the ring, as the judge for that ring scrutinized every move made by both dog and handler. Dad often remarked that Kylie could always bring out the best in every dog that he showed. I also remember that my dad taught a young kid, Archie (Humpty) Houston, how to groom, train, and work with his dogs. I knew Archie's sister, Marion. I believe that their parents had died and the county placed them in Ms. Mitchell's home. When our country entered WWII, Archie joined the Navy. He was stabbed to death while on duty in Florida.

As children, we were never allowed to get to know these dogs. We couldn't play with them, pick them up, love them, take one for a walk, or take one into our house. However, Dad often allowed me to go in the fields with him when he was training his pointers for an upcoming field trial. This was always very exciting because I saw a dog in action as he flushed out birds in the brush or cornfields, then watch him stay motionless, pointing until he reacted to the sound of the shotgun. For me, this was an unforgettable moment.

I fell in love with Dad's dogs and admired what my father had accomplished. Carl Sillman wrote me, "You should be proud of your father and his dogs. It was very hard to earn American Kennel Club (AKC) championships back in the 1930s and 1940s: so few shows compared to today. Getting the five champions in only five/six years was considered a real feat." Dad's kennels were considered as good as some of the other famous kennels back then.

CIRCUS TIME The one thing that we always looked forward to in the spring was when the circus would come to town. As a small child, this was truly one of my most anticipated moments, much like my waiting for the arrival of Santa Claus. Daddy would say, "Everybody into bed early tonight. Tomorrow morning the circus is coming to town." Who could sleep knowing that! Oh, our imaginations were stirred to a boiling point in anticipation of such an exciting event. Somehow or other, we managed to drift off to sleep only to be awakened (in what seemed like only a moment) by Daddy saying, "It's time to get up and get dressed. It's circus time!"

The time was *only* 4:00 A.M., and that, in itself, was unbelievable. How many times did we ever have a reason to get up that early, get dressed, and go somewhere? Our envisioning of the coming show was definitely apparent on the second floor of our house. We never stopped talking the whole time we were trying to get dressed. We seemed to be in each other's way for no reason at all. Mother always managed to have breakfast waiting for us before we left for our big adventure. Our usual breakfast consisted of hot oatmeal, homemade bread with honey, and cocoa. As a rule, we always enjoyed Mother's cooking, but on this occasion, we felt there was no time for eating. We just wanted to get going.

Soooooooo, on to see the circus come in! The extravaganza would arrive by rail, and the cars were shunted to the freight yard. There would be large open boxcars that carried all of the wagons, equipment, and other items necessary for the circus. The closed boxcars contained all the animals, which were kept in cages except the horses and elephants. These animals were used as haulers to pull wagons and equipment off the train, through the town, and up to the circus grounds. They used them to put up the tents and to pull equipment whenever it was necessary.

There were streamers on the wagons, which made them look festive. Some of these wagons were used as housing for the performers and workers. They reminded me of the gypsy wagons that meandered past our home every spring on their way to a campsite. As we waited for the circus people to unload everything, we could hear a furious roar of a lion somewhere in that maze of cages. Florence and I would move closer together each time we

heard another loud, deep roar. People were crowded around, many standing on tip toes, necks craned, eyes wide with excitement, not wanting to miss a thing, just waiting to see what would be unloaded next.

I couldn't help but notice the people who worked in the circus. I never saw the likes of them. Some wore bands around their foreheads. So many of them had only a few teeth. Most had old clothes that appeared to belong to someone else because they were much too big or were badly torn and worn. There were faces of many colors, all weather-beaten and rough. Their bodies were strong looking, giving them an even meaner, sinister look. As I looked at these men, I felt frightened. I decided that I'd better not run away and join the circus. I'd better stay at home where it was safe. They really looked mean!

Some of the circus men spoke in languages I had never heard before. Cuss words were heard repeatedly. Of course, that was nothing unfamiliar to us, since we had heard Dad use all of them whenever he became frustrated and angry. My father told us that these people were the ground workers who would put up the tents and get everything ready for the afternoon perform-ance. Now I understood why they looked so dirty, sweaty, and sinister, and why I was having second thoughts about running away to join the circus. Perhaps I would do it next year when the circus came to town!

The animals came last. What a thrill! Large and small monkeys were already performing for us as they passed by in their cages. An organ grinder walked by playing his music while a small, cute-looking monkey hung by his tail around his master's neck and chest. Even the clowns with their suits and make-up on, running along side all the cages, gave a wonderful preview of the coming event.

My father placed my little sister, Pauline, on his shoulders so she could see and enjoy the sight of the oncoming parade. We were getting more and more excited. Oh, just to be a part of this! The great desire to run away with the circus was, again, bouncing about in my little mind. The afternoon seemed hours away.

Some clown came down the street banging on a large drum, trying to skip, jump, and play all at the same time. Several dogs were running around him. Tied around his waist was a long rope that was being used to lead a

large elephant that was pulling a wagon. My older sister and I looked at each other when we saw several very pretty girls dressed in scanty costumes standing on the steps of the wagon and waving to the crowd as they passed by. They had big smiles, showing beautiful white teeth against their wild make-up. They were thin, with bodies that made them look like paper dolls.

I began thinking how easy it would be to do what those girls were doing. I could join them. I could smile like they did. I could fix my face like theirs. No one would need to know I had run away from home. If I couldn't be one of them, well, maybe I could be a clown. The world loved clowns. They appeared to be trying to dance, but the area was much too small for all of them to perform. Some ran about the street throwing kisses to the crowd. They were wonderful! All of them had captured the crowd's excitement and before we knew it, an uncontrollable bedlam was in the making.

By now it was 7:00 A.M., and daylight was well on its way. The sun was rising, showing us that it was going to be a nice day for the circus. Slowly, the circus wagons moved down the street, carrying all the animals in their cages. The stench was becoming almost nauseating as we tried not to breathe until the wagons had gone well past us. The noise was captivating. Everyone was clapping and shouting as the animals paraded by. They, too, had reached a height of excitement and bellowed so all could hear.

The crowd was definitely ready for the circus. Many children were running alongside the large wagons and equipment, trying to keep up with the parade, laughing and shouting and keeping in tempo with the atmosphere surrounding them. Everyone loved it! The excitement had overcome everyone! We followed the parade in our car up to the circus grounds. The excitement was even greater there because the workers were starting to put up the tents and unload the wagons.

The animals' wagons were uncovered and put into place. There was a lion in one cage and several brown bears in other cages. Monkeys and chimpanzees were in numerous cages. A beautiful tiger was pacing up and down one cage, occasionally putting a paw through the bars as if to grab at something. However, no one was allowed to get close to these wagons, which had been roped off from the general public.

The large main tent was laid out by a series of pulleys and ropes, looking to the unpracticed eye like a tangled mass of spaghetti. The elephants, hitched to the main poles by means of this maze of ropes, were an important part of this operation. On the command of the trainers, they would start their slow, ponderous walk, and the poles with the tent would rise as if by magic. The workers, who I learned later were called roustabouts, were amazingly proficient in their work: no seemly hurry, no shouting, no confusion, just each person doing his job at precisely the right moment—teamwork at its best.

The bleacher seats were set up. The trapeze ropes were hung. The ticket wagon was situated in its place, and all seemed ready for the afternoon performance in just a few hours' time. The horses were fed and watered. The animal cages were cleaned out and washed down. No foul odor existed now.

The elephants were chained by one leg to large stakes driven deep into the ground after they had been fed and watered and allowed to rest for the coming performance. Other performers were now busy getting their costumes and make-up ready as well. The smell of popcorn popping seemed to hover over the circus grounds. Colorful pink and white cotton candy was being made for the expected afternoon crowd. All seemed in readiness for the gala events of the afternoon and evening. By now it was almost midmorning and time for us to return home for a short rest before we ventured back for more excitement at the circus.

VENDORS OF THE 1930S   As far back as I can remember, Mr. Walter Weeks, the milkman, came every day with his supply of milk. The quart-sized milk bottle, back then, was glass, not heavy cardboard or plastic like today's containers. The milk had several inches of heavy cream on top. There was always an argument over who was going to have the first taste of such a treat. It was the best! Mr. Weeks had the milk brought into his small bottling plant, Ravenwood's Dairy, which was located for many years on the corner of Speedwell and Walker Avenues. Believe or not, the old plant is still standing, but certainly not in use. There he would bottle the raw milk and deliver it to his customers. Milk was not always pasteurized by the individual dairy at that time, since it was not yet a federal law. Home delivery lasted through the war years.

The most important home-delivery person was the iceman. It was necessary for him to come every couple of days to replace the ice that cooled our icebox. Up through the 1930s, he came by horse and wagon. I can remember the many times his horse would suddenly bolt, wagon and all, down the hill because one of us kids gave the horse a good slap on his rump. The poor iceman was either left stranded, depending on how far the horse went before he stopped, or had to run like hell to catch him. In the meantime, the one (or ones) who had slapped the horse would be laughing like crazy. Quickly, the air would be filled with cursing and unkind words directed only at us kids. Refrigerators did not exist during the 1930s (and were not readily available until after World War II).

Around 1939, our iceman bought a truck with an open bed that held the ice. There was a step-up where he could stand to chop the correct amount of ice needed. Between deliveries, the ice was covered with a large tarpaulin. It was similar to the one he had used with the horse and wagon. This tarpaulin would keep the ice from melting as he made his deliveries. Everyone usually put a sign in their kitchen windows to tell him how much ice they would need for that day. That way, by looking at the sign, he only had to make one trip to the house. Once the iceman started delivering by truck, our fun in making the horse run away became only a memory.

Another person who came into our neighborhood on a daily basis during the summer season was the vegetable man. He had an old truck that pulled a wagon containing all kinds of vegetables. He would ring a large bell to announce his arrival. The women would surround his wagon within minutes, inspecting and touching the many different fruits and vegetables. He had the patience of a saint. However, during the war years, many neighbors planted their own gardens. People were afraid of not being able to get vegetables, due to all kinds of food shortages.

Whenever the knife-and-scissor-sharpener man came, usually once a month, he would also announce his arrival with an old school bell. We always knew when he was in the neighborhood because his bell was loud as hell. This man had all of the necessary equipment in the bed of an open truck and did all of his sharpening on the spot as each customer waited for her cutlery. Because women did a great deal of sewing in those days, this

gentleman was very important since he kept their scissors, as well as their many knives, sharp.

Another man came every couple of months selling only spices and vanilla. He had the first closed, van-like truck that I can remember. We would go out to his truck and get my mother's order. The Fuller Brush man was a constant visitor. He always came with a suitcase filled with all kinds of brushes and cleaning supplies. Once an encyclopedia salesman found a family with children, he became a regular as well. Of all the salesmen, this fellow had the best sales pitch. It was hard to refuse this man and twice as hard to get him out of the house, but Mother knew better and never fell for his line.

GRANDFATHER RITTER'S DEATH   Grandfather owned a landscaping business during the late 1800s and the early 1900s and worked on the many mansions located on Madison Avenue in Morristown. He was considered the best landscaper in the area up through the 1920s. Granddaddy was active in local politics and was elected as an alderman for several years.

Grandfather Ritter died in 1935 when I was about six years old. A black wreath was placed on our front door to show that there had been a death in our home. Strange looking men arrived, carrying what looked like a huge chest. We were told that they had come to prepare Grandfather for the viewing and that the huge box was called a casket. They brought the burial box into our guest living room and put it catty-cornered in front of the stairs leading to the second floor.

Florence and I soon noticed that, by the time we got to the third step on the stairway, we could turn around and see Grandfather lying in it. He appeared ghostly white, very stiff, and looked even sterner than usual. He was wearing his favorite black Sunday suit, and it wasn't even Sunday! We found ourselves using the back kitchen stairs that led to the second floor a great deal more during this difficult and emotional time. The sight of Grandfather lying in that thick, white satiny burial box terrified the two of us long after he departed Knollcroft.

His casket was surrounded by many beautiful flowers, which sent a sickening aroma throughout the entire house. An endless stream of people kept

coming into our home. Each person who entered the room immediately went over and stood gazing down at Grandfather. After a few minutes, they quietly turned and walked over to the family to convey their sympathy and then became lost amongst the other viewers. Numerous mourners walked around eating assorted foods supplied by the neighbors and friends. Many sat quietly, wiping away occasional tears. Others tried not to cough too loudly. Many tried desperately to make as little noise as possible when they had to blow their noses.

However, it was a custom that the entire family was expected to take part during this grief-stricken and agonizing period. Pauline was about two years old, and Mandy took charge of her during the viewing. Since this was our first experience with death within our family, we were expected to act completely bereaved. We weren't bereaved nearly as much as we were frightened by what was happening. Many questions concerning death began to invade and haunt our thoughts, but they disappeared as quickly as Grandfather did.

Mother, Dad, and Aunt Love's grief seemed to linger throughout Knollcroft for many months. However, Hubert, my sister, and I almost felt relieved at not having to see Granddaddy's stern, disapproving, and scrutinizing expressions anymore. We always seemed to be in his way, or he was always too busy to talk to us or do anything with us. He never gave hugs, let alone kisses—God forbid! I think Florence and I were scared to death of him. Secretly, we were glad Granddaddy was going away, but why was he leaving in such a strange way? We hoped he had a one-way ticket.

One day, the black wreath was taken from our front door, and much to our surprise, life began to return to our home. Dad was the only one whose tremendous grief refused to let go of his beloved father. The death took an awful toll on him. It took many more months before Dad smiled or seemed like his old self.

After Grandfather's death, Aunt Love and Hubert remained at Knollcroft into the mid-1940s, when Hubert married Sylvia. They rented an apartment down the street from our home, taking Aunt Love with them. Within a year, they were blessed with a son, Bert.

"The Martians Are Coming!" During the last week of October 1938, Orson Welles presented his famous Halloween radio production of H.G. Wells' *The War of the Worlds*. It is a story about aliens from the planet Mars who had landed in New Jersey and were proceeding towards New York City with deadly force. It was presented in the format of a news bulletin that interrupted a musical program. Although this had all been explained at the beginning of the program, many people, including my own mother, did not realize it was only a dramatization. Many took it to be fact and reacted as if it were true.

Panic erupted all over New Jersey and New York City. It took hours before people realized what had happened. Mother was in the kitchen, singing, as she put the finishing touches on tomorrow's morning bread and dinner rolls; we were playing in the living room. She was always convinced that her singing sounded as good as Kate Smith, a famous singer of that period. (Mother's recipe for Cloverleaf Dinner Rolls, which she was baking at that moment, can be found in Appendix B.)

A short time later, she turned the radio on just as a special bulletin was being read. We heard Mother gasping, "Oh, my God! Oh, my God!" Immediately, we knew something was wrong. Florence and I listened as the announcer's terrified voice intoned those unforgettable words, "'Ladies and gentlemen, I have a grave announcement to make. Incredible as it may seem, [. . .] those strange beings who landed in the Jersey farmlands tonight are the vanguard of an invading army from the planet Mars. The battle which took place tonight at Grovers Mill has ended in one of the most startling defeats ever suffered by any army in modern times; seven thousand men armed with rifles and machine guns pitted against a single fighting machine of the invaders from Mars. One hundred and twenty known survivors. The rest strewn over the battle area from Grovers Mill to Plainsboro, crushed and trampled to death under the metal feet of the monster, or burned to cinders by its heat ray. [. . .] . . . At this time martial law prevails throughout New Jersey and eastern Pennsylvania. We take you now to Washington for a special broadcast on the National Emergency . . . the Secretary of the Interior . . ..'"

Seconds later, Mother ran into the living room, screaming, "Oh, God, we're being invaded! Girls, get up! Help me, Christ; get up off the damn floor! We're being invaded by Martians! What should we do? Florence, hold Pauline! Don't let go of her!" Within moments, Mother had gone totally out of control.

We never saw her so frightened. She was running around like a chicken with its head chopped off, screaming. She frightened us more than the Martians, whoever they were. By this time, we were all crying. Mother locked the front door, screaming for us to follow her. We ran around the house not knowing where to go or what to do. Daddy wasn't home, which only made it worse as Mother cried, "You bastard, you're never around when I need you. God, I'm so afraid." She sank to the floor as we watched the energy drain from her helpless body. Florence grabbed her arm and began shouting, "Mother, get up. We have to do something to keep them out." Mother's face was as white as a ghost. She looked pathetic as she got up.

Her realization of the moment made Mother come to life. She began yelling, "Move! Move faster, damn it!" Florence and I shoved, pulled, and carried furniture to stack against the windows and front door. We were ready to do anything to keep the Martians from devouring us.

Dewitt Compton, our neighbor, heard our screams. He also knew that it was just a Halloween story. He began banging on our front door. "Areta, open the door. Open the door for God's sake!" She kept bellowing, "Save yourself, Dewitt, go home, go home!" We could hear his body smashing against the door, trying to get in. Mother continued her wailing, hearing nothing Mr. Compton was saying.

Florence and I were frozen with fear, staring at each other in disbelief as we huddled behind the couch. The next thing we knew, Mr. Compton was in the room, shaking Mother. His voice dominated the entire area. "Areta, Areta, it's only a radio program, nothing more," he blurted out. "You're in no danger! There are no Martians!" At that, Mother sank to the floor, trying to digest the news, trying to regain her composure. Slowly, normalcy returned to Knollcroft. We were safe. It was all a hoax. However, when we went to bed, the darkness would not allow us to sleep. It was a long, torturous night.

Mother wasn't the only one who had panicked that night. Many in the area loaded their families in automobiles and trucks, trying to get to the hills where they might be safe from these unknown creatures. Everyone was out to save himself! Lunacy swept over the community, the state, the entire country. For several days, the majority of people talked about the mass hysteria that ran rampant, devouring all common sense. Some people didn't want to talk about it. Many were still reliving that horrific moment. It all happened so quickly; ending as quickly as it started.

1930S–1940S: FAVORITE ICE CREAM STORES

I remember Silverstein's Ice Cream store, located on Speedwell Avenue, directly across from Cutler Street. I was extremely thin and sickly as a child, and the doctor ordered a malted milkshake every day to try to put weight on me. I never missed a day going to Silverstein's. Dorothy, the owner's daughter, worked behind the counter and always added extra ice cream in my malted shakes. I could hardly get myself up on the stool and, at times, needed a helping hand. She would talk to me as if I were her younger sibling. She made me feel special. When we were fortunate to have a few pennies in our pockets, we ran to Dorothy's store. Allowances were unheard of during my entire youth. Comic books were considered a special treat and something that we seldom asked for. A slap on the side of the head or on our small behinds usually took care of that little question.

Ad for Shalit's Drug Store, owned by the parents of renowned movie critic, Gene Shalit.

Shalit's Drug Store was the other store we made frequent trips when the few pennies we had began burning our pockets. Shalit's was down the street from Silverstein's, but they had a larger selection of everything we liked. The Shalit family included two sons, Nathan and Gene, the well-known movie critic on NBC. Their home was on Cutler Street, which was within the boundaries of our neighborhood. He and my

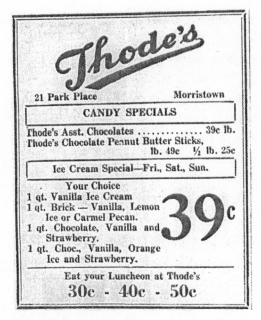

A 1934 ad for Thode's, the best ice cream shop in Morristown.

sister, Florence, graduated from Morristown High School in 1943. Occasionally, when we had a heavy snowstorm, Gene would join us sleigh riding down Elliott Street. Most of the time, he was too busy working in his father's store, which was located at the apex of the triangle dividing Sussex and Speedwell Avenues. He had little time for playing. I never forgot Gene's mother. She worked in their store covering the three counters. One was for ice cream; one for newspapers, candy, and magazines; and the other for drugs. She was a sweet lady who helped us more than once when we didn't have enough money. As we got into our teen years, we made more trips to this store.

"THOSE GIRLS" During these early years of schooling I found myself faced with what became my worst nightmare. It involved three girls who were my classmates throughout our grammar and high school years. Although Mother was not involved with their mothers socially, she did know them. Whenever she ran into one of them, the conversation always revolved around their daughters and their social activities. These chats seemed to irritate

Mother and, naturally, by the time she arrived home, she had worked herself into a livid state. Mother turned on me with vengeance and disgust. In her eyes, these three girls represented everything I wasn't and everything Mother wished I were. I lived being questioned why I didn't act like Jean, Carol, and Joan. Mother thought they were such little ladies. They always looked so pretty and acted so proper. Terrible feelings of anger and inadequacy became a part of my life. I retreated more and more within myself. I began avoiding Mother as much as I could. I learned to avoid "those girls," as well.

As the years went by, I became very aware of my own unique skills that set me apart from those girls. These skills only added more fuel to the fire that was raging in Mother. I had become a total humiliation to her. I knew that they couldn't shoot a gun like I could! I became a skeet shooter or "skeeter," that is, one who could shoot clay targets. They wouldn't dare pick up one of those dead muskrats that I would trap and then skin so I could sell their fur!

They would never climb to the top of our handsome copper beech tree. They never knew what a wonderful tree was all about, like *I* did. Its branches seemed to cradle each of us as we climbed up into its bosom. It was almost like a mother cradling her child to her breasts for protection and love. This wonderful tree kept us safe as our imaginations created images of characters such as Tom Mix hiding in it from Indians, soldiers hiding among its branches as an enemy army below searched them out, or Tarzan swinging from one branch to another.

I would have loved to have seen Jean, Carol, or Joan put a big, juicy worm on a fishing hook as its innards oozed all over the hook and their hands. They never had the fun of working a hunting dog in the field and flushing out a pheasant or quail, only to take it down with one quick shot from a shotgun. My father had taught me well. I was his boy! He was proud of me! My mother was infuriated to think that her daughter was being taught activities that didn't fit into a young lady's lifestyle. Again, those girls were, in my mother's mind, everything I wasn't. Each of them always looked neat and cute in whatever they wore. They never looked messy or dirty. I was so different. Ah, my poor dear Mother. I drove her crazy.

By the time, those girls and I got into the upper grades, I knew I had nothing in common with them. They had taunted me all of my schooldays, and not one of them ever knew it. They brought me such misery, such disapproval from my mother, and they never knew it. They haunted me for most of my life and, once again, they never knew it.

Occasionally, I would run into one of them as the years went by, and I wondered why Mother was so impressed with them. I don't believe one of them could have walked in my shoes and survived. Reality can be difficult to accept, but looking back, I got stronger as the years passed.

THE CHERRY, MULBERRY, AND CHESTNUT TREES I have already mentioned the copper beech trees that we climbed and played in as children, but there were also several other trees that played a part in my childhood. We had a beautiful cherry tree that was next to one of our many garages. The flavor of those cherries was superb. My mother would make delicious cherry pies and gave every child a chance to pick enough for their mothers to do the same. It became a neighborhood tree and everyone waited for its fruit to ripen.

First came the cherry blossoms, always predicting a large quantity of cherries. When the cherries began to ripen, a great deal of excitement and anticipation amongst the neighborhood was noted. Picking was right around the corner, and each mother was making the necessary preparations for the arrival of such a delicacy. A cherry pie, not to mention everyone's favorite homemade cherry jam, would soon be forthcoming on every neighbor's table.

This tree served us well for many years in several different ways. It was a ladder for us to climb onto the top of the roofing garages where my father kept his homing pigeons. The entire neighborhood found these birds fascinating. Dad always made his trips to release the birds on weekends, and when the news went out that he and his birds were on the road, everyone began to look upward for the first sighting of their return. I would help Dad load the birds into their cages, hoping he would allow me to go with him. He had spent many long hours training the homing pigeons and never rested until the last one returned to its cage. He was very gentle with each one and always released the pigeons with pride, concern, and care.

The cherry-tree ladder also allowed us to get on top of the garages and play our games of cowboy and Indians, cops and robbers. The guys who managed to get on the roofs always became the heroes because they were able to shoot everyone below. We made all of our weapons, such as our bows and arrows, slingshots, and wooden pistols. Occasionally, one of us would get a store-bought water pistol or a Hopalong Cassidy rifle. Whenever this happened, our games would always end up in a real fight between the toy's owner and the rest, who just wanted to be able to say that they had shot a store-bought water pistol or rifle. Wow! It was well worth the pain.

Another favorite tree that the entire neighborhood enjoyed was a mulberry tree. It was located on Walker Avenue, right next to the roadway, making it very easy for any of us kids to climb and pick its fruit. We would come home with our clothing nearly ruined by the stains from the juice from the berries we had eaten. Our stained hands and faces would stay purple for days. All of our mothers would make jam or pies when the fruit was edible.

The huge chestnut tree located on Sussex Avenue just across from the beginning of Lake Road also played a small part in our young lives. This tree was magnificent in structure and produced large chestnuts. We would gather up these nuts and make pipes out of them by cleaning out each center with our small penknives; then we would make a hole in the side of the nut and insert a stick as a pipe stem. Every autumn, we would pick up the nuts that would fall from the tree and take them home to our mothers for roasting and cooking. We often hid behind that tree when we played our pocketbook trick on April Fools' Day. However, we couldn't climb it because its branches were too high for us to reach.

As the years went by, our chestnut tree became infected with a disease that eventually destroyed it as well as all of the chestnut trees throughout America. Because of this, chestnuts were shipped into this country from Europe. It was discovered within the past couple of decades that European chestnut seedlings that had been brought into this country were surviving well. Arborists hoped that eventually they would restore our chestnut trees to their rightful place as both a shade and commercial resource. However, our tree was never replaced, but its memory still remains as part of our past.

MY SIXTH GRADE TEACHER, MISS COWAN   Alexander Hamilton
School, located on Mill Street, went up through the seventh grade. From
there, we went to Morristown High School, which covered all the remaining
years of schooling. However, my favorite teacher, and the one teacher I never
forgot, was Miss Cowan, my sixth grade teacher. It was in her classroom that
I discovered my real love of nature. We would take nature trips out into the
swamps, the woods, and the open fields to see what we could find. Our
entire class loved this very special lady. She was fun and exciting, even
though she was considered an "old maid." At this period of time, the late
1930s, becoming an old maid was usually considered the worst thing that
could happen to a young woman. Because of our admiration of her, none of
us would ever have said anything to hurt her. Miss Cowan was as thin as a
pencil but always stood very straight, which made her look much taller than
she really was. Her short, black hair surrounded a stern face. Her looks never
bothered any of us because she was so exhilarating as a teacher.

I believe she was the only teacher in the entire school who made all of her
students both eager to learn and eager to please. Her nature-study walks,
regardless of when they occurred—during school, after school, or over a
weekend—always became top priority for her students. None of us wanted
to miss any of her trips. Miss Cowan turned her teaching into an exciting
and informative event.

We studied many of the local birds while on our walks. We also learned
to recognize their calls and songs. To this day, I still look for many of the
birds, but so many of them have disappeared from our area due to the
growth in population, homes, and businesses. To find a little hummingbird
today is most unusual, at least where I live. Yet I have gone to Arizona and
Georgia and found large numbers of them there.

I can remember the excitement we all felt when we would come across
a slow-moving wood turtle, painted turtle, or a box turtle. Where have
they all gone? I never see them anymore. I always made my father stop the
car if I spotted a turtle in the road when we were going somewhere. Miss
Cowan taught us the importance of each living animal, no matter what
species it was.

Miss Cowan taught us to check under rocks and stones for the many types of tiny insects that lived under them. Our most impressive find would be to lift up a rock and find a salamander staring up at us. That was the greatest because it resembled a miniature lizard. The only thing missing was the fire that we imagined coming from its mouth. To get that slimy salamander into a jar and carry it home would have been truly an act of bravery. Miss Cowan never allowed this, since she felt nature should stay untouched. While the other girls in the class cringed at the thought of touching a salamander, I was the only one who dared to pick it up in order for each of us to look at it more closely. Miss Cowan always made sure I placed it back under the same rock.

Are the children of today even aware of these interesting small creatures? What about tadpoles? I always had some kind of jar filled with something slimy sitting in my bedroom or playhouse. It was exciting to watch them slowly evolve into frogs. The tiny spring peepers with their shrill piping call made one aware that they were around. Their call was heard only when evening set in. Then it sounded like there were hundreds tucked away in the trees. The bullfrog, larger than a softball, made one think there were a multitude of them instead of only one. There were so many different types, and we got to know just about all of them. Such wonderful discoveries were typical of everything we came across during our many nature hikes with this very special teacher. Thanks to Miss Cowan and her teaching, I am still alertly looking for the unique. She definitely left an impression on me, and I don't think I will ever forget her. Now when a person can truthfully say that sixty-five years later, that's what I call an *excellent* teacher!

"THE OLD LADIES" My association with Auntie Young took another path as well. As I got older, around the age of ten, I began to play the clarinet. Mother was excited about this, since all of her friends had their daughters playing some type of musical instrument, and she was finally able to say, "My daughter, Teeny, plays the clarinet." Yes, that was true! I played quite well. Before I knew it, Mother had me co-starring with Auntie Young as the entertainment for her monthly social functions at Knollcroft.

Auntie Young would play the piano, and I would play my clarinet. We became a team. These were some of the few times Mother appeared proud of me. Unfortunately, they were only for the moment. I knew my total lack of sophistication was infuriating to her. Once the show was over, she would retreat back to her never-ending disapproval of me. Mother would constantly remind me to smile. These were her guests! In my eyes, those old ladies seemed to sit as if they were glued to the chairs. There wasn't even one smile amongst them. Each face had a stern and mean look.

When Auntie Young and I would complete our musical program, Mother's guests would stiffly clap their prim-and-proper white-gloved hands, which produced only barely audible applause. Their hands hardly moved, and their fingers scarcely touched each other. The more I looked at them, the more I began to see a distinct resemblance between the "Wicked Witch of the West" and each one of them.

Auntie Young and I would play "God Bless America" as our opening piece. She would play the first half of the song alone. She considered this a patriotic song and felt that it should be played strongly and sung with the greatest pride. I was expected to join her as a duet when she got to the part, "from the mountains, to the prairies, to the oceans, white with foam." We were great together! I blew that clarinet as hard as I could, completely caught up in the spirit of that moment. Those last few bars, "God bless America, my home sweet home," even sent chills up my spine. We played one stanza after another several times.

Spunky, our pointer, was never allowed in the living room when Mother was entertaining. However, there were times when he managed to sneak in and hide under some table or chair. He knew just the right moment to announce his presence. It seemed as if every time the ladies would sing, Spunky would let his appearance be known. He would throw back his head, releasing long, painful howls. I had all I could do not to laugh.

I stood before the group, glaring icily, determined that our playing was going to be heard over their singing. My mother, in the meantime, would be busy trying to get Spunky out of the room before any of the ladies realized that he was only trying to stop that terrible bellowing they were inflicting on him. They kept on singing. He resumed howling.

As I watched Mother struggle to remove Spunky from our presence, I wanted to give him a big hug, but I continued playing. He continued to wail on his trip to another part of the house. The more they sang, the louder I played! My thoughts turned to Kate Smith. Those wide and hideous mouths that I was forced to stare at and listen to could never produce her version of "God Bless America." I do believe they all thought they sounded like her. They were terrible! Kate Smith was the only person who ever sang that song the way it should be sung.

"The Star Spangled Banner" was always our closing song. Once again, the ladies had their chance to perform while we played. The moment we began our finale, the ladies immediately stood at attention, and proudly ended that part of the social affair by singing as loudly as they could, "Oh, say can you see, by the dawn's early light . .. .." Off in the distance, we could hear Spunky still wailing his cry of distress.

After the entertainment, I was expected to help Mother serve her guests. By this time, I was tired of all that was hiding under the façade of those smiling, self-righteous faces. I would set all the fancy sandwiches, small cakes and Mother's home-baked cookies on the dining table. My orders were to step away from the table, assist only if someone was in need of help, and above all *smile*.

These women never failed to descend like vultures upon Mother's fancy sandwiches, small cakes, and assorted cookies. Whenever she entertained, it was always overdone. The table was set to perfection with Grandmother's silverware and one of her lovely white linen tablecloths. At this point, Mother was enjoying her own self-induced high. Prouder than a peacock, she strutted up and down the length of the table.

Even as a young girl, I could read Mother's mind as she paraded around the room, secretly concealing her country-girl background from all. She was a proud woman who loved belonging to all the local societies, and these moments made her life in the social world come alive.

To this day, I can still hear Auntie Young and me playing at Mother's many social affairs. Whenever I hear or sing our national anthem or "God Bless America," the scene of our playing together flashes before me. It leaves me with a slight chuckle and a feeling of peace as I proudly stand at attention.

FOURTH OF JULY An annual tradition in our family was making home-made ice cream on the Fourth of July, followed by the neighborhood picnic, which was finalized with a beautiful explosive display of fireworks by the neighborhood fathers. Fireworks were easily obtained and available to buy at any store anytime during the year because there was no law to prohibit their sale. The complete agenda was essential to create the mood of America's birthday! Patriotism seemed to sweep over our backyard only to gain momentum as the day progressed into the late evening. My father had three ice-cream makers churning at the same time; each one held a different flavor; vanilla, chocolate, and strawberry.

Early on the morning of the Fourth of July, Daddy would gather us kids by the outside cellar entrance, announcing that it was time to make the ice cream! Oh, the excitement from this anticipated message created an exhila-ration only equaled by our thrill of seeing the first large exploding firecracker of the evening. None of us liked having to turn the crank handles, but it was a rule that we all had to help if we wanted any of the finished product.

Mother would prepare the creamy, smooth liquids to go into the ice-cream makers while Daddy packed the space around liquid-filled containers with ice and salt. Dad would set the buckets by the outdoor cellar entrance. He kept extra ice in a large sink in the cellar so it would not melt until we needed it. We would then take turns in turning the crank handles, wanting each turn to be the last so we could finally taste the results of our hard work. The more we turned, the more we craved that first taste.

Even the neighborhood kids would come and help turn the crank handles once the news spread. This manual job was very difficult because a person's arm would become almost numb from constantly turning the handle. It seemed as if it only took a few minutes before one was looking for the next kid to take over. The reward was well worth any agony we had to suffer. There was always a dispute amongst us about who was going to get to "clean" the paddles once Daddy removed them from the containers.

All the neighborhood women would bring special dishes for the event, which was always held in our backyard. The highlight of the holiday finally came. It was time to relish and devour the fruits of our labor. It was ice-cream

time, party time, and time for the fireworks! An abundance of assorted foods was arranged neatly on the many picnic tables: fried chicken, barbecued pork, potato, macaroni and vegetable garden salads, homemade baked beans, deviled eggs, and many different types of cakes, pies, and other wonderful desserts.

We always knew when it was getting time to eat, as one of the father's would be designated to be the chef for grilling the hot dogs and hamburgers. Dad had a large BBQ grill built in our backyard for such occasions. It was the only grill in the neighborhood. In just a short time, the assigned cook would have the aroma of his cooking floating over the entire area. Beautifully decorated cakes and desserts were displayed as well, tempting all as we gazed upon such a feast.

Scattered about the yard were well-packed tubs of ice, which held the many sodas and cold beers. Of course, the beer was only meant for the men, but there was always one kid in the crowd who would manage to sneak a few beers out of the tubs. These beers were passed, quickly and quietly, around to the kids who were brave enough to take a swig. Naturally, this kid became bigger than life in our eyes—at least, for that evening. Wow! To take the beer right under the noses of all our parents was really a tough thing to do. The more we sipped from the stolen and forbidden beer, the more we giggled. Our parents never noticed our shenanigans; at least that was what we wanted to think.

One of us always ended up getting sick as a dog as our sampling continued well into the evening. We later learned that our parents were very much aware of our folly of those evenings. They were good sports. A fun time was had by all, and as the last crash from the bursting fireworks enveloped the area, we felt the pride that went into the final moments of such an important birthday: "Happy Birthday, America!"

VISITING GRANDPARENTS IN NORTH CAROLINA From my early years up through my early twenties, my family in North Carolina consisted of Grandfather and Grandmother Whorton, their sons: Elmo and his wife, Marguerite; Freddie and his wife, Jessie; Howard, married once, but divorced eleven years later; and Julius and his wife, Clara. They were the ones

who captured my heart at a young age. I was fascinated by the differences in our lifestyles. Their warmth and love overwhelmed me. They made me feel important. It was something I never felt in my New Jersey family. I belonged! I lived for the moment when my mother would make her yearly announcement of my going to North Carolina to visit Grandmother and Grandfather Whorton. My two sisters never found the same kind of joy or love that I captured in the small village, called Oriental, where my grandparents lived. My sisters went once and never went back. Those times in Oriental were some of my happiest times as a young girl.

Me in front of Grandmother's house in Whortonsville, 1932.

When I was a small child, Grandfather would take me in his mule cart to visit family members who lived in other small villages in the lowlands of Pamlico County or to travel to New Bern for supplies. This always made me feel special. Riding in that cart ignited my imagination and always made the excitement of the day difficult to conceal.

Granddaddy would shout all kinds of obscenities at his mule, snapping his whip as it cracked above its back. The next minute, he would sound more like a lover as he leaned over to pat its rump. Sometimes, the mule's pace would suddenly change to a fast-moving gallop (for a mule that is), for which both Granddaddy and I were totally unprepared. Immediately, Granddaddy would pull back on the reins, forcing the mule to calm right down. That mule knew who was in charge. Granddaddy always portrayed himself as a great muleteer with fascinating stories wrapped around the bravery of those men. In my eyes, as young as I was, he was my great muleteer.

When my imagination would nearly reach an exploding point, I would beg Granddaddy to pretend with me. Before long, he would join in. We would pretend we were back in the old days trying to outrun a group of

Bethel Free Will Baptist Church in Whortonsville, where Grandmother's father, Timothy Martin, her little brother, and many of the Whortons are buried.

attacking Indians or that we were outlaws eluding the sheriff. Sometimes Granddaddy would let me hold the reins and sit in his seat just like one of his storybook muleteers. That was my special moment. I held on to those reins as if my life depended on them as I guided the mule down the dirt road. Our trips to visit family members usually took about an hour. How I hated to give the reins back to Granddaddy, pleading, "Not yet! Please, Granddaddy, just a little longer!"

Our trips to New Bern, however, always took on a more serious mood. Granddaddy would harness two of his larger mules to his four-wheeled wagon. Getting the monthly supplies was a time-consuming job. It was all business once Granddaddy secured the mules and went into the store with his order. Talking was out of the question until Granddaddy had everything loaded onto the cart. I learned just to follow him around, be quiet, and never ask for anything. Once he completed loading the wagon, the afternoon took on a more relaxed mood as we traveled back home.

Arriving back at Grandmother's for one of her delicious suppers seemed to conclude another perfect day. Back then, the roads below New Bern were mostly dirt. Asphalt roads were only common within city limits.

Transportation in the lowlands was mostly by mules, horses, and carts. Only a few more fortunate folks had cars or trucks. Granddaddy had an old truck that hadn't been used in ages and a beat-up old car. However, he had more faith in his mules to get him where he wanted to go. The car, when it was operating, was used only to take the family to church.

Another exciting adventure occurred when my cousins would take me to school with them. It was a one-room schoolhouse, and I was, on that day, the most gawked at person in the room. When I think of it today, it was exactly like I had just arrived from another planet in their eyes. New Jersey seemed so far away. Yes, at that time, the mid-1930s, it really was far away!

It was with many of these children that I first heard gospel music and gospel singers. When the Negro tent revivals would come to the village, we would sneak under the canvas and wait as men, women, and children filed in. The Negroes considered these revivals their source of survival. It eased their pain and the hardships that still existed in the 1930s. I was intrigued the moment I saw and heard the enthusiasm that poured from the people within the overcrowded tent. The beautiful and exciting music, as well as the preacher's words, quickly turned the revival into a passionate frenzy. Many instantly leapt to their feet shouting, with their arms reaching upward toward the heavens, and then, when exhaustion overtook them, they collapsed onto the floor. The ground shook beneath us as many stomped their feet and clapped their hands. Their elation had risen to a new level of hysteria. I was mesmerized. The air was filled with the smell of their sweat and the odor of many perfumes and heavy powders. Even though we were speechless and motionless spectators, we began to feel the excitement that was bouncing off the sides of the canvas tent.

One time in particular remains fresh in my memory. One evening, when the Negro revival came to the village, several of my cousins and I once again crept under the canvas to wait for the unknown and watch for the unexpected. The preacher began walking up and down in front of the small wooden table that served as an altar. When he first started to preach, his voice was calm and gentle. A few songs were sung. An occasional "Sweet Jesus" was heard from the congregation. The preacher's voice became

stronger with an excitement that began to move his flock. One parishioner after another slowly rose up from the wooden benches with arms outstretched, singing, bellowing, "Holy Jesus, amen!" Many were overcome with a spiritual excitement, I had never seen before. The preacher's voice swelled to a thunderous intensity. We kept looking up for fear the tent would collapse under such a commotion. By now, every person was caught up in his own spiritual ecstasy. The preacher began moving his hands a little more until his whole body was trembling. He had captured his audience as he wallowed in his accomplishment. Again, we heard the loud shouts, "Thank you, sweet Jesus!" The next thing we knew the entire congregation was shouting and singing.

Our eyes got bigger and bigger. We were too afraid to move. We were wedged in tightly together, hoping we would not be seen. The fear of these strange people and their antics, along with the fear of God, began to play tricks with our little minds. We dared not speak. We could not move. The bottom of the canvas that laid over us seemed as if it were getting heavier and heavier. A woman with arms outstretched, jumped up from her chair, shouting words I never heard before, and ran up to the preacher. She fell down and began gyrating on the ground. What a sight! Then, before we knew it, others came forward and began doing the same. We watched in disbelief. One by one they began to stop, each lying motionless. Our imaginations had spun out of control by now. Was Satan behind all of this? They were either dead or the preacher had put a spell on them!

The excitement was overwhelming. Time seemed to stand still as we stared and waited to see some type of movement from those poor crazed creatures. One by one, they began to get up, some wailing, some dancing and clapping, and some with exhausted voices echoing, "Thank you, sweet Jesus. Thank you!"

By now we began to feel guilty. Perhaps Satan was instigating our boldness? That thought scared each of us. Even *we* began to feel the preacher's words, and our watching suddenly seemed wrong. These people were good and truly loved God. What in the hell where we doing there? We wiggled out from under the canvas and started to run. We never looked back, silently hoping we could make it to Grandmother's house before the devil caught us!

The white peoples' revivals, though, lacked the enthusiasm and the emotional excitement that was so much a part of the Negro revivals. However, the white revivals with their music, their singing, and the preacher's soothing words made me feel safe as I sat under the canvas tent. Just enough excitement abounded. Perhaps that is why, today, I play my gospel music on my organ with such joy and peace. The stroke of each key provides me with that same feeling that I experienced way back then.

Another memory that I cling to passionately was my grandmother's complete delight in preparing unforgettable feasts. My grandparents had so little, yet the table was always filled with the most succulent foods imaginable. Homemade hot biscuits, heavy cream and fig preserves, and Grandmother's wonderful country sausage! It is impossible to find treasures such as these today. The tastes remain with me. The shrimp and crabmeat dishes are just as luscious in my mind today as they tasted to me as a child. Oh, not to be forgotten, Grandmother's seven layer cake. Wow! Only she knew how to create such a delight. I have tried to carry her spirit over to my own grandchildren so they will have a chance to experience the love that really made those dishes so special.

The front of my grandparents' home in Oriental, 2002. They moved here from their place over the crab plant.

The hardships Grandmother endured never surpassed the joy she constantly showed throughout my visit. As a child who never had to experience any type of hardship, I was fascinated watching Grandmother do her weekly wash. Grandmother never saw a washing machine like my mother had! Her so-called washing machine consisted of a huge well-blackened iron pot, filled with steaming hot water, placed over burning pine logs that sent the aroma of pine pitch through the air. Grandmother made her own oversized, homemade soap (made of borax, lye, and the fat from the meats used at her food table). When she would put it into the boiling water the water became, to our amazement, a glistening mass of bubbles. This homemade soap was known as the "clean-wash suds" during the 1930s. The recipe had been handed down from one generation to another until it was mass-produced and sold in all the local general stores. Grandmother had a long wooden pole that she used to stir the clothing around, just like she was making a cake. This was difficult work.

A section of back of my grandparents' house showing the screened porch where Granddaddy always sat in his rocking chair, smoking his pipe and swatting flies, which he claimed we kids let in every time we opened the screened door. This summer picture from 1949 shows my younger cousins. Back row (l–r): Leroy and Wyman. Middle row (l–r): Paul, Danny, and Diana. Front row (l–r): Carol and Barbara. They remembered Granddaddy acting the same with them, and we all had a good laugh. Those were fun times.

She took such pride as she hung her clean wash to dry. A rope wrapped around four long, thick wooden poles was her clothesline. She always seemed to place a small pinch of snuff (very finely ground tobacco) on the inside of her cheek before getting involved in any of her daily jobs. A little snuffbox was always tucked down in some pocket of her outfit, ready to be opened whenever she felt the need. Her spit can was close by, never out of range. However, I tried to distance myself from Grandmother when she was dipping and spitting, just in case she missed her can and hit me.

Grandmother was a tiny woman whose black hair was always rolled into a tightly wrapped bun. Wisps of her hair occasionally fell from her severe hairstyle. There was hardly a wrinkle on her gentle face. Her soft blue eyes sparkled. A very strong woman was bound within that small frame. She was a woman who was never afraid to take on any job that would provide her family of nine children with a decent lifestyle, obtained through the providence of God and her own hard work.

She was raised as an only child. Even so, she had the ability to instill in her children the importance of loving each other and keeping a family together. Sharing was a part of her. Selfishness never entered her life. She lived every day of her life as a representative of the full meaning of family and love. Besides her four daughters, Grandmother had the five sons I have mentioned: Rommie, Fred, Elmo, Julius, and Howard. These five men carried the beautiful traits of my grandmother throughout their entire lives. They were raised with principles and values that were never questioned, destroyed, conveniently discarded, or compromised. Although no one ever said it, we all knew that Grandmother was definitely the pillar of strength that held the Whorton family together long after her demise.

Grandfather Whorton was a hard-working man, gentle, kind, and loving to everyone, but with reservations. I never saw Grandfather without his corncob pipe, which always dangled so precariously between his teeth. It seemed like a source of security and comfort for him.

He was a rather short man in stature, with a slight fullness creeping around his waistline. He had whitish, thinning hair. This seemed to make his ruddy, smooth face appear large. He was wrinkle free, considering the

hardships he had to endure. I loved to hear Grandfather laugh because it seemed to make his round little belly jiggle.

Grandfather's rocking chair remained on the porch. He loved to rock. I can still see him sitting there. In one hand he held a well-used, nasty flyswatter. He hated to see a fly invade his area. Many times we felt that he was about ready to use it on us as well. He was constantly complaining about us running around, opening, shutting, and banging the old screen door as he sat directly across from it. Letting his nemesis "the fly" penetrate that opening would never do! It was a constant war between Grandfather and "the flies." We annoyed him to no end, but we kept him busy and out of Grandmother's way. He swore that we were on the side of the flies. Grandmother would always scold him when he was acting so nasty. He would then behave just long enough to make sure Grandmother was out of sight. Nevertheless, I found this man to be very caring and refreshing to be around. I loved him. It was a silent and shared affection.

The stories Grandfather would tell us kept us entranced and glued to our chairs. One of his favorite stories was about when he owned and operated a large cotton field just after the turn of the century. He had many Negroes working in his field. They cared for Grandfather and, at that point in the story, Grandfather would always sit back, looking satisfied, commenting, "Yes, they really loved me!" By now, we had become so used to his way of telling the story that we waited with childish anticipation for the next sentence. We thought that the buttons on his shirt would surely pop: "I loved them as well! I was good to them!"

A loud and deep sigh was always due about this time. Grandfather shifted his body so it seemed to fit more snugly in the chair. With another sigh, he would sit back and continue his story. They worked hard. He knew their misery as he worked with them. What they endured, Grandfather endured. Bleeding fingers and hands, badly torn by the rough cotton balls, had become a way of life for each of them, adding to their suffering. They had to tolerate living with never-ending back pain from bending over the seemingly endless rows of cotton, just to earn enough to provide food for the evening meal.

Their discomfort was often temporarily alleviated when one of them would break into song. Instinctively, the huge field would come alive with faces looking upward to the heavens as if God Himself were overseeing them. The most enchanting singing and breathtaking chorus would envelop the entire field, momentarily, distracting them from their suffering and stimulating their cramped muscles, making it possible for them to continue once more until sunset ended another day in the field. By this time, tears would stream down Grandfather's cheeks as he, once again, stated how he could still hear that beautiful music whenever he thought of that time and could see his cotton

Granddaddy and Grandmother with my younger cousins. Back row (l–r): Howard, Wyman, and Leroy. Front row (l–r): Danny (sitting) and Judy. Lorraine, Judy's mother, is in back of my grandparents.

field as it once was. How he loved their singing, their faith, their joy in just being alive, living so meagerly but thankful for the little they had. When misfortune came to Grandfather in the form of losing everything he had worked for, the remembrance of the struggling, hard-working Negroes inspired him to keep his faith in God and move on, since tomorrow was another day. He survived!

Grandfather often told us stories about his travels during the early 1900s on his coaster supply boat. He traveled along the coastal tidewaters of the Albemarle and Pamlico Sounds, which eventually took him into the Chesapeake Bay area. During this time, Grandfather owned a cotton gin. He would buy cotton from the local people, take this cotton to his gin, and put it into bales.

Grandfather loaded the many cotton bales onto his boat, carrying them to Norfolk, where he sold them. He had a crew of about eight hands to man

the boat. It took a total of ten days to make a round trip. On these trips, he would shop for necessary supplies not only for all the local people in his area, but also for the general merchandise stores along his water route. He would bring these supplies back, distribute them, and then start all over. He did this for many years. His general store and the cotton gin were mysteriously destroyed by fire within a short time of each other; thus ending his career as a coaster supply boatman. He then began to make his living by fishing and crabbing in the local waters and farming his land.

Besides their large farm, which surrounded their home, Grandfather at one time owned the only general store in the area. While Grandfather was running the coaster supply boat, Grandmother ran the general store because she had a better educational background than Grandfather. As a young girl, Grandmother had the opportunity to attend private school. In those days, that was considered a privilege only enjoyed by the wealthy. An older woman called Aunt Hattie watched her children while she operated the store. Aunt Hattie lived with them, so the family was never apart.

Grandfather and Grandmother were the first people in Pamlico County who had a telephone and a piano. The general store became a success, and life was becoming easier for the family. Grandmother was proud of her accomplishments. However, a vengeful local man who owed Grandfather a

Granddaddy's crab plant. In later years it became the Jessie and Freddie Whorton Crab House. (Photo, circa 1939, from At Home in Oriental: 1878 to 1945, *compiled by the Oriental Centennial Committee.)*

large and long-overdue sum of money set fire to the store. My grandfather apparently was not a shrewd businessman. He kept many people on his books for food and supplies at his own expense, never placing any pressure on them. He always had faith they would pay their debts, but the fire destroyed all the records, and the losses were never retrieved. With the burning of his general store and, just a few months later, the mysterious burning of his cotton gin, Grandfather went back into fishing, shrimping, and crabbing for a living. They left Whortonsville and moved to Vandemere, a small village on the Pamlico Sound. A couple of years later, they returned to the old homestead in Whortonsville, where he farmed and continued fishing.

In the late 1930s, Granddaddy opened his own crab plant in a neighboring village called Oriental. This opened up jobs for the local people, both Blacks and whites. They became crab pickers and workers in his small plant. He had helped make the area a productive community. This was his life for many years to come, but unbeknownst to him, the many coastal storms were slowly draining him of his drive in this business. His life was full of disappointments in attempting to achieve financial independence. He was a driven man with a dream of overcoming the odds, but unfortunately, he never really succeeded.

When I was visiting my Aunt Affie in August 1995, she mentioned that my grandparents had a little boy named Robert Algar Whorton, born August 26, 1898, and died on May 19, 1899. He was their first son. I never knew this before and had never heard his name mentioned in all the years I visited my southern family. Affie said that he drowned while Grandmother was bathing him. She left him for just a minute to open the door for a visitor. When she returned, he was dead.

From that day on, Grandmother never spoke a word for over a year. When I asked my cousin, Wyman, if he knew of little Robert and his tragic death, Wyman said that Robert had toppled into a large pot of boiling water in the backyard. Granddaddy and some of the local men were slaughtering and boiling their pigs. Granddaddy had placed Robert on a table next to the pot while he was getting another pig ready for slaughter. Robert crawled over to the edge of the table and fell into the boiling water. The men got him out,

but he was badly scalded. Someone grabbed the first mule that was hitched to a cart and went for Dr. Daniel, who stayed with Robert until he passed away that night. He died from pneumonia and scalding. Wyman said that Affie could never accept the true story of his death and had always said, "He drowned." It was true; Grandmother never spoke a word for over a year after that horrific accident. The family continued to grow.

As young boys, my uncles had to work the farm, but made fishing their livelihood as young men, hoping they would be more successful in beating the odds against the elements than their father had been. Like Granddaddy, all my uncles were great storytellers as well. They could make us laugh and cry with every story. How we loved to hear them tell stories of their youth. How they relished telling stories about their father and all the aggravation they brought to him as young men growing up on the farm.

Little did I know, as a child, what a tremendous inheritance I had received from my family in Whortonsville and Oriental. The pride and love that my grandparents exhibited in everything they did have never left me. Quality was the important factor, not quantity. Just a note of interest: I was given Grandmother's Christian name at birth and as a result of my marriage, I carry her exact maiden name, Lavenia Ernestine Martin. Grandmother's parents were Timothy and Susan Lincoln Martin.

My grandparents had none of the nice conveniences we had in our home up north. Just getting a drink of water was a task. If a large amount of water had to be obtained, that was torture. The pump was the only source of water in the house. This pump rested securely on the edge of the old galvanized sink in the kitchen. A ladle always lay against the body of the pump. It was our drinking cup, since its deep bowl held the water nicely. How tired our arms would get if we were asked to pump a bucket of water for some chore or for a necessary Saturday night bath. That bucket never seemed to get full. One would almost begin to think it was bottomless.

Going to the outhouse was an adventure, especially at night, even though a slop pot was under every bed. We, as children, hungry for as much excitement as possible, would take the well-used oil lamp and head down the crushed-oyster-shell path to the little wooden shed. Our imaginations

Oriental Harbor in the 1940s. (Photo from the Irma Midyette Collection, found in At Home in Oriental: 1878 to 1945, *compiled by the Oriental Centennial Committee.)*

burned as brightly as the lamp. Believe it or not, there was always a thick catalogue sitting on the floor in that outhouse. In no time at all, I learned the real reason for it being there. Not everyone shared us children's hunger for adventure; what looked like fancy chairs in a couple of the larger bedrooms actually held chamber pots with lids, much to the solace of the older folk. As Grandmother would say, "Just to make it a little more convenient."

Whenever we arrived, I can remember my cousins spotting our car and running as fast as they could, all the time hollering, "They're here! They're here!" What excitement! Our little faces would be pressed so tightly up against the back window, pushing each other out of the way to get a better look at the small gang running so hard to keep up; we wanted to make sure they were still following. At this point, one of us would always be hanging out of the car window, letting them know that we saw them and how excited and happy we were to be there at last. It seemed like the whole village knew we had arrived, and everybody was a relative.

I remember the old homestead in Whortonsville. It was situated on the main road leading into Whortonsville and consisted of sixty acres of farmland.

(The home of Will Whorton, my Granddaddy's brother was at the beginning of a dead-end road that led down to the creek.) Both homes had been built to hold large families. Granddaddy's home had a beautiful front porch that went almost completely around the entire house. We could run and play on it even when it rained because the roof extended beyond the porch, which kept us dry.

It was an all-wooden structure mounted on many large pilings of cement blocks so that the house was off the ground. Most of the homes in the area were built this way to protect them from the Neuse River and Broad Creek whenever they overflowed their banks during the many storms. The home had large rooms on each of its three floors, with each room appearing larger than the other. Our favorite floor in Grandmother's house, other than the kitchen, was the third floor because that was the bedroom for all the grandchildren.

Their general store and cotton gin were located on this dead-end road where a wooden dock extended out into Broad Creek. Both the local fishing boats and Granddaddy's large boat for traveling up to Norfolk and back (to get supplies and sell his cotton) were tied up at this dock. There we fished, crabbed, swam, and watched the local people being baptized in the river. This, and the open fields that completely surrounded the family homestead were our play areas.

As the years passed, this home always seemed to have sufficient room for one more occupant whenever the families would decide to make the annual visit back to the old homestead and their family roots. The yard surrounding the house consisted of mostly sand or dirt with occasional patches of so-called grass. My grandparents had many pigs, chickens, cows, and, of course, mules. These animals were always a delight for us because we had an opportunity to feed and care for them.

Whenever Grandfather would get one of the mules hitched to one of his different types of wagons and carts, we always tried to get him to take us with him. This would make us feel like we were back in the pioneer days. He was very particular about his mules and never wanted us to bother them.

I loved his two-seater wagon. Only a couple of us would fit in it once Granddaddy sat down. When he would pull his supply wagon out from the

shed and start hitching it up to one of the bigger mules, we knew he was going to get supplies, and we would hang around him until he motioned for us to get in if we wanted to go. He never said no to any of us.

Looking at the rooms through the eyes of a child, they appeared large, filled with furniture I had never seen before. Each of the bedrooms had a small but lovely table upon which a large water basin and pitcher were placed. The most popular and necessary chairs were only in two of the larger bedrooms. Each one had a lid as the seat, and they had more than one purpose. Their home had no plumbing other than the hand pump in the kitchen. Several of the rooms on the first floor had large fireplaces. On the second floor, three of the six bedrooms had them as well. Sitting right next to the bedroom fireplaces were some of the most beautiful fireplace screens, which my great-grandmother Martin had made years before. The ceilings were much higher than ours in New Jersey.

The beds were high off the floor, which made it difficult for us to climb into them. However, the beds were only for the adults, not the children. We only used the beds when just our individual family was visiting. Grandmother made the third floor into a huge bedroom for all of her grandchildren and kept many small mattresses ready for when we all arrived. We would pick out which mattress we wanted to call our own during our stay. That way, if our cousins wanted to spend the night with us, and they usually did, the sleeping arrangements were already taken care of. Some of the family came from quite a distance, making it more practical and easier for them to just spend the night. This way we were able to spend every moment with our favorite cousins.

As children eager to impress each other, we would go upstairs, sit on our mattresses, and tell our many stories. We spoke of our adventures, our school year, our life at home, and our pets. We tried to think of the many things that had happened since we saw each other last. We hardly ever ran out of words while we were all together.

All of Grandmother's furniture throughout the house, no matter how old it looked, was beautiful. Every window seemed to sparkle and shine. Grandmother's home was her pride and joy as it gleamed with all of her

tender loving care over the years. The curtains were crisp, fresh and wrinkle-free. Her ironing was done with irons, which she placed on her wood stove to get hot, and then she would iron the clothing on a large board that she would place on her kitchen table.

It seemed like Grandmother and the large woodstove in her oversized kitchen knew what each other expected. Grandmother wanted to please and satisfy her family with the delightful aroma, delicious appearance, and the delicate flavor and taste of her well-prepared meals. The stove knew how to keep just the right temperature to help create it all. Story-telling time always began after everyone finished dinner. My uncles were always trying to outdo each other's favorite story.

When my grandparents moved to Oriental, they lived above the crab plant because it was now just the two of them. We missed the old homestead and the adventures surrounding it, but new adventures awaited us in Oriental, as well as the neighboring military bases. Our country had been at war for about a year. I was now a teenager and was suddenly exposed to the sights and sounds connected with military training. It was an exciting time to visit my grandparents. I began to see a side of life that I had never imagined. It was a glance into adulthood, as well. We would sit on the steps leading to my grandparents' living quarters and watch the Marine Corp planes practice dive-bombing over the Neuse River. Cherry Point Marine Corp Base is directly across the river from Oriental. It was exciting for the local kids and I to listen to the explosions from their practicing, which let us imagine them attacking and sinking a Japanese ship.

I noticed more and more men in uniform as each war year went by. When Aunt Love and I went south, we traveled by train. The trains were always loaded with ever-moving military personnel. It was difficult for most civilians to find seats not to mention trying to sleep. The noise in the different cars was always loud, which made sleep impossible. We got off in Wilson, North Carolina, where we had to take a bus to New Bern. Army camps were plentiful, as were the soldiers. It was an exciting time to be a teenager.

Every now and then, my cousins, Ray and Tommy, would borrow one of our uncle's old farm trucks and drive us kids to Minnesott Beach, where

all the marines went for a night of fun. We didn't want to miss any of the action. From the local band's music to the dancing, drinking, and brawls that would break out, our eyes and ears took in every rip-roaring scene. For a bunch of kids, this was the place of all places to be on a Saturday night. I hesitate to mention sex, but it was as much a factor in what we saw as were the constant fights.

There we saw the rougher side of life. The marines were young, out for a good time, and nothing was going to stop them. The local "good ol' boys" resented the marines' bad attitude and arrogance. Competition between the two groups always intensified once the local Southern belles came on the scene. The MPs would come shrieking down the road in their jeeps, getting ready to end yet another brawl, one way or the other. Ladies of the evening would pass by, still seeking out their prey for the evening, while we watched amazed by every move they made. Anything could happen and it usually did. We waited. We watched. We always left, counting the days until we could return.

We all stayed close together, a little scared, but filled with excitement. The area seemed to be wrapped up in the feeling there was no tomorrow, only tonight. Music played loudly, and everyone had to shout in order to hear each other. The noise itself created an excitement of its own. Everybody wanted to dance. The military men were looking for partners, some even settling for a buddy, if a girl was not available. The music was fast because the jitterbug was one of the more popular dances at the time. The excitement of the moment spread amongst the young crowd. It was tantalizing. No one was spared. The mood around the beach on those evenings was that of young men and women trying to live their entire lives in one evening, behaving as though there would be no more tomorrows. It was crazy, but we loved it.

My best friend was Georgia Mae Mason. She was a little older than me (maybe by a year). However, this was never a problem, since we shared many adventures together and our likes and dislikes were similar. We were more like sisters when we were together because Georgia Mae was the only girl in her family, and I was the only one of my sisters who traveled to Grandmother's as a youngster and teenager. Thus, our relationship became

*My best girlfriend in North Carolina,
Georgia Mae Mason.*

very close. We would sit on the docks with our fishing poles (made out of long bamboo sticks) and fish by the hour.

In no time at all, we would be surrounded by the other local boys and girls. They would join us in everything we did. Blanche Gilgo; her sister, Jane; and two brothers, Jimmy and Paul, were always tagging along behind us, just waiting until we would acknowledge their presence and give them the okay to join us. Several of the Lupton kids were part of our little gang. We would get Granddaddy's small rowboat and end up way down stream or well out into the Neuse River, which was strictly against Granddaddy's rules.

One time in particular, Georgia Mae and I got terribly sunburned while rowing the boat across the inlet in order to get to one of the local farmer's watermelon patch, which was located at the edge of the river. We never realized how burnt we had gotten nor did we feel the terrible pain that usually goes with it. We were so busy eating, we never noticed that we were turning as red as the inside of those melons. We were laughing, playing, eating, and just having a great ol' time when we noticed the farmer's truck. The dust cloud from the dirt roads gave him away, but by then it was too late. He had come to pick a load of his melons to take to market, and we knew we had been caught.

The farmer came over and asked us if we found his melons to be good and ripe. Of course, all he had to do was look around and there was all the evidence lying amongst the vines of other melons and around our own bare feet. When he found out that we had arrived by boat, he suggested that we get ourselves back home the same way we came and told us that he would see us later. However, he decided he could use our help in picking and choosing the best melons to take to market, since we seemed to be so good at it.

We dared not argue with him because we hoped that if we helped him, he would not come to our homes for reimbursement. I can't remember what was worse, the terrible sunburn we received or the angry words of my grandfather and Mrs. Mason. They made all kinds of verbal threats. However, we were spared from any physical punishment: they both felt that our sunburns were painful enough.

The homes around the village were old. Many had been built before the Civil War, but many were neglected because their owners were poor, without the money for the repairs that most of these homes needed. Those people had all they could do just to scrape enough money together for the real necessities, like food and clothing. It was still hard times down in the lowlands. However, they always sat down to a generous meal.

One of the funniest stories I remember involved my Uncle Howard. Howard's favorite stop after work was the local saloon. He lived with Grandmother and Granddaddy Whorton on and off because of his divorce and alcoholism. They had moved from their quarters over the crab plant to a nearby bungalow that gave them a little more room and privacy. There were several ways of getting to their house from the main road. However, everyone always cut through Raymond (Granddaddy's

Jane, me, and Blanche.

cousin) and Myrtle's backyard because it was the quickest route to Grandmother's. Myrtle was always washing, and her clothesline was usually full; because of this, we found this shortcut could be very hazardous.

Myrtle was a *huge* woman, in spite of the fact that she was short, not more than five-foot-one. My guess was that she was wider than she was high. She was a happy woman, who proudly displayed her great love of her duties about the house. Myrtle's son, Ray, Jr., was also *extremely* large—definitely taller and twice as wide.

As children, my playmates and I enjoyed watching Myrtle hang out her wash as we gathered around Grandmother's backyard. We found her entertaining as she strutted around that line, singing one of her favorite gospel songs. She handled each piece of clothing in such a loving, proud manner that one would almost believe they belonged to the Master himself.

Never having seen such humongous clothing, we laughed because each piece appeared larger than the one she had just hung. This always irritated Myrtle, and she would start hollering at us, "You young'uns better stop your laughing and go play. Stop watching me! You all go away, now, before I tell Veenie" (Grandmother's nickname). We would pretend to leave, all the time watching her. We knew it was only a matter of time before she would display the most fascinating item in her well-used, broken-down, wooden laundry basket.

Every time she pulled out another item to hang, we would hold our breaths. We would close our eyes, count to ten, and then quickly open them in hopes that we would be gazing upon that gigantic piece of clothing that always left us speechless and motionless. Those unbelievable *drawers*! With our mouths opened wide in amazement, the only audible sounds were our gasps of "Oh! *Oh!*" and our giggles. One of us always ended up saying, "My *God*, they are *huge*!" Myrtle would get a long stick and shake it at us. We would run, hollering and laughing at the sight of their colossal drawers. Those drawers! Those *huge* drawers! I had never seen anything like them before. I didn't know they made them that *big*! They were unbelievable to any child's eyes.

One day, Uncle Howard was coming home after making his usual stop for a drink or two and, as usual, he took the shortcut through Myrtle's backyard. It was getting dark, but that was never a problem. He did well in maneuvering past her front yard, considering his unsteady stride and occasional fall, but this was not to last. He thought he had passed the heavy-laden clothesline, but he suddenly found himself caught up in her drawers. He turned and turned some more until he found himself unable to get out of the huge piece of underclothing. His head became entangled in one of the leg openings; an arm was thrust through the other opening. He was in a mess.

He fell down, pulling the drawers tighter around his own body. He got back up, only to stagger and reel around the wash. He began hollering for help. No one came. He tried to call out again but he had turned in such a way that his head was completely covered again by the *huge* drawers. Again, he tried to call out. Still, no one came. He fell down, bringing the complete line of wash down with him. He tried to get up, but matters only got worse. More clothing entangled him. Now he was caught up in Ray's huge clothing as well.

A formal portrait of Georgia Mae Mason.

In the meantime, a couple of young Black men were nearing Myrtle's house when they spotted a white object, flailing, kicking, and falling around in her backyard. Their mouths fell open and their eyes widened as each heard the other whisper, "Ghost!" They stopped. One of them said, "What's that?" The other responded, "Lordy, let's get out o' here!" Howard stood up just long enough to let out a terrifying, drunken holler. They took off faster than they had ever moved before. However, they, too, had been drinking as the story goes. They ran back to the colored people's saloon, telling everyone that a ghost or something terrible was thrashing about in Myrtle Whorton's backyard. They had never seen anything like it before. "Go on down and see fo' yo'self," one of them said. "I's goin' home. I's afraid o' that thing."

The two's excitement and terrified looks sparked their drinking partners' curiosities to the point that they all stopped and left the bar to go see for themselves. In the meantime, the story of the first encounter had spread into the white folks' bar. They, too, joined the noisy procession as both groups ran excitedly toward Myrtle's house. They could hear the many strange sounds coming from the backyard. None of them would approach the yard as they stood, looking at the unbelievable sight, now so visible to each of them. It was exactly as the Black men had described. "My *God*, what is it?" several of them whispered. They stood gawking at the strange sight, not knowing that it was Howard.

Again, Howard fell down. This time, he attempted to crawl, only to fall flat on his face. He got to his knees and began crawling, as best he could, trying to get away from whatever kept him captive. Finally, Grandmother heard all the noise and ran out in the backyard to see what was wrong. At the same time, Myrtle heard the noise and came running. It was a sight never before seen by anyone. Howard was somewhere within all that clothing. Grandmother suspected it was he, but Myrtle could not believe anyone could get in that kind of a mess.

Some of the white men came running over to help the two women as they all tried to see what the ghost-like thing was that had frightened the young Blacks. They arrived just in time to see Myrtle and Grandmother unwind Howard. They couldn't believe Howard was the "thing" until they actually saw it. Their laughter devastated Myrtle. Because many of the men who patronized the local saloons (both Black and white) were watching the entire scene unfold, her drawers immediately became *the* local joke. Poor Myrtle. Before the rooster crowed the next morning, everyone in the village had heard of Howard's entrapment in Myrtle and Ray's *huge* drawers.

From that time on Howard referred to those drawers as the largest sailcloth he ever dealt with. It was days before Myrtle would hang any of their drawers on that clothesline. In fact, it was days before Myrtle showed her face around the village. And it was a *very* long time before Howard again took the shortcut to Grandmother's house.

A few of my relatives on my mother's side still reside in Pamlico County. Over the years, the majority of Whortons packed up and left the area because of the extreme hardships of living along the coastline. Hurricanes had become the enemy. One severe storm after another always turned the Pamlico River into a raging mountain of water, flooding everything the families owned. Before they and their belongings were completely destroyed, they moved down along the Georgia coastline to continue fishing, shrimping, and crabbing.

Many beloved memories of this area are embedded in my mind, rekindled at the slightest thought of my youth and the time spent with those dear country folk. I loved this region, the people, and their simplicity, which

seemed to mask the real hardships that existed there. Many years later, I realized that Mother felt intimidated by me throughout my childhood and teenage years because I had become a constant reminder of where she came from. I was her past! I was one of them! I was her awkward, ugly, unsophisticated, and introverted Saturday's child.

VISITING FAMILY IN BRUNSWICK, GEORGIA This was the area to which most of the family from North Carolina eventually moved after the devastating coastal storms finally broke them spiritually, as well as financially. However, the final migration did not occur until the early 1950s.

Before this time, back in the late 1920s, Mother's older sisters, Leonia and Lillie—along with their husbands, Gordon and Sam Lewis—moved to Brunswick, Georgia, and Jacksonville, Florida. Uncle Sam opened a crab-and-shrimp company called Golden Shores Seafood in Brunswick. Aunt Lillie created a frozen Shrimp Creole that was shipped to several large food-store chains throughout the United States. (For Aunt Lillie's Shrimp Creole recipe, see Appendix C.) Uncle Sam shipped this product using trucks with cooling systems for carrying seafood and other perishable foods long distances. Aunt Lillie and Uncle Sam never had any children of their own,

Uncle Sam, Aunt Lillie, Uncle Gordon, and Aunt Leonia (l–r).

but Aunt Lillie eventually raised my Uncle Howard's two children, Judy and Howard Jr. Life was good to my family in Brunswick. Money was plentiful.

Aunt Leonia and Uncle Gordon had four children: Willie, Euclid, Binkie, and Claire. However, Leonia and Gordon left Brunswick and moved to Jacksonville, Florida, where they lived and opened their own crab plant. Uncle Sam and Uncle Gordon were brothers, creating two close-knit families. They had tremendous success with their crab plants and were well known throughout the South.

My Uncle Rommie Whorton and his wife, Mary, followed them to Brunswick and became employees in the crab plant. They had five children: Edith Marie, Dorothy, Madison, Elwood, and Ann Bryan. The need for work and their love of making their livelihood from the sea and living near the water was the force behind their remaining in Brunswick.

Howard was the next Whorton to follow the clan. His life fell apart, eventually ending in an early death. Time passed, bringing more Whorton men to Brunswick as employees in Lewis' crab plant.

Elmo and Marguerite left North Carolina during the early fifties and took their children, Paul, Carol, Diana, and Michael, to Key West. Elmo enjoyed being a self-employed fisherman. After a period of years, they returned to Brunswick. My cousin, Euclid, owned the ferry that ran twice a day to Cumberland Island. He needed a captain who was familiar with the waterways and hired Elmo. For many years, Elmo remained captain. He was loved by everyone who shared a small part of his life.

Julius, Clara, and their three children—Leroy, Danny, and Barbara— became victims of the coastal storms along the North Carolina shores, as well. Finally, after much hardship and devastation, they packed up and moved to Brunswick. Their lives never seemed to prosper or become easier, and the move ruined Julius, physically, mentally, and financially.

After their move, Howard and Julius slowly became victims of their own self-destructive impulses. They became alcoholics, and both died tragic deaths within a month of each other. However, I remember their sober moments, the good times when we would all sit together and laugh, eat, and enjoy more of the stories of their youth and the so-called better days. These

The Whorton family (l–r): Uncle Rommie, Aunt Leona, Grandmother, Uncle Elmo, Uncle Howard, Uncle Freddie, and Aunt Lillie. Mother and Aunt Affie were not living in Brunswick when this was taken, and Uncle Julius is also absent.

scenes became unforgettable. Today, my heart still feels the love and the warmth wrapped within those precious moments.

My Uncle Freddie and Aunt Jessie were the last of my uncles and aunts to leave North Carolina and move to Brunswick. This move was the results of financial difficulties and backstabbing by others. They were completely disheartened and found themselves unable to forget their wounds or accept their new lifestyle in Brunswick. They felt put down and lived rather depressed and unhappy lives. They had one son, Wyman, who was born and raised in North Carolina. He was one of my favorite cousins. Wyman was younger than I, but we shared being family. Years later, Wyman married Glenda. They had one little girl, Maria, and it was through Maria that my aunt and uncle enjoyed what little happiness was left in their lives.

A state of underlying hostilities between the Whorton and the Lewis families had been created and continued to fester for many years. However, with the passing of the older generation and my generation, these feelings have subsided amongst our children's generation. My generation, however, still remembers the way it was.

As I look back on all three of my family groups, I realize that the family from North Carolina had instilled in me a better understanding of the values

that accompanied the simplicity of their way of life. It grew out of love, affection, and an unpretentious lifestyle. A person's worth depended on what was in his heart, not the size of his wallet. A common bond made me one of them. I belonged, much to my mother's horror.

THE RIDE THAT MADE ME CLAUSTROPHOBIC An incident that is impossible for me to forget occurred when I was eight years old. It created a terrible dilemma for me and still remains with me. I suffer from claustrophobia. During the summer of 1937, I went to Brunswick, Georgia, with my Aunt Affie and Uncle Bud. At that time, his car was a two-seater with an oversized trunk. It was exactly like Walter's "old jug" car, except it had a trunk in place of a rumble seat. Well, we had no trouble going down to Brunswick, since both Affie and I were small, and we fit well on the passenger seat.

Auntie was always impressed by Uncle Sam and Uncle Gordon and loved their attention. During the late 1930s, these two uncles began to make a great deal of money from their crab plants. Affie admired their ambition and their lifestyle when everyone else was still hurting from the Depression. When it came time for us to go home, Affie and Bud decided to bring my older cousin, Claire (Uncle Gordon's daughter), home with us. She was about thirteen years old.

No one, not even me, saw the pending dilemma until Uncle Gordon and Aunt Leonia began saying their goodbyes. Uncle Bud beckoned for the three of us to get into the car. Claire got in, and Affie followed. When it was my time to get in, I stood there, looking, thinking, "Hey, wait a minute!! There's a big problem, here!!! It's *me*!" Where was I going to sit? How were the three of us going to fit in that small passenger seat?

Uncle Bud moved to the back of the car and stopped. He opened the trunk and began moving our suitcases around as if to make room for something else. He looked up and beckoned to me. I thought he needed help, so I innocently hurried to the back of the car. Quickly, he said, "Okay, honey, hop in." I looked at him in disbelief and then looked at the almost-filled trunk. I heard myself say, "No, I'm not getting in there." Bud continued to rearrange things, and then he laid a quilt in the small empty area. Laughing,

Bud said, "It's either in the trunk or you'll have to walk home." I continued to stare at my unexpected situation. What do I do now? "Uncle Bud, please don't put me in there. I want to sit with Aunt Affie."

My begging turned into crying as he lifted me into the cramped trunk. He pushed me down onto the thick quilt and held me so I could not move. I knew there was nothing I could do. Cringing, I pulled my shaking, small frame into a ball as I watched the trunk close. A darkness I had never experienced enveloped the entire space. I lay for hours in a frozen, terrified state as a strange odor filled my inky area. Later I learned the smell was gasoline.

During the trip, Aunt Affie would occasionally call out, "How are you doing, Teeny?" I could hear laughing and talking coming from the other side of my prison wall. The car seemed never to stop. When I would become aware that we had stopped, no one opened the trunk. Several times I heard the tank being filled with gasoline. The fumes became worse whenever this happened. I heard Auntie and Claire laughing and walking about; then the car would begin to move.

Aunt Leonia had made sandwiches, fried chicken, and biscuits for our trip home. Motels and interstate highways were not in existence during the 1930s. I waited, hoping that Uncle Bud would stop the car, open the trunk, and hand me a sandwich and something to drink. I could hear the three of them eating and talking. I banged on the partition, trying to get their attention. Aunt Affie finally heard me and said that she would give me something when Uncle Bud stopped for gas. I was hungry. I had no choice but to wait.

I lost track of time. The trip seemed endless. Had they forgotten where they put me? My thoughts haunted me. My panic was quieted only when sleep overpowered my living nightmare. I looked forward to those moments of drifting off to a safe place. By now, I knew I had wet myself, not just once, but several times. I was terrified, embarrassed, uncomfortable, and *hungry*.

Hours later, the car stopped. I heard both doors open, and Aunt Affie's voice rang out. "Bud, open the trunk. Teeny has to see the White House." I watched the trunk open to an unexpected and beautiful scene. It was night. Lights were lit all around the area, and, in front of me, stood the White House. It was a sight I had never seen. Uncle Bud lifted me out of the trunk.

I could hardly walk. Aunt Affie and my dear, sweet cousin, Claire, whom I now "hated," were squealing with excitement at such a picturesque setting. Auntie handed me a ham sandwich. I savored each bite.

I drank in the night air. It felt good to move about. I was even feeling their excitement and, for the moment, forgot my hours of misery and fright. Uncle Bud's announcement, "Enough, gang, let's get back on the road," abruptly ended our sightseeing. I heard, "Get back in the trunk, Teeny." I looked at that threatening, empty space I just came from and said, "No, I won't get back in there," and began crying.

I could feel myself backing away from the car. Uncle Bud stood by the trunk with his arms outstretched, waiting to help me back into my cell. By now, I was on the sidewalk screaming. I began jumping up and down, hollering, "No, I'm not getting back in there!" Auntie had Claire get into the car and then came over to me. "Now, honey, be reasonable and stop screaming. You can see there's no room up front. Please, be a good girl and let Uncle Bud put you back in there. We're almost home." I stood there crying. My back was pressed against the huge gate to the White House. I wanted the gate to open so I could run up into all that beauty. It looked safe and lovely, not like that terrifying gaping hole of blackness that was waiting for me to re-enter.

Aunt Affie could see I was out of control. She and Uncle Bud began arguing. I couldn't keep up with who was saying what. All I knew was that we had a big problem here and I was crying—loudly! All of a sudden, I saw Uncle Bud throw up his arms, slam down the trunk, and briskly walk to his side of the car. He shouted, "Okay, hold her on your lap, damn it! Let's go." Auntie grabbed my arm, pulling me in the direction of the car. "Now stop crying, Teeny. I'm going to hold you. We'll be home in a few hours." I didn't have time to tell Auntie that I was wet until I sat on her lap. She never said a word, but I knew that she was as uncomfortable as I.

Well, six hours later we arrived home. It had been a nightmare of a trip. When I told Mother what happened, she thought I was acting silly and had no reason to have been so frightened. Dad, on the other hand, was furious. He felt that they insulted him and put his child in a precarious situation. Nobody was going to do that and walk away with out hearing from him first.

Well, he lit into both Aunt Affie and Uncle Bud. They knew he was upset, and I looked lovingly at my wonderful Prince Charming as he attacked Auntie with one curse word after another. The more he yelled, the madder he got. "You're a nurse? What damn school did you graduate from? I can't believe you allowed this!" Uncle Bud was next. I watched and listened as Dad ranted on. "How could either of you do this? You're a Princeton graduate? I always considered you an intelligent man." Bud tried to interrupt him, but Dad quickly told him to shut up. He wasn't finished yet. "My God, I believe my dogs have more sense than you! Your degree must have been in *stupidity*! Do you realize what you put this kid through?"

After that trip, I was never able to get into an elevator or any enclosed-area alone. *I had developed claustrophobia.* Mother took me to several doctors who tried to help me deal with this problem, but they did little good. After all these years, the memory of that ride still haunts me.

THE GYPSIES From the very beginning of the 1900s through the early 1940s, after wintering in Florida, the gypsies would return in the spring to their campsite on Lake Road in Morris Township. This campsite was only a short distance from our neighborhood, making it easy for any of us kids to venture to their site. Word *always* spread quickly among us that the gypsies were coming.

We couldn't wait to start our spying from the high bluff above the Whippany River, atop the ruins of one of the old estates that overlooked the gypsies' campsite or from behind the high shrubs just a short distance from their encampment. To watch this most unusual group of people setting up their site for another lengthy stay always held us in awe. Their lifestyle was so unique, nothing like ours. We were completely captivated. We dared not speak of our spying to our mothers or fathers. All hell would have erupted.

The area where they camped was actually purchased in 1926 by Naylor Harrison, known as "King of the Gypsies." Other groups of gypsies had camped on the Lake Road lot many years before Harrison bought it. This group gave all the gypsies that came into the area a bad name since the Morristown Police were always receiving complaints from the nearby

neighborhoods concerning their behavior. The tales of their destruction and thievery became widespread. They were finally driven off of the Lake Road site by Harrison after he purchased it.

On the way to their many different campsites, their wagons with fancy and brilliant trappings along with a large drove of horses would pass our home. Once again the cry would go out, "The gypsies are coming! Here come the gypsies!" Yes, the gypsies had arrived for another season. They were back! Oh, what excitement!

Mother would come out to join us just to make sure we did not venture off the porch. That would only make the fancy caravans appear more mystifying. Mother warned us again not to leave the porch. Wagon after wagon would pass by, some highly decorated, some looking very mysterious, none looked dilapidated, despite the fact that the entourage usually consisted of at least twenty or more wagons. The majority of gypsy wagons were always thought to be decrepit and rundown.

One wagon in particular held our interest because it belonged to the palmist. Little did we know that this particular wagon once belonged to the Queen of the clan. She knew everything, or so we thought; our little minds began to run wild, especially after seeing the sign painted on the side of her wagon: "Fortuneteller—See What Your Future Holds." That, alone, was a frightening thought for each of us. A large hand, palm outstretched, had been painted on the other side of the wagon with the word "Palmist" directly under it. One by one the wagons passed.

Then one year the majority of wagons changed to small trailers, except for one trailer that was being pulled by a large Cadillac. We decided that it had to belong to the king and his queen! It looked like it was elegantly equipped as a traveling home.

The other trailers belonged to his eleven children—each child had his own. Young boys and girls ran alongside the wagons and trailers. They were laughing, singing, waving to passersby, and giving the appearance of being very free and happy. Their clothing was not as tawdry as that of other gypsies who came into the area. It was similar to our own, as a matter of fact. We knew they had to be gypsies though; no one would ever get that

close to the wagons or those seemingly menacing people who rode inside them if they weren't.

This particular group of gypsies was of English stock and considered themselves above the average gypsy clan (usually of middle- or eastern-European background) that settled in the Morris County area. Harrison's clan was known for having a very unique and semi-permanent gypsy camp (very unusual for gypsies) and for being led by the most extraordinary man who founded it. His queen, Louisa Harrison, helped him build their own fortune through her fortune telling. They became millionaires over the years, owning a great deal of real estate throughout the country, as well as being known as two of the wealthiest gypsies in the world. This man was well known for his honesty and tried to instill this in his clan.

Our only problem was that we never knew which gypsy clan we were watching until we saw the fancy trailers; therefore, Mother was always cautious about the caravans that rode by. Harrison had died in 1928 at the age of eighty-five, and his wife died two years later. It was their children with whom we became familiar and whose annual arrival we awaited so eagerly each spring.

The site on Lake Road was beautiful. From the roadway, we could stand and look in at their encampment. The wagons, trailers, and tents were scattered about, looking like they were expecting an Indian attack. We would never think of putting one foot on their property for fear they would put a spell on us.

In one area, we saw the beginning of a garden. In another area, there was a supply of firewood. Behind the encampment was the Whippany River, which ran into Speedwell Lake. This section of the river was lovely. We always loved to explore the banks of it and finding many of its water creatures, such as frogs, turtles, snakes, and muskrats. To spot a fox, a rabbit, or deer was very common since they were just as plentiful. The grass along its edge was always so green and untouched. Many swamp flowers and plants surrounded the area as well.

We always felt so brave when we would come across a Jack-in-the-pulpit flower. This is a most unusual plant because it is carnivorous or, more

accurately, insectivorous. This plant has an upright club-shaped spadix arched over by a green and purple spathe. It made our imaginations run wild. We could picture ourselves being caught up by it, being sucked down past the strange, sharp, projecting tongue-like object, down the smooth stem into the cavity of the plant, never to be released. These plants were very plentiful, but we treated them with tremendous respect. We considered it a true sign of bravery if one of us actually picked one of them and carried it out of the woods without being devoured by it. We dared not go near the gypsy camp with a Jack-in-the-pulpit plant in hand for fear the palmist would put a hex on us or make the plant devour us at her command.

We knew when we were approaching the gypsy campsite because the smell of many skunk cabbages reigned over the area. It is said that even cattle will not touch this plant because of its stinging acrid juices, regardless of the tempting tender, fresh, bright green foliage. The odor of these cabbages resembles a combination of skunk, putrid meat, and garlic. Because there were so many different flowering plants surrounding the area, we never went home without some type of bouquet for our mothers.

There were several large weeping willow trees that looked like an umbrella covering and protecting the encampment. The beauty of the area would be quickly spoiled once the gypsies moved in. They would accumulate all kinds of junk within a very short time after arriving. Things such as car parts, broken-down furniture, bicycles, and broken-down small wagons were left lying wherever they fell. An old washing machine sat near one wagon, unusable for the lack of electricity. Bonfires would glow at night around each wagon and trailer, displaying strange looking shadows from all their junk. It was an eerie sight.

Just a short distance from the gypsies' campsite was an area known as the sandpit. We played in this sandpit for hours, building all kinds of imaginary towns, etc., while trying to gather up enough courage to creep closer to their campsite. The sandpit was the base for another bluff from which we were also able to observe the activity within the encampment. Many building contractors in the area obtained their sand from this pit because it was so pure it did not need to be washed.

One day while we were spying on the campsite, a young gypsy girl, in her mid-teens, came out of her wagon and began to tend the open fire. We were fascinated to be so close to her and able to watch her every move. Suddenly, she turned and spotted us, gave us a warm smile, and beckoned us to come in. We all slowly backed away.

The gypsy girl beckoned again. She called us to come out. She gently moved the fire around to get more heat for her impending cooking. She had rather dark-colored skin, which gave her a weather beaten appearance. Her long black hair flowed down past her shoulders and surrounded her small, thin face. Although we could not see her legs, she appeared to be quite tall. A colorful skirt hung down to her ankles with a cloth belt accenting her small waist. An off-the-shoulder blouse with a ruffled neckline slightly exposed her small breasts. We started to move towards her. She smiled as we approached.

The fire was starting to crackle, making the sparks fly in all directions. Suddenly, she spoke, "My name is Rose. This is my wagon. Come in and sit down by the fire. I would like to talk to you. Do you want to hear about my life as a gypsy? No one in my camp will hurt you. Don't be afraid."

We were excited. Her quiet and soothing voice made us feel comfortable. Our fears began to leave us. We sat around the fire for a long time just listening to her tell of her travels around the country, how she lived, and how her aunt taught her because she didn't attend any school at all. This was the only campsite that these gypsies stayed at for any length of time.

From that time on, every time we went to spy on the gypsies, Rose would come out and beckon us to come into the campsite. She would take us around to meet other young gypsy children, and before long, we felt safe among them. However, we never entered the campsite without being invited by Rose or one of the other young gypsies.

THE ELLIOTT STREET GANG   Our imaginations helped to contrive the games and activities of the period between the mid-1930s through the mid-1940s. We never had the privilege of having store-bought games until we were well into our teens. By then, "Monopoly" was considered the most popular game among the young people. We spent hours playing it.

When I look back, I can't help but remember how ethnically diversified our neighborhood was. We were a mixture of Irish, English, German, Black, Italian, and Jewish. However, no one ever argued over our differences. We were just a bunch of kids, only concerned about what we were going to play or do together. Our parents had the same attitude.

Nancy Liedell (right) and me.

Our neighborhood consisted of the upper part of Lake Road, all of Elliott Street, Cutler Street, Ralph Place, and the upper part of Sussex Avenue as well as the "Sherman Hill" section. These areas were considered our playground, our territory, and our borders. No other gang dared to invade our private kingdom.

Several large estates had been located within our playground. These properties had been owned by some of the country's wealthiest men. "On the Hill" was the thirty-acre estate of A. Emilius Outerbridge. "Glen Arile Farm" was owned by H. Elmer Gibb. Its twenty-seven-room mansion was at the center of the estate's twenty-seven acre farm. Barns, cottages, extensive greenhouses, stables, carriage houses, and beautifully designed flower gardens had all been part of these estates. The three-story frame "Outerbridge" mansion was built to the rear of the Gibb's tract off a narrow lane from Sussex Avenue.

These mansions had been razed and left to decay during the early years of the Depression. For years, gloom hung over the acreage until the excitement of children laughing, running, and playing awakened the openness of its pathetic surroundings. Life returned to the landscape, thanks to the Elliot Street gang. The fields had become our private sanctuary. It became our ivory tower, our hideaway, our refuge. Our imaginations ran wild when we walked through the rusty, broken-down iron gates. Robin Hood, Tarzan, cowboys, Indians, and soldiers came alive. It was in these fields, grounds,

and gardens where my happiest years were spent, where my dreams of tomorrow were created, where I was free from my mother.

The passage of time and the terrible neglect the area had suffered did not interfere with the hidden, underlying surprises that awaited us during spring, summer, and fall. Pussy willows always announced the arrival of spring as we waited patiently to touch their silky, soft shields. Slowly, the gardens began to expose their hidden treasures. Tulips, daffodils, lilacs, and azaleas, disguised by their wild coverings, would burst into view. The excitement of their loveliness and their mass array of colors put each of us into a hypnotic state.

Tenderly, we would pick them, pretending that we were the young maidens who lived in such luxury. The area had become our private garden, our castle, our fort.

Located on one of the sites today is the Sussex Avenue School of the Morris School District. All that remains of the Gibb estate are decaying fences and two handsome copper beech trees. It is in one of these trees that my initials still lie embedded, a reminder of yesteryear's love. The entranceway leading up to the large mansion had beautiful pillars on which the large iron gates had been mounted. These pillars and iron gates remained standing long after we all became adults.

Eunice Daily.

To this day, when I drive pass this area, I only see the young children of yesteryear running and playing happily over the open grounds. All our dreams of tomorrow were visualized as we sat on the ruins of this once beautiful mansion. For just a second, I allow my ghosts from the past to come alive with their shouts of excitement as they swing from the branches of the massive copper beech trees. Freedom reigned, allowing nature and those innocent spirits to live together in harmony. I still find myself uttering a deep sigh as this precious moment disappears from sight.

"Ridgewood Hall" was the name of another mansion that felt the terrible effects of the Depression years. It was located at the top of Sherman Hill, just a short distance from Elliott Street. Dr. Frederick H. Humphries purchased it in 1890 from a Mrs. Bryon Sherman. He enlarged the dwelling to include a music room with an organ, a bowling alley, a gymnasium with an indoor slide, a greenhouse, carriage houses, and several formal Japanese and terraced gardens.

According to our parents, the Humphries owned a large medicine business that failed during the Depression. They had to claim bankruptcy, selling the home to a man by the name of Spanjers. This man was in the real-estate business, but left the entire estate untended for many years, and over time, the home slowly began deteriorating, as did its surrounding grounds. Many hobos and tramps used it as a place to escape the elements. More than once we found one of them asleep on the large front porch or inside, enjoying the warmth from one of the many fireplaces. These men never frightened us. We knew it was hard times and accepted them as they were.

It was here at Ridgewood Hall (we always referred to it as Spanjers') that the Elliott Street gang spent much of their childhoods, playing inside and

Alice White in a school photo.

outside this scary, empty, yet magnificent mansion. We were able to enter the house through a half-open window located on the side of its wrap-around circular front porch. The other entrance was at the back of the house where its huge black door always appeared threatening to intruders like us. This entry area was scarier because it was always very dark. There were no windows, only a long hallway with a small, dark room on one side and the cellar door on the other side. The thought of entering the back door alone was terrifying. We either went in as a group or sent Eunice in first because she was always the bravest. If she came out, then the rest of us went in, with her leading the way. Once we got in

Spanjers, the old spooky mansion.

the kitchen area, our object was to go up the back stairs, which led to the second-floor bedrooms.

Our greatest discovery on the second floor was a beautiful, large gymnasium with a slide. Wow! As scary as it was, if we reached the gymnasium safely, we felt very brave. The slide was breathtaking. To this day, I have never seen one that equaled its beauty or its speed, considering its years of neglect. The slide became magnetic to anyone who dared to venture up its winding and narrow stairway or down its well-preserved, slick and fast surface. The passageway was dark and frightening, but the thrill of that ride proved stronger than the fright that stirred within us; the dash upward always triumphed.

Sitting at the top of the slide, awaiting the swift descent was exhilarating, yet a twinge of fear silently rekindled within us at the thought of being *up there alone.* In addition to the slide, there were many ropes that hung down from the high ceilings. We used those ropes for climbing and swinging. For years they hung there and never deteriorated as one might expect.

Another event that I never forgot took place in Spanjers' kitchen. The boys in the

Barbara Coe with cat.

Standing to the right of me is Cynthia Husk from Cutler Street, as my sister, Pauline, squats on the ground.

neighborhood had overheard us girls talking about going up to Spanjers' to play detectives. We loved sitting on top of one of the carriage-house roofs, looking down on the grounds and imagining some sort of mystery in the making. The boys, unbeknownst to us, apparently decided to beat us up there. When we got there, they appeared terrified, screaming that Elwood had been hurt and was lying in the kitchen covered with blood. They did not know what happened to him except that they had found him lying there, unable to move. We opened the back door, fearful as usual of the unexpected, pushing Eunice first.

We huddled together and slowly proceeded into the kitchen. There by the back stairway was Elwood, covered with blood. We screamed in horror. He didn't move! He looked dead! We were panic stricken. Our screams bounced off the walls, only adding more terror to the entire scene. "My God! They weren't kidding! We've got to get help," screamed Nancy. We made a dash for the back door. The sight of daylight increased the speed of our charge.

Once outside, we were stunned by the funny look on the boys' faces, considering poor Elwood was in that house either terribly injured or *dead*. We knew something was wrong. We couldn't take our eyes off of them. All of a sudden, we realized that these guys had all they could do not to laugh. We had made their day! In the meantime, neither Eunice nor Elwood was aware of the scene that was taking place outside nor did we know what was happening inside.

Eunice was still in there. She was always the last one to leave. She saw Elwood getting up. Angrily, she stepped out from the shadows, shouting at him, "We thought you were dead. How could you guys do this to us?" She realized at that moment that he wasn't even hurt. What we saw was ketchup,

not blood! Elwood and Eunice appeared together at the back door with Eunice swinging the empty ketchup bottle over Elwood's head. The boys had played a joke, a cruel joke, on us. They stood before us like proud victors.

It took us several minutes to realize what was really going on. The boys began jumping up and down, laughing hysterically, with their fingers pointed at each of us. Elwood was the only guy who wasn't laughing. He was a mess as the ketchup dripped down his face, clothing, and shoes. Once the boys had their fun, we found ourselves exhausted. They scared the daylights out of each of us. We decided to go home. We would never forget the sight of Elwood covered with the so-called blood, pretending to be dead on Spanjers' kitchen floor.

Even though Spanjers' was deteriorating, the library was one of the few rooms in which the fireplace mantle remained completely intact. I remember how fascinated I was with its beautifully carved markings and designs. They held me in awe, even as a child. The many beautiful bookshelves surrounding the mantle were also unmarred. We had no fear of being in this room, the dining room, or the living room. These rooms had large windows that allowed in plenty of light. This made us feel a little less scared because we could exit quickly if we had to. Every room had a fireplace, but none could compare to the well-preserved one in the library.

The cellar area was completely out-of-bounds for us girls. It was pitch black, and none of us, including Eunice, was brave enough to venture down those long, dark cellar stairs. The cellar entrance was located in a small alcove off the kitchen. This area was scary and darker than any other room in the house. To get to the cellar door, open it, and peek down those stairs was considered a very brave feat. An old, locked steamer trunk had been left by the owners when they moved, and so the story went, whoever opened it would be cursed. The boys, of course, bragged about going down into that terrible darkness. We often wondered if they really had enough courage to do that. They spoke of seeing the old trunk and even talked about how they tried to unlock it. We never believed that part of their story.

They told us they had heard rumors from the older boys in our neighborhood that something terrible was locked in that trunk. The person who

opened it would be cursed for the rest of their life. Awful things would happen to them, and they would die before they ever reached old age. The more the boys talked about this rumor, the colder we girls felt and the more foreboding their story sounded. The thought of having such a curse put on us, suffering painfully, and dying in an agonizing way scared us. They told us that there was a bowling alley down there as well. However, none of us was ready to go down there to see if that was true or just a lot of talk as well.

Another story that comes to mind took place on an early summer evening. Again, we girls decided to go up to Spanjers'. It was time for us to show the guys that we were as brave as they said they were. No play today! Our mission: the *cellar*. We decided to use straws to see which one was going down first.

Marie and Ruth Ecklin
with my sister, Florence (l–r).

We crawled through the library window and proceeded through the kitchen area until we reached the cellar stairs. We huddled together as we stood looking down into the terrible darkness. Who was going to get the shortest straw? Who was the one who had to enter the unknown?

Flashlights went on as each of us took a straw and held her breath as we looked down on that tiny straw. God, I got it! "Jesus," was all I heard myself say. I wanted to run the other way, but the lucky ones eagerly made way for me to move forward. Well, I had no choice. After all, I was the leader of the pack, right? *Wrong*—at least not at that moment. They were all lined up behind me, waiting for me to take that first step. I gave a sigh as my flashlight lit up the doorway.

Shaking, I opened the door as my flashlight moved up and down the walls and steps, creating weird shadows out of the decaying plaster. Suddenly, I realized that there was a figure or something staring back at us. "Oh, my God!" was all I heard as our screams filled the dingy area. Terrified, we quickly turned, pushing and shoving each other as we made a mad dash

for the back door. The words "Oh, God! Oh, God!" traveled with us down the seemingly endless hallway leading to the back door.

A loud banging noise followed us. It got louder and louder, but none of us dared to turn around to see what it was. Puffing and panting, we flew through the back door, desperately wanting the safety of the outdoors. We headed for the carriage-garage roof, concealing ourselves behind its large parapet wall. As scared as we were, we sat, trying to catch our breaths, waiting for the unknown to appear. The banging noise continued, getting louder and louder. We knelt as we peered over the wall, waiting, waiting. The back door began to open. A ghostly figure appeared, pulling the "forbidden trunk" onto the small back porch. I could feel the sweat starting to run down my forehead into my eyes, burning and stinging them. My hands shook as they wiped away the many droplets.

However, the desire to flee was stifled by our curiosity about what was in that trunk. Silence invaded our space. Our hearts were pounding. Our breathing seemed harder. We watched frozen as the figure raised its arm and, with a crashing blow, smashed the lock on the trunk. We dared not move. The ghost-like figure pranced around the trunk, muttering strange words, interrupted only by an occasional penetrating screech. Suddenly, the trunk lid flew open, allowing a cloud of dust to float out from it.

As the dust cleared, an eerie sound began to emanate from the trunk. As much as we all wanted to scream, we found ourselves paralyzed by fear as events continued to unfold before our eyes. The ghostly figure was still circling around the trunk and gesturing wildly. With no warning, the figure dropped to the ground, unleashing a terrible wail, rolled over, and jumped up. Another ghostly figure vaulted from the trunk and began running toward us!

The figures were closing in on us. Screaming, we jumped off the roof and ran in the direction of our homes. We dared not look back for fear those ghostly figures were following us. Even though our homes were close by, fear made us feel that we had miles to go before we would be safe. Those five minutes seemed more like hours. Our feet felt like they weren't moving at all. The normal farewells—"See you tomorrow," "So long," or "Good night"—were impossible to say. *Home* was the only thing on our minds.

The next day, we said very little to each other because we had no words left to describe our frightening ordeal. We didn't reveal those torturous moments to anyone because we felt that no one would believe us. That curse! That terrible curse! For three months, we lived not knowing if we had been cursed or, if we had, when it might strike.

Grant Edwards and
Elwood (Elmer) Kenzler.

A couple of weeks before Halloween, the boys asked us if we wanted to go trick-or-treating with them. Excitedly, we began describing our costumes. The more the boys described their unique ghost-like costumes that could give off a smoke screen, the more we began to stare at them in disbelief. It was them! Those bastards! How could they have scared us so badly that summer evening and never let us know? To have kept that secret all that time and still not admit it was them! We were ready to kill!

There was no time to plan revenge. In one split second, we lost control of our emotions. One of us screamed out, "Get those bastards!" The next thing I knew, we flew into them, punching and yelling until we dropped to the ground from exhaustion. We were amazed as we viewed the results of our unleashed anger: boys' faces scratched and bleeding, clothing no longer repairable. The results of our unexpected, chaotic attack made the scene look like a real battlefield.

The boys, never expecting such a response, found themselves on the ground before they knew what had happened. Revenge was no longer necessary because this sudden attack proved more satisfying, more successful, and longer remembered by the boys than any other retaliation we could have planned. We were the victors for that moment!

The neighborhood was divided between the girls and the boys. We were like a large family: everything we did, we did together in some way or other.

We shared the good times and the bad. It all started when we were small kids and only grew throughout the years. It was a great neighborhood. A great bunch of kids.

The principal girls were Eunice Daily, Nancy Liedell, Alice White, and I. The other neighborhood girls—Ruth and Marie Eicklin, Barbara Coe, Grace Osborne, and Cynthia Husk—joined us whenever they could. The boys were Grant Edwards, Elwood Kentsler, Richard Daily, Charlie Cullen, Dominic DiPrimo, Ralph Gallagher, Jerry Evangelista, Rudolph and Anthony Vito. They outnumbered the girls most of the time, but that never bothered us. We could hold our own!

One of our favorite games was "kick-the-can." This was very similar to hide-and-seek. To determine who was going to be "it" one said, "One potato, two potato, three potato, four, five potato, six potato, seven potato, *more*," as she pointed to each of us and herself in turn. Whoever ended up being pointed to when she said "*more*" would be "it." The rest of us had to run and hide as soon as one of us kicked the can. "It" had to run and get the can, put it where it originally was, and then find everyone.

If one of us was able to sneak out and kick the can again, "it" had to stop searching for us, run and get the can, put it where it belonged, and start the search all over. While "it" was trying to find everyone, someone could sneak out and kick the can again. "It" had to run back, get the can, put it back where it had been and start looking all over again. The first person "it" found would be "it" for the next round, and the game continued in the same way. During summer vacations, this game was constantly being played. It sounds confusing, but it was a lot of fun.

APRIL FOOLS' DAY Our favorite joke on April Fools' Day was to play the pocketbook trick. In the late 1930s through the early 1940s, we would go up Sussex Avenue where two gigantic trees stood. They were slightly away from the edge of the roadway and made an excellent hiding place for us. Back then, traffic on Sussex Avenue was light, and cars were never in a hurry. It was at this spot, in the center of the roadway, where we laid a pocketbook with a string attached. We would be sure we were well concealed behind the two trees.

When an oncoming car would stop to allow a person to pick up the pocketbook, we would reel it in quickly, shouting, "April Fool!" In some cases, the person who had just been tricked did not always react as we expected. We found ourselves running in all directions as the chase after us began.

As a rule, most of the people whom we tricked would just laugh, drop the pocketbook, and wave to us as we hollered, "April Fool!" However, once in awhile, one would stop, get out of their car, pick up the pocketbook, look in it, and then actually take it with them. That left us holding just an empty string with their words "April Fool" echoing back at us as they drove away.

CRAIG'S BOBSLED   Another well-remembered time was sleigh riding down Elliott Street. Our street was considered the perfect hill for such fun. During the winter months, the entire neighborhood came alive as everyone came out to sleigh ride. One of the older neighborhood boys, Craig Compton, had a large bobsled. It was made of thick wood with slick, shiny, steel runners. It stood at least eighteen inches off the ground. The ropes for steering were attached to the front ends of the runners and extended the entire length of the sled. It was everyone's job to pull the correct rope when attempting to negotiate a curve. This bobsled held at least fifteen to twenty people and always took off with its maximum capacity. It was the most fantastic ride as we flew down Elliott Street and into the woods, going as far as what we called the Duck Pond.

The section of Elliott Street we used for bobsledding. My dog, Spunky, is running up the hill, which was fantastic for sleigh riding and took us deep into the woods.

It took everyone who had the thrill of riding down the hill to help pull the bobsled back up to the top. Sometimes, if we were lucky, a neighbor driving up the street would allow us to hitch the bobsled to their bumper. That baby was heavy! So when that happened, we considered it being in the right place at the right time. There was always a group of neighbors waiting at the top of the hill for the next ride down. No neighborhood in the Morristown area experienced such a thrill or the privilege of being able to ride on Craig's treasured bobsled. The white snow lit our way as we flew down the steep slope, holding on for dear life. Our screams of delight lingered long after the bobsled came to a complete stop. Our fearful yells pervaded the atmosphere.

ICE SKATING The Duck Pond was a small pond in the woods at the end of Elliott Street. It always seemed to freeze over before any other pond, lake, or river, allowing us the chance to ice skate long before other people. Few people knew of its whereabouts, which made it even nicer. The older boys in the neighborhood would make a large fire in a huge steel drum that they placed near the pond, or sometimes, they would just build a fire from all the fallen wood lying about. This fire was a welcome sight because it kept us warm. We would roast marshmallows and hot dogs over it. They always had something hot to drink and *always* shared with us, the younger kids on the block. Henry, Robert, and Edward Daily; Craig Compton; Sammy and Donald Karn; Hubert Whorton, my cousin; Dudley Tiger; Teddy Melick; Walter Critchley; Adolph and Willie Reinish; and Donald Woods were known as the "older" boys in our neighborhood.

Speedwell Lake was another favorite spot for ice-skating, but it took much longer to freeze because of its size. It was just a short distance away from the Duck Pond, and many people skated there. However, we felt that the Duck Pond belonged exclusively to our neighborhood. Another popular area to ice skate was at Burnham Park, which was located in Morristown. Occasionally, because of the distance, we had to have one of our parents drive us. However, this was a real inconvenience for our parents, so we seldom went there.

WALT'S "OLD JUG" CAR AND SIDECAR CYCLE We loved the attention the older neighborhood boys gave us. They never walked by without taking time to talk to us. They made us feel very important. Walter had an old roadster with a rumble seat. It was the neatest contraption we ever saw. No one in the area had a car like it. Walter had named his jalopy "the Old Jug." We would line up on the curb, waiting for him to come by, hoping he would stop and say, "Hop in!" Oh, just to take us for a spin around the block filled us with enough excitement to last for the next few days. We loved his attention and the thrill of riding in this very special old car. We fought among ourselves about who would be the ones to ride in the rumble seat. It only held three small people at a time. Walt allowed two of us to sit in the front with him. Thank God, we were small. However, it was never as exciting as sitting in the rumble seat, where the rushing air and the wind whipped around us and made us feel so free.

Walter also had a motorcycle that had a sidecar attached. When we saw him driving down the street on his unique cycle, we would all wave, jump up and down, and holler. Oh, how we wanted him to stop so one of us could have a ride. We thought that was the neatest looking cycle. He could see our excitement and seldom disappointed us. He was our special neighbor, a nice young man.

"MONOPOLY" AND SWIMMING My older sister, Florence, played with us on occasion, but she usually played with Ruthie and Marie. On rare occasions, these three would join us in playing kick-the-can or venturing down near the gypsy campsite. They were a little older than our group and felt, most of the time, that we were too young for them. It was not until we all got into our mid-teens that they decided we could join them. By that time, "Monopoly" was their number-one game. We had a very large porch, and it was there that we would set up the old card table and begin playing. Once we started playing, it became a real challenge to see who would be the winner. A game of Monopoly could last for several days.

All the kids in the neighborhood enjoyed swimming at Mt. Kemble Pool, located between Morristown and the Bernardsville area. In order for us to get there, one of our parents had to drive us there and pick us up. Each parent

took turns doing this, which meant we were there for the day. A membership was required, but members could bring a guest for the day by paying a minimal charge. Not everyone in our two gangs (boys/girls) had memberships, but no kid was ever left home because of this. If one went, we all went. There was a stand where we could get hot dogs, sandwiches, snacks, and cold drinks.

We spent many wonderful days at this pool. There was a sandy beach right by the pool where we would set up all of our belongings. There were also two regular diving boards and one high diving board. By the time summer was over, each of us had jumped off the high dive at least once. By the following year, we had to start all over again because our fear of the high dive took a long time to overcome. The pool always had lifeguards, and as each year passed, those young men looked better and better to each of us girls. Rivalry between our two gangs was put on hold while we swam and enjoyed the pool. We were all dependent on each other for our transportation to and from the pool. We also had to look out for each other while there. Today there are no signs that this lovely pool ever existed.

The Morristown public pool, known as Burnham Park Pool, was free. A person only needed to apply for a badge and prove he was a resident of Morristown. Because of all the mishaps that seemed to take place there, our parents preferred the Mt. Kemble Pool even with the additional cost. When none of our parents was able to take us to Mt. Kemble Pool, we would bike-ride to Burnham Park Pool, sneak in for a swim, cool off, and ride home.

ARCHIE'S ROAD STAND Back in the mid-1930s through the 1940s, restaurants were not popular because the lack of money stopped most people from eating out. Road stands (of which there were only a few in our area) were popular because they served inexpensive hot dogs, hamburgers, French fries, and cold drinks. They could be considered similar to today's McDonald's. Archie's Hot Dog and Hamburger Stand, located on Whippany Road, was known for having the best grilled food in the area. It was considered a very special place for both young and old. Because of the way it was growing, additions were constantly being made, making it look most unusual, almost a hodge-podge of additions to additions.

This road stand became a regular hangout for many teenagers and young adults. Just before we entered World War II, these young people were relishing the luxury of their own golden era. They never realized that their innocence and youth would soon be shattered by the forces of war. They would arrive at Archie's in a variety of different cars, which were now slowly becoming more affordable for the working class. Each one of their cars always held several persons more than what the car was designed to accommodate. This fascinated us to watch how they maneuvered themselves into positions so they could actually fit everybody in. How we envied them!

These young people's approach to Archie's was announced by their loud laughter and the excitement of the evening. The noise of squealing brakes indicated their arrival. Their radios blasted out music from such popular bands as Tommy and Jimmy Dorsey, Glenn Miller, Gene Krupa, and Benny Goodman. We were well into the big-band era. Our eyes would light up with amazement just watching them, wishing we were old enough to be one of them. Their laughter seemed to fill the entire area. Archie's would turn into bedlam as one car after another arrived in the same fashion. Friday, Saturday, and Sunday evenings were the busiest times, when Archie's was patronized by young and old alike.

When my father would suggest we get ready for him to take us to Archie's, no one argued or kept him waiting. It was a rush to the car! It was the excitement of the day! We suddenly became famished! During the war years, Archie's was one of the first places where the local community noticed the absence of young men. It was strange, no longer the way it was. Something was missing. The excitement was gone. It was another time. It was World War II.

Sometime during the later part of the war or right after the war, Archie's became known as Lou Rich's Bar and Grill. It never had the same appeal or the atmosphere that Archie's had. The excitement of those days was now just a memory. We had been through a war. Many of the local young men did not return home. Their absence was noted! The land was eventually sold, and today a residential area sprawls over this memorable site. I can't help but wonder if the enchanting laughter from the ghosts of yesteryear continues to echo throughout this small tract of land.

UNUSUAL CHARACTERS IN OUR NEIGHBORHOOD We had several unusual characters that either lived in or just beyond our neighborhood. Because these people left such an impression on each of us, I feel I must mention them, as they were a part of our childhood.

Old Man Beech and His Wife During the 1930s, there were a man and a woman known by the local people as "Old Man Beech and his wife." Everyone presumed that they were married, even though, as I would later learn, his wife, Mary, kept her maiden name, "Jumbo." They lived in the woods, in a tumbled-down shack off Sussex Avenue. Once a week they walked to Morristown for their weekly supplies. This was actually a good three-mile walk each way. Whenever they came into town, they always had an old baby carriage with them. As soon as someone in the neighborhood saw them walking either up or down Sussex Avenue, word spread among the kids: "Old Man Beech and his wife are coming."

We would gather in one spot to watch them pass by. Their strangeness became our fascination. We never stopped gawking at them until they were well past us. Together, they made a bizarre couple. We would shake our heads, giggle a lot, and one of us always had to spurt out some kind of nasty comment. We were kids who could not understand why anyone would want to live in such an unusual way. Our faces showed many different emotions, since each of us had different feelings regarding this strange couple.

They never hollered at us. It was like they never saw us. They were so filthy. Their clothing was always tattered, including shoes that were either too big or too small and were usually full of holes. Their faces were wrinkled, terribly weather-beaten, showing the effects of their hard lives. There was nothing gentle looking about either of them, but we knew they would not harm us. They did not walk upright at all; their bent bodies had an awful, deformed appearance. What disturbed us most was the fact that no one could get close to them because their stench was terrible. They hitchhiked rides on occasion, but few people ever allowed the two in their cars once they got a whiff.

According to the gossip among local merchants, the only time they ever got bathed was when one of them had to go to the hospital. Old Man Beech would push his wife in the baby carriage whenever she became too exhausted to walk

any further. It was an unbelievable sight to see an old man pushing a baby carriage with an old woman trying to lie in it. Her thin body gave the appearance of being forced into it because her legs dangled over the sides of the carriage. They were never known to beg or ask anything from anyone. Old Man Beech always seemed to have enough money to buy their necessary supplies, much to the amazement of the local merchants. This couple was devoted to each other. They appeared in the area right after the 1929 Depression and always kept to themselves right up to their deaths. No one knew their real ages or their next of kin. I believe that they both died as mysteriously as they lived.

Just a note of interest regarding this odd couple: Last June 2002, I attended a graduation party and met Betty Windt, who was also born and raised in the Morristown area. We talked about the past and the many people we knew. I mentioned these characters and to my surprise, she remembered them. I was shocked and excited when she told me their first names. I couldn't believe it. After all these years, I heard them referred to as "Freddie Beech and Mary Jumbo," not "Old Man Beech and his wife." It gave a little dignity to their pathetic and difficult existences. It really never mattered if they were or weren't married. They were never apart!

Old Dickie Hunt Another interesting character who was a part of our lives as children was Dickie Hunt. He had the appearance of a wild man. His eyes were always cold, empty looking, and bulging. They were set deep within his strained, wrinkled, and unshaven face, making his age almost impossible to determine. His slick, grayish hair had the look of total neglect. It was severely matted, unwashed, and hung down his shoulders. It appeared to weigh heavily from the combination of oil and dirt. His clothing was in complete disarray and in desperate need of washing. He had a large frame with arms that seemed to dangle aimlessly at his sides. His walk was similar to the "goose step," since he never bent his knees. We would hide behind the trees when we spotted him coming up the street, hoping he would not see us. He never said a word or bothered any of the children in the neighborhood. His cold, hard stare made us feel afraid of him.

He lived in the foundation of a half-built shack at the bottom of Elliott Street. He built this foundation out of cement blocks as the cellar of his

home. Unfortunately, that was as far as his building went, and he lived in the area of the cellar that was completed. On occasion, Dickie Hunt would disappear from the area. Only God knew where he went! He always boarded up what windows and doors he had. One time, the boys, knowing he was away, tore down the boards from the windows and entered his so-called castle. They found many World War I manuals, like *How to Be a Soldier*, as well as items, souvenirs, and medals that showed he had been in the military during the Great War.

I remember Grant told me how guilty they all felt and how sorry they were to have invaded his domain. The boys left everything intact, boarded the windows back up, and never again ventured into this strange man's private world. This news spread quickly. The entire neighborhood looked upon their wild-appearing neighbor differently. His strange behavior was no longer a problem.

During the summer, everyone had their windows wide open (air conditioning was uncommon back then), and their radios blasted the music of *Your Hit Parade*. Many of the nightly programs would shatter the stillness of a hot summer night. Sounds from the radio shows such as *The Shadow*, *Lux Theater*, *Amos 'n' Andy*, and many others would penetrate the blackness of the night.

Apparently, Dickie Hunt would become extremely upset by all the noise pervading the hot summer air. He would come out of his shack with a washtub and hammer and bang away, goose-stepping up and down the hill. It was as if he was competing with the noises of the summer night. The next-door neighbors feared that their radios were irritating him or frightening him. Everyone on the street felt that when he needed to create this tremendous commotion he must somehow have been reliving one of his war experiences. No one ever complained to the police or caused this man any more pain than what he was already going through.

The only time anyone ever saw Mr. Hunt clean, shaven, and dressed in a suit and tie was when he came to pay his respects to my family on the death of Grandfather Ritter. Grant and his father were standing on the curb in front of their home when he passed by. He commented that he was going to say his goodbyes to Mr. Ritter and express his sympathy to Paul and his

family. Mr. Edwards was taken aback by this unexpected comment. This strange and unfriendly man who no one knew anything about was filled with a great amount of sympathy for a neighbor's loss. My father, mother, and Aunt Love were deeply touched by Mr. Hunt's desire to convey to the family his sincere sympathy. Within this strange man was concealed a very gentle, tender person. He never revealed this very private side of himself again. Sometime during 1941, he left the area and never returned.

Old Mrs. Gordon and Her Daughter, Edna The last of our unusual characters who lived within our neighborhood were old Mrs. Gordon and her daughter, Edna. During the spring, summer, and fall, our mischievous ideas were endless. Boredom was usually behind it all! We loved to ring the Gordon's doorbell and then run for our lives as we heard one of them approaching their door. We would run behind a large tree, a hedge, or anything that was fairly close to their home and watch how upset they would get. Mrs. Gordon and Edna would parade up and down their porch, cursing and shouting at us for bothering them. They never disappointed us: they always acted exactly as we expected them to act.

Mrs. Gordon looked like an old witch with her sharp, pointed nose and mean, dark eyes. She was very thin and had a voice like a screech owl. Edna was similar to her mother, except she was much heavier. She knew every curse word there was, and of course, she screamed every one of them at us. We could upset her so easily. Our fun would begin when we would stand close enough to be seen by them as they paced up and down their porch, but far enough away so that they couldn't catch us. They would no sooner go back into their house, than one of us would run and ring their doorbell again. The door would fly open. Out they would come, cursing and hollering, while we scattered in all directions.

The most fun was when either Mrs. Gordon or Edna (or, at times, both of them) would dash off their porch in hot pursuit of us. Just what we wanted! The great chase had begun! Oh, what fun! At this point, a couple of us would remain behind to move a couple of their porch chairs onto their lawn. We had these two half-crazed ladies totally out of control, and we were enjoying every moment.

By the time we reached age thirteen, removing their chairs seemed wrong, no longer fun. We often thought that our actions toward those poor souls were cruel and wondered why we ever thought it was fun. The biggest shock for us came when we learned the truth about them. Edna was mentally retarded. Mrs. Gordon's husband had been decapitated in an accident at work. This was why Mrs. Gordon appeared so irrational.

We found it difficult to mention their names or to pass them without feeling pangs of guilt. Each one of us secretly wished that we could erase the torment we had inflicted upon those two women. We wanted to tell them how sorry we were, but no words could undo the so-called fun we had forced upon our unfortunate neighbors. However, on Halloween nights, and only then, we would still ring their doorbell, but we never hung around for candy!

THE HOBOES, TRAMPS, AND THE CCC CAMPS After the beginning of the Depression in 1929, more and more men found themselves financially destroyed. Thus, a multitude of hoboes and tramps sprang out of nowhere. They hitched rides all over the country by climbing on freight cars. It made no difference which direction the train was going. Our local area was no different from the rest of the country because we, too, had our own hobo camp. It was located in the woods behind the Alfred Vail School.

This camp was set up close to the railroad tracks, owned by the Delaware, Lackawanna and Western (DL&W) line. Many long freight trains, as well as the well-known passenger trains the Buffalo Express and the diesel-powered Phoebe Snow, ran on these tracks. These two trains had their main terminal in Hoboken, New Jersey. The DL&W trains passed through Morristown and the many other towns on their way northwest. They made stops only on notification of pick-ups before arriving in Buffalo, New York. They would then continue on to Chicago, Illinois. The freight trains were the main transportation for the hobos and tramps. They offered a direct route to the west and became most popular trains to hop. The freight cars would attract so many hoboes and tramps that the railroad companies had special police to try to keep the trains free of these characters.

The difference between the hoboes and tramps was that the hobo was willing to work for his handouts. I remember when my mother would allow

a hobo into our kitchen to eat whatever extras or leftovers remained from the previous meal. We would sit around the kitchen table, frozen to our seats, watching and listening to his stories of woe and the places he had been. Hoboes were basically good people who found themselves in dire straits. Tramps, on the other hand, would never offer to work for their handouts. Mother considered her offering an act of Christian charity, and no one was turned away without a good thick sandwich for his next meal.

I learned that the hoboes had a way of leaving markings, often made with chalk, on a fence or elsewhere on the grounds of homes where the people showed them kindness. I found myself looking for their mark every time one of them left our home. To my surprise, I found several such marks on a small section of our fence.

Around 1933, a Civilian Conservation Corps (CCC) camp was built just a short distance from Archie's road stand on Whippany Road. The CCC began just after Franklin D. Roosevelt took office for his first term. This program was part of his famous "New Deal." The CCC camp was inhabited by young men (known by us as "the boys"), veterans of World War I, and Native Americans. They had to be single, jobless, in good physical condition, and needy. It was a lifeline for the undernourished sons of the Depression. They earned only a dollar a day, but left behind a heritage of parks, dams, bridges, buildings, roads, and hundreds of conservation and restoration projects throughout the country.

Their camp always held a certain amount of fascination for us girls. We had never seen this type of living where young men wore uniforms, lived in barracks, and worked on local projects as a group. These boys worked very hard, and their accomplishments turned out to be awesome. Many of them had a chance, for the first time in their lives, to learn some type of trade. This was their way both to survive those hard times and to help their families back home get through the Depression. During 1942, Congress stopped funding the CCC, and most of "the boys" changed their CCC uniforms to military uniforms because our country was already at war.

SPUNKY AND THE WEDDING CAKE One day, Dad gave me one of his pointer pups as my very own. I named him Spunky. From the moment I

brought him into our house to show him to Mother, he became our house-dog. Even Mother loved him, and soon there was no mention of his returning to the kennel. No matter where I went, Spunky was always right by my side. I had this dog for many years.

A cute story comes to mind. It was my cousin Hubert's wedding day. The wedding and reception were to be held at our home. Hubert and his fiancée, Sylvia, were still sleeping because it was early in the morning. There was nothing more either of them had to do except to get themselves ready for the day's events. On the other hand, Mother, Aunt Love, and Ida, our cleaning woman, were busy getting last-minute projects completed before the wedding began. Mother had asked me to dust the living room and the dining room.

Upon entering the dining room, I noticed Spunky was there. He came over to greet me with the strangest smile on his face. "What are you doing in the dining room, Spunky?" He just wagged his tail and left the room. I was too excited about the wedding to give Spunky any more thought. The table looked lovely with Mother's silver and china. It all looked so festive including the wedding cake, which the bakery had just delivered. Mother had placed it on the table with tender loving care, making sure it was not too close to the edge.

All was going just as planned, and once again, Spunky appeared with an even bigger smile on his face. By now, we were all in the kitchen receiving instructions for our next project. Mother remarked how funny Spunky looked, adding that the white glob around his mouth looked like he was ready to shave. She laughed and continued working at the kitchen table. Spunky quietly walked over to Mother and laid his head on her lap. She gently patted him as a large glob slide from his mouth onto her clean, fresh dress, then another and another. Suddenly, Mother became aware that the white substance was falling on the kitchen floor. Her face turned white. This was not shaving cream. Mother jumped up and headed for the dining room, uttering a loud cry: "My God, the cake! Spunky has been in the cake." Panic and despair poured from her. She stood by the dining table, looking at the cake, wailing, "Oh! My God, he's has licked the icing off one side of the cake." Mother began to weep.

Sylvia and Hubert, awakened by all the commotion, came running down stairs. Sylvia looked at the cake. With globs of icing still around his mouth, Spunky followed the family into the dining room. Everyone gasped. No one said a word. Globs continued to slip from Spunky's face as he looked up at Sylvia as if to ask, "Is something wrong?" Sylvia and Hubert looked at us as we stood around the table with faces of disbelief. The beautiful wedding cake was a mess, a disaster. They began to laugh. They quickly reassured Mother that everything would be all right. Mother regained her composure and called the baker. He suggested that she bring the cake back and he would re-ice and redecorate the section that had been licked off.

The violated cake was immediately repaired, and no one who attended the wedding ever knew the difference, except those few who had witnessed the earlier scene. The wedding day proceeded with no other disasters or distractions. Much to his bewilderment, Spunky was removed to another part of the house until the affair of the day was over and all the guests had left.

I could do anything at all with Spunky. Many times I dressed him up in my pajamas. Spunky loved to sleep in my parents' bed. I would put a pair of pajamas on him, then lay him on his back and extend his front paws out from under the covers. He enjoyed my messing with him as I placed a book between his paws and put Daddy's glasses on him. There he would stay until my parents came to bed. He never moved. Spunky loved the attention as much as I loved giving it.

Spunky always felt that whatever Mother cooked was meant for him as well. This was especially true on Sundays, when we always had some kind of roast. Spunky's head seemed to rest very nicely on our dining room table. Because of this, we had to always make sure that the meat was never too close to the edge. There were occasions, however, when we forgot to do this, which always created a disastrous Sunday dinner. Spunky would devour the meat so fast that no one realized it was gone until we were at the table. In the meantime, Spunky, feeling very full, was having a nap upstairs, away from all the pending upset. At these times Mother always swore that she was going to put him back in the kennel. We knew they were only threats and nothing more. She loved Spunky as much as I did, so I never worried.

HALLOWEEN   Another exciting time was Halloween night. As it approached, every kid was busy trying to decide what he or she was going to be: a soldier, a witch, or some hideous and scary character or creature. It was a night of merriment and mischief, as well as a night filled with ghosts and goblins. No two Halloween nights were ever the same. Some years, we would go out as a neighborhood gang. Other years, only three or four of us would team up and go out together.

By our ninth year, our route was well established. First, we went across the street to Mr. and Mrs. Hall's home. Then we traveled to Lake Road were Mrs. Mazzocchi lived. There was no messing around until we visited our favorite two houses. These neighbors gave us special treats. The Hall's didn't have any children, but they were always well prepared for Halloween. I believe they loved it as much as we did. You must remember, I am talking about the 1930s, when the Depression was being felt by everyone. Most neighbors gave an apple or penny candy, but the Hall's gave each of us a nickel *plus* a five-cent candy bar. What fools wouldn't head there first? As we ran up to their front door, our excitement and anticipation filled the air. We could already feel and see that shiny nickel. It was always a race to see who was going to be first in line, each of us fearing that Mr. Hall would run out of nickels before we got ours.

The kid who rang the doorbell never took his finger off the bell, making it sound like it was stuck, until Mr. or Mrs. Hall opened the door. Mrs. Hall made a fuss over each one of us and pretended she didn't know who we were. We tried not to look impatient as we shifted from one foot to the other, wanting her to hurry up. However, we were not going to spoil her fun. We hadn't gotten our goodies yet! The big moment came when Mr. Hall would appear with a large jar of coins. We know exactly what to expect. He would shake the jar just enough to make the nickels jingle and then watch our reaction. Of course, we were bewitched by the sight of so many coins. It was a tantalizing moment. We held our breaths until he placed a nickel in each of our extended hands. Then it was Mrs. Hall's turn. She always placed a five-cent candy bar in everyone's bag. Wow! We savored those moments.

We hooted and hollered as we raced to Mrs. Mazzocchi's home. We would arrive, breathless, anxious to see and taste her surprises. We were

immediately invited in. Every year, our eyes quickly moved to the dining room table. There they sat, tempting and teasing, a large platter of home-made doughnuts! No bakery in town could match her delicacies. After the many years of stopping at Mrs. Mazzocchi's home, we knew her routine. She had to talk to each of us about school and other things that we considered to be unimportant. We were anxious to dive into her goodies. Those few minutes seemed like hours. We were anxious to eat and get going.

Mrs. Mazzocchi always had a large pitcher of cold cider waiting to quench our thirst. She knew exactly what we needed. On our departing, she would give each of us a small bag filled with homemade cookies and a Halloween cupcake. What more could we ask?

Mrs. Mazzocchi was special in her own way. She wasn't rich like Mr. and Mrs. Hall, but she worked hard to make this night special for us. We knew her goodies were made with a lot of love and caring. After making the important stops, we would, then, just go to house-to-house. Sometimes we tried to go back to a house that had just given something special, but we always got caught. No one ever got mad at us. Instead, they just laughed and said, "Weren't you just here?" Halloween was, indeed, a night to be passed on to the next generation. It was always the most fun night of the year.

To this day, when Halloween comes around, I can't help but think of our neighborhood, the old gang, and the fun we shared on this special night. Our parents never bought us costumes nor did they have the time or money to make them. We had to do our own improvising if we were going out. Our costumes consisted of anything we could find laying in the old trunks in our attics. These trunks were filled with treasures from the past, such as the World War I U.S. Navy whites that belonged to my father when he was in the service. Dad served for a period of three days, then he was discharged (honorably) due to a severe influenza epidemic. He worked as a medic over in the Brooklyn Navy Yard. When he came home, he had everyone believing he was a real hero during his short stay in the navy.

Dad's navy whites and navy pea coat were just as exciting to put on as my grandmother's dresses. She apparently had loved the frilly clothing of her day. There were many to choose from because neither Granddaddy nor Dad

had thrown any of her clothing away. They had placed every piece of it in several large trunks. We would squeal with delight as we dressed up in one outfit after another.

We found other treasure as well, including Grandfather Ritter's knickers! I often heard Granddaddy speak of a very special cap that he wore with those pants, but I never saw it until, lo and behold, one day, while scrounging through the many trunks, I found it. It had been wrapped carefully in tissue paper and placed in between some of Grandmother's lovely clothing. I couldn't wait as I gazed at Granddaddy's most prized possessions. My mind went into overdrive as mischievous thoughts began to whirl within it. All I could think was, "What a find!" I threw off my clothing and, to my surprise, I began dressing up in his things. Naturally, the knickers fell below my knees, but with the help of a small piece of rope, they stayed up. I paraded up and down the back attic pretending I was Granddaddy out on an afternoon stroll. Once again, my imagination took over. I walked, as he had, with head held high, arms swinging by my side, and a stride that bespoke importance. I loved wearing his prized cap.

If Granddaddy had still been alive, I would have never touched his prized possession or put it on my head. He would've seen that I got a good spanking while he stood and watched. Naturally, he would have had a smirk on his face. He never liked us kids. Everything we did aggravated him. It was hard for me to think of him any other way because he never seemed happy around us. His stern look and cold attitude gave us a reason to keep our distance. He often bragged that no man could ever walk in his shoes. As I sat there remembering him, I carefully folded the clothing, and placed it back into the old trunk. As I closed the heavy lid, my afternoon ended with great satisfaction.

I remember the day, I found Grandmother's old fox-fur stole. I had never seen anything like it. Shocked, I dropped it quicker than I had picked it up. The animal still had its head and feet attached! It had a funny black mouth that would open and close if you pressed it in a special spot. Its little feet dangled and moved every time I moved. It scared me even though it was dead. My mother told me that women wrapped these fur pieces around their

necks. I was fascinated by it. I didn't want to put it back in the trunk. I just wanted to wear it and see how it felt.

Mother was furious with me for bringing it downstairs. She hated it and hid it, thinking no one would ever find it. She was waiting for her own beautiful mink coat. When Dad saw the stole, he told Mother how pleased he was to see she was wearing it again. He wondered why she never wore it anymore. After all, that was a lovely fur piece. It had been his mother's pride and joy. So much for Grandmother's fur stole. Unfortunately, Mother waited many years before she ever owned a full-length mink coat.

The fox-fur stole now belongs to my little granddaughter, Kelsey. To my surprise, Kelsey wore it when we went to the Madison Hotel for our 2002 Thanksgiving dinner. She looked like a little lady, all dressed up. I'd forgotten that I had given her that fur piece. As I gazed at it, a scene from yesteryear flashed before me.

WINE MAKING AND WINE TASTING   Knollcroft was well known for its large cellar, which was divided into many different rooms. However, the most-used ones were the laundry room, the bathroom, and the large game room. There was also a back cellar, which had storage bins for potatoes, onions, turnips, and apples. Huge, long shelves extended the length of the canning room, which also held the massive tables were Mother's canned goods and preserves were kept, neatly, always in order. However, the most popular room belonged to Grandfather and Daddy. It was a small area located just off the back cellar. This area was used as their winemaking room because it was always cold, regardless of the season.

For years, the family heard stories about the prohibition days when Granddaddy and Dad made their own supply of wine and then had a big wine-tasting party. They kept the wine barrels stored securely along one wall. Their equipment for making the wine was stationed on the opposite side. It was well-organized and well-planned to take care of their thirst. The barrels never had a chance to empty. So long as the drink was plentiful, a new supply was always in the making. Mother's teetotaler beliefs never penetrated that particular area. She was ordered to stay away from their room, which

she did. Her job was to make sure Knollcroft carried the appearance of a picture-perfect home. It was anything but that!

As kids, we knew we were taking one hell of a chance whenever we entered the most forbidden room within Knollcroft. Stinging cold always met us the moment we opened the heavy steel door, but it never kept us out or discouraged our entering. It was a great adventure, so long as we didn't get caught. The wine made us feel good. It made us feel grown-up as we sipped ourselves silly. The coldness we had felt disappeared as the wine began to take effect. The drink became more and more soothing as we became more and more relaxed.

As children, we could not resist the temptation of such an enjoyable and fun-filled feat. Mother would have gone into hysterics if she had ever caught us. Granddaddy and Dad would have been in big trouble as well. In other words, all hell would have let loose. The ritual she always performed when Daddy came home from the dog shows smelling of drink would be nothing compared to her dramatization of us kids playing with the devil. God! The thought of that scene would scare the Devil himself.

Many times Grant helped my father make the wine and store it in the large wine barrels, so he knew which wine was the most flavorful and ready to drink. We would take one of the little cups that we hid for our own use, place it under the nozzle and slowly release the knob so a little wine would flow into it. We took turns getting a drink, all the time hoping that no family member would find us sampling Daddy's specialty. The more we drank, the better the wine tasted. Our wine-drinking days lasted as long as the wine continued to flow from the barrels.

Approximately ten years after my grandfather passed away, my father lost interest in making wine. The wine barrels held enough wine to last for a few months. Thus, our supply and our fun-filled moments continued a while longer. Mother could never understand why the neighborhood kids loved to play in our cellar. Thank God for the outside cellar entrance. More drunken kids went through that door than I care to mention. None of us ever got caught, however, and we often thought God had to have been on our side!!

Me as a young teenager in 1942.

OLD-FASHIONED FUN Because of the size of our cellar, I held many girls-only parties in the large room. Mother would never allow any boys except the neighborhood boys, but they never wanted to come. We would decorate the room according to the type of party it was going to be, and as we got into our teen years, we would have a radio or phonograph to provide music for dancing. None of us knew how to dance, but it was fun just jumping around and pretending we were dancers.

As young children, we would put on shows in this large room. One of us would pick her favorite storybook character, and then we would base our play around that character. A large sheet hung as a curtain to conceal the stage until the show began. We spent hours putting our act together. We practiced for a couple of weeks, gathered the necessary costumes, and then one of us would go about the neighborhood selling tickets for our big performance. A few of the mothers bought tickets if for no other reason than to see what we had been up to. These were very busy times for us. Our imaginations overflowed in the entertainment field. We were never bored! We were the first young entrepreneurs in our neighborhood!

Eunice, Nancy, Alice, and I would set up a lemonade stand in front of Knollcroft and sell lemonade on hot summer days. Our mothers would let us have some of their store-bought cookies to give to our customers, but never their homemade ones. We would sit by the curb all day, waiting for our first customer. The boys in the neighborhood would come by, laughing and jesting at how ridiculous we looked, but even they returned eventually to buy some. We had good lemonade! We only charged two cents a glass and felt that our customers were getting a good deal. Our table was made out of a piece of plywood set on two wooden horses that my dad provided. Once we had put

a pretty tablecloth over it, it looked good. By the time we added a vase of flowers and our large pitcher of lemonade, it looked even better. We used paper cups that we could threw away when our customers were finished.

A little cigar box was our cash register. Eunice was usually the cashier. We had small chairs to sit on as we waited for our customers. When a car stopped, it was an unforgettable moment. Naturally, each of us wanted to be the first to help our customer. Breathless and almost speechless, one of us, meekly, spoke out, "Can we help you?" In the meantime, six hands were trying to get into the package of cookies, six hands were pulling at the paper plates, and six hands were handing the customer a napkin. We were trying so hard to impress this kind person who was helping to make our day. Plus, our thoughts had already turned to the possibility that maybe this customer might stop again on his return trip. Our entrepreneurship opened our eyes to the many ways of making money.

As we all played together, games were on top of our list of activities. We would play Chinese checkers, jump rope or jump double-Dutch, hide-and-seek, giant steps, or puss-in-the-corner (four clothesline poles, a kid at each pole, and one person in the middle who was "it"). My mother had this type of clothesline, so we had to play puss-in-the-corner in our backyard. As I look back, Knollcroft was the social center of the neighborhood anyway. For some reason, it had a bewitching attraction to those looking in.

Eunice Daily and Alice White.

We would have marble tournaments between the boys and the girls of the neighborhood, as well as tournaments at school. Marbles were a big thing back then, and we were dead serious on winning whenever we had a chance to be in one of those tournaments. I had a beautiful bag of marbles, including my very special shooters (they were the large

ones). I was out to win; not lose. Hours were spent kneeling on the ground. We surrounded the large stick-made circle like a bunch of vultures gathering around freshly killed prey.

Our marbles lay inside this circle as if waiting for someone's special shooter to knock them out of it. No matter how many times we played, the wait was agonizing. No one said a word once that special shooter hit the ground and began rolling toward the circle. Eyes popped; breathing stopped. Each one of us watched and wondered if this was going to be the moment when that prized shooter missed its mark. The game of marbles drew blood

Nancy Liedell in front of our famous cherry tree.

many times, especially when someone felt that he was being cheated in some way or other. Many good friendships were destroyed, at least for the next two or three hours. The bond we all shared wouldn't allow any long-term anger to interfere with our fast-moving lifestyle. Each of us knew that we needed the others. No way was anger going to end our bonds of friendship.

Bike riding was another favorite pastime. We would ride for hours and pretend we were touring the country or whatever. Our imaginations were always working. We would pedal out into the country, which, back then, was only about two blocks away. We would ride to the

local ice-cream shops or, on occasion, bicycle into Morristown. We felt very grownup as we pedaled around and among the moving traffic.

To venture beyond our neighborhood was always exciting. By the time we reached our mid-teens, we pedaled miles into unfamiliar areas. We were never afraid to ride our bikes into someone else's neighborhood because we knew we could take care of ourselves. We knew how to fight! If we found we had a problem, we would ride back, gather the gang, and return to resolve it. We all stuck together in times of need because we were bonded by our shared territory.

We had an understanding that it was up to the person having the problem to take care of it. The gang was there only for support, not to fight the battle for him or her. These times were few because none of us liked fighting anymore.

Henshaw was our private swimming hole. We had either to walk or ride our bikes because it was in the area where the gypsies camped. Years earlier, the older boys in our neighborhood had attached a rope to one of the tree limbs that extended over the water. They spent hours swinging and dropping into the

Jeanne Monahan, a good school friend.

water. Once we came on the scene, we did the same. That piece of rope stayed on the branch for years after we no longer went swimming there. Henshaw was home to all kinds of small insects, beavers, muskrats, deer, and foxes. It was their watering hole as well.

During our youth, Eunice, Nancy, Alice, and I went to the movies whenever our parents gave us money. The Park, the Jersey, and the Palace theaters were the local movie houses. The Community Theater opened in 1937. We patronized all of them when we had money. Movies were a great entertainment for us. For a change, we let the many different movies create their special magic within our tiny minds. They also opened our eyes to the outside world for less than twenty cents.

The old Palace Theater on Speedwell Avenue charged the least: ten cents per person. Because this theater was patronized by a wild bunch of kids, we were expected to go to one of the others. If something good were playing, we would go to the Palace but never tell our parents. Somebody was always throwing something around, hollering some dirty remark, or chasing someone up and down the aisles. As a rule, the chase ended in a fight, and those involved were thrown out by the management. Most of the time, we found this gang of kids more exciting than the movie we had come to see.

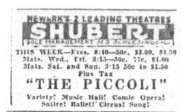

From the Daily Record, *March 23, 1933.*

From the Daily Record, *March 23, 1933.*

*In 1933 you could go out to
dinner for 30–50 cents!*

Movies featuring stars such as Hopalong Cassidy, Roy Rogers, Tom Mix, and Our Gang were shown at the Park, Jersey, and Palace theaters. Those were exciting and happy times for each one of us. Our imaginations were always inspired by such movies. The Park Theater was torn down during the 1950s. The Jersey Theater was torn down just a couple of years ago.

After seeing one of the local movies, we never went home without first stopping at Thode's for our favorite ice cream soda or sundae. A "Dusty Road" sundae was my number-one choice. It was yummy; it was the best. It consisted of vanilla ice cream with hot chocolate fudge, malted milk sprinkled on top of chocolate, topped off with a big glob of real whipped cream, and naturally, a cherry on top of that. Need I say more? Just writing about it still makes my mouth water. Oh, just to have one more, exactly like those of yesteryear.

The Community Theater was considered the nicest of the four, simply because it was newer. What attracted the populace were the velvety cushioned seats, unlike the hard, leather seats in the other theaters. The refreshment stand had much more to offer in the way of popcorn, candy, ice cream, and sodas. The restrooms were situated on the first floor, making them more convenient than the other theaters' restrooms, which were located in their

basements. Patrons could sit for hours and never find themselves uncomfortable, especially, when it came to long movies such as *Gone With the Wind*. The better movies were shown at this theater, and children had to be accompanied by a parent. The Community Theater was closed and unused for many years as well, but recently it reopened (in 1994) for concerts and performing arts groups.

From the Daily Record, *March 23, 1933.*

EXPLOSION AT HERCULES POWDER COMPANY   During my seventh-grade school year (1940), we were having one of our usual geography lessons when we suddenly heard a loud boom. Frightened faces found themselves looking back at other frightened faces. No one moved. For one moment, an eerie silence took over the classroom. We watched the windows bend, swaying back and forth, books and supplies fell from shelves to the floor, and our desks moved. Every one in the room reacted differently, including our teacher who had instantly lost control of her class. A few students fled into the hallway, while some stood against the blackboard, away from the windows and any possible flying glass. Several students, too frightened to move, were being comforted by others.

We heard another loud boom. The building shook badly for a few seconds. We could feel the explosions before we heard them. There were more explosions. Then someone shouted, "There goes Hercules!" Another kid yelled, "No, it's Picatinny Arsenal! Wow!" Little more was said, except an occasional whisper, "Yeah, you're right. It's gotta be one or the other."

Hercules and Picatinny were government arsenals that made small-arms ammunition, artillery shells, bombs, grenades, and other munitions for the military. They both were located about fifteen miles from Morristown. This

was considered the worst accident Hercules ever experienced. The local areas, such as Wharton, Roxbury, Succasunna, and Ledgewood, absorbed the brunt of the explosions. Hit by flying glass and other debris, a large number of workers at Hercules became casualties. Many police units and ambulances arrived within minutes. The smoke overpowered everyone. It was chaotic. However, by the grace of God, only about fifty-some people were killed, which was remarkably few, considering the terrible damage. If I remember correctly, over one hundred people were seriously injured.

World War II was going on in Europe at this time, and England was buying ammunition from these two munitions plants. Every kid in our class realized how lucky we were. No one was hurt. We had just experienced what many kids over in Europe were living through on a daily basis.

Little did we know that the horrors of war were right around the corner or how deeply it was going to affect the American populace. Our way of life was just about to end, bringing us into the realities of World War II with all its tragedies and sacrifices. A whole new way of life was about to unfold.

WORLD WAR II   Pearl Harbor was bombed on Sunday, December 7, 1941, at 7:55 A.M. (Honolulu time). When the news was released to the American people, the country was shocked. We were listening to one of our favorite radio programs when a special bulletin announced the horrific bombing. Most people didn't know where Pearl Harbor was located. We had to get out our geography books to look for it.

Our neighborhood was no different from all the other neighborhoods throughout America. One by one, young men, eighteen years and over, were either signing up for the particular branch of service that appealed to them or being drafted into the military. Many kids who were only seventeen also went into the service after obtaining parental permission. Patriotism climbed non-stop to new heights. Its driving force spread throughout our entire country.

Walter Critchley lived with his friend, Dudley Tiger, and Dudley's family, our neighbors, while he attended Morristown High School. Even though Walt's parents lived in Valley Stream, New York, Walt stayed in Morristown because he had an opportunity to be on the Morristown High School foot-

Some of the older boys in our neighborhood, most of whom served during WW II or the Korean War, in happier, more innocent days (l–r): Grant Edwards, held by Dudley Tiger; Milton Emmons; Sam Karn; Don Karn; Henry Daily; and Edward Daily.

ball team, which was his first love. Walt was considered one of the school's gridiron heroes. He was also very active in working with the youth in the Presbyterian Church, showing that he was not only tough on the football field, but also had a gentleness that we, as well as other kids, had experienced many times. After Walter graduated from Morristown High School in June 1940, he went to work for George Green and Sons in Morristown.

Walter joined the U.S. Marine Corps shortly after Pearl Harbor was attacked. He did his basic training at San Diego, California, and was eventually promoted to corporal and sent to the Pacific theater. Walt was killed sometime between November 20 and 24, 1943, during the invasion of Tarawa, one of 985 young American servicemen who died on that island. His name is inscribed on the World War II Tablets of the Missing at Honolulu National Memorial Cemetery of the Pacific, located in Honolulu, Hawaii. That monument displays the names of 2,369 other U.S. Marines who died in the Pacific theatre during the war.

Robert Matthews, a friend of Walter's who had a chance to visit Tarawa after the invasion, describes the final resting place of Walter and his fellow servicemen: "Because there was very little space for a cemetery and so many men were killed during the invasion, the bodies were laid to rest in what we would call mass graves. These graves were dug to accommodate fifteen or

twenty bodies. The burial grounds were made up of many small plots of about twenty-foot squares, each enclosed by a white picket fence and a small arbor at the entrance with a plaque containing the names of those buried in the plot."

The entire neighborhood mourned Walter's death and, for the first time, felt the pain of war. He became our beloved hero, the first young man from our neighborhood who sacrificed his life for our freedom. The memory of Walt piloting that jalopy, "the Old Jug," and his famous "sidecar cycle" around the streets of Morristown will never be forgotten by those who knew him.

Another young neighbor, Donald Karn—or "D.K.," as he was called by everyone who knew him—joined the army shortly after he graduated from Morristown High School on June 16, 1944. He was inducted into the service just ten days later, on June 26. By December, D.K. had been sent overseas to become part of the 319th Infantry Battalion, 80th Division, Third Army, under General George S. Patton. This unit was heavily engaged during the Battle of the Bulge. Private Donald Karn was killed in action on January 13, 1945, in Luxembourg. D.K. had turned nineteen years old just one month before he was killed. He is buried in Luxembourg American Cemetery. Before the war, as we, the younger kids on the block, reached our teens, D.K. had often joined us when we went bike riding, played "Monopoly," went to the movies, or just went into town for ice cream. Again our neighborhood felt the pangs of war: now two homes each had a service flag with a blue-bordered gold star hanging in one of its front windows, signifying that a family member had died in military service. A picture of D.K. horsing around with Ralph Gallagher in a section of our backyard helps me remember him.

Donald Karn and Ralph Gallager (l–r). Donald was killed in WWII.

Donald's older brother, Samuel, was already in the U.S. Army. He had reached the rank of lieutenant by the time D.K. was inducted into the service. Sammy was closer to Walter Critchley's age and was one of the older boys in the neighborhood. He was with the 333rd Infantry Division of the First Army in Belgium. Shortly after D.K. was killed, Sam learned of his death when he saw his brother's name on a casualty list posted on a bulletin board in the army headquarters where he was then stationed. Sam survived the war and came home.

Craig Compton joined Army Air Corps and became a pilot, flying in the European and African theaters. Dudley Tiger was a pilot in the U.S. Navy Air Corps, where he received his commission as a naval air officer and spent some of the war years training other pilots in the United States. Dudley married Marion Pierson shortly after receiving his commission, and Robert Daily was his best man. Both Craig and Dudley survived the war, came home, and got on with their

Craig Compton, who was one of the older boys in our neighborhood and owned the famous bobsled, in his flight suit during WWII.

lives. I know little of them after they were honorably discharged, except that they both married and had families. I remember hearing that Craig moved to the Springfield, Massachusetts, area after he married.

The stories of the three Daily boys—Henry, Edward, and Robert—from the time they graduated from Morristown High School until the end of the war, are fascinating. Henry was accepted at Princeton but did not get a scholarship. He graduated from American University in Washington, D.C., before joining the Army Air Corps in January 1941. However, a medical condition resulting from a childhood mastoid operation proved to be too painful on his eardrum when changing altitudes rapidly, so he was honorably discharged after flying some thirty solo hours. He was then accepted into the Merchant Marine Academy at Kings Point, Long Island, from which he

graduated in early 1944 as an officer in both the Merchant Marine and the U.S. Navy. He served in the European theater until war's end and was discharged at an Italian port in January 1946.

Edward entered Fort Schuyler Merchant Marine Academy in 1938, graduating in 1940 with both a third-mate's license in the Merchant Marine and an ensign's commission in the U.S. Navy. Edward served most of his naval career in the Pacific and at one time had his own command. After the war, he was honorably discharged as a lieutenant commander while serving as the executive officer of a troop transport.

Robert entered Princeton on September 1, 1939 (the same day Hitler invaded Poland) on a full scholarship and planned to become a State Department diplomat. Robert sensed that his life and those of all the other young men were never going to be the same. The change began with the bombing of Pearl Harbor. Robert was accepted into the Marine Corps Reserve Officer's Training Program on condition that he accelerate his educational program, which he did. He graduated from Princeton early and went into the service. His commission as a U.S. Marine Corps officer was presented at Quantico by Senator John McCain's grandfather, Vice Admiral John S. McCain Sr., then Chief of Naval Aeronautics.

Robert was assigned as an intelligence officer to the 27th Regiment of the 5th Marine Division, then being formed in Camp Pendleton, California. The division was largely a combination of Guadalcanal veterans and raw recruits like him. His roommate was Jack Chevigny, a man in his late thirties and an ex-football great under the legendary Notre Dame coach, Knute Rockne. Jack pretty much took young Robert under his wing. Because of Jack's Hollywood connections, he was asked to seek out a "sweetheart" who could preside over the ceremonial presentation of colors to the new division. Jack took Robert to Hollywood, where they visited several movie studios and had the opportunity to meet Anne Blythe, a well-known starlet.

In 1944, the division replaced the 2nd Division at Camp Tarawa, a forward base in Hawaii. In early 1945, they joined a naval flotilla to invade the tiny, strategically located island of Iwo Jima, just 600 miles south of Tokyo, which was heavily defended by some twenty-two thousand Japanese.

The island was being used by Japanese Zero fighters to intercept American B-29s en route from the Mariana Islands on bombing raids of the Japanese mainland. The airfields at Iwo were considered key to the Allied success.

Robert and his forward-observation platoon landed at Red Beach Two, between Mt. Suribachi and Motoyama Airfield One, early in the morning of February 19, 1945. He spent his first night in a foxhole that was constantly caving in due to the heavy artillery and mortar fire the Japanese were lobbing from the top of Mt. Suribachi. The following morning, the regiment's colonel called Robert to his command post and told him that Jack had been killed during the night while serving as liaison officer with the 4th Marine Division on Yellow Beach Two. Robert replaced Jack as liaison officer to the 4th Division.

For the remaining one-and-a-half-month struggle, Robert, accompanied by a Navajo Indian code-talker, kept his regiment's commanding officer apprised of enemy positions. The Japanese were not able to decipher the Navajo language that the code-talkers used to send radio messages, which turned out to be a significant strategic asset. Despite this advantage, a total of 5,931 marines were killed and 17,272 wounded on Iwo. Many members of Robert's platoon were among the casualties. During the battle for Iwo Jima, Robert received a field promotion to first lieutenant and a Naval Citation for bravery under fire.

After Iwo Jima was secured, Robert's unit returned to Camp Tarawa instead of going on to Okinawa as originally planned. Robert's division replaced the 2nd Marine Division, which had just invaded Tarawa Island, where Walter Critchley had been killed. A letter that Robert had sent Walter was returned a short time later. Immediately, Robert expected the worst and told me that he has never been able to destroy that letter because it is a remembrance of the horror and torment of war that took the life of a close friend and neighbor. In Hawaii his division prepared for the imminent invasion of Japan. Robert was to be one of the first to land; his job would have been to disarm Japanese mines. Fortunately for Robert and countless others, President Truman saved many thousands of lives (both Allied and Japanese) by authorizing the use of the atomic bomb on Hiroshima and Nagasaki.

After the Japanese surrender, Robert spent six months in Japan as part of the occupying force before being discharged with the rank of captain.

Richard Daily, the youngest of the four Daily boys, told me the stories of his brothers. Looking back on all these many years, I can't help but feel proud that our neighborhood created so many interesting, intelligent, and honorable young people who left an inspirational legacy for their families and others. Richard graduated from Princeton University, as well, and became as successful as his three brothers. Eunice, their sister and my best friend during our youth, graduated from Northwestern University, again proving what an amazing family they were.

Like many young men, my cousin, Hubert, tried to enlist. However, the military rejected him because they found that he had a medical problem that made him 4-F. This was the most humiliating and devastating period of his life as he watched his buddies go off to war. Back then, patriotism—love and devotion to our country, our flag, and our freedom—was nearly universal in the United States.

When the Korean War began, Grant Edwards joined the U.S. Navy on September 6, 1950, served just shy of five years, and was honorably discharged on September 2, 1955. He was assigned to the U.S.S. *Oriskany*, CV-34, based, I believe, at the U.S. Naval Air Station in Norfolk, Virginia. Grant attained the rank of aviation electrician's mate, third class. The *Oriskany's* cruises during his service covered much of the South Pacific, as well as the entire Atlantic coastline and the Caribbean, including voyaging "around the Horn," (passing Cape Horn at the southern tip of South America into the Pacific). Grant died on Saturday, August 8, 1998. A note of interest: One of our get-together parties occurred on Tuesday, August 4. Grant died at home alone just four days later. He had volunteered to have the next get-together at his home. We were all shocked when we heard the news.

Elmer (also known as Elwood) Kenstler joined the U.S. Navy on September 26, 1950. He served as a hospital corpsman, 2nd U.S.N.-1, and was honorably discharged on July 13, 1954. Grant and Elmer were like brothers. Their friendship and closeness lasted their entire lives. Elmer died on November 9, 1994, at age sixty-five and a half.

Another of our playmates, Dominic DiPrimo, joined the U.S. Navy on October 12, 1950. Dominic served nearly four years, attaining the rank of petty officer, third class.

Now, in this new millennium, I look back to my younger years and realize how our times and beliefs have changed so drastically. Before we were involved in the war, school classes began with students saluting the American flag by extending our arms while saying the Pledge of Allegiance. However, this was stopped during the war because it resembled the Nazi's "Heil Hitler" gesture. After that, we just placed our right hands over our hearts and said the pledge.

Before World War II, airplanes were not part of our daily lives. Strange sounds from the vastness above preceded the rare sighting of a plane. We automatically stopped whatever we were doing and looked up in utter amazement. It was a spectacular and unbelievable sight. However, life changed quickly once war was declared. Air-raid drills at school became a weekly occurrence. Our country, for the first time, realized that our shores were no longer as secure and safe as we had always assumed.

During the war years, we experienced all kinds of shortages, which was a shocking experience for the American people. Rationing went into effect. Gasoline was the first noticeable restriction. Rubber tires, new cars, and new appliances were impossible to find. Items such as sugar, spices, coffee, chocolate, butter, and shortening were disappearing from grocery shelves. During the war years, cigarettes became hard to find because the military had a bigger demand for them. However, one was able to purchase them through the black market. Every family was entitled to a certain number of food stamps and gas stamps. These stamps were traded among neighbors and families, depending on each one's need for a particular coupon. Red-point coupons were issued for meat, butter, and fats; blue points for canned and processed foods.

The black market acquired the name "Mr. Black" and became widespread throughout the country. All one needed was to know the right person, and one could get almost anything for a price. It was considered a social stigma if one patronized "Mr. Black." Some of my father's friends were in the black market, so we never did without anything. Motorists were assigned either A, B, C, or E (emergency vehicle priority) and were issued gas coupons accordingly. The

government imposed a nationwide thirty-five-mile-per-hour speed limit and banned pleasure driving. Ladies' silk stockings were impossible to find because silk was used to make parachutes and gunpowder bags.

Practically every family had a Service Flag hanging on the inside of their front window. It was white with a red border and one or more blue stars in the center. Each blue star represented a family member serving in one of the military services. As I already mentioned, if a member of the family was killed or died in service, a blue-bordered gold-star service flag was used. It was sad when one saw a gold star hanging in someone's window. Whether we knew the family or not, it gave us a sense of reality because it brought the war home.

Women went into the defense plants and took over men's jobs. This is where the character "Rosie the Riveter" came from. She represented all the female defense workers. Songs and films, but especially posters and magazine covers, portrayed her with a look of determination to finish the job. We were at the age where we admired her and wanted to be just like her. She had a small but perfect body that was always wrapped in tight-fitting coveralls, accenting her bulging arm muscles. Her face was beautiful, but her body carried a masculine force with tremendous strength. After the war, however, such women had learned the feeling of independence and the advantages of receiving a paycheck. Many found it hard to give up their jobs as the men began returning home.

A multitude of posters invaded our lives, stressing the importance of everybody working together and doing their jobs for freedom. Magazine covers, especially those painted by Norman Rockwell for *The Saturday Evening Post*, portrayed the American family surrounded by the flag and apple pie that symbolized our freedom in some way or other. Everyone loved Rockwell for his ability to capture the spirit and the down-home atmosphere of the American people. Many cherish his paintings because they represent the American way of life before, during, and after the war. As young as I was, I was completely drawn to his paintings. No one has ever captured a period of time and touched my heart as did Norman Rockwell.

The American people reacted to war exactly as the government wanted and expected. All the large auto companies kept their names in the public

eye through posters, magazine and newspaper advertisements that showed they, too, were helping the war effort by building tanks, ships, planes, guns, and munitions. According to my father, most people didn't realize or care that the cost of these messages was being added to the bill for war products. Citizens themselves were paying for the advertisements through their taxes. This angered my father especially, because his so-called drinking partners could never understand what he was complaining about. Mother worried for fear he would speak his mind once too often in one of the local bars and end up in the hospital.

One would have thought that Dad was against our government, but he was afraid that the American people would slowly begin to loose their independence. Once Social Security went into effect, he swore that this was the beginning of the government manipulating our lives through their many controls. Dad resented this because he felt he knew how to handle and save his money and needed no help from the government. He felt that he could have made a lot more money if the government hadn't put Social Security into effect. He liked saving for his own retirement years. He needed no help and resented having to pay for those people who were too lazy to work and/or had already learned how to use the system to benefit themselves. Social Security disability payments were another matter. He went along with that with no complaint. Again, his ideas were often expressed freely and angrily after a few drinks at his favorite pub.

The war had also turned our economy around, and full employment was prevalent. Money was again filling men's and women's pockets. Industries were enticing workers by offering high wages, something that was very unusual in the past. Defense jobs became easily obtainable. Today, when I look back on it all, propaganda was taking over our lives, and most people never saw it.

Small towns were overwhelmed by the influx of women and children who took up residence close to the newly erected military bases. These bases also meant jobs for the surrounding areas. These towns were not prepared to handle such a sudden impact. They didn't have the buildings to insure decent facilities for these military wives and families and the others that needed

work. Shantytowns sprang up outside the towns' and cities' limits. They were a combination of trailers and tents with no sanitation and waste disposal. Unfortunately, these shantytowns became breeding grounds for disease.

I also remember when over 110,000 persons of Japanese ancestry were imprisoned in many relocation camps in remote and desolate parts of this country. Persons of German or Italian extraction were not subjected to any restrictions. Our country was afraid these Japanese could be spies for Japan. This was the government's way of protecting us from them and vise-versa.

This internment was declared, years later, to be one of the most serious breaches of civil liberties during wartime. I remember seeing these camps in the many different newsreels, which were always shown before the featured movie. Of course, our young-teenager boos and hollering at these pictures proved that we were just puppets being played by our government. We didn't understand the seriousness of what was taking place. Today, I realize that they were pretty much like concentration camps, except that there were no atrocities inflicted on these prisoners. These Americans were placed in over-crowded conditions with very limited supplies. Most of these people were natural-born citizens of the United States who had been unjustly imprisoned.

The newsreels always shocked us as we watched the war being presented right before our eyes. When pictures of England came across the screen showing the buildings, laying in rubble and the injured being taken away, it made us shudder. We saw American GIs struggling, fighting the enemy as they walked across Europe. In the winter, they experienced the terrible cold, snow, and ice. In the spring, summer, and fall, it was mud, heat, and the smell of death all around them. During these newsreels none of us spoke a word as we watched this horror, thanking God we had an ocean to separate us from all the madness.

Blacks also found that the military services as well as the defense plants were not always ready to accept them on an equal basis. They were still being separated from the whites. I saw this every time I visited the South, both as a child and during the war, but I never gave it a second thought. I never asked why this separation was necessary or why Blacks were not considered the same as us. All I knew was that it was the way it was. I look back now

and can see the injustice of it all. It is a part of our history that we can't erase nor should we. We can't pretend it never happened. It did. There were strikes, protests, and confrontations because of this racial discrimination. For the first time in our lives, we were seeing the beginning of racial protests.

Bodies began floating ashore all along the Atlantic coastline before our country entered the war, and their number increased soon afterwards. The beaches of both coasts, primarily the Atlantic, were marred by great blotches of black, sticky oil. Bathers soon realized that these were actually oil spills from tankers (under flags of other countries) bound for Britain that had been sunk by U-boats not far from our shores. People saw burning ships off Cape Cod and Cape Hatteras. The California coastline, north of Santa Barbara, had actually been bombarded by shells from a Japanese submarine. Suddenly, for the first time, the American people began to realize how vulnerable we were to our enemies. We were no longer secure behind our "moat" of oceans.

To help the war effort, we collected tin cans, cut the ends off and then flattened the cans so we could turn them in at the nearest fire station. Paper had become very scarce, and paper bags were retrieved and refolded for carrying groceries. Mother constantly reminded us that the average paper bag could be reused five times. Saving, bundling, and tying newspapers became a new chore for us. The school gave us packets of vegetable seeds so we could start our own Victory gardens.

My father became a Civilian Defense Corps air-spotter during the war. Their job was to sight any enemy airplanes that may have ventured into our area. He had to go once a week to a high tower that had been built for this purpose. It was located on Columbia Turnpike, in the same area where the Morristown airport is today. His best friend, Emil Pozzi, joined him. To listen to them talk about their nighttime air-spotters patrol, one would think that they were on the front lines, facing an enemy that was attacking from every direction. Their stories grew every time they told them.

Mother joined the Neighborhood Civilian Defense Patrol in which she was responsible for seeing that everyone was obeying the blackout. When the sirens sounded, she would dash out of the house to patrol the entire neighborhood, wearing her air-raid-warden's helmet, carrying her much-needed

flashlight, and wearing her emergency whistle around her neck. These helmets were actually old tin "doughboy" helmets from World War I that had been painted white with the Civilian Defense Logo painted on the front. No lights were allowed to be visible when the sirens starting wailing. Everyone waited for the all-clear whistle to blow, hoping this was just a practice alert. We secretly considered her far braver than Dad because her job appeared to be much more dangerous. She walked about the neighborhood in total darkness. Anyone could have jumped her, or she could have fallen or been injured in some way so easily.

MY SISTER, FLORENCE   My sister, Florence, began driving around 1942. On occasion, she would take some of us kids for a ride. I remember one time in particular when Dad gave her permission to drive the family car. She asked several of us kids to take a ride in the country with her because it was fall, when the countryside abounded in colorful beauty. We spotted several apple trees located fairly close to the roadway, and she stopped the car and told us to run over and pick up a few apples. There were no signs that read, "NO TRESPASSING."

As we filled our jackets with apples, the farmer who owned the land and trees took us by complete surprise, as he seemed to appear out of nowhere. We stood there not knowing what to say. He thanked us for doing such a good job of picking up all of his apples. He suggested that we put them into the bed of his truck. We felt terrible. What could we say? We gave him all the apples and even picked up all the others that were still on the ground. He took our names and addresses and told us he was going to call our parents. Florence, still sitting in the driver's seat, never moved. She became panicky when we told her we had to give our names to the farmer. She asked if we gave her name as well, and I said, "Yes. You were with us, even though you never left the car." She was very upset.

On the way home, Florence said that she would never take us with her again. We both went into the house looking sheepish for fear the farmer had already called. We never heard from the farmer, and if my parents did, they never said a word. We suffered silently in fear of that long-awaited phone call, which apparently never came.

During that same fall, a very similar incident occurred, but this involved black walnuts. Once again, we joined Florence on a ride in the country. This time, we drove by a beautiful black walnut tree. Many of its nuts were lying all around the ground. Florence pulled the car over to the side of the road. We all got out and began filling our bags with the nuts. We each had a full bag when the owner came by and caught us. He took our bags and thanked us for gathering up his black walnuts. He suggested we call him or stop by his house in the coming year to let him know exactly when we would like to help him pick his black walnuts again.

The farmer continued speaking as each of us stood shaking, hoping he hadn't noticed how scared we were. We became even more uncomfortable when he asked for our names and addresses so he could call us in case we forgot. He also mentioned how much his wife was going to appreciate all that we had done. The black walnuts meant a great deal to her,

My sister, Florence, as a teenager.

especially when it came to her baking. The man continued talking to us in a friendly voice. He mentioned that his back had become very painful and made it difficult for him to bend over. He felt that we were a real godsend. He shook each of our hands and said how much he appreciated this unexpected help. Once more, what could we say? We had blown it again, but this man made us feel like we had done something nice, even though our intentions hadn't been honorable!

Once again, Florence swore never to take us for a ride. Well, not very long after the black-walnut incident, she asked us again to take a ride into the countryside. It sounded great, so without giving it a second thought, we hopped in. We were several miles from home when Florence stopped the car just opposite a farmer's cornfield. She said, "What could be better than fresh-picked corn for dinner tonight?" With that thought, we made a dash into the cornfield. The next thing we knew, Florence blew the horn, hollered

"Goodbye," and drove off. We stood there in disbelief. How could she leave us so far from home? We knew she wasn't coming back for us.

To make matters worse, a farmer drove up and asked if that had been us in his cornfield. We told him, "Absolutely not! It was probably that other bunch of kids we saw running back into it when they saw us. We would never do that!" The farmer smiled. As we looked at each other, not knowing what to do next, we noticed that some of the silk from the corn was clinging to our clothing. He never said another word. He got back into his truck and drove off. There was nothing else for us to do except start walking. It took almost four hours to get home. We were exhausted, hungry, and angry. We never asked her for a ride again, nor did we ever get in when she offered one to us.

I had experienced Florence's revenge more than once, especially when she felt that she had been wronged or things hadn't gone her way or that I had gotten something better than she had received. Florence hated for me to have anything more or better than she had. When I look back now, it was most noticeable whenever I had a birthday party. She would not stop pestering me until she got those birthday gifts of mine that appealed to her. She would take them away from me by badgering, threatening, and tantalizing me until I gave in to her demands.

Older brothers and sisters often teasingly threaten their younger siblings, not realizing how damaging such threats can be, even when they aren't meant literally. As a child and a teenager, I often feared that Florence would carry out one of her threats, and I became the victim of my own fear. From my perspective, our thinking seemed as different as night is to day, so it was difficult for me to predict how far she would go. And, because I never knew what to expect from her, my imagination usually took over: Could I wake up with her holding a pillow over my face to let me know how easy it would be to smother me during the night? Would she "share" her favorite drink with me and then casually mention how easy it would be to poison me? Justifiably or not, I truly feared her. I knew from experience that she could hurt me by pinching, punching, and kicking whenever she got mad at me or I didn't obey her, but I didn't know if her selfishness and jealousy knew any limits.

I tried to tell Mother and Daddy about her actions, but they always turned a deaf ear to any of my complaints. Even when I showed them my

bruises, it seemed to make no difference. Dad would give me a sweet smile and a pat on the head, always adding, "Keep out of Flossie's way and you won't get hurt." Mother's comment was always the same: "What did you do to provoke her?" At that, they would go about their business, and I would be left feeling furious and rejected.

If my parents ever confronted Florence about my accusations, I never knew. I would try to avoid her just in case Mother had confronted her. I would go around for days, angry, punching and kicking everything in sight, secretly wishing it were Florence, and trying to get some sort of satisfaction. I hated those feelings. I was younger and smaller; I couldn't hurt her like she could hurt me! I was angry with myself for not standing up to her, for not striking out at her. I felt disgusted by my inability to deal with my feelings. Florence considered herself the smartest of us three girls. Yes, that was true. She was shrewd, calculating, and clever. She had to control and dominate every situation. From my point of view, she was downright *mean*!

My fun-loving and witty father was also a man who loved to play dangerous mind-warping games. He was excellent at playing favorites among us kids. For years, he played us against each other, bringing out such hideous emotions as jealousy and envy from each of us towards the other. We were too young to understand, and by the time we understood, it was too late. The damage had already been done. During the 1960s, when I was nearing my mid-thirties, I began to understand what he had done and was doing to us.

I realized that we had been fools not to see through his destructive amusement and what a dysfunctional family we had become. He meant no harm to any of us. It was a game with him. We didn't know how to handle the situation correctly! I began to take control of my emotions and feelings towards my family. Auntie's help and understanding taught me how to deal with my dad's thinking. I began to see myself as an individual who was emerging from the cocoon that had hidden, protected, and covered me for so much of my life. It took years, however, before I was able to challenge him concerning his actions toward his daughters. My father saw this change in me and, of his three daughters, I became the daughter that he respected and admired most before his death. He was completely surprised by my unexpected

courage in standing up to him and giving him my opinion when I felt he was being unfair and wrong in his thinking and actions.

Even though my father saw, too late in his life, the terrible results of his devious actions, he died never having accepted any of the blame for the hatred that he had cultivated within his family. He himself, both during his lifetime and even after his death, became a victim of Florence's scheming. Over the years, he became frightened by her love of power and the hatred she was able to exhibit. We never realized her potential to generate the havoc that would eventually destroy our family with these emotions. As the years passed, we never understood the depth of hate that she allowed to grow so savagely within her.

When I look back at the terrible unhappiness that began to spread throughout the family, it seems to me that Florence must have put together a cunning and well-calculated scheme that would eventually affect my life, my children's lives, Aunt Affie's and Aunt Clara's lives, and those of many of mother's friends around Brunswick. We all suffered tremendous grief and sorrow, which continued even after Mother passed away.

One of the few times Florence and I experienced a truly sisterly relationship was during 1947 and 1948 when we both commuted to New York City together. I attended Katherine Gibbs Business School, and Florence was employed as an executive secretary at the Bankers Trust Company. Florence seemed like a different person. She was being nice, and it felt strange. I kept waiting for some hint of her true nature to emerge.

Standing by the train tracks, watching for our oncoming train, I always moved slightly away from Florence. My fears of her childhood threats never left me. I had become very cautious about my safety no matter where we went. Even though I knew my sister well, I tried to enjoy this new image of her. It was a special time because of its rarity.

The only other special time was during August 1969 when she and I took our children camping just outside of Wildwood, New Jersey. I had just had a hysterectomy, and after discussing the pending camping trip with my doctor, he gave me permission to go as long as I didn't lift anything and took it easy.

I gathered everything that my three boys and I would need and drove up to Florence's home to pick her and her two children up. Pamela was Kevin's age, Michael was a year or two younger than Paul, and Brian was the youngest of the group. We loaded the tent and all the camping equipment into our cars. Florence had a large station wagon with a luggage carrier on top of it. We headed for Wildwood and our week of camping.

It took several hours for us to get unloaded, but we had completed the job and were well settled-in before dark. Sitting near the open fire, we had our first meal and then continued just sitting, singing, and having lots of fun, filled with laughter. It was the most fun I ever had with my sister, as well as the last.

For one week we lived the life of real campers. We cooked everything over a small gas stove. We covered our table with netting so the bugs and flies wouldn't bother us. The kids played all kinds of games, running everywhere in the campsite and swimming every chance they had. Our campsite was close to the ocean, so we were able to walk to it. The weather also stayed clear for the entire week. We were very lucky. Our time together was coming to an end. There was only one other time that we shared being together as sisters, aunts, and cousins: Easter 1983.

When Pamela, Florence's daughter, had her ninth birthday party, Mother and I were invited. We went, looking forward to a lovely time. Florence had invited the mothers of the other children as well. When Mother and I arrived, her husband, Ray, immediately ushered us into the kitchen. We were never introduced to any of their guests. Ray told us that Flo needed help in the kitchen so she could entertain her lady friends. We prepared the fancy sandwiches and drinks. Ray kept bringing in dirty dishes and empty plates. We were kept busy as we washed and cleaned up the kitchen. We never saw Florence or Pam. I thought it was strange because it seemed as if Ray had become our overseer. I think that, between the two of us, we may have had half a sandwich and a cup of coffee as we worked. Then we got ready to join the group to watch Pam open her gifts. At that moment Ray told us that he didn't want us to mingle with Flo's friends. They were all college graduates, and we had nothing in common with them. Mother and I looked at each other,

not quite believing what he had said. After a moment of thought, I suggested that we should leave. Pam never came into the kitchen to see either of us. I often wondered if that child even knew we were there. Ray made damn sure that we got his message. That was the last time I was ever in their home.

There were occasions when we all would be invited to Mother and Daddy's home for a holiday dinner, but it usually ended as a very strained affair. Ray seldom came. No one missed him. And when he did show up, his attitude made everyone wish he hadn't. By the end of the holiday get-together, everyone felt it was not worth the trouble just to be together. Our mixed emotions left us exhausted.

Many years later, in the mid-1980s, I felt that Florence was totally out of control in her desire to have complete control over Mother and her life. I also believed that the blueprint for my banishment from the Ritter family had been put into motion. I wanted to think that Pauline was only a follower, not the instigator.

I believed that Florence's scheme was to gain complete financial control of everything that involved Dad's estate. I felt that my sisters had never gotten over the jealousy that existed among us for so many years. Throughout the years, however, I never allowed these feelings to control my actions to such a degree as my sisters seemed to. One incident after another, throughout our lives, only made the trail of deceit, hatred, and jealousy more evident.

After Mother told Florence and Pauline about transferring the deed to her home into my name, my life suddenly became a sea of torment. I could never imagine what was about to take place and found myself devastated by disbelief when it did. It seemed as if, overnight, my mother became a woman who was wrapped in nothing but hate. Almost immediately, Mother stopped visiting me. My sisters were now constantly visiting her and bringing her to live in their homes for periods of time. Mother began calling me, more and more, using profanity, hateful words, and accusations that Pepper and I were thieves and dishonest. I was beginning to think that Mother was being brainwashed and wasn't responsible for her terrible behavior. Whenever she called me, I was afraid that she would have a heart attack. No matter how much I tried to calm her, it was impossible to have a conversation with her.

I tried to speak to Pauline, but her only comment was, "Return the house to Mother," and she would hang up. One by one, those who loved Mother were slowly being alienated from her. I was shocked. I felt that my sisters were behind this, simply because Mother's entire lifestyle was suddenly turned upside-down, and she was filled with hate and revenge. Who was responsible for this? Why did all this begin once the girls arrived on the scene? Anyone with a conscience would never deliberately turn a loving person into a hateful and vengeful human being.

I realize that I can't prove it, but, in my heart, I feel that I know who was behind my removal from the Ritter family. Unpleasant though it is, how could I possibly eliminate this part of my life in my memoirs? I am left feeling that Mother was a victim of manipulation and brainwashing. Mother was too much a Christian to think such evil thoughts and then put them into action. Living a happy and carefree life in Brunswick, Mother had no money problems. She never mentioned selling her home or that it had become such a terrible burden to her that she had to move into something smaller. She loved her home, loved entertaining in it, loved having me and my kids visit her, and loved having her sister, Leonia, stay with her for weeks at a time. After all is said and done, I will let my readers draw their own conclusions.

MY YOUNGER SISTER, PAULINE   Pauline, on the other hand, was always considered Daddy's little girl. She was ten years younger than Florence and five years younger than me. Therefore, we never played much with her. Pauline had acquired the nickname "Piggy" by the time she was three years old. It remained with her for a good ten years. Throughout most of her life, Pauline stayed heavy. Occasionally, when Pauline would go on a diet and loose weight, she would become a real beauty. However, she was never able to keep the weight off. Pauline was a private person, very much like me, because neither of us had no confidence or faith in ourselves at all, and both of us hoped that the rest of the world would never notice. Florence hardly bothered with her. Pauline and I played on occasion, but we were never really close as sisters. Dad's mind games took care of that. Like Grandmother Ritter's furniture, Pauline was just there.

Pauline (r) and her girlfriend,
Helen Louise Zellka, who lived
in our neighborhood.

I remember one time when Pauline was just a small child, no more than three years old. Star, my father's English setter, followed Pauline and me downstairs. We were playing when Star knocked Pauline down, and the next thing I knew, he was on top of her. He had her pinned to the floor. She began screaming. I ran over to help her, but Star began growling, snapping, and wouldn't let me near him or Pauline. He kept pounding harder and harder down on her. His face covered hers and I knew by his growls that I couldn't pull him off.

I began screaming. Mother and Florence came running and tried to pull Star off. The dog was biting Mother. Her arms and legs were bleeding. Daddy came running when he heard our screams. Florence and I didn't understand what was happening. Dad threw Star off Pauline. By this time, Mother was in a state of complete hysteria. She grabbed Pauline off the floor and screamed for Aunt Love to call the doctor. Dad took Star outside and locked him in the kennel. After that, Star was never seen again. Dad never spoke of him and never said what he had done with him. The doctor came and examined Pauline. All hell broke loose. Star had done something terrible to her. We didn't know what it meant. Florence and I were sent to our rooms with orders not to come out until we were called. We had never seen our parents so angry and upset. This incident was never mentioned again. However, I never forgot it.

MY BUDDY, SID   I mentioned at the beginning of my stories how my father always wanted sons but, unfortunately, ended up with three daughters. During my childhood, Dad befriended several young men, and one of these, a young boy around nine years old, really touched his heart. He took

him under his wing the moment they met. Dad treated him like a son, taking him fishing, hunting, and teaching him many things about guns and dogs. This young boy's needs were a perfect match to my father's: he was looking for a father while my father was looking for a son.

His name was Sidney Schneider. He lived on Mills Street (just a short distance from our neighborhood) with his father and two older sisters, Ruthie and Sadie. His father was elderly and unable to enjoy doing all the things a man would like to do with his son. Sid's mother had died when he was a small child, and his sisters had raised him. Theirs was a devoted Jewish family who cared a great deal for each other.

Meanwhile, Sid missed having a father who was active in all kinds of sports and activities. On occasion, he and another young boy, Jackie Rosoff, played with the boys in our neighborhood, and we got to know them. Apparently, Grant mentioned my father's name and his interest in fishing, hunting, dogs, homing pigeons, and all the other outdoor sports he could think of. Sid became fascinated by these stories and especially by the man behind them. In no time at all, he decided that this person was going to be his mentor and male role model. All he had to do was figure out how he was going to meet this Mr. Ritter. The sign on our front yard advertising "Puppies for Sale" had tantalized Sid. He longed to have his own dog and decided to use this as an excuse to meet and talk with his new mentor. That was it! That was going to be his reason for entering the grounds of Knollcroft!

Sid held his breath as his long, thin finger reached for the doorbell. He knew that there was no turning back now. Fear seized Sid as he watched the door open. Quickly he looked down, realizing that two large feet were standing in front of him. He looked up and there stood the man he admired. Sid felt flushed, as a sheepish smile seemed to spread from one ear to the other. With a nervous gesture, he brushed his brown hair away from his forehead. An air of excitement enveloped him. My father sensed this immediately and smiled.

Sid shifted from one foot to another as he blurted out, "Do you have a puppy for sale, Mr. Ritter?" My father looked at the young boy again and heard the same apprehension in his soft voice as he spoke again: "Excuse me, sir, do you have a puppy I could buy?" "What's your name, son?" my father

asked. "Does your family know you've come to see me about buying one of my pups?" By now Sid's cheeks had a brilliant red blush, and he quietly said, "My name is Sidney Schneider, sir. Uh, uh, you can call me Sid."

Sid was starting to sweat. His cheeks felt flushed, and his mouth had become very dry. Panicking, he thought, "God, my tongue is stuck to the roof of my mouth. I can't talk." He tried to answer my father's question. Praying that his own anxiety would not be noticed, he answered, "My father knows I want a dog." His knees were shaking. My father motioned for Sid to come in. That was the beginning of a warm and fun-filled friendship between a young boy and a man. Their friendship never died.

To this day, many years after my father's death, Sid still talks about and cherishes the warm memories of the wonderful times he enjoyed with my father as a boy and young man.

When we first met Sid, we saw a typical-looking young boy, clean in appearance and wearing what had been, earlier in the day, well-pressed clothing. His neat cotton shirt was hanging over his loose-fitting pants. My sisters and I looked quizzically at this kid who had just entered Knollcroft.

Once Sid got past the family introductions, not to mention the excitement of meeting my father and being invited into his home, he relaxed. Having his own puppy was no longer his priority. Mother's warm personality and her strong southern accent only added to Sid's desire to settle right in. He found our home fascinating. It was a magical mansion. From that point on, whenever he visited, he hated to go home when one of his sisters would call for him. Mother always sat another plate at the table whenever he came for a visit, since they were usually around our dinnertime.

I never envied Sid for the love and affection my mother gave him. I was glad that he enjoyed coming to Knollcroft. Other than Mandy, Sid was the only other person who made me feel comfortable in my own home. He was sincere in everything he said and did. He was naive, kind, gentle, refreshing, and I loved him. He was like a brother. I welcomed him as he became one of my constant companions all through my school years.

My sisters and I shared very little togetherness, concern, or love during our childhoods. My sisters were usually involved with Mother's projects while I was made to sit on the sidelines. Mother never included me in any of their

plans, but when Sid became a part of our lives, I turned to him. Sid was like a new toy. I was glad my mother didn't look down on him. By now, she knew how fond Dad was of Sid, and in no way would she hurt his feelings or say anything that might destroy the relationship between Dad and Sid.

Sid loved Mother as if she were his own, and today, the memories of her remain within his heart. He would devour every one of her deliciously prepared meals, and with each bite, he would let us girls know what a great cook and mother we had. He knew how to impress Mother. Regardless, he was completely sincere, which made me love him even more. He was no phony!

As time went on, our friendship grew into a lasting one. We shared our many insecurities, our dreams, our likes and dislikes. I was amazed at how easy it was for me to talk to him. I could say anything, and he would sit and listen. He truly loved me as I did him.

I was a year older than Sid, but that didn't matter. His personality bubbled with excitement when we would go hunting, fishing, and shooting with Dad. He loved helping Dad's trainers with the dogs, always showing gentleness with each dog he had to work with, still longing for a dog of his very own.

A few months later, as my father became more and more aware of Sid's gentle traits, he decided to give him one of his very own pointers that had already been broken for hunting. Dad felt Sid was ready to appreciate and understand the full value of one of his dogs. This bitch was considered very valuable because of her excellent hunting abilities. Her name was Gay. She was beautiful with brown and white markings.

When Gay ran, her legs moved with the swiftness of a deer. Whenever she picked up the scent of a bird, her entire body was in motion, excited by the smell. The only problem with her was that she could not go into the fields with other field dogs because she would attack them. She never attacked a dog for any other reason. My father felt this would not be a problem for Sid or the bitch, since no other dog would be involved. He made this very clear to Sid before he turned Gay over to him. Sid never had any trouble with Gay. They became a team, each loyal to each.

By now, Sid was feeling right at home. One day he came across a bunch of old phonograph records in his attic. He knew we had an old wind-up phonograph in our cellar and decided to bring them up to our house, hoping

we would enjoy hearing them. Mother fell in love with each record and every song. While she did her ironing, she would listen to them. When she was doing her wash, she would put them on, enjoying the gentle sounds of yesterday. She often said Sid put joy into her laundry day. He had her completely wrapped around his little finger, and she never knew it.

Sid would kid and joke with Pauline and Florence, but that was all. They felt Sid was a threat in their relationship to Daddy. He sensed this and backed away from them. However, he never forgot that they were Mr. Ritter's daughters. With me it was different. Our relationship blossomed, day by day.

Sid had established a second home with our family. He had now acquired a place within our gang as well and became just another kid on the block. Sid's first love was sitting with my father in the evening, listening to Dad speak of his youth, his travels, and his adventures in sports. Sid never forgot the many beautiful and funny stories. Once Dad knew he had an audience, nothing stopped him. Sid always found himself completely spellbound by those creative stories and never questioned their veracity. They were entertaining, and that was all that mattered to this wide-eyed, innocent young lad.

One day, Sid and I took my father's favorite and most valued dog, Jake, on a walk without permission. What we failed to realize, however, was the dollar value placed on him. The stud fees set for him at that time made him even more valuable. He was beautiful, well groomed, and colored in multiple shades of brown and white. Jake was an English setter, well behaved and completely trained. He knew and obeyed every command we gave, so I felt we would have no trouble.

Well, the damn dog had different ideas. Before I knew it, Jake had slipped out of his collar and started running. He had suddenly discovered freedom. He would run a little distance, stop, look back at us, and go bounding off as if he wanted us to give chase. I knew that we were in big trouble.

Jake was enjoying his moment of freedom a bit too much. We had to get that dog back, and we had to do it quickly. That was all I could think about. We called and called. He would look at us from a distance, run, and stop just out of our reach. He wagged his tail and gave a slight bark as if to say, "Come on, let's play!" and then took off running. I never saw him act so carefree.

Sid kept saying, "Everything will be alright. We'll get him." About two hours later, with Jake still enjoying his freedom, we were trying to figure out what we were going to tell my father. We knew we were in serious trouble.

By now, I was in tears. I glanced over by the roadway, and to my horror, I saw my father's car pulling up. It stopped, and Dad got out. Jake also spotted my father. To our complete surprise, Jake came swiftly over to us, sat down, wagged his tail, and looked up at us as if to say, "What's the matter with you guys? I'm back."

My father approached us, looking bewildered, but accepting what he saw. He began praising us for catching Jake because he thought the dog had gotten loose and had taken off on his own. "You kids were in the right place at the right time. Thank God." My father gave a sigh of relief. What could we say?

Secretly, we both swore we would never take one of his dogs out again. At first, we wanted to kill Jake, but after it was all over, we gave him a big hug. I still swear that Jake knew the trouble all three of us would be in if he didn't cool it, and, that's what I call a damn smart dog!

We decided it was time to go back to the gang to enjoy our usual walks along the Whippany River, bike ride all over the countryside, swim in the old swimming hole at Henshaw, roam all around the grounds of the estates, and watch my father train his dogs, alone.

Sid and I were the best of buddies. We did many things together without the rest of the gang. We decided to try our luck muskrat trapping, since Sid's uncle, Mr. Rosenberg, was in the business of buying skins. As soon as the weather became cold and wintry, we would gather up our traps and head for the Whippany River.

One of the most beautiful sights when we were trapping was when the first snow fell and we would have the thrill of descending into the woods to be the first ones to see it untouched, undisturbed, wrapped in its solitude and beauty. The woods would resemble a winter wonderland with the snow lying on the branches of the trees, fresh and not yet fallen. Soft, pure, white snow as fluffy as a goose-down pillow, laid neatly like a blanket covering the ground, disturbed only by the occasional footprints of some animal that had been roaming about.

The river, now barely moving with its thin coating of ice, looked so innocent with its deadly beauty hidden under the protection of the new-fallen snow. Here we would set our traps, baiting them with a piece of apple and making sure they were set well under the water or right along the water's edge or bank.

Once the weather turned cold, we knew we would have to put our hands down into the freezing water in order to set our traps correctly. This was a painful ordeal. When we touched the cold traps with our wet hands and fingers, already burning from the freezing cold, they would stick to the metal, making the pain even worse when we tried to let go. We would attach a piece of wire to the trap and then secure the wire to a large stone or small tree. In that way, once we trapped the animal, it would not be able to drag the trap away and end up dying before we found it.

We had to get up at the crack of dawn in order to check our trap lines before school started. There was no time to play around. Most of the time we would find our prize securely locked in the trap but there were many times when the muskrat would chew off a leg just to escape the painful deathtrap. Sometimes the muskrat would be trapped but still alive, which meant we had to put it out of its misery before we could go any further. This was a business, and we couldn't let this bother us. We suffered in our own way with the cold, snow, ice and freezing waters. It took a strong stomach to overcome some of the things we had to do. The money was worth it; trapping paid well.

Sometimes, Sid would skin the muskrats, stretch the pelts, and let them dry before we took them to his uncle's garage. We would get extra money when we brought the entire muskrat in to Mr. Rosenberg because he would save the muskrat meat and sell it. I drew the line when it came to skinning the animal. The thought of anyone eating the meat was nauseating to me. Never! With the coming of spring, we knew that was the end of our trapping for the season. We put our traps away and once again looked forward to the approaching seasons, filled with sports, games, bike riding, and swimming.

Another incident that comes to mind occurred when Sid started going to church with my mother, my sisters, and me. One day, much to Mother's

surprise, Sid mentioned how impressed he was with her religious background and asked if he could go to church with us. He wanted to see and hear this man about whom my mother raved so often and whom dear Polly loved to aggravate. Mother was not sure about Sid's intentions. Perhaps he was teasing her about her strict Baptist background. She had many Jewish friends whom she loved. Religion never entered into those friendships nor was it ever a problem, at least in our little family circle. Mother truly believed in the idea that "We are all God's children," even though she feared being ostracized in her little social circles. In our household, all religions were good. Believing in God was all that really mattered. Today, I have friends from all walks of life whose religious beliefs and skin colors have never interfered with our friendships. Respect of the person was, and still is, the important factor.

Mother felt that she could not say no. What would Paul say if she did? Would he give her "holy hell"? She felt uncomfortable about the dilemma in which she found herself. More and more questions seemed to pop into her mind, but the terrible *fear* of his being Jewish and her taking him into a Christian church scared her to death, but she couldn't refuse his request. God would be angry with her.

I kept watching Mother as she became more and more nervous. I prayed, "Oh, God, please, don't let her do another one of her theatrical shows! Please don't let her say something that will hurt him. If Sid is here, and she makes us all sit while she does her performance, I'll die. God, he will think she really is crazy."

As Sunday approached, Mother continued to worry. How could the parishioners ever look down on her for bringing this young boy to church with us? She had no intention of trying to change his religion. She convinced herself that her rationale sounded pretty good. Reverend Hoorseman and the congregation would never scold or berate her. She was bringing a lost soul into Christ's flock, if only for an hour. God would praise her! That did it! Sid could go to church with the family. She had eliminated all her fears!

Sid was impressed by his first visit to the First Baptist Church. Everyone was friendly. As we left the church, Mother proudly announced that she would

be rewarded in Heaven for her good deed. I wanted to throw up. Anyway, Sid continued going to church with us. Mother continued thinking the pearly gates were open, waiting for her appearance, and that Heaven was a sure thing! All I could think was "Put a lid on it, Mother. Enough is enough!"

In the meantime, his family had no idea that he was attending the First Baptist Church. Mother made the mistake of presuming they knew about it. Reverend Hoorseman was impressed with Sid's attendance and spoke to him about joining the church. Sid declined but informed the good Reverend that perhaps one day he might consider it. Sid played it very cool, much to my mother's relief.

One day, Reverend Hoorseman decided to visit Sid's home and meet his family. Sid's sister, Sadie, answered the door and was the first family member to meet Reverend Hoorseman. Because she was about twenty years older than Sid, the good Reverend thought she was his mother. She was bewildered by this unexpected visit. Confused because this man standing in front of her was a minister, not a rabbi, she thought, "What does he want? Does he want a donation of some kind?" Apparently he was not aware that the family was Jewish and practiced the Jewish faith.

Sadie led him into the living room where they sat and chatted for a while. However, the visit was beginning to annoy her. "What does he want?" she asked herself. At that moment, the truth was about to unfold! Much to her surprise, Reverend Hoorseman asked if Sid was at home. He wanted to talk to him and his family about his being baptized, since he had been going to the First Baptist Church for such a long time. The good Reverend informed Sadie that he was very impressed by Sidney's attendance and felt that it was time to meet his family. Baptism was going to be given within the next couple of weeks, and Reverend Hoorseman suggested that even she, his mother, would be welcomed. His mother! Sadie was really ticked off now. How dare this man presume she was Sid's mother!

Sadie was totally unaware of Sid's activities, especially his attending the First Baptist Church. She left the room to calm down before she involved her father and Sid in this disturbing conversation. After talking to her father about the caller in their living room, Mr. Schneider entered the room, looking rather confused by this unexpected news and visitor.

Sadie, meanwhile, went to look for Sid so he could join the group. When Sadie told him that Reverend Hoorseman was waiting in the living room to see him, Sid knew this was bad news. His family would never understand. Sadie assured Sid that they would settle this matter after the Christian left the house.

One look at his father's flushed face made Sid decide it might be safer to sit next to the good Reverend. Mr. Schneider began to explain that they, including Sidney, were Jewish and that he was confused to think his son would want to change his religion. Sid knew that he had to get the Reverend out before all hell broke loose.

Mr. Schneider was sounding more and more annoyed. Sid knew that he was in trouble, and the more the Reverend spoke, the worse it sounded. It was up to him to end this visit. He took the Reverend's hand and held it tightly, trying to look and act as sincerely as he could. He thanked Reverend Hoorseman for inviting him to join his church but said that he felt he was not in a position to change his religion at the moment.

Sid never returned to the First Baptist Church, and I never asked why. I knew he was terribly embarrassed by the whole episode. From that day on, Sid's feelings on religion changed. He even stopped going to his synagogue, feeling that it was not necessary to belong to any particular church in order to believe in God. He never cared about what religion one belonged to. What mattered to Sid was what was in a person's heart and how a person treated others. For him, that was all that was necessary. To this day, Sid's belief is the same as it was fifty years ago. He represents a little piece of every religion, and I am proud to say I know and love him!

Meanwhile in 1944, the war was still going on. One story still remains dear to me regarding the unusual friendship Sid and I shared. Both of us were so innocent in our thoughts about each other. There was no sexual activity between us because sex was not important to bond our relationship. Besides, we were too naive for things like that! When I think about it, I guess what we had was just complete trust in and respect for each other. I never had any fear of Sid making advances on me, since he was as much a virgin as I. His innocence was based entirely on his total lack of thinking or doing anything bad or harmful, but mischief was okay in his eyes. I agreed.

Many times we romped around the tall grass, pretending we were grown-ups. It was nothing unusual for us to give each other a hug. We were innocent, and our feelings were natural. We knew that there was a line that we could not cross because it would destroy our friendship forever. We both held that dear. In our mid-teens, our friendship was stronger than ever, with both of us enjoying what was just a beautiful relationship as young teenagers.

Our lives were slowly changing due to the war as well as our own matu-ration. However, we were still trapping every winter, enjoying bike riding with the rest of the gang, and playing our many games of Monopoly. We continued going to the movies, hiking, partying, and dancing. The most popular dance of the 1940s was called the "jitterbug." Because we had no one to teach us, we made up our own version.

During our many parties (with only the neighborhood kids, never any outsiders), we would teach each other what we thought might resemble jitterbugging. The parties were fun and totally innocent. We did about everything that made up a fun party: eating, dancing, laughing, playing spin the bottle, and, last but not least, playing strip poker, always stopping just before either of the last two pieces of clothing was removed. We never let nakedness enter into the game. Well, maybe once or twice! It was all in fun.

It was during this period of time that I encountered my most touching moment with Sid. It was just a tender moment between two kids until gossip and my mother got involved. Sid gave me a ring that his mother had left for him when she died. It was beautiful. A note was attached that simply said, "May our friendship never be tarnished by the passing of time." How could I not accept it?

Sid told his sister, Sadie, that he had given me the ring. She was surprised but knew how much he cared for me and felt that it was all right. A short time later, Sadie mentioned this to one of her friends. The news began to spread. Several of Mother's church friends heard it. Our phone began ringing. Gossip had twisted our friendship into something dirty. I had, once again, humiliated Mother. She was shocked, horrified, unwilling to listen to my side of the story.

By now, gossip had Sid and me, not only engaged, but getting married because I was pregnant. It went from bad to worse. My God, we were only

sixteen years old! The misery that unforgettable ring carried! It almost ended my mother's social life. The ring suddenly seemed no longer lovely; it seemed more like a curse on our friendship.

Once again, I felt those terrible feelings of inadequacy and disapproval, triggered by Mother as she continued to question Sid and me about what was going on. We tried to explain that it was only a friendship ring, but she was in no way ready to accept our so-called flimsy story. She believed all the gossip. The household literally exploded. For the first time, she called me a slut, a whore, and ending with the phrase "just a piece of white trash." Mother banned Sid from Knollcroft. It was my turn to be completely humiliated and embarrassed by her bitter words.

Mother cried hysterically for days and verbally attacked me whenever I came in her sight. My father appeared unconcerned about the whole episode. He just allowed her to act out her viciousness.

My father's thoughts and reaction turned into laughter. He thought the whole affair was ridiculous and told Mother that he would handle any further problems concerning Sid, the ring, and me. She had done enough damage to Sid and me. Sid was no longer banned from our home. The ring was returned to Sid and never mentioned again, and our beautiful friendship continued only in our hearts. We were not engaged, nor was I pregnant. After all was said and done, Sid and I went in separate directions. However, the original thought and meaning of the ring is still buried deep in my heart even now, sixty-some years later. We were soul partners with a special bond then, and today this bond still ties us together.

The Korean War was going on when Sid joined the local National Guard, and shortly after he joined, his unit became federalized. He was a member of the 695th Artillery and was sent to Fort Knox, Kentucky. He joined the Army and was accepted into the 38th Reconnaissance Group, gorilla warfare. During his training, which involved learning to blow-up bridges with different types of explosives, Sid was struck in the head by debris and spent five months in an Army hospital. They kept weights on his feet to keep pressure off his brain. Finally, the Army retired him.

While he was in Kentucky, four or five of Sid's army buddies all chipped in and bought an old broken-down taxi to get around in. One day, while Sid

was out driving, the car broke down. He was in the mountains and realized he had a big problem. He needed a push, but no one was around. A short time later, he spotted four girls walking toward him. He asked them to give him a push. One of them was Cecile, the gal who eventually became his wife. A short time later, they ran into each other at a YWCA dance. Cecile recognized him as the fellow she and the other girls had pushed down the road. He asked her to dance, even though he didn't know how. She, in the meantime, wanted to dance but she didn't know how. When they realized that neither of them knew how to dance, they decided to try it anyway.

That was the beginning of a beautiful romance and a marriage that has lasted more than fifty-one years. Cecile lived in Corbin, Kentucky, at that time. It was located not far from the Daniel Boone National Forest. Lo and behold, Sid began to go to church with Cecile, who was a member of the Southern Baptist Church. Sid fell in love with Cecile. She was surprised when Sid told her that he had gone to the First Baptist Church in Morristown with the Ritter family many times and that this was nothing new for him. Before long, he asked Cecile to marry him. A rabbi married them and told the newlyweds to get off the base right away because he felt the marriage would never last any longer than it would take them to reach the gate. Fifty-one years later, they continue to be one. Sid was proud to tell me how he met Cecile, and I was happy for him. I loved him.

MY JOB AT WESTERN UNION   My first job in the business world began around the end of October 1943. One day, I saw an ad in the *Daily Record* (our local newspaper) seeking a young person with the ability to type incoming and outgoing messages from telephone customers and willing to learn the Teletype machine. The job was with Western Union in Morristown, and it was for weekends only. I applied because I was an excellent typist. Plus, I knew I could do it. My typing teacher had used me as a tutor for other kids and had exempted me from having to take any tests.

Miss Foster, the manager, told me the job paid fifty cents an hour. The thought of making that kind of money left me dumbfounded. Talk about visions of sugarplums dancing in my head! I did extremely well on the

interview, which consisted of typing, spelling, and speaking. Miss Foster was impressed, asking, "Can you start this weekend?" With no hesitation, I said, "Yes!" I was hired on the spot.

Miss Foster was impressed and soon asked me if I would like to work an occasional weekday evening in addition to my usual weekend hours. Once, again, I said yes. The job consisted of typing a message as the customer spoke it to me over the phone. I wore a headset that covered my ears so I could hear the client. Attached to the headset by a wired cord was a microphone that I positioned in front of my mouth. This allowed me to talk to the customer as I typed. It was the same type of contraption worn by the telephone operators of that day. The headset cord was plugged into the telephone board, which connected me to the customer.

This job was exciting. I began to feel my own importance to the person calling in. Everyday, many tragic messages would come though our Teletype machines. I also received exciting messages from all over the world. I was fascinated as my small world began to expand far beyond my imagination. I was sending messages to places in our own country that I never heard of before. I was suddenly being exposed to names of cities, towns, and villages throughout Europe, Asia, and the Far East—again, places that I never knew existed. I found myself being a messenger of joy and sorrow. For the first time, I began to see the misery that can and does exists in people's lives.

Western Union was one of the many ways our government notified families that their loved ones had been killed, wounded, or were missing in action. I would remove the message from the Teletype and paste it on an official Western Union message form. This was delivered to the serviceman's family by the Western Union delivery boy on his bicycle during the daytime only. This type of message was never allowed to be delivered during the evening or late at night. This spared the family one night of their impending grief. Sometimes a military officer delivered the message. The war was at its peak, and these messages and visits were the most feared.

During the Christmas season, the phones and Teletype were buzzing with messages to and from people coming or going home for the holidays. The local businessmen who used our services would drop off all kinds of goodies.

I began working every day during the summer of 1944. It was a great escape from home, and I loved it. I was fascinated by how small the world suddenly appeared to me, especially during the summer months when vacations took priority over the war for some people. I pictured myself visiting areas that had never existed for me before.

I worked during my junior year in the same manner: weekends, when I was in school, as well as an occasional weeknight, and part-time on weekdays during the summer. During my senior year, I continued working at the Western Union office because they needed me (mostly on weekends and during holiday seasons). Miss Foster had had to hire a permanent, full-time person during the weekdays by then due to the increased volume of calls. This worked out well for me because I had a little money that was mine, which gave me a feeling of independence.

EVENTS LEADING UP TO GRADUATION DAY The war finally ended in August 1945. During 1945 and 1946, I found myself eagerly awaiting my high school graduation day. Even those years added to my emotional difficulties. Much to my mother's disgust, I was not one of the "bluebloods" who roamed the school's hallways like a bunch of little gods. "Those girls" were. Naturally, this infuriated Mother. She could not understand my choice of friends, whom she considered beneath me. Constant arguments between the two of us had become a way of life. I was not sophisticated and knew I would never meet her standards. Christ, this tore at my guts.

I liked my friends: I felt comfortable around them. I could be myself, and that made me happy. We went to the movies; took long hikes, bike rides, and sleigh rides; went roller-skating; and enjoyed all the other simple things in life that kids did then. Mother's disappointment in me grew deeper. She never realized that her prudish rules were behind all of this. If I couldn't use make-up and had to wear clothes that made me look like a *nun* (covered from head to toe) and wasn't allowed to date or go to any dances, what in the hell did she expect? I felt defeated. It was an impossible situation. I would never be her "most popular girl in school," and by this time, I could have cared less. I was miserable.

A few of my friends and classmates during my high school years.
Front row (l–r): Helen Izykowitz and Jeanne Monahan. Back row (l–r):
Mary Buchanan, Frances Swindell, and Clementine Depetro.

My association with the opposite sex consisted of only the time I spent with the neighborhood boys and Sid during those years. It was easier this way, at least for me. My two sisters never had this problem with Mother. Florence was the smart one who made Mother proud of her. Pauline went to a private high school, which Mother used to gain more entry into the many social groups. Sex was never mentioned in our house nor did Mother ever attempt to talk about it. The subject was considered unmentionable.

When I, as a child, would ask Mother, "Where did I come from?" she would just walk away without giving an answer. It was as if she never heard me. Mother's favorite saying concerning sex was simply, "When you get married, you'll find out." That was it! My girlfriends and I often discussed this taboo subject among ourselves because they, too, had the same problem with their parents. Our discussions usually ended in giggles and snickers and sometimes produced a reaction of repulsion and disbelief. Mother was right. When I got married, I learned quickly, with no help from her.

During my junior and senior years, several of my girlfriends occasionally took the train down to Newark and went shopping. Back then, a magazine called *Seventeen* appeared on the magazine racks and became popular among

Celeste Fornaro, my good friend, in 1946.

our age group. Because of the magazine's success, Bamberger's, a large department store located in Newark (which has since become part of Macy's), started a club called "Seventeen." My friends joined and commuted to Newark at least once a month to attend its Saturday meetings. I went for a while, but once I started working at Western Union, I had to stop. The girls felt like real "hot-shots," but I had a job and was earning money. Back then, the city of Newark and the town of East Orange were considered the shopping areas for the more affluent people in northern New Jersey.

OBTAINING MY DRIVER'S LICENSE As soon as I had reached the age of seventeen, I applied for my driver's permit. I was excited because that little piece of paper represented freedom and a chance to see beyond Knollcroft. By then, in 1946, most families had at least one car. However, most people were still carrying around the terrible suffering of the Depression era. While money and jobs were becoming more and more available, saving had become extremely important. Dad had a new Buick by the time I was ready to learn how to drive. I loved that car: it was sleek and long, with two large, fin-shaped rear fenders.

Dad taught me the basics and never got upset or angry if I made a mistake. No lectures! No insulting names! I was nervous, but as time went by, Dad's kind and gentle ways gave me the confidence I needed. In no time, I passed the driver's test and received my driver's license. There were now four people in our family who drove and only one car. As one can see, that was a big problem. Florence and I had to ask permission every time we wanted to use the car. Dad, of course, had priority because he used the car for business. However, I was lucky. Dad did a lot of his estimating in the evening, and he always took me with him so I could drive. This kept me on top of my driving. Dad was good to me.

PREPARING FOR HIGH SCHOOL GRADUATION AND COLLEGE

There were several teachers throughout my high school years whom I felt were exceptional. My Latin teacher, Miss Little, kept my interest in learning this old language. It made Miss Lippincott's French class so much easier. My typing teacher will never know how many times throughout my life I wanted to thank her. She was an excellent teacher. Her course opened the doors to many different jobs for me. I knew the value of it the day I was hired by Western Union and in all the many other jobs I had traveling down the road of life. I still type, but now on a computer rather than the old-fashioned typewriter.

My last year in high school was filled with growing thoughts of graduating. As seniors, we were granted certain privileges. One of the most cherished was our being allowed to use the front stairway as a gathering place for seniors only and as a convenient access to the second floor. The seniors, who pompously sat on those marbled stairs, made many exciting plans and dates for the coming evenings and weekends. The stairway consisted of two lovely, curved white-marble stairs that faced each other like open arms. Smooth mahogany railings rested securely on heavy black iron balusters.

No student, other than a senior, dared put a foot on those steps. Those who did, and were caught, suffered the consequences of their actions at the hands of the group who caught them. They never attempted such a transgression again, or at least so go the various stories of their capture and punishment.

Well, of course, the senior prom came and went. My friends were excited as they talked about their gowns, hair, shoes, and jewelry for the most important dance of their high school years. I was never asked by anyone to go. If I had been, Mother would have said no, so what was I suppose to do? My only consolation was that the boys all knew I wouldn't be allowed to go. Word had spread over time that I wasn't allowed to date. It made my life so much easier. My husband, Pepper, was right: I missed a great deal throughout my high school years, especially when it came to the social relations between boys and girls.

During my senior year, Mother decided that it was time for me to start looking into colleges. Aunt Affie suggested that Mother call Uncle Bud's cousin, Florence Puzon, who was a college guidance advisor. The next thing

I knew, the three of us—Mother, Aunt Affie and I—were on our way to her home in Suffern, New York. As soon as the introductions were over, Florence asked Mother and Auntie to wait in her living room because she was going to give me an IQ test. This was imperative to help determine which direction I needed to go. Now, when it comes to tests, I do absolutely terribly. It seems as if my mind goes blank. I told Florence this, but she insisted that I get started right away. "Show me how smart you really are," she said as she, too, left her office. I shrugged, took a deep breath, and began. An hour later, I sheepishly handed Florence the miserable test. I knew I had done badly.

The three of us waited while Florence quietly went over the test results. I couldn't help but feel the tension rising around me. Finally, Florence returned and began to speak. It was terrible. I was humiliated and wanted to crawl out of the room. To put it nicely, one might say, I had an IQ just above an idiot's. What could I say? I had tried to tell her how nervous I always got whenever I had to take a test, but she had refused to believe me.

Auntie and Mother rushed me out of the front door. Both appeared terribly embarrassed. "God, how could you have done that to me?" Mother screamed. I couldn't understand why she was so upset. I was the one who was applying for college, not her. I decided to be quiet because I knew I was about ready to get smacked in the head. Poor Mom; along with everything else wrong with me, now she had an idiot for a daughter. The ride home was quiet. The three of us had little to say.

A few days later, Mother received a phone call from Florence, who told her that she had found a college that might accept me even with my low IQ. I immediately realized that it was not good news for either of us. I was being labeled as a real dummy. For the first time, I felt terrible for my mother, but that didn't last long.

Florence suggested I apply to Greenbrier Junior College in Lewisburg, West Virginia. She thought I needed a less stressful environment than that of a large university or a well-known college. Greenbrier was a small junior college located at the foot of the Allegheny Mountains. When Mother got off the phone, she turned to me and said, "You should do fine there; you'll be with a bunch of hillbillies with about the same IQ as yours." Words

would have been useless at that point, so I left the room, glad it was over. A few weeks later, I received notice that Greenbrier had accepted my application for admission.

HIGH SCHOOL GRADUATION Graduation took place in the Community Theater because the school auditorium was not large enough to handle the entire class plus all the families who would be attending. Many of the later graduations were held on the high school's football field. That did not last long because the weather frequently presented some kind of a possible threat that could cause the cancellation of the pending graduation.

The Community Theater, in its day, was considered an extremely beautiful theater. On our graduation night, it seemed as if its beauty became even more pronounced. The excitement of that evening exploded all around each of us as we walked on stage for that special, hard-earned, well-deserved diploma. Our individual dreams of tomorrow seemed to surround each of us. Time seemed to stand still as our names were called to come up on stage and receive our diplomas. All we wanted was to get the commencement over.

Even to this day, some of those unfilled dreams occasionally tug at my heart to let me know they are still alive and waiting to be lived. No matter how old I may be, I still want to feel that I can reach for the moon. It is this drive that makes life exciting and creates fascinating situations. Our innocence only lasts for a short time, but life's reality and how we live it really says it all. Few people succeed in fulfilling their special dreams.

My husband (who will enter my story presently) made an audio recording in 1996 about his World War II experiences. After his death, I decided to transcribe his story from the tapes. It took me many months. When finished, I had put together the interesting story of his life as a young G.I. during World War II. His story is in the Library of Congress in Washington, D.C. I feel very proud of what I accomplished. I left a little of Pepper behind, never to be forgotten through his story. I never dreamt of the responses I have received from men who were with him during the war. The most satisfying feeling I received was when a few of our children's generation wrote me. Their fathers had been in the same regiment as Pepper, but they

had passed on. They requested a copy of his story because they, too, never heard their fathers speak of the war. Never give up on your dreams!

Our years as children had come to an end. Our lives were going in many separate directions, raising the possibility (and probability) of never seeing each other again. Many of us would attend college and total strangers would become our newly acquired "families." However, many of my peers went directly into the workforce upon graduating. Many of their families were still struggling from the Depression and money was not readily available for things like college. Therefore, they had no choice but to go to work and help their families financially. The nation was on an upswing after the war, and opportunities in the workforce were countless.

After the war, the government passed the G.I. Bill, which offered many benefits to veterans. However, many of these men went into various different trades later, becoming their own bosses and self-employed businessmen. Back then, employment and promotion did not depend on a college diploma. People still believed that one could be a self-made person and desired to become one. Opportunity was out there, and one only had to have the drive to achieve success. Time was moving fast for each of us, and we were finding ourselves anxious, yet enthusiastic, about what lay ahead.

GREENBRIER JUNIOR COLLEGE   It was time for me to start thinking about my own life and what I wanted. I was interested in sociology and

Greenbrier Junior College.

journalism. Greenbrier Junior College offered these two courses of study. I was excited and eager to start college life. I was happy to be going to a small and insignificant school.

I spent one year at Greenbrier. Upon arriving, I was informed that the school had decided to discontinue their sociology and journalism courses. Unfortunately, there was nothing I could do except sign up for the liberal-arts curriculum, which included one year of psychology.

I lived that year at the McElhenney Lodge, also known as "The Lodge." It was separate from the main dormitory. Miss McMahon was our house-mother and showed real concern and interest in each one of us. Most of my newly acquired friends lived there, and in no time, we were like a big family.

My roommate, Yolanda Urriola, came from Panama with her two sisters. Lelia was a junior and Eneida, a sophomore. These three sisters would dance in their native dresses. They were fabulous, and I felt lucky to have had Yolanda as my roommate. They were constantly talking about their country and how much they missed their family and customs. We lived listening to their music because they brought many records to entertain all of us who lived in The Lodge.

Me and my Panamanian roommate, Yolanda Urriola, as we started out on our hike.

My pals were Shirley Johnston, Barbara Lawton, Margaret Wade, Martha "Mickey" Michelfelder, Jackie Smith, and Johanna "Jo" Westley (my Eta Upsilon Gamma sorority sister). The first couple of months were hard as I adjusted to an entirely different environment, but before long, I was just one of the gang.

I joined the horseback-riding club, "Bit and Spur." We had two shows, one in the fall and the other in the spring in which I won a small horseshoe-shaped pin as a trophy for my riding abilities. I recently gave that pin to my

little granddaughter, Kelsey. We had riding classes every Monday afternoon. On the weekends, breakfast rides and picnics on some of the most scenic trails took priority over everything else as far as I was concerned.

I remember the time I fell off my horse. It was a hard fall. It not only hurt my tailbone, but also badly deflated my pride. We were having a lesson in cantering when I fell. The instructor came over, asked if I was all right, and immediately pulled me up and said, "Get back on, right now!" I knew, by the tone of his voice, he meant *right* now. My tailbone hurt for days, but my pride and confidence were on a real high. I learned a very important lesson that day: "If you stumble or fall as you go through life, get back up, and keep going." Looking back, I did that many times over, and every time I did, I silently thanked that man for those few words.

A "Hell Week" adventure:
Johanna Westley, Shirley Johnston,
and me, dressed as babies and waiting
to go into town as Gamma pledges.

Another fun time was when I was invited to join the Alpha Zeta Chapter of the Eta Upsilon Gamma Sorority. Miss McMahon was also our sorority sponsor, which delighted me. We had Hell Week from March 3rd through March 8th. We had to dress up and act like babies by drinking from our bottles while our sorority sisters paraded us around the center of Lewisburg. They made us play ring-around-the-rosy in the center of the main street. All traffic had to be stopped. We also were made to sing "Daddy" and "Playmate," popular songs of the day, as the cadets from the Greenbrier Military School, as well as many of the local townspeople, stood watching. Everybody was laughing. We felt so embarrassed and a little humiliated as we stood looking at our ridiculous reflections from the store windows.

During this initiation period, our sorority sisters had us dress up as clowns for our next visit into town. This time we had to play leapfrog up and

down the main street while we sang Kay Kyser's number-one hit from 1939, "Itty Bitty Pool" (words and music by Saxie Dowell):

Down in the meadow in a itty bitty pool

Swam three little fishies and a mama fishie, too.

"Swim," said the mama fishie, "swim if you can,"

And they swam and they swam all over the dam.

Years later, I would sing this silly little song as a diversion for my two grandchildren whenever we were traveling. They would laugh so hard, all the time trying to sing it as well as "Buddy." (My grandchildren call me "Buddy" rather than "Grandmother.") The miles passed quickly. That's all it took! It's as if "everything old is new again!" I loved singing it because that brought back such pleasant memories. Once again, our reflections in those store windows, this time as clowns, said it all. We were ridiculous. We laughed uncontrollably as we watched each other doing cartwheels, somersaults, and backbends, which I was never able to do. At the end of an exhausting week of nonsense, filled with satisfying laughter, we were accepted into the Eta Upsilon Gamma Sorority. Life in the sorority was rewarding. Our motto was simple: "Be strong in the truth."

One of the most important events each year at Greenbrier was the October coronation ceremony for the new queen and her ladies-in-waiting. We had to vote for the girl who we felt would best represent us as our queen for 1946–1947. The queen of 1945–1946 crowned our new queen, Bettejane Mackenzie, as she knelt before her predecessor. Dorothy Mogge was her maid of honor and Nannette Robinson was attendant to the queen. I remember how beautiful

Shirley and me just after we got back from town dressed as clowns for "Hell Week." What a day! What fun!

they looked in their exquisite gowns with long, flowing trains. How proud they appeared as they received these honors. It was a festive and exciting day for everyone. The music with its regal tone blended in well with such an occasion.

After the ceremony was over, everyone was ushered into the gym for more festivities. The gym had been decorated to resemble a courtyard. The queen's ornate chair faced the long rows of tables for the oncoming feast. We were all asked to sit until the queen of 1946 and her entourage entered the room. Then we were to stand at attention in her honor until she was seated. It was more fun than any of us had imagined. Several vigorous jesters came bounding into the room, flopped down by the Queen, and began plucking at their mandolins and lutes. Their plucking produced rich musical rhythms of the Elizabethan era. The room broke into a frenzy. Many girls from the senior class began appearing in eighteenth-century costumes and carrying trays laden with all kinds of food and drink. In one corner of the room was a huge table where more food was being placed. It was fabulous. The senior class provided all the entertainment, as well as the food.

Yolanda, Lelia, and Eneida performed several unusual Panamanian dances. They never said a word to any of us. They appeared in their beautiful and colorful native costumes, and before long, everyone in the room was completely mesmerized by the exotic and graceful movements of their dances. One of the seniors put on a puppet show. To everyone's regret, the affair concluded; the final act was an astonishing magic show, performed by one senior's father. It was a day none of us would ever forget.

Around February 7, 1947, we had a very severe snowstorm. Upon waking early that morning, I looked out and saw how beautiful the snow appeared. It was unsoiled and looked more like a fallen, fluffy cloud that just settled all over the area. It was breathtaking. I remember hearing the sound of sleigh bells ringing from afar. As I continued to scan this new and beautiful landscape, I spotted a horse and sleigh coming in our direction. The silence that prevailed over the entire area was awesome, yet the jingle of those bells, as they invaded the stillness, added a delightful touch. They helped to create this winter scene, a pristine winter wonderland. It continued to snow all day and most of the night.

The next day we were allowed to go out. We were like a bunch of kids, laughing, playing, and romping in the snow. One of us came up with the idea of making a snowman on the front lawn of the college. We began to roll the

snow into large balls until the snowman finally began to take shape. Upon completion of our masterpiece, we stopped, stood back, and gazed upon him.

A carrot became the snowman's nose, two slices of red pepper were his lips, and two green peppers were inserted as ears. We had one lemon, cut in half, that we used for his eyes. We managed to find a red scarf to wrap around his neck. A corncob pipe was stuck between the two red peppers. A black felt hat was placed upon his head. A large, wide cloth belt was wrapped around his waist, and to this we attached a large sign saying, "Welcome to Greenbrier." Our snowman's picture appeared on the front page of the local paper with several of us sitting and standing next to him. Dean Marion Currie remarked how good we all looked around our masterpiece. It was a fun day that proved we were still kids at heart.

During the spring session, Betty Lou Nedell, who also lived in The Lodge, had her mother arrive for a visit. Betty Lou lived in Hollywood, California, because her mother was a movie star, charming and beautiful. Even now, I occasionally, see Mrs. Nedell (Olive Blakeney, wife of actor Bernard Nedell) in some of her old movies that are shown on TV. Among her many roles on stage and screen, she played the title character's mother in the nine "Henry Aldrich" movies that were made at Paramount Studios in the 1940s. James "Jimmy" Lydon, who played Henry in those movies (and who also made many other movies), later married Betty Lou Nedell!

However, the *most* exciting event for me while I was attending Greenbrier took place in the Lewisburg County Courthouse. Our psychology professor, Mr. Graybill, received permission for our class to attend a murder trial that was being held there. Everyone in the class was excited. A pretty seventeen-year-old Allegheny Mountain girl had been found murdered not far from our area. She had been stabbed many times as well as beaten and raped. She was found near one of the lesser-known openings leading into the Lost World Caverns just north of Lewisburg. Only the mountain people would have been familiar with this particular area.

The local police began their investigation. Apparently, the young girl tried to fight off her assailant or assailants, since a great deal of blood was found surrounding the area. The ground around her body was badly trampled,

showing that the attack took place there and that more than one person had possibly been involved. A trail of blood leading away from the spot showed that either the assailant or someone else had been cut. A jagged-bladed hunting knife, popular amongst the mountain people, was found close to her body with a great deal of blood on it. Her feet and hands had been bound—"hogtied," as the local newspaper reported—with homemade rope, made only by mountain people.

The investigation led the police deeper into the Allegheny Mountains. The mountains in West Virginia were considered a very dangerous place for a stranger to venture into. The people that lived there had their own rules and laws and did not like or want intruders. They did not feel that they had to abide by the laws beyond their boundaries.

The police learned that the girl and their prisoner were going to marry, but she had begun seeing other men. Their investigation uncovered testimony that the young mountain man had become extremely angry when the girl broke off her relationship with him. He told many of the local people that he would kill her if she married anyone else. A short time later, the girl met with this young man and asked him to take her back. She realized that she had made a terrible mistake because she loved him. He refused and an argument broke out.

In the meantime, the other man she had been seeing told many people in their small village that he was finished with her because she was only trouble. Just after the murder was discovered, he disappeared from the area, along with several of his buddies. No one had any clue about their whereabouts nor had anyone ever heard anything more from or about them. Many of the mountain people were afraid of these men because they were considered more dangerous to them than any outsider.

No matter what direction the police's investigation took, it seemed to lead back to the young prisoner. Their evidence consisted of a hunting knife with a jagged blade. The young prisoner told the officers that his jagged-bladed knife was missing and that he didn't know where it was. This type of blade could inflict the hideous wounds that tore her flesh apart so badly. The prisoner's boot fit the plaster mold of a shoe print found at the scene.

The prisoner had several severe cuts on his arms and many bruises on his chest and back, which he claimed had come from a recent fight. The blood was sent to one of the state's forensic laboratories for analysis and came back as being the same blood type as the prisoner's. Even though his blood type was the universal type, the police felt there was enough evidence to arrest him. They brought him back to Lewisburg for incarceration, where he remained until his trial.

In the meantime, the town was being inundated with mountain men. They were coming to support one of their own. They were angry with the law for invading their mountain, property, and people. They stood on the corners of Lewisburg talking to no one in particular about their anger over the local authorities. I never saw people look so filthy, neglected, and unusual. Each man wore a wide-brimmed hat made from either black felt or dirty brown straw. These hats were pulled tightly down on their heads, covering a portion of their faces, making them barely recognizable.

Their thick, long beards almost covered their entire facial area. Their eyes were dark and seemed to peek out from all the hair hanging down from their unkempt heads. When the men stood talking to each other, we were able to see the terrible condition of the few teeth any of them had. It made us sick to look at them.

Many of the men wore no shoes or boots at all. Those who did walked as if the shoes were either too small or too large. We decided that they must be hand-me-downs from someone who had died. Many of them had corncob pipes dangling from their half-hidden bottom lips. Their overalls were torn, dirty, oversized, and looked as if they had never been in water. For the few who were wearing a shirt under those baggy overalls, it was hard to say it complimented the outfit. Many didn't wear a shirt at all, exposing their broad and heavily haired chests. Their thick arms and muscles looked power-ful and frightening. One could almost imagine being completely helpless if challenged by men like these. We stirred in disbelief at these creatures that were supposed to be men.

Their women didn't appear in town until the day of the trial. They came in dresses that hung to their ankles. Each one wore a hat similar to those of

their men. Most of them had long, lifeless hair, showing little care. Their dresses fitted them like large burlap bags with holes for their heads to pass through and two holes for their arms. Tied around their waists were pieces of rope as belts. We couldn't take our eyes off of them. I truly believe that they never realized how filthy and dirty they were. When any of them smiled, we could see that they, too, were in dire need of dental attention.

All the women had stern, callous faces with many lines and winkles that reflected their hard lifestyle. Most of them were thin, almost emaciated looking. Like their men, they also smoked corncob pipes. The courtroom reeked from the odor of their tobacco and the stench of their bodies. They hardly made an effort to speak to each other, and when they did, it sounded more like a grunt. It was difficult for any of us to understand their jargon because it seemed almost foreign to our ears. They appeared just as frightening as their men. These mountain people had come with a purpose. The victim's family wanted to administer their own code of mountain justice. The prisoner's family wanted him back under the protection of his own clan. This, in itself, meant that the trial would have the atmosphere of a classic mountain feud. We could feel it in the air.

The trial began. The family of the victim sat right in front of us. They were angry, and every movement and gesture of their bodies indicated to us that their anger was building as each hour passed. They wanted that mountain man for themselves! Now the family of the prisoner was working up a good sweat from the other side of the aisle. They kept watching the victim's family, making grunting remarks about the dead girl and waiting for one of the family to respond.

Mr. Graybill was beginning to feel uncomfortable because he felt that we could be hurt if trouble erupted. The courtroom was overflowing with many of the local townspeople, making it impossible for us to move to a safer location. As students of psychology, we were captivated by the individuals embroiled in this unfolding drama. We didn't want to leave! The judge was constantly banging his gavel and shouting, "Quiet!" or "Sit down!"

The lawyers began bickering, and every few minutes they asked to have a meeting with the judge. The feuding families were getting louder with

their hellish remarks, thrusting themselves into the face of their foes and with shaking, raised fists, taunted their opponents to go one on one. The judge ordered that more police be brought into the courtroom to help maintain order. Bedlam was on the verge of erupting. It seemed as if the room was getting smaller, and because there were no window fans (no one had air conditioning), the warm, stagnate air was making our breathing difficult. We were into the afternoon. The foul odors were nauseating.

In the meantime, the prisoner seemed to be totally bewildered, sitting and acting as if he didn't have a care in the world. Every now and then, he would turn around as if he were searching for someone. When this happened, one of the family member's would jump up, wave his arms, and holler, "We're here, boy! We're here! You're goin' home!" The prisoner would try to stand up, only to be pushed back into his seat by his lawyer. The judge would bang his gavel several times, shouting, "Stop that, or I'll have you removed from this courtroom!"

Once again, the lawyer had to force the young prisoner back into his seat. The police finally dragged several of the mountain people from the courtroom before a real fight broke out. Those remaining vented nasty slurs, once again disrupting the proceedings, as they watched their kinfolk being removed. The lawyers continued on with the trial. It was difficult to sense the feelings of the jurors. They sat, looking at the players in front of them with such deadpan faces, yet concentrating intently on every word the lawyers and witnesses were saying.

A great deal of circumstantial evidence was presented. However, we felt there was enough reasonable doubt to prevent a conviction. Could this defense lawyer prove to the jury that his client was innocent? We felt that he was shattering the prosecutor's case.

It was now late in the day. The trial was coming to an end as the jury went out to determine the guilt or innocence of the prisoner.

Mr. Graybill suggested that we return to the college before the verdict came back. He was afraid for our safety and didn't know how long the jury would take. We looked at him in disbelief. No way could we leave now! We were too involved with our own mixed feelings as to whether he was

innocent or guilty. The evidence presented was not enough to really convict this man because the defense attorney seemed to destroy the credibility of the prosecutor's case.

Our tremendous interest in this case impressed Mr. Graybill so much that he agreed to let us remain until the end. We went out for a quick supper. The verdict was announced within a couple of hours: *not guilty*. The courtroom went silent. The victim's family jumped up and ran out of the room, screaming that they would get revenge. He was a dead man.

The prisoner was released within the hour. As we sat in the ice cream shop, one of the girls looked out the window, and saw the young man and his kinfolk coming down the street. We rushed outside as they passed, headed in the direction of their mountain home. They were all, including their women, frolicking and singing over their victory while sharing a swig of moonshine from a large earthenware jug. As we watched this clown-like group disappear from view, we knew we had been introduced to a society of people with whom we would probably never come in contact again.

We returned to Greenbrier very late that night. However, none of us could sleep because we were filled with the overwhelming emotions of the day. A few days later, we learned that the police had reopened the case. They were looking for the man and his buddies who had disappeared after the murder. I always felt that they knew that they had the wrong man by the time the trial was over. The circumstantial evidence was not enough to convict the young mountain man to a life sentence in prison. There was enough reasonable doubt to find him innocent.

My one year at Greenbrier was coming to a close. It was now almost the end of May, and we were busy gathering and packing our belongings and saying our goodbyes. It was an exciting year. Many wonderful friendships were to become a memory, even though we promised to keep in touch.

KATHERINE GIBBS BUSINESS SCHOOL During the summer of 1947, my mother told me that I would not be going back to Greenbrier because she wanted me to go to Katherine Gibbs Business School in New York City. My sister, Florence, had just graduated from there with highest honors as

"Best Gibbs Girl" of the year. Florence had accepted a job offer on Wall Street as an executive secretary to the president of the Banker's Trust. Mother was proud of her and felt that I should follow in her footsteps. I tried to tell her that I needed to find a college that had courses in sociology or journalism. She would not hear of this and informed me that she had *already* enrolled me in Gibbs and that I had been accepted. In September 1947, I became a student at Katherine Gibbs.

This school believed in preparing students for the business world; this preparation included classes in the proper dress and apparel code for a Gibbs graduate at work and at home. Proper etiquette training was on the same level as learning shorthand, typing, spelling, and English grammar. It was a combination of all of these things that made Gibbs girls so outstanding and in demand.

A Gibbs girl always wore heels, stockings, gloves, purse, and a hat to work. She entered the business world looking extremely striking and confident in her qualities and thorough training as an executive secretary. She was taught how to walk correctly with head held high, how to speak properly, and how to be socially correct, regardless of the problem or situation. She would never chew gum, regardless where she was. This was considered vulgar and cheap looking. Cigarette smoking was socially correct only if a young woman was sitting. A Gibbs girl would never walk anywhere with a lit cigarette in her hand or between her lips.

Florence and I had to travel the same route every day. Before we knew what was happening, we began enjoying our commuting together. Mother or Daddy would drive Florence and me to the train station each morning. We would take the 7:15 A.M. train out of Morristown. After our train arrived at its terminus, Hoboken, New Jersey, we would travel across the Hudson River on the Lackawanna Ferry. We would then proceed to walk a short distance, which took us through the Fulton Street Fish Market and eventually to the subway, which, at that point, took us in different directions.

We shared a wonderful year together exploring the city with all its fascinating points of interest and all its treasures. We seemed to put our differences aside for the time being. We became sisters for the first time in

our lives. It was fun and gave me a nice feeling. This was something we had not experienced before. After my day ended at school and Florence's workday ended, we would meet at a designated point and begin our adventures touring the city. We toured the city on weekends as well.

Broadway plays became our favorite pastime. We became connoisseurs of the better restaurants throughout the city and patronized as many as possible. Madison Square Garden was another hot item on our entertainment menu, particularly the Westminster Dog Show and the Championship Equine Show. Florence's love of horses made the Equine Show important to her. I just went along. The Madison Square Garden Circus was always a thrill.

We toured many museums, each more interesting than the other, but each had its own specialty, such as the Museum of Modern Art and the Museum of Natural History. The Bronx Zoo was usually an all-day affair. We covered Wall Street; the fur and diamond districts; the Bowery; Chinatown; Fifth Avenue; Central Park, with its famous Tavern on the Green restaurant; and the East Side with all its quaint shops and restaurants. The Waldorf Astoria was another favorite stomping ground; we would often eat lunch or dinner in its famous Green Room. The Plaza Hotel and the Russian Tea Room, both near Central Park, were also favorite spots. Carnegie Hall was another spellbinding experience.

Florence seemed like a different person, not my real sister at all. We were actually enjoying each other's company. However, during this time, I kept waiting for some hint of Florence's true nature to emerge. I felt guilty every time I had second thoughts about her. I wanted so much for her to be a sister to me. Standing by the train tracks, watching for our oncoming train, I always moved slightly away from Florence for fear she might take advantage of a convenient opportunity and fulfill her childhood threats that I still recalled so vividly. Though previous experiences, I had learned to become very cautious about my safety no matter where we went together. At times, I felt my feelings bordered on paranoia. Even though I knew my sister well, I tried to enjoy this new image she was portraying. It was a special time, even more so because of its rarity.

My time at Katherine Gibbs was a wonderful experience. I only wish I had applied myself more than I did, but secretarial work was not my true calling,

and I never wanted to compete with my sister. However, I made a good living from the many jobs I held in my lifetime that involved secretarial duties.

At this point, I felt that my real goal of being a journalist or a social worker had been lost forever. I tucked them away and went on with my life. They would occasionally pop into my mind, letting me know that the longing was still there. Somehow, I have been fortunate in keeping the desire to write alive. With very little training and with so many years behind me, I hope that I have the ability to recapture my many, unusual, funny, and wonderful experiences, as well as my trials and tribulations, which, when put together, become my life in words.

MEETING AND DATING PEPPER MARTIN   During the Christmas season of 1947, Florence's boyfriend, Ed, and a friend of his, Pepper Martin, stopped by to wish her a Merry Christmas. I answered the door because my sister was upstairs getting ready to go out on a date with someone else. She asked me to get rid of them quickly because her date, Ray, was on his way to pick her up. When Ed and Pepper arrived, I told Ed that Florence was ill. I noticed Pepper's lovely smile. Ed left a Christmas gift for Florence, saying he would call her. Ed and Pepper went on their way. Within a matter of minutes, the doorbell rang, and Raphael Moss stood before me.

Just before Christmas, I went into town to finish my last minute shopping when I ran into Ed and Pepper. The boys stopped, and we talked for a few minutes. My heart began pounding, my face felt flushed, and I wasn't sure if my legs were going to hold me up. My only fear was that I hoped it didn't show. I couldn't keep my eyes off this young man. The gleam in his eyes went along with his funny name, Pepper. His coat was unzipped, and I gazed at his body. God, he looked beautiful: lean, muscular, and very sexy. His height was perfect for me. He was dressed in dark brown clothing, which seemed to add to his great appearance. I liked what I saw, and I believe I fell in love right then and there.

The following weekend, Pepper called and asked me out. I was flattered and excited, but scared to death. I was eighteen years old and had never dated before. *I* never went out with a young man! God, I was embarrassed. That evening Pepper met my parents and faced all their questions. I figured

I would probably never see him again. I began to have a hopeless feeling when he told my folks that we had better get moving. When we arrived at The Spinning Wheel, a dancehall located in Mt. Freedom, Pepper asked me what I would like to drink. I had absolutely no idea what kind of drink I should order. I had never done this before! You talk about being naive! Well, that was me, a real jerk. I just looked at him and told him the truth: "I never ordered a drink before. What would you suggest?" He looked at me in a rather stunned way, and, suggested a rum and Coke with a small amount of rum. In other words, he wasn't taking any chances on my reaction to alcohol. He didn't want a drunk for a date. I knew exactly what he was thinking. I felt foolish, but at least he didn't jump up and rush me home, thank God. We danced, and I'm sure it took him less than a minute to realize that I could hardly dance either. If I remember correctly, I believe he was holding me up to keep me from collapsing on the floor out of sheer embarrassment. I know he never danced with a gal who held on to him as tightly as I did. After a couple of hours, he took me home. My first date with a nice guy! Yeah, I figured that when he said, "Goodnight," I wouldn't see him anymore. When I closed the door, I had mixed emotions—happy, yet sad. Again, the thought, "What a jerk I am," came though, loud and clear. My inadequacies really showed.

A week went by, and I heard nothing from Pepper. Every time the phone rang, my heart skipped a beat. I wouldn't answer it. As much as I wanted to hear his voice, I didn't want the disappointment of hearing someone else. The phone became my tormentor. Another week went by, and I was back answering the phone. My self-image was shattered. I thought, "One night of me was enough for him." Then, out of the clear blue sky, he called and asked me if I would like to take a ride up to Sussex County on Saturday morning. I didn't want to act too eager, but at this point, I didn't care. I said, "Sure!" Saturday was a lovely day, perfect for a ride. We stopped for lunch. I guess I was a little nervous. I put salt in my coffee instead of sugar. He started laughing. I felt like a fool.

A few days later, Pepper called and asked me out again. We went to a movie and later stopped and had something to eat. Well, it happened again. I was just about to put salt in my coffee when Pepper took my hand and held

on to the salt. He didn't laugh; instead, he gave me a nice smile. I guess I was a little more nervous than I thought. Oh, well, chalk it up to whatever.

At this time, I was still attending Katherine Gibbs. The school's yearly spring dance was announced. It was going to be at the New Yorker Hotel. I asked Pepper if he would like to go with me, and he said, "Yes." It was a formal affair, which meant we both needed appropriate clothing. No problem. We went and had a great evening. From then on, Pepper called me. The Spinning Wheel became our favorite hangout. It was rustic and had a warmth of its own. I knew we were falling in love. I continued to order rum and Coke, but I no longer found myself putting salt in my coffee.

Our Wedding, August 21, 1948

The house bustled with excitement. Laughter was never so prevalent or greeted more enthusiastically. It was my wedding day. Pepper was not only my hero and love, but also the handsome, strong man of my dreams, the man I was preparing to marry on this unforgettable day, August 21,1948. A wonderful feeling of intoxication seemed to blanket my entire body. Even though I was anxious to have the day over, I was amazed by my own calmness.

Mother, Aunt Love, and Affie were busy hustling about the house, trying to complete the last of a long list of projects. One knew that a very special event was about to take place. Every room sparkled, groomed to perfection. Knollcroft, once again, was indeed a lovely and beautiful home for such an important occasion. Ida, who had replaced dear ol' Mandy as our cleaning woman, was busy giving the many pieces of furniture their last, quick dusting. The door chimes announced the arrival of the florist with vases of flowers. I could hear Mother giving instructions about where each vase was to be placed. By the time I came downstairs, their fragrant perfume had already combined with the delicious aromas that floated from the kitchen. Grandmother Ritter's sterling silver sparkled as small rays of sunlight filtered into the rooms, striking and reflecting the true beauty of the many pieces.

Several weeks before the wedding, Ida had spent hours cleaning and polishing the many pieces of silver. She had to wrap each piece in its individual silver cloth to prevent any tarnishing before my wedding day. It was a big job. Mother always inspected every piece, regardless of the occasion, as Ida watched for Mother's approval. Throughout the years, Mother and Ida managed to turn

this particular job into a real ceremony. Mother portrayed the matriarch while Ida took the part of the devoted servant, always ready to do her best. It was so silly. Ida was more like family than a servant. We all loved her.

Decorations were hung securely, running from one room to another with a multitude of white balloons and large and small white bells with all their trimmings clinging together. For the first time, I noticed how beautifully Mother could create an exciting and lovely atmosphere. I was proud of her. I knew that I loved her, and for the first time, I felt she really cared about me to have gone to all this work.

The reception was being catered by one of the better catering services in the area, but Mother insisted on preparing her own favorite dishes, as she remarked, "only to add a touch of down-home flavor to all this fancy prepared foods that's coming." It was the only time I ever heard her speak with any pride or loving feelings about her unrevealed roots. There was a purpose for every part of Knollcroft on this festive day, including the back-yard. Many tables and chairs had been placed around the grass for guests who preferred to sit outside. Dad had set up a special table to be used as a bar for the folks who were enjoying the outdoors.

Mother had envisioned having the wedding reception in one of the private rooms at The Winchester Inn, The Harbor, or The Manor. Daddy had other ideas: he wanted his three daughters to be married in the family home. As he so often remarked, "The girls were born upstairs. They will get married here as well." This idea shocked her. However, she had no choice but to accept it. As the wedding plans moved forward, many angry words were vented by Mother to voice her disapproval of having the reception at home and worst of all, in the basement. She was terrified of being socially ostracized. Daddy refused to give in to her frustration and anger. His only request was that we were not to go into the basement until he was finished re-doing it.

A great deal of activity started as more and more men entered the base-ment for one reason or another. We could hear their banging, cussing, talking, and singing. Dad was completely wrapped up in his project. Mr. Pozzi, a dear family friend as well as an excellent artist, became Dad's right-hand man. Two days before the wedding, Dad announced that he was ready

for us to see what he had created. We hurried down the stairs, and when we walked into the big room, we were in awe. The walls were freshly painted and decorated for the occasion by Mr. Pozzi. A large section of the basement's cement floor now had a slick, highly waxed, wooden dance floor with an area reserved for the band. Throughout the rooms were potted plants nestled against the walls. Lovely rugs had been placed over the old cement floors. A large table for the wedding party was ready to be dressed and decorated, as were the other tables. The wedding gifts were to be displayed on a separate table.

Every room in the basement had a purpose, and each room was presented as part of the reception area, including the laundry room. Dad had even gone as far as to hire a decorator for the final touches. We all agreed that he had done a magnificent job. Dad was prouder than a peacock as he pranced about each room. No one questioned how much this project cost. Money was never an object. Whatever Dad wanted, he got. Apparently, he had hired highly skilled men to help him. Mother and Affie couldn't wait to get started preparing and setting up the tables as the final touch.

Because I was not Catholic, we were not allowed to be married in St. Virgil's Church. That was a rule of the Catholic Church! Therefore, I had to be married in the rectory. Mother insisted that my gown should be an afternoon garden dress rather than a white wedding gown because of this ruling. I couldn't believe it. Pepper said that it made no difference to him and that the rectory was fine. That was it. No white wedding gown, no flowers, nothing—just married in the priest's office.

I was very upset, but there was nothing I could do or say. Mother and Pepper had everything under their control. Suddenly, I found myself in a situation where I had no voice. I was completely devastated when Mother presented me with my wedding dress. It was a hideous bronze-tannish color. I felt like anything but a bride. I couldn't bear to look at myself as I passed by Grandmother Ritter's very old, magnificent, huge mirror. I shrugged my shoulders, wiped away my tears, and went downstairs wrapped in complete defeat. The wedding was at 10:30 A.M., and the reception was to start at 11:30 A.M. Only our two families went to the rectory and saw us married.

Thank God for Knollcroft. At least we had a beautiful reception. About three hundred people came. Dad was in his glory, and Mother was doing her best to keep the food moving, the drinks flowing, and everyone laughing and having a good time. I will say that both my parents were great that day. Mother actually seemed to enjoy watching everyone drink. Most of the drinking did not come from the non-alcoholic punch, either. Uncle Bill, my father's uncle, got drunk and kept the party in great spirits. I think we had half the mafia there as well. These were the guys who had kept us well supplied with sugar, gas, tires, etc. during World War II. Aunt Effie and Uncle Dave, on the paternal side of my family, were there. As usual, Dad had hired one of his workers (with strict orders) to stay with Aunt Effie because she was a great one who could fall, so easily and then sue the hell out of the property owner. Dad always had us kids watch her whenever she and Uncle Dave came for a visit, so I knew he was only protecting himself. Uncle Dave was a nice man. He was my grandmother Ritter's brother.

Some of Dad's roofers were there, more drunk than sober. All the neighbors were invited. Pepper's family was there: Pop, Kitty, Larry, Lucy, Bruce, and Maureen. Pepper's side of the family was small but was supplemented by about thirty of their friends. An aunt and uncle from the New York City

Pepper waiting to leave for our honeymoon.

came with two of his cousins, which was a nice surprise. The reception consisted largely of my family's friends.

Everyone, young and old, danced, drank, and ate the afternoon away. It was a fun party. One of our friends, I believe it was Harry Sander, took a movie of the reception, which I still have. Every now and then, I will get the film out and watch it. I have to laugh to see the antics that some of our guests came up with. The house was full of wedding gifts, most of them still wrapped, which had arrived with the

many guests. They were placed upstairs, in both living rooms, as well as in the dining area. We were not aware of all these gifts until we came home from our honeymoon.

Knollcroft was at its finest. Many guests enjoyed sitting in the formal living room, where they were able to have a more quiet conversation. Many took comfort in Knollcroft's charming dining room, where lots of extra goodies and finger foods were placed for their convenience.

Me in my green "going-away" outfit.

OUR HONEYMOON   By the time we changed into our traveling clothes, it was nearing late afternoon. We went around to each table and said our good-byes and thanked everyone for making our day so special. It was time for us to get on the road because we wanted to drive as far as possible before darkness set in.

Our car was a sleek, black 1947 Ford. We were heading west on Route 46 toward the Delaware Water Gap. Pepper was driving. I looked over at him and smiled. He was beautiful, strong, everything that I wanted or expected in a man. I loved him! He smiled back. I wondered what he was thinking. He was wearing a casual light brown shirt and dark brown pants. They were definitely his colors!

I looked down at my green suit. "God," I thought. "What a color! Why did I buy it?" Suddenly, I realized that I was still wearing my hat. It was a wide-brimmed green hat that I bought as part of my going-away outfit. Mother insisted that every bride wears a hat when departing from the reception. "I never wear hats," I thought. "Why did I listen to her? Why did I buy it?" My eyes shifted downward as I stared at green shoes. Everything I was wearing was green except my pristine white gloves, which sat on my lap as if they had never been touched. As I glanced across the seat, I saw my small

green pocketbook. My hands touched my face. Had it turned green to match the rest of me? I began to laugh as I felt the stress of the day leaving me. It felt good.

Pepper looked over at me, flashed a warm smile, and said, "Butt me, babe." Our eyes met, and again I thought how beautiful he looked. I pulled a cigarette out of my bag and lit it. One of his hands remained on the stirring wheel; the other reached out as I pressed the cigarette between his fingers. I watched him as he slowly inhaled the strong, yet flavorful Lucky Strike. How pleasing they both appeared: one for his manly beauty, the other for its satisfying taste. My attention turned back to my outfit: "God, I look like a green toad sitting on a lily pad." For one split second, I wanted to rip everything green from my body. Instead, I took out a cigarette, lit it, and sat back to enjoy the moment, the ride, and the events of our day.

It was our honeymoon, and we were headed for Niagara Falls. We were young, in love, happy the wedding was over, and excited about becoming man and wife. Few words were spoken as we drove west. I would light up a cigarette for Pepper every time he said, "Butt me, babe!" Occasionally, we would touch hands or flash a smile at each other just to reassure ourselves that neither of us was dreaming. We were married!

The highways at that time consisted of only two lanes (one coming in one direction, one going the other). Fancy motels and hotels were not part of the highway scene; an occasional inn, a few rough-looking cabins, or a rare tourist home were about the only overnight facilities available to motorist, and they were usually miles apart. Traveling was not like it is today. Realizing this, we decided to stop at the first cabin we saw because it had been a long day.

We were just outside of Scranton, Pennsylvania, when we spotted several rustic-looking cabins just off the highway. We stopped and inquired if a cabin was available. After checking it out, we decided we had better take it. An outhouse and washroom were available a short distance from our cabin. The owner brought us a basin of water once we were settled in. The cabin had an old iron bed, one dresser, a hard-backed chair, and a washstand. There was no radio, television, or, any nice, cushy rug to rest our bare feet

on. It had none of the comforts available today. The bed was only a three-quarter-size bed. It was small, but we managed. No problem. We were too excited and happy to think about anything other than ourselves, together as man and wife. At least the bed had clean sheets and a light blanket.

Mother had had Ida pack a nice supper for us just in case we couldn't find an eatery that evening. Restaurants were not as common as they are today along the highways. The supper Ida had packed was food from our reception: turkey legs, rolls, ham, roast beef, and some of our wedding cake. We picnicked on the bed and enjoyed every morsel of food. We were happy as we laughed at our surroundings and glad to be off the road. It was a long night.

I was a virgin and completely naive. Mother never sat down for an old-fashioned mother-and-daughter discussion before my marriage. I was happy with what little I did know. It was nice, sitting together, enjoying our tasty cuisine, and the quietness of the night. Finally, our first night together as man and wife was about to take place.

No matter how quiet we tried to be, the rusty old bedsprings squeaked something terrible. I don't know why we were worried. We were the only travelers spending the night, or so the owner told us. The unevenness of the cabin floor didn't help. We couldn't move without it sounding like a herd of elephants on the rampage.

From the time we started our honeymoon till we consummated our marriage that night, the complete scene will remain with me forever because it still ignites the love I had for Pepper. It was the beginning of the end of my youth, my innocence, my naiveté.

The following day, we arrived in Niagara Falls. We could hear the thunder of the falls as we drove through the small town looking for a hotel room for the night. It was exciting. We found one just a short distance from the falls and decided to see if it had a vacancy. The desk clerk mentioned that if we would agree to be interviewed by the local radio station, the hotel would give us the bridal suite as a gift plus several other surprises. We would be perfect candidates because we were an out-of-state couple who came to the most famous honeymoon spot in the world. We decided it would be fun, so we accepted his offer.

We drove to the radio station, where we were ushered into the studio. The interviewer asked the usual questions: Where we came from? How had we met? What kind of wedding had we had? I was given a coupon for a rose corsage from one of the local floral shops. I picked it up the following day just before we left to go over to the Canadian side of the falls. Pepper received a tie and a girlie calendar. The interviewer sent us back to the hotel, where we were given the bridal suite. Once we were settled in, we decided to take the famous ride on the boat called "Maid of the Mist," which went under the falls. They gave all the passengers yellow rain coats so we would-n't get too wet. It was exciting. That night we roamed around the area until the magical lights were turned on, making the falls a mass of color. We were told that the Canadian side was more beautiful than the United States side.

The next day was a complete surprise, weather-wise that is. We had arrived just in time for a very unexpected heat wave for this part of the country. Temperatures climbed over the one-hundred-degree mark. We had only fall clothing with us because we had been told that the area would be chilly even though it was the end of summer. We had to go shopping for cooler attire. However, we made the terrible mistake of not changing before we left the hotel.

As we were crossing the international bridge into Canada, I began strip-ping. The wool slacks were making me sweat to the point where I was getting a rash. This became a project I had not encountered before. I began scream-ing at Pepper to slow down. I wasn't out of my slacks yet and the border-crossing station was just ahead. I looked ridiculous as we pulled up and stopped. I had frantically pulled my wool slacks off and was in the process of putting my shorts on when the inspector looked into our car. I could feel my face burning with humiliation as I noticed his eyes become fixed on my problem. Pepper acted like nothing was wrong as he answered the officer's questions. I blurted out how hot it had gotten and how unpre-pared we were. What else could I possibly say?

The inspector nodded his head while his eyes continued to survey the inside of our car. I rattled on with senseless comments as I sat with my shorts halfway on. The minute his eyes shifted to the backseat, I quickly pulled

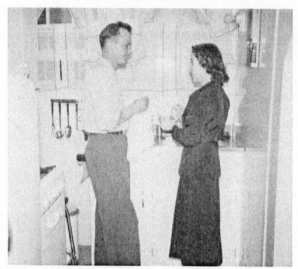

Enjoying and sharing the moment together as we arrive home at our small third-floor apartment.

them up. My face felt like it was red-hot. The word "embarrassment" is not strong enough to describe what I was experiencing. I believe that dear man could see my distress and the terrible predicament I found myself in. The officer commented that he noticed that I had a problem but was glad it was now resolved. He gave us the go-ahead.

We continued driving until we reached the outskirts of the town of Hamilton and decided to start looking for a place to stay for the night. We came across several small cabins that were available and picked the one that appeared to be furthest away from the roadway. The heat traveled with us. There was no such thing as air conditioning, but the cabin was neat, clean, and had everything we needed. We spent most of the night outside, talking, laughing, and making love. It was romantic, even though we were trying to capture the occasional breeze. The night was all the more mystifying for the sounds

Pepper and me in 1970.

of nature and the serenity that surrounded us. The moon was full, displaying our naked bodies to the entire valley below. We were happy. We were young. We were in love, and we were married. Boldly, we made passionate love as we lay under the beauty of a summer night. We decided to return to the states the next day.

The heat wave was unbearable as we crossed back into the states, so we continued driving just to keep cool. Sightseeing was no longer a priority on our list of things to do. We headed home, hoping to out-ride the sweltering temperatures. We had just experienced the worst heat wave in that part of Canada and the northern sections of the United States. We arrived home exhausted but happy.

Our Marriage

Dad had converted Knollcroft into three beautiful apartments during the early part of 1948. My parents kept the first-floor apartment for themselves. Pepper and I rented the third-floor apartment. During the summer of 1949, Dad bought waterfront property at Lake Mohawk, New Jersey, and decided to build a home as soon as possible. He wanted to spend more time enjoying the rewards of his hard work.

Pepper worked for Sturgess Brothers, who were considered the *finest* builders in the Morris County area. By 1951, Dad hired them to build his dream house. By the time they finished the lake home, Knollcroft had been sold. It took no time to find a buyer. Pepper learned a great deal from the Sturgess men, especially the importance of quality workmanship. He enjoyed building, but his greatest pleasure came when he looked upon his "finished product." Dad was very impressed by Pepper's work habits and his knowledge of building. He asked him to come into his business and learn the roofing trade.

By 1956, Pepper saw that there was no future working for Dad. He was treated just like any of the other roofers in the yard. He had no medical benefits, no paid vacation, and no pension. He was the only worker who showed up everyday. The other hired men were drunks and not responsible at all. Dad knew that Pepper made a good impression on his customers. He was always clean-cut and shaven, never swore while working, and never smelled like booze. His work was excellent. Even though Dad knew this, he still gave him nothing other than his weekly wage. He was on no salary, and

he was paid only for the hours he worked. However, Dad taught him how to measure all types of roofs, how to figure estimates for these jobs, and how to deal with all types of customers. Once Pepper learned how to do all of these things, Dad no longer went out estimating. He sent Pepper, but did not pay him for doing it. Dad kept all the profits. For some reason, this arrangement did not seem fair.

Pepper worked hard at proving himself, but the two men were too much alike. Within a few years, Pepper decided to go out on his own. In 1956, he opened his own business and called it North Jersey Roofing Company. I became his secretary, doing all the necessary paperwork and answering the phone. My day was full. Between my home, family, and office work, I didn't have time for outside interests. I didn't mind at all. I liked keeping busy. It made my life easier. The business became a success. He operated this business for forty-five years and did extremely well. However, it turned a young man into an old man, long before his time.

OUR FIRST CHILD, PAUL J. MARTIN   On December 18, 1950, our first son was born. We named him with both of our fathers' first names, Paul Joseph Martin. Of course, we all agreed that he was the most beautiful baby. I can't imagine any family saying anything else about a newborn. Naturally, we spoiled him to death. When he was three, we took him down to the Morristown Fire House so he could ride on a fire truck. Pepper knew most of the men, so Paul was given all the attention a kid could ever expect. They put a helmet on his head, and I took a picture of him, which I still have. We had a black cocker spaniel named Joe at that time, and when we brought Paul home from hospital, we had to introduce the dog to his new competitor. Dr. Ferris had given us instructions about how to do this. She was a great dog lover and didn't want Joe to feel that he was no longer important. Until I had my second child, Paul was exposed mostly to adults.

By the time he was three years old, we felt he needed to be with children. I enrolled him in Mrs. Trottman's Nursery School for a few hours a day, three times a week. He enjoyed the school and attended it until he went to kindergarten. Mrs. Trottman never forgot Paul. As the years passed, she always

called on Pepper and Paul to handle her roofing problems. Mrs. Trottman always took an interest in Paul's life.

Paul was a typical kid. We lived on Elders Drive for his first ten or eleven years, and he was bussed to Alfred Vail School. There were a few children in our neighborhood at that time. I have a cute picture of Paul wearing the famous Davy Crocket coonskin cap. He loved that cap and wore it every time the kids played cowboys and Indians. Once he reached his teenage years, his first loves were cars and

Paul showing off his catch of the day at his grandparents' home at Lake Mohawk.

motorcycles, and then racing them. My heart stopped beating more than once when I watched him race. Pepper taught his sons how to work at very early ages. He had them out cutting people's lawns, raking the fall leaves, and plowing snow out of driveways. They were taught how to save money.

We never gave them a weekly allowance. Anything that needed to be done in or around our house was done without pay. Pepper believed that because we were a family, everyone should do what needed to be done without pay or argument. I went along with that because I felt it was good training. No complaints. By the time Paul reached his sixteenth birthday, he had saved enough money to buy Dr. Delpho's Mercedes Benz convertible. It was one beautiful little car. However, he wasn't allowed to take it out of the driveway until he had his driver's license. When Paul would allow Pepper and me to ride in it, we were not permitted to smoke in it, even when the top was down. Pepper loved the feel of that car.

Once Paul had his license, he entered many different motorcycle races, covering most of the eastern seaboard. My heart was always in my throat when he went off to race. We went to several, but I found them frightening and stopped going. He was injured several times, but always got back on his cycles.

Paul met his future wife, Debbie Vroom, during his senior year in high school. Paul attended County College for one year, but quit because he liked working with his dad. That was Paul's decision. Pepper always wanted his boys to earn their livings with their heads, not their backs, but life doesn't always turn out the way you want it. Pepper then made him a partner, and they worked together until Pepper retired. At that time, he gave Paul the business.

Paul and Debbie went together for a couple of years, and then, in May 1976, they were married. A few years later, my first granddaughter, Elizabeth Huntington Martin, was born on February 4, 1982. She was a beautiful baby and grew into a lovely young woman; she is attending University of Vermont in Burlington. She plans on getting her Masters in Education and becoming a teacher in the lower grades. Two years later, Ryan Francis Martin was born on January 11, 1984. Ryan was also a lovely baby. As he matured into a young man, he left behind a record of real accomplishments, and I admire him for that. He was a member of the Presbyterian Church Bell Ringers, and their yearly tours gave them an opportunity to visit England, Scotland, Germany, and France. Their tours also included trips to many different states along our East Coast. These tours included invitations to perform. This young group of bell ringers was amazingly good. Everyone who knew of them and heard them play admired their ability to make such beautiful music with bells. I was very proud to think Ryan was part of this

Paul's family: Ryan, Paul, Elizabeth, and Debbie (l–r).

group. I loved to hear them in concert. He also was involved in the Boy Scouts for many years. He made me very proud. Ryan was an excellent student, achieving high marks throughout his school years and earning a four-year scholarship at Colgate University. I always felt that these two grandchildren loved us very much, but their lives became so busy once they were in high school that we saw little of them. Both Beth and Ryan have great futures ahead of them. I hope that they use their lives wisely. They hold a big part of my heart.

MY GUARDIAN ANGEL   Another story that comes to mind is one that I shall never forget.

I began hemorrhaging almost immediately when I became pregnant with my second baby in December 1951. We were still living in our third-floor apartment at Knollcroft. I had to buggy-lug everything—including my little boy, Paul—up and down those stairs. It was very difficult for me. When I began hemorrhaging, finding a donor became a challenge because of my rare blood type. However, Doctor Ferris located one woman in the Morris County area with the same blood type who was willing and able to donate her blood. Throughout the entire pregnancy, she kept me alive.

I was a constant patient because I would no sooner be discharged than I would have to be re-admitted. My life had become a nightmare: I lived with the constant fear of bleeding to death. However, during my sixth month, an incident occurred that left me feeling that someone up there was watching over me.

I was nearing the end of my sixth month. Weakness and exhaustion were my steady companions. I was angry with myself for getting pregnant, angry with the Catholic Church for not permitting birth control, and angry every time Mother made her disapproving remark, "You're turning into a breeding machine for that damned Church." My life had become hard and difficult. My sex life became a living hell because I never knew from one month to another whether I was pregnant. I tried to embrace Pepper's strict faith. Every time I attempted to discuss these issues, Pepper would remind me that I had no business complaining because I knew where I stood before I ever married him. He was right. I did know. Guilt had also become my steady

companion, and when these emotions clashed, I would become devastated. Why did his mental and physical strength overpower me, always leaving me to hide in the humiliation of my failures and weakness as an individual? I found myself controlled once again and too weak to stand up for my rights, my beliefs, and my desires. I was ashamed of this person who was I in all reality. I knew how screwed up I was getting.

My little boy had become as confused and upset over my situation as I. He could not understand why he was always being sent to Grandma's house. Mother took him every time I went to the hospital. How can you explain something like this to a small child? If I tried to clean, cook, or do anything that required walking, I would hemorrhage, and off to the hospital I would go.

Dr. Ferris continued to warn me about the seriousness of my condition. I just wanted it over with. I knew my child could be born prematurely or dead if I did not follow the strict orders of Doctor Ferris. Neo-natal care was not as advanced then as it is today. Premature babies had little chance of surviving. My life was on hold until my pregnancy ended. I was restricted in every way. Bed rest was imperative to prevent a possible premature birth or my own death from hemorrhaging. There was no escape. My family was feeling the effects of my frustration and uncertainty as well. Life was miserable. My guilt over my immaturity and disregard for my unborn child ate at my very soul. I knew my actions and my thoughts were wrong, but I continued to act like an angry child.

I was in the early part of my seventh month when I had to be re-admitted to the hospital. The transfusions had become more and more frequent. Doctor Ferris always appeared smiling and cheerful, but I felt her anxiety and concern for me and my baby. It was during one of these admissions when I experienced a most unusual encounter.

I was awakened in the middle of the night by the sound of someone moving in the direction of my bed. I thought it was one of the Sisters who had come to take my blood pressure. Moonlight kept the ward from total darkness. To my surprise, I saw the outline of what appeared to be a young girl coming toward me. Her nightgown made a swishing sound around her bare feet. As she approached me, she reached out and very gently touched

my arm. Her eyes met mine. Her hand touched my hand. It was warm, and that warmth seemed to flow into my body. She startled me, for no child should be wandering around the maternity floor during the middle of the night! Who was she? Where did she come from?

Before I could say a word, she began speaking in almost a whisper to me, "God loves you, and He will take care of you." I could feel the hair on my arms begin to stand on end. Goose bumps followed as I lay back on my pillow, never taking my eyes off of her, not sure if I was awake or dreaming. As she continued talking, I knew that I was experiencing a strange and mystical encounter. I never heard a child or anyone speak so beautifully, look so angelic, and speak of God in such a loving way. I was mesmerized by the beauty of the glowing light that now seemed to be wrapped around her. Was it a reflection of the moonlight? Her small, pale face and her frail body gave the appearance of a very ill child. However, her voice was soft, her words gentle, yet powerful and strong, making it difficult to believe they were coming from such a fragile frame. Short blond hair surrounded her gaunt face. Again she spoke of God and His great love for all of us. "You must believe in Him," she said as she held my hands between her own.

Her warmth and her tremendous faith captivated me. I felt uncomfortable as I found myself wishing, almost to the point of being envious, that I could have the same kind of love and adoration of God as this child had. How could she, so young, have such faith, and I have so little? I felt ashamed as I listened to her speak of her great love and faith. The glow remained around her. I could not move, nor did I want to. I was completely hers. Still holding my hands, the child told me that she would always be with me, and God would carry me when I needed Him the most.

"Love God, and He will be with you, and he will take care of you both," were her last words as she released her small hand from mine and began to move away from me. The glow went with her. I stared in disbelief as she seemed to just float away, evaporating into the darkness. I lay back against the pillow. Her warmth was still with me.

I waited for morning to appear, trying to understand what I had experienced. At the first sign of daylight, one of the Sisters came into the ward. I

asked her to sit down because I wanted to tell her what had happened. I felt foolish as I began talking. Suddenly, I felt frightened as I watched her face take on a puzzled and strange look. I stopped. I couldn't help but wonder what she was thinking. Did she think I made it all up? Perhaps I had frightened her with such an unbelievable story. The Sister asked me to continue. I could feel tears roll down my cheeks as I spoke of my brief encounter with this sickly, but beautiful child.

Sister told me that a young girl had been admitted to the hospital last evening. However, there were no beds left in the children's ward. "The youngster was dying. It was only a matter of a few hours or less before she would pass away," the Sister whispered. "She was an orphan, a ward of the state. Mother Superior insisted that we find a room for the child," the Sister quietly added, "and because the maternity ward had several private rooms available, she was placed in one of them." The Sister paused, then said, "She died during the night." Silently we sat, looking at each other, deep in our own thoughts. Finally, the Sister took my hands, held them in hers, and quietly said, "Perhaps, she was sent as your guardian angel!" With those few words, I knew my encounter was the greatest moment in my life. Truth is stranger than fiction!

On June 14, 1952, Joseph Patrick Martin was born prematurely during my seventh month. It was a difficult breech birth, causing injury to his tiny under-developed body. Doctor A. Mintz, our pediatrician, found him to be in grave condition with little chance of surviving. Our friend, Margaret Courtet, was one of the nurses present at the birth. Recognizing his precarious condition, Marge baptized him shortly after the birth and requested to stay with him as his private nurse. Joseph died twenty-four hours later.

Mother told me that my baby was beautiful and that it broke her heart to have to bury him. I felt, for the first time, that Mother was truly sorry and felt our pain. I never saw my little boy because he had to be placed in an incubator as soon as he was born and could not be taken out of the nursery. My condition after the birth was considered serious. The delivery left me weak and unable to walk, and I had to receive additional blood transfusions. My mother and my husband picked out Joseph's casket and burial clothing and buried him before I was released from the hospital. That was the only time I ever saw Pepper cry.

Go for the House   Around the end of September 1952, Pepper and I went into New York City for a day of fun. This was something we had not done in a long time. By now, the pregnancy was behind me. I was back on my feet and able to do a few things. Both of us needed a day off, a day away from every thing. Our first stop was at the observation tower in the Empire State Building to see the fabulous view of New York City from such a height. While there, we heard the NBC Radio tour was about to start, and we decided to sign up. The tour took us into several different studios where we saw how different sounds were created.

A radio program called, *Go for the House*, was picking contestants by asking them, "Why do you want a house?" Pepper told me to wave my hand, and by gosh, the announcer stopped and asked me that question. I was sitting on an aisle seat. I told him that I had had a baby just a couple of months ago, but due to all kinds of complications, the baby had died forty-eight hours after his birth. I also mentioned that we lived on a third-floor apartment and that it had become extremely difficult for me. There was no elevator. Well, by the time I told him my whole story, he sent us up on the stage to participate. He asked us about five questions, and Pepper answered all of them correctly. We were on the last question, which called for the name of a certain song. My mind went blank, and Pepper gave the wrong name. We won a kitchen set (a yellow Formica-covered table and four chairs), but missed the one question that would have given us the house. Even if we didn't win the house, it was exciting. I still have the table and one chair. Every time I look at it, the entire scene flashes before me.

During the early spring of 1953, Pepper and I bought a house on Elders Drive in Morris Township. He watched it being built and knew it was well constructed. Even after we moved to Maple Avenue in Morris Plains in May 1963, he still felt that his first house was his real home.

THE DEATHS OF MY GRANDPARENTS   It was September 7, 1953, when my mother received a phone call from Grandmother Whorton with the sad news that Granddaddy had passed away. We all knew how ill he was because his doctor said there was nothing more that could be done to help him. Granddaddy died from cancer of the mouth, lip, and jaw. Pepper and

I had gone south earlier that summer and stayed with my grandparents. Howard took us fishing and shrimping every day. It was fun. However, it was the last time I saw Granddaddy. Uncle Howard was living with them at that time, thank goodness. He was a big help to Grandmother when no other family was there to help her. They watched Granddaddy slowly deteriorate until death took over.

About six years before Granddaddy's death, my grandparents had bought a small white stucco house, just down the road from the crab plant. However, after Granddaddy passed away and Howard's drinking became worse, Aunt Lilly moved Grandmother to Brunswick to live with her and Uncle Sam. She sold the house in Oriental. By now, most of the family lived in Brunswick, so it made little difference to anyone. It was hard on Grandmother because she missed her home and was no longer in control of her life. Grandmother died in April 26, 1965.

THE SILENT TREATMENT   The real beauty in any newborn child is its pureness and innocence. The road of life, however, has its own twist and turns, which can destroy gifts that God placed in each of us. Detours lead down paths where love and other gentle emotions become entangled with the more destructive emotions. Anger, power, control, and greed can destroy when they are put into motion. A troubled childhood, lack of love, some type of abuse, or guilt and anger from a horrific environment, such as war, can create these mixed emotions. Meanness becomes a weapon of controlling force as it creates a life of hell for those involved.

It takes a strong person to endure years of living with an individual who refuses to talk because of an argument or because his nose got out of joint for some reason. Until one experiences the "silent treatment," one will never understand the mental abuse it involves. It is extremely cruel, especially if its victim is the least bit sensitive. As silly as this may sound, silence can be as hurtful and harmful as any physical abuse. At times, it can be worse, depending on how long the silence continues. It is a maddening experience, one in which I found myself shortly after we were married. It occurred, on and off, lasting longer and longer, as the years turned into decades.

Unfortunately, one is not always exposed to these realities until situations unmask a person's true and troubled identity. I often wondered what caused Pepper to act as he did when we had a disagreement or I did something of which he did not approve. I knew his life had not been easy. Money was scarce. The Depression years were hard on his family. He felt that I had been born with a silver spoon in my mouth and never knew what it was to do without. To my surprise, he used this as a way of punishing me. If I asked for anything, wanted to buy something or go somewhere, his answer was "No." He would stop talking, sometimes for a day, sometimes for a week, depending on the situation. Again I was living the same kind of life I had before I married him. I felt worthless, unloved, and completely controlled. If Pepper wanted to do something, however, that made a difference. I had to be a part of it because I had no choice. He would make me beg for grocery money, take the car keys so I couldn't go anywhere, put his fist in my face, and dare me to confront him. Our marriage had turned into heartache and pain.

I wondered if World War II had anything to do with his actions. Pepper experienced the wrath of war and suffered terrible nightmares from it. For a long time, he suffered from frostbitten legs and feet as well. Was he full of guilt and anger because of these events? Why was his anger always addressed to me? Was it me? Did I create the situation through my own imperfections? That thought frightened me.

I knew that I was young when I married him and knew less of the world than he did. He often remarked how normal his high school years were and how screwed up mine had been. I also knew that I had escaped from Knollcroft by marrying him. For the first couple months, our marriage seemed typical of most newlyweds. I was surprised when I realized how little I knew him. I'm sure he was just as surprised to see my flaws. Our honeymoon came to a screeching stop once we began living with each other's faults and differences. As the years passed, our feelings toward each other had become a love-and-hate relationship filled with physical abuse, unkind words, and my fear of being "white trash," as Mother so often called me.

At first, I thought Pepper was just being funny by showing me how stubborn he could be. As time went by, I knew our marriage was in big trouble.

His silence was real and was meant to hurt. The longer he kept up this type of punishment, the stronger his determination seemed to become. This attitude was killing to me. He had no trouble living without talking because this had become another weapon in controlling and degrading me. If a situation came up and he didn't like it, his reaction was the silent treatment. If we had an argument, it usually ended in the same way. In the beginning of our marriage, his silence would last only a couple of hours: then it became an entire day. As the years passed, a month, two months, even six months of not speaking was nothing unusual. I felt like he was Goliath and I was David, but without a stone or a sling.

The local police were becoming frequent callers. It was terrible to live in a house under such conditions. I wanted to run away, but where was I going with three young boys (Paul and his two brothers, whom I will introduce shortly) and no money of my own? I didn't have the courage to uproot them. How could I ever provide a decent life for them on a typist's salary? Where would I go? Everything was in Pepper's name, including the car. During our many arguments, I often shouted, "I'm leaving; I'm taking the kids and we're going!" Pepper always got in the last word: "Go ahead, leave. Just remember, when you walk out, you loose the rights to this house. Don't touch the car, or I'll have you picked up by the police. You better think about it, baby!" His cutting words always left me feeling weak and helpless. I had three kids who needed me. I was trapped. An emptiness filled my entire body. So much was missing from our lives. I did my everyday chores, but nothing changed. I thought, "How can people live like this?" It was impossible to talk to him. If I questioned his love for me, he would only answer, "Grow up!" This living hell became a big part of our life. Those times our hate relationship was at its strongest. Physical abuse joined our living hell. No matter what, I couldn't fight back. He was stronger than me. I felt helpless. There was no love, only tormented, never-answered questions; we were left with only our actions, wondering how we ever got to this point. "Love" became a meaningless word in a torturous environment.

Pepper knew how to play the game well. Whenever we had company or friends stop by, he spoke around me. At the dinner table, he only addressed

the kids. No matter how hard I tried to be a part of the conversation, he had a way of keeping me out. He never looked at me or spoke to me. He made me feel like I didn't exist. No matter how long the silence continued, it tore at my guts. I felt like I was being destroyed mentally. I could never understand what pleasure he got by acting like that. I would beg him to talk to me. I would cry, throw things at him, anything to try to get him to talk. I acted like a child having a tantrum. I couldn't stop myself as I watched the expression on his face change from anger to delight. He was proud of his meanness. Years passed and nothing changed. Goliath continued to win battle after battle while David was still searching for a way to fight back, trying not to fall apart completely.

Pepper never spoke of his service years, and whenever I asked, he always said he was glad he had come home alive. I never knew how much the memories of World War II remained within him. Pepper never told me about the nightmares he experienced after he was discharged from the service. During the first few months of our marriage, his screams, outbursts, and thrashing about in our bed would wake both of us. I would try to calm him as we paced back and forth in our small bedroom. It made me realize the agonizing pain he was carrying.

Beside his mental anguish, there were mornings when he couldn't get out of bed. His legs and feet would be swollen and too painful to stand on. Finally, I convinced him to go to the Veterans Administration hospital in Newark for help. While he was overseas, his legs and feet had been frostbitten. He refused to sign up for any veteran's disability benefits. There was little the VA could do to help him. They tried to alleviate the pain in his legs and feet, but nothing worked. He didn't want anything from the government. I often wondered if any of his anger came from the toll the war had taken on his body.

OUR THIRD CHILD, KEVIN TIMOTHY FERRIS MARTIN   Kevin was born on June 20, 1956. He, too, was another charmer. About three months later, I started working at home by taking care of working mothers' children. Kevin grew up with a gang of kids and never knew a home empty of

Kevin holding the fishing rod while Paul displays his fish and I pet Bubbles, our dog.

Kevin, Morris Township, New Jersey, police officer.

children. He enjoyed all his playmates. Like Paul, Kevin gave me little trouble. He always minded me, and I never had to do much hollering or spanking. Maple Avenue was a good street to raise kids on. The boys were always outside playing with the other neighborhood boys. At the end of the street was a large, empty cornfield (now known as Simon's Playground). There the boys played all kinds of games. Billy Dempsey, Kevin Frain, John Boudreau, and Chris Grant were his buddies. They shared a great, fun-filled childhood. They were typical boys who never got into any serious trouble. Their teen years were also good years. Kevin joined Paul in his love for motorcycling and racing.

When Kevin was about six years old, I noticed his heart was pounding.

I had never seen anything like that before. Pepper was in the office, and I called him to come and look at Kevin. We took Kevin down to the emergency room, and the doctor found he had WPW syndrome. His heart would beat extremely rapidly, 220 beats a minute. He had to go on special medication and for years lived with this problem. A few years ago, a new operation was available that could, we all hoped, correct this medical problem. Kevin had the operation in 2001. It was successful.

WINNING A CAR: MY 1956 RED FOUR-DOOR PLYMOUTH It was a delightful Sunday afternoon late in September of 1956, a perfect day to take a ride out into the country and buy the last fresh-picked corn and a few

tomatoes. The season was pretty much over for vegetables such as these favorites. Pepper's football game wasn't going to be on TV until late in the afternoon, so I suggested that he could drive us and that perhaps we could stop for a hamburger or hot dog. With some hesitation, he agreed, so I got the kids in the car, and we were off.

Well, it became a disaster shortly after we left the Morristown area. Both kids began crying. Pepper was getting upset and kept telling me to make them shut up. Family outings were not one of Pepper's more favorite things to do. No matter what I did or said, I could not quiet either child. A short time later,

Kevin's wife, Mindy, and their children, Kelsey and Travis, with Papa and Baby Beau, our dog.

Pepper said he had enough and that we were going home. He turned the car around, and we headed back home. It seemed as if total quietness pervaded our surroundings by that time. By now, it was too late. The ride had been ruined. The kids had stopped crying!

As we were going up Speedwell Avenue, I noticed a raffle stand that had been set up by one of our local church organizations. They were selling tickets for a car that was going to be raffled off the following evening. The organization was having a dance, and at 11:30 P.M., they were going to pick the winning number. I asked Pepper to stop so I could take a chance (for only fifty cents per chance). He kept on going. I asked him again to stop, but he would not. I shrugged and said, "Well, I thought I might have a good chance on winning, seeing the car is going to be raffled off tomorrow night." That was it.

About two blocks down the avenue, he pulled over and said, "Now, if you want a ticket so bad, walk back, and get one." I was surprised by his actions. As I opened the door to get out, I said, "I'm going to win that damn car just because of your nastiness." He laughed. I walked back to the stand and bought my one ticket.

Me, summer of 1959.

The next evening, I decided to go to bed early and suggested that he wait up because I was going to win the car. Pepper just said, "Go on to bed." As I started upstairs, I said, "Be sure to answer the phone when it rings." Again, he told me to go to bed and knock that nuisance off.

Well, at 11:30 P.M. the phone rang, and, guess what—Pepper answered the phone, and to his surprise, his friend, Johnny Courtet, told him that *I had won the car.* Johnny was attending the function, and when my name was announced as the winner, he told the committee that he would call me because he knew us.

Pepper was shocked and immediately woke me. After my conversation with Johnny, I turned to Pepper and said, "You see, I knew I was going to win when you made me walk two blocks back to get one fifty-cent ticket." I shook my head and went back to bed with a very big smile on my face.

The next day, we went down to the dealer who had the car. Pepper asked me if I had the money to pay the taxes. I looked at him with complete bewilderment and said, "What do you mean?" "Well," he said, "if you don't have the money, I guess I'll have to pay for it. If that's the case, I want the car in my name; otherwise, you can just leave the car where it is." I couldn't believe it. He was dead serious. He paid the taxes, and the car was put in his name. He was the owner! It was his car! What could I do? I had no money of my own except my weekly grocery money, which never lasted very long.

PROMISES AND DEMANDS OF THE CATHOLIC CHURCH   When I married Pepper, I had to make several promises: (1) We would not use any form of birth control; (2) Any children we had would be brought up in the Catholic faith; and (3) We must be married by a Catholic priest and live by the Church's rules. I knew little about the Catholic faith. I was still a member of the First Baptist Church, even though I seldom went. However, as time

went by, I began to realize that we should be worshiping together as a family. It was not until after my encounter with my guardian angel that I realized the importance of this.

I knew I was still living with all my fears. I also knew that my phobia, or whatever a doctor might call it, was taking over my life. I was going downhill and couldn't stop myself. My panic attacks usually got worse during church services, especially when I wanted to take Communion. Living in fear of possibly fainting or making a fool of myself as I walked down that long aisle to receive the body and blood of Christ suffocated me. What could I do? Pepper couldn't understand my problem. Just watching him shake his head at me said it all. He refused to listen to me. I needed his help, understanding, and most of all, some concern from him about the hell I was going through. Where were his love, his gentleness, and his caring? Emotionally, Pepper chose anger to deal with my problem. He refused to even talk about it. I felt lost and ashamed. I wanted to shrink into nothing. It seemed as if I was reliving my past with all its mixed emotions. I was alone then, and alone now, trying to survive in an atmosphere of turmoil.

It took me years to overcome these feelings, but I have often thought that my survival was due to the help I received from my guardian angel. I found myself praying and thanking God for getting me though each day. My prayers were quieting for me. I wanted desperately to unravel this frightened shell of a person and find the real me that had stayed hidden for so many years. Each step was more painful than the previous one, but a force inside me gave me the courage I needed. I no longer carried the guilt of that second pregnancy because I believed God knew I was losing what little strength I had.

He sent me my angel to protect me, guide me, and give me the strength I needed to get though today and tomorrow. He spared my little boy from a life of terrible pain he would have had if he had survived. God took him to rest peacefully throughout eternity, wrapped within His special love. What more can I say? Has my angel been with me all these years? I want to believe she never left me and is still that force that comes through when I need it the most.

PEPPER'S SIDE OF THE FAMILY It was June 20, 1963, around 7:00 P.M. when we received a call from Lucy, who was married to Larry, Pepper's brother. They lived just a few doors down the street from us, as did Pepper's father and stepmother. She told me that Larry had hanged himself in their

Pepper's mother, Bridget Mary Delehant (seated) on her wedding day, 1917.

Pepper's mother and father, "Pop," with the family dog.

cellar. His son, Bruce, had just found him. We were shocked. Lucy and Larry had four children, Bruce, Maureen, Michael, and Peter. We never dreamed Larry was that depressed or had problems that would cause him to commit suicide.

It was a painful time for the entire family. However, I admired Lucy for her strength and courage. After the funeral and the initial shock were over, she returned to nursing at All Souls Hospital. Lucy worked the night shift and kept her home going as if nothing had happened. I really don't know how she did it. She cleaned, cooked, baked, washed, attended PTAs and church activities, fixed and repaired things that broke down. She was an unbelievable woman. She created a family that, to this day, remains a strong force. They still have a special closeness.

A few years later, Lucy decided to move the family to California. It was a complete surprise, but as she said, "We need a change in our lifestyle." She and the kids began packing. Maureen had just graduated from

nursing school. Michael and Peter were eleven and nine years old, respectively. It was going to be their adventure of a lifetime, and that is exactly how it turned out. They settled in the San Diego area.

Since Pepper and I had never been to California, we flew out several times to visit them. Every time we went, Lucy and the kids had our trip all planned. We never stopped. Old Town was one of our favorite places to visit. Lucy introduced us to an original Marguerita drink. My, they were good. We drove down to Tijuana, Mexico, and left with mixed feelings about this city. The poverty was unbelievable. Lucy took us on top of one of the local hills to show us the horrendous squalor in which the poor Mexican people lived. She also warned us not to get out of the car. They lived in cardboard shacks without water or sanitary facilities. One shack after another sprawled as far as the eye could see. Pepper got out of the car, and within seconds, he was surrounded by small children going through his pockets, hands held out, begging for money. It was a pathetic sight. He had all he could do to get back into the car. Lucy and her children took us up to the Hearst Castle. We went from poverty to riches. Seeing that castle with its over-abundance of wealth was sickening when, just a hundred miles south, people were living worse than animals.

Francis Matthew "Pepper" Martin at age three.

When Maureen was married, we flew out to attend her wedding. On the day of the wedding, the groom's pants zipper broke. Ed, the groom, got a safety pin, hoping it would solve his unexpected problem. However, it didn't work. Ed was desperate. Guests were arriving. The family was running around, trying to find someone who could fix it. Maureen knew that I sewed, but I had never fixed a man's zipper. Aunt Teeny became the hero of the day. It was a most unusual affair because they had a

Standing (l–r): Lawrence, Mary, and Pepper. Pop squatting in front.

luau on the beach as well as an indoor reception in their oceanfront home. It took us all by surprise. Instead of a bar, they had a figurine in a fountain where the drinks just kept pouring out. I had never seen anything like it. Their black Labrador retriever bounced between the ocean waves and the luau food. Filled with laughter and fun, it was the most informal wedding we ever attended.

As the years went by, the boys married and started their own families. The only one who did not go west was Bruce. After he found his dad dead, he developed many mental problems and stayed in New Jersey. Pepper tried to help him, but it was impossible. Bruce finally married a girl from Pennsylvania and had two children. It was a difficult marriage. Pat, his wife, stayed with him until he died of lung cancer in the early 1990s.

On August 2, 1966, Pepper's father, Joseph Patrick Martin, died at All Souls Hospital. He also lived on Maple Avenue across the street from Larry's home. "Pop" as everyone called him, died on my son Brian's birthday. Pop was born in Clagy Beg, Armagh, Northern Ireland, and came to this country when he was seventeen years old. He had a sister over in Ireland, Mary McGuire, whom Pepper and I met when we went there. Pop's other sister, Lillie McKenna, moved to Australia when she was a young woman. Little

was known about his background because the family seldom spoke of it. I know his had been a hard life.

Pop's mother was from Northern Ireland, and his father was from southern Ireland. His mother died after having several children. His father separated the children by placing Pop in the hands of the local parish priest and sent the other children to Northern Ireland to be raised by their mother's family. (I wish I knew their entire story. Perhaps it would explain the terrible coldness and lack of love that seemed to exist within the family over a multitude of decades.) At that time, Ireland was wrapped in terrible misery, and hatred reigned. It was a divided country, each side hating the other. Only the wealthy landowners had a decent life.

I know little about Pepper's mother or her family except that she had died on July 18, 1943, while Pepper was in service. Her maiden name was Bridget Mary Delehant. She was born in Ireland on May 10, 1887, and came to the United States around 1915. She was approximately ten years older than Pop. Upon arriving in New York City, she worked as a domestic in many wealthy homes. After she married Pop, she obtained day work around the Morris Plains area as a cleaning woman. I remember hearing Pepper say that when he was a child, she took him with her and had him help her. Whenever he spoke of his mother, it was always in a loving way. I feel that their entire life had been hard and lacked the gentler emotions.

Pepper had a sister, Mary, who also suffered a terrible life. When Pop married Kitty, a year after Pepper's mother died, Mary was committed to Greystone Psychiatric State Hospital in Greystone Park, New Jersey. Kitty had three children, but because the house was very small, only the youngest of them, Robert, lived with his mother

Pepper in full field pack, including steel helmet (note cartridge belt).

*Lucy Martin, our sister-in-law
and a great lady.*

*Our niece, Maureen, and her
husband, Dr. Edward Nowell,
on their wedding day.*

*Our nephew, Michael,
and his wife, Kathy*

*Our nephew, Peter, and his two
children, Patrick and Sarah*

and Pop. The other two, Patricia and Edward, lived with other family members. I know that Pepper was shocked when he come home from the service and found his sister in the local state mental hospital. He always felt that Kitty was behind Mary's incarceration.

Mary remained in the state hospital for thirty years. After living in this environment for so long, she became completely "institutionalized." Pepper had a hard time accepting his sister's so-called mental condition. I visited Mary many times and even brought her to our home for an afternoon. She loved being with my kids, but they never understood Mary's problems and lacked the excitement she felt. My heart ached for this poor creature because she always carried the stigma of being a patient in a mental institution. It was a sad and horrible story. Mary died around 1993 from emphysema.

During the late 1970s or early 1980s, a law went into effect that gave every person in mental institutions individual rights, and the state began releasing many patients. Mary was released and ended up living in several different boarding homes around East Orange, New Jersey. The State of New Jersey provided money for these patients. After this move, her life was no better than it had been when she was hospitalized. I saw the pathetic conditions in which those patients lived. It was a law that should never have been passed. These so-called boarding homes helped to create the massive number of homeless people. Many left those homes because they found it better and easier to live on the streets. Once they had been left on their own, many failed to take their medication, and this has become a big problem for our society.

PAULINE AND HER FAMILY During 1951, Pauline met Andy. He lived in Ogdensburg, about five miles from Lake Mohawk. She had just begun her senior year at St. Elizabeth's Academy for Girls when the family moved into their new lakefront home. However, by November 1951, Pauline found herself pregnant. Mother insisted that she continue with her education at the Academy. Each month, Pauline was showing more and more.

It was all so strange. I will never forget how Mother handled Pauline's pregnancy. It was like nothing had happened. Life went on just like everything was fine. Few words were spoken about their problem. No one cried,

shouted, or bothered to load the 12-gauge for a shotgun wedding. Mother kept saying, "It will go away. Let's not talk about it. I know it will go away." That was it!

I honestly felt that Mother lived in denial for months. Florence and I were not allowed to talk to Pauline about her "condition" or what she should expect. Mother preferred the word "condition" rather than "pregnancy." God, I felt sorry for Pauline. The one time she needed support from her family, she received nothing. I can't help but feel that she suffered a great deal mentally. I never asked her, and she never said anything about it. Pauline continued going to the Academy, getting larger as each month passed. The world outside our family was buzzing with the news of Pauline's pregnancy. Quietly, Mother, Dad, and Mrs. Hete, Andy's mother, made arrangements for Pauline and Andy to marry. Pauline, eight and a half months pregnant, graduated from St. Elizabeth's Academy. My heart ached for her. I honestly don't know how she managed to hold it all together. Pauline's diploma came in the mail. She was a pregnant child, a married child, and a soon-to-be-mother who was still walking in the shoes of a child. Andy was working in the mines in Ogdensburg. Their daughter, Susan, was born in July 1952.

In the meantime, Dad found a small house that was perfect for Andy and Pauline. The rent was affordable, and it was located just outside of Lake Mohawk. We loved visiting them because it was like a dollhouse. The sound of the swift-moving stream that ran nearby would have moved any poet or artist. Even the birds became a part of this back-to-nature scene. The weeping willow trees that lined the banks of the stream were the backdrop for the many different songbirds. This shallow stream also served as the watering hole for many local animals. It was a serene scene, one that I never forgot. The newlyweds had settled in by the time Pauline had Susan. Somehow their love for each other survived. I believe that they were just a couple of young kids who needed each other desperately for whatever reason. This charming and peaceful home became a source of solace that generated some of their happiest moments.

In 1955, their son, John, was born. As best I can remember, he was a little runt, skinny, tough, and at times, as cute as a button and at other times, a

terror. As he grew though, he became uncontrollable, extremely active, and unpredictable. When John was around six years old, he and the kids were playing a game when he ran into a tree with such force that Florence and I could not believe he was still standing. However, he dropped quickly to the ground. By the time we got to him, he was dazed. I screamed for someone to call an ambulance, but the family felt that he would be okay and made no effort to get medical help. His forehead resembled the bark of the tree, which had left pinhole marks across its entirety. Blood began to run down his face. I picked him up and ran to the house, where Mother cleaned and bandaged his wound. By the next day, his face was horribly black and blue. I often wondered if this severe blow to his head helped create the many problems he had throughout his life.

John and Kevin were less than a year a part, and their relationship as cousins became close. Pauline and I had a good relationship as sisters, at least during that time. Pepper was always fond of Pauline and accepted Andy because he knew that Pauline loved him. After a move to Randolph and, later, to West Orange, they found an old but charming country home near Califon. It had everything that Pauline needed: a large stable for several horses, an ideal area for raising her dogs, an in-ground swimming pool with a patio, and lots of privacy provided by the large fields that surrounded them. By now Andy was working in Dad's roofing business.

John's grammar school years were hard because his short attention span and difficult attitude had become a concern to everyone involved with his education. The school was unable to met John's educational needs. His emotional needs were being seriously neglected, since he did not respond to any help that Pauline tried to get him. A special-education teacher spoke to them concerning John, but unfortunately, they turned a deaf ear. By the time John reached the age of thirteen, the entire family began going to Family Services for help.

The family continued with one problem after another. Susan had become very defiant. Terrible fights took place between John and his father. Pauline and Andy had one more child by this time. His name was Paul, but because of the difference in the boys' ages, he grew up pretty much as an only child. Paul did not have mental scars like his other two siblings.

When Susan was a teenager and staying with my parents, I received a call from Mother, who said that Susan had hit her when she asked her to clean up the kitchen. To make a long story short, I called her mother, Pauline, and told her to come down and take Susan back home because Mother could no longer control her. I tried to talk to Susan, but it was useless. She made it very clear that I was to mind my own business. She was right, but definitely wrong in her actions. Pauline finally arrived and took Susan back home. Within a week, Pauline had had enough of Susan's nasty disposition and brought her back to live with her grandparents. This constant moving from her home to her grandparents home became a way of life for Susan until she graduated from high school and married. I saw more and more signs that our entire family seemed to be seriously dysfunctional.

I began to see a change in Mother's attitude toward me. I was the only one of her girls whom she called when she needed help or had a serious problem. Florence and her family had stopped all relations with our parents about a year after they were married. That all began when Ray asked Dad if he could borrow a large sum of money to pay for some equipment he needed. Dad told him he had to think it over and see if he could afford to do this. However, Ray didn't wait and went ahead and bought the necessary items. When he came to get his money, Dad told him that he wasn't able to loan him any money and that Ray should have never ordered the equipment until Dad had given him the okay. Ray went a little nuts, screaming and cursing at Dad. I heard him from my third-floor window and knew something was very wrong. I looked out and saw Ray pacing up and down the yard screaming at my dad. That pretty much ended what relationship there was between Dad and Ray. After that, we saw very little of the Moss family.

Pauline and her family depended on Dad for a lot of their luxuries. Pauline had two Great Danes that were considered housedogs. They loved her, especially Ajax. At the same time, she and Susan got involved in riding horses and she eventually owned several. My father usually paid for whatever this adventure called for. Between her dogs and horses, Pauline found her life rewarding. She was more comfortable around her farm animals than she was around people. A lovely pond on their property was occupied by a family of wild geese.

According to Pauline, one evening, she and Andy got into a heated argument. As Andy approached Pauline, Ajax jumped over the gate, growling, showing his teeth, and heading toward Andy. Pauline screamed. The dog was powerful and ready to defend Pauline. Just at that moment, John came into the room and managed to get the dog off Andy, and he put Ajax in the basement. When John came back upstairs, all hell broke loose.

Pauline called Pepper and asked him to meet her and John in the emergency room of the Morristown Memorial Hospital. She told him that Andy and she had an argument in which John had gotten involved and injured his dad. Pepper left immediately, and when he met Pauline, she told him what had happened. John had picked up a sickle and struck his father in the neck, a quarter inch from his jugular vein. Andy had bled like a stuck pig. Pauline had called the police to get an ambulance to the home immediately, and then she had called Pepper.

Andy needed stitches because the cut was deep and severe. The doctor told Pepper that John was very lucky he hadn't killed his dad. The police wanted Andy to press charges, but Pauline told him that if he did, she would leave him. Andy did not press charges.

Pauline told the police that the family had been in family counseling many times, but apparently it hadn't helped their situation. I believe the police noted that John needed immediate help, and they were going to issue an order for his parents to get it. Pepper told me that John struck out at Andy because he knew what his father had been doing and he didn't want his Mother to be hurt. Pepper asked the police to wait and bring Andy home. Pauline and John were exhausted and needed to calm down. Pepper stayed until the police arrived with Andy, and then he came home.

During 1974, when Kevin was in his senior year at Bayley Ellard High School, the school sponsored a skiing trip to Mt. Saint Anne, outside of Montreal, Quebec, Canada, for a week. Kevin was into skiing at this time and was excited about going. We gave our permission and, then he told us that he asked the people in charge if John could go with him because he loved skiing as well. They gave their permission because other students had

also asked if they could bring along a friend. Pauline and Andy gave their okay, and we saw the boys off. As their bus rolled out of sight, I prayed that nothing would go wrong.

Kevin felt a great deal of compassion for John and was always trying to include him in things that he thought John would enjoy. However, it was during this trip that Kevin began to see that John was heading for big trouble. Every night, they and the other students left the lodge to wander about the French-Canadian village. They were eager to take in the atmosphere of the local pubs. The locals spoke French, and even though Kevin had had four years of French, the only French that he remembered was "deux beers," which means "two beers." In the evening, these pubs harbored the local young people, known as "Canucks." These young men were rough and ready to rumble with anyone who wanted a go-around. They were used to hard living, and this was their entertainment. This was their "turf." Kevin said, "That was all John needed to see. His delight was in looking for some way to get a fight going, not as a participant, only as a spectator."

Later that same winter, Pauline allowed John to go to Switzerland on a skiing trip organized by a local group in their area. The trip turned out to be a disaster. He had no sooner arrived at the ski lodge, located near Zurich, than he began calling home. He said that the CIA was after him and that he had to return home immediately. Pauline tried to convince him that everything was all right. No one was after him. She tried to encourage him to stay. He swore that the government wanted him dead. No matter where he went, "they" were lurking, watching and waiting for the right moment to take him. John was terrified. After a couple of days of trying to cope with all the voices, he came home. John had become a paranoid schizophrenic and needed help. Again he was calling out for help, but when it was available, he refused to get involved. He blamed all his problems on his family and was haunted by the fact that he had almost killed his father.

A few years after Pauline and Andy moved to Montana during the mid-seventies and eighties, John began living, on and off, with Pepper and me in the late-1970s and through most of the 1980s. Throughout these years, I saw John in many different situations and observed his troubled mind. I had

to admit him several times to the psychiatric department of Morristown Memorial Hospital, as well as the Greystone Park Psychiatric Hospital. When he became impossible, I had to ask him to leave our home. He would then become homeless until he either came to my door for help or some one called me about him and his condition. When he was discharged from one of the hospitals, he would be placed in state boarding homes. But when he got tired of those places, he would go back to the streets, living in deserted cars, boxes, benches, deserted buildings, or any place where he could lay down. Occasionally, he would go to one of the local shelters or mission houses to get a meal, a shower, and a bed for the night. John was left to live whatever way he could.

I know how much John longed for his parents' affection from the time he was a youngster, but apparently he needed more than they were able to give. Neither parent knew how to cope with their troubled son. They feared him, which I can understand. John seemed to be getting more and more involved with drugs and alcohol, and we all worried that substance abuse could become a way of life for him. Judging by his constantly changing array of "girlfriends," sex was becoming his hobby, and it seemed to me that his partners were in the same shape as he, lost souls drifting toward oblivion.

To this day, John remains in my thoughts, even though I haven't seen him in many years. I can't help but feel sorry for him. I just pray that he is no longer using drugs and that he is taking his prescribed medication on a regular basis. He had so many opportunities to overcome his problems; I sincerely hope that he has managed to put together a decent life for himself.

1960s THROUGH 1980s During these years I began quilting. Mother was very involved with the quilting group at the Presbyterian Church in Morris Plains, and I occasionally would go with her to their get-togethers because I wanted to learn the hand stitch used in quilting. Today, many quilters use sewing machines to do the work, but this quilting group did every stitch by hand. I quickly learned the stitch and began working on the Dresden-plate pattern. It took me three years to make Paul's quilt, which was for a full-size bed. I made a beautiful gold background. Each square

consisted of a multi-colored Dresden-plate design within so many squares. I cut out everything, and every stitch in my quilts was by hand. I made the same quilt for Kevin, but with a lavender background. It took me another three years to make that one. Both quilts were beautiful, and I was very proud to see what I had created. I used the fence-rail pattern, which has a more masculine appearance, for Brian's quilt. He preferred this pattern to the Dresden-plate design.

I enjoyed doing needlepoint and crocheting, but crewel was my favorite. It was good for the nerves, and I needed something to hold my attention when I had to wait up at night for one of my boys to come in. It was better than pacing the floor, wringing my hands, or working myself into a state of hysteria. When Kevin was ten years old, he earned enough money by raking fall leaves to buy me a needlepoint kit for a pillow cover. It was my Christmas gift from him. Kevin always loved one of my finished crewel pieces, which had a forest scene with a skunk, raccoon, and a chipmunk standing among many wild flowers. Just before he married, I had it framed and gave it to him.

Raising kids during the sixties and seventies became a constant confrontation between parents and their offspring. To quote Charles Dickens, "It was the best of times; it was the worst of times." Money was plentiful. Business was on an upswing. Prosperity was all around us. Our kids were still safe as they played on our streets. They could wander far beyond their neighborhoods without any fear of being harmed. We never had to worry about where they were when they were playing. The majority of women were still at home as wives and mothers, tending to their families' needs. Latchkey kids were not common then.

Hard drugs were now appearing on the scene, but had not yet invaded our neighborhoods or our schools. Sex was on the increase among our young. Virgins were considered old fashioned and were becoming as rare as the proverbial hens' teeth. Shacking up for a night or living together was now the lifestyle of our young adults. Homosexuals were coming out of the closet, gathering momentum as they grew in number, no longer afraid of public opinion. We felt safe because these problems only happened in other

families, other neighborhoods, or other areas of the country. Certainly not in ours! Never!

As I look back, changes came slowly. We believed that they were fads, but unfortunately, they were here to stay. It was easier not to face the truth and just laugh them off. We tried frantically to overlook the seriousness of the times, but these changes and new beliefs were worming their ways into our young peoples minds. We sat back, angry and disgusted, waiting for our children to get tired of living and thinking such radical beliefs. We only shook our heads, still not realizing or believing how the changes would eventually affect everyone's morals and values.

By the time these changes had invaded our homes, it was too late. We read about it in our local papers. We heard about the changes through song and dance. We watched the Vietnam War come into our living rooms through the news media every night. Hell was becoming our daily companion as we observed the ravages of war with all its violence and death. We saw and heard the many different anti-establishment groups emerge on every street corner throughout the country screaming against patriotism and loyalty towards one's country. They created disunity within families concerning morals, values, and principles.

Music was no longer soft and gentle. The anti-establishment groups sang their protests through the lyrics of their music. The dress code and appearance of our young took on a look of complete slovenliness. Young men were now wearing their hair very long, tied back in ponytails, hanging down over their shoulders, or covering their faces. The new fad invaded the homes of the wealthy as well as those of the poor. No family was spared.

Anti-establishment groups were prevalent throughout many of the colleges and universities, provoking riots and disharmony within them. The murder of the young people at Kent State by our own government left the country in a state of shock and created disillusionment with the government. A group of students began protesting against the war and the establishment by rioting on the campus. It got out of hand and the government sent in troops to squelch it and disperse the students. They never believed that the National Guard would fire live ammunition at them. Questions about why

this happened and how the situation reached the point of murder still remain bewildering. Chaos had invaded our country as well as our lives.

America's young men were once again going off to war. It was the Vietnam War era! At first, Pepper and I believed that each young man had a responsibility to his country. However, as the war continued, we began seeing the unfairness in the government's drafting of the men in this country. Because this war was never declared an official war, any young man who didn't want to be drafted and had enough money behind him, entered college, left the country, or went underground to disappear within the anti-establishment groups. We began hearing our friends talk about how they weren't going to let their kids be sent over there. This was not a declared war! We could not understand their thinking, but as time passed, we changed our minds and felt as they did.

A demonstration against the war was held on the Morristown Green in 1970 by the local hippies, among whom were many of our own children. Marijuana, as well as more severely mind-destroying drugs, was being used heavily by the youth. These hippies were well known for carrying peace signs and creating a disturbance wherever and whenever they felt they had a cause. They hitchhiked around the country on a dime, holding up cardboard signs showing their destination, waiting for a car to pick them up. They were filthy with their long hair, beards, and ragged garments.

The young men who did go to Vietnam came back home only to be cursed by the public, looked down on as drug addicts, drunkards, and killers of women and babies. The American people plus our government did a terrible injustice to these men who gave up so much. It was twenty-five years later before our country finally recognized them and gave them the respect and honor they so well deserved, even though the damage had already been done. "The Wall" in Washington, D.C., gave the Vietnam veterans a sense of pride and closure for the first time. The American people realized the terrible wrong our country did to the returning Vietnam vets. As we gazed at the number of names on "The Wall", it sent shivers up our spines. It showed the world the awful waste of young men who were killed or missing in action by a war that was never declared a war.

MY MANY JOBS   During 1954, I began part-time employment at Morristown Memorial Hospital. I worked in the accounts-payable/accounts-receivable department as a clerk. I worked odd hours that did not conflict with my duties at home. I remember one particular male co-worker. Because he was younger than I, I was surprised by his kindness, his willingness to help me, and his innocent ways. He lacked everything that was typical of macho men. I found myself fantasizing about being married to a man with this type of personality and compared him to the men who were a part of my life. I had little experience with any men other than my dad and husband. The few men whom I did know were only casual acquaintances. My shyness and fears kept me a good distance away.

One day, my co-worker came to work wearing an elegant raccoon coat. Everyone in the room looked up, but to my surprise, no one was impressed. I was mesmerized. It was something out of the Roaring Twenties. Most of us would have only seen a coat like that in some movie. I said, "Oh, my God, what a beautiful coat." To which he replied, "My friend gave it to me, Teeny. Thank you. I love it." Again I looked at him and watched his face beam with delight. I sighed, "Oh, I wish I had a friend like that." He took my hand and patted it.

I heard my other co-workers giggle as if something were funny. I turned and asked, "What's so funny?" Eleanor came over and suggested that we go on break. The thought of a good cup of coffee sounded nice. I joined her and the other women, never thinking that there was a reason behind their unexpected invitation. On the way to the cafeteria, they began to tell me about my co-worker. They said that he was homosexual. To their shock, I said, "What in the hell is that?" They starred at me, disbelieving that such innocence still existed. Immediately, they all began to speak at once. I looked at them, each one, wanting to educate me on this very shaded side of life. Having never heard the word "homosexual," I now had a new word to add to my vocabulary. Finally, they quieted down and began to explain its meaning. I sat in disbelief as I heard the definition. "God! Is that what it means? Why didn't you tell me this long ago? Why did you let me sit here and make a fool out of myself?" They admitted that they had no idea I was

so uninformed about life and people. In a way, I wish I never learned about my co-worker's private life and what the word "homosexual" means. I resented having my own innocence exposed by my co-workers. So much for the word "homosexual." However, I could not hurt this kind and gentle man by disassociating myself from him. Our friendship continued over the many years we both were employed by the hospital. I worked over a year in the accounting department.

As I have mentioned, after Kevin was born in 1956, I began watching working mothers' children in my home. Kevin never knew our home to be without kids as he grew up with many of them. Some of these children, I watched for years. I always felt that this helped Kevin have such a nice disposition. Paul never liked my babysitting. These children took my attention away from him. He could not adjust to any of this and was too young to understand why I had to work.

My babysitting job came about when Pepper told me that I needed to bring in money without going out to work. He needed to re-invest his money into building up the business. He had it all figured out that my job could cover the household expenses. I was puzzled about what to do until I came up with the idea of babysitting for working mothers. The first thing I had to do was get a Morris Township Board of Health license, which would allow me to take care of children in my home. It also entitled the Board of Health to come into my home anytime of the day or night. I also obtained Lords of London Insurance on my services. This protected me in case I was sued by any of the parents. This insurance also covered the child in case of injury or accident while in my home. This type of policy was extremely expensive, but it was absolutely necessary.

Before I knew it, many mothers who just needed to get away for a couple of hours also left their babies or children with me. My business grew. I had to hire two women to come in every day and help me. My home was always spotless. I had some kids who stayed with me while their parents went away for a week or two. I did extremely well. However, all of the money I earned went into the household expenses. I took care of children for ten years and, as everyone knows, it was very hard work. I amazed myself by what I was

able to accomplish on my own. Oh, Florence Puzon, where are you now with your test showing my IQ was that of an idiot? I learned quickly that I had a lot to offer and knew how to work.

For many years, on and off, I continued working in different departments throughout the Morristown Memorial Hospital. These positions were on a part-time, weekend-only basis, working 3:00 P.M. to 11:00 P.M. or the midnight shift. My favorite job was as a medical secretary in the emergency room. I found the environment fascinatingly unpredictable because a different situation was always presenting itself. Between gun shot wounds, heart attacks, broken bones, bleeding, traumas of all kinds, etc., I became acquainted with another side of life I had never seen. Dealing with the public was an education in itself. The confusion that seemed to erupt out of nowhere kept each of us on an emotional high from the beginning of the shift until we were well on our way home.

It was in this part of the hospital that I began to feel myself changing. During 1977 through 1980, I worked full time in X-ray, transcribing pathology, autopsy, and general X-ray reports. We watched as our workplace grew, but we came to feel that "bigger" only meant "corporate." The comfortable family environment we had worked in was disappearing.

At this time, I joined a team of volunteers who were taking courses through the Morris County Courts in order to learn how to work with juvenile delinquents. I found this work exciting, and it gave me a better understanding of the breakdown of families and how it affects the children involved. Before long, I was asked to work with women who had been released from prison but were still on parole. I had to make weekly visits to their homes and put together information for their parole officers. It was interesting. For the first time, I felt as if I were experiencing an inside view of what sociology was all about. I was surprised to find that my earlier dreams of going into journalism and sociology were still gnawing at my gut. I did this type of work for a few months, but the areas that I had to visit were making me feel threatened, and I decided I should do something less dangerous.

I began working at AT&T in 1981. My family needed full medical benefits, leaving me with no choice but to continue working. AT&T paid well. I

opened my own checking account and stopped contributing toward our bills. I obtained an American Express card in order to build my own credit record. I was finally becoming my own person. The different departments that I worked in always had a great deal of overtime, which I loved. My paycheck looked great. I just wish Florence Puzon could see one of them. I was proud of what I could do and accomplish. An IQ of an idiot! I don't think so.

By the time Pepper had to retire, I had accumulated six years with AT&T. I was an excellent employee, always receiving high appraisals, always completing every task to the best of my ability. I took my job seriously. I was responsible, accurate, and never afraid to tackle any job that was given me. Many district managers asked for me when they needed a secretary or clerk. They considered me a professional. I earned every penny, however.

The fears that I had lived with for most of my life were beginning to leave me. I began to recognize my own abilities in the workforce; something that I had really never experienced before. At work, I felt good. I began to notice how inept so many of my younger peers were. Most could not write a simple letter, nor spell correctly, nor create huge worksheets. However, it was they who became management. To make matters worse, I was in my mid-fifties and began to realize that it was my age that kept me from being promoted. I had reached "Level Six," which was the highest level for occupational workers, and I knew that I would never go any further. The older women did the real work. That really hurt! That was how the corporate world operated during the 1980s, but they would never admit it. Sex discrimination is no longer accepted, but nothing else has really changed. Even now, in 2003, the corporate world often gives a raw deal to both women and men over the age of fifty!

I did question, many times, why I was never promoted. Their excuses were ingenuous, which left me frustrated. However, twelve years later, I had to admit that my years at AT&T paid off well. My benefits, pension, and overtime made up for my disappointments in never becoming "management."

During 1988 through 1990, even though I was employed full-time with AT&T, I went back to the emergency room, working every weekend for those two years. In other words, I worked continuously, seven days a week.

It became a source of therapy for me as time passed. It was my excuse and escape from Pepper, his illness, and the seesaw emotions we were living with. It felt good to be among my old co-workers and to be tackling, once again, the one job I truly loved. I always went home feeling good. It made me realize that my problems were small compared to those of many patients who came through those emergency room doors. I liked the confidence I was gaining through exercising my own abilities.

AT&T never gave me that feeling, but I no longer needed their approval. I knew I was a damn good worker, highly skilled in secretarial work and any other type of job they needed completed. My favorite job at AT&T was working in the Human Resource Department, Sickness Disability Group.

During these years, I also volunteered as a cook in the Presbyterian Church's shelter for the homeless. It seemed as if Morristown had a huge influx of homeless people who suddenly seemed to take over the park benches, many of the small alleyways, as well as our local railroad station. No matter where you looked, you saw the sad results of liquor, drugs, and mental illness in a group of decaying people. I'm sorry to say that my own nephew, John, was one of them. Once a week, I went to the shelter and became the cook for the night. I felt that I was giving back to a church that fed John and gave him a place to sleep and wash up when I could no longer have him in my home. I did this for a year or more, but some of the homeless men were becoming very aggressive, and I stopped before I was injured or raped. My dreams continued to stir within me as I found myself more and more involved in parts of society that most of us have never seen. In my own simple way, I felt that most of my jobs were wrapped around a small area of Sociology's perimeter. I got great satisfaction, and it made me feel good.

OUR FOURTH CHILD, BRIAN FRANCIS MARTIN Brian was born on August 2, 1961. Within a very short period of time, he developed severe colic. By his ninth month, his problem had become serious. Nothing was working. Finally, in desperation, I called Dr. Mintz. After trying every formula one could buy, Dr. Mintz ordered goat's milk for him. No more formula. At that time, goat's milk was hard to find, but one local dairy,

Kevin holding Brian on his christening day.

Alderney, had goats, and they made the milk available for us. It helped a great deal. Brian had to stay on it for a couple of years.

We no sooner had this problem solved when Brian began running off on me. As soon as he could walk, he was gone. He learned how to unlatch the back door by using the broom handle. That kid was always two steps ahead of me. By the time Brian was three and had disappeared from home several times, the police suggested that I get an identification bracelet and put it on his arm. Pepper put a fence up in the backyard to keep Brian in, but that was a waste of time and money. Brian would wiggle the fence until it just fell apart, and then off he would go. He was impossible to keep down. He was always a hyper child. As he grew, he became even more hyperactive. His kindergarten teacher told me that she could not handle him, and she thought that he and I needed to visit a psychiatrist. Dr. Mintz put Brian on Ritalin, hoping that would calm him down. Brian remained on that medication until he got into his teen years.

When Brian was ten years old, he developed mononucleosis. However, it took several months before this illness was diagnosed. Shortly after this, he began to develop a great deal of pain throughout his body. He had come down with juvenile rheumatoid arthritis. These illnesses never interfered with his determination to do what he wanted. His childhood and teen years were filled with fun. His stamina was unbelievable. Our neighbors, the Dempsey family, were Brian's second home. Pat Dempsey and Brian were inseparable. There friendship is still on going. They are like brothers.

In June 1980, Brian graduated from high school and went right into the U.S. Air Force. His basic training was in Texas, and from there he was sent

to several different bases. During 1981, Brian was sent to Mathers Air Force Base, outside of Sacramento. We decided to fly out to San Francisco, stay there for a few days, and then drive over to his base. I was thrilled to see how happy he was. When he said, "Boy, this is my life. I love the military," I thanked God.

After visiting Brian, we flew down to San Diego, to visit Lucy and the kids. While there, I collapsed and was taken to the local hospital. Maureen's husband, Ed, was a doctor in the emergency room, and he placed me under the best pulmonary doctor in Southern California. They found I had pneumonia and emphysema. The doctor had me drink freshly squeezed orange juice every time I wanted a cigarette. It worked. I never smoked after that. I remained in the hospital for ten days, which meant our visit had to be extended.

Brian had almost completed three years in the Air Force when he became ill. His sergeant had recommended him for promotion, but his medical condition worsened, forcing him to retire. He came home devastated because the military was going to be his career. For two years he was despondent. I didn't know what to do to help him. I was frantic. I knew the pain he was suffering, mentally and physically. Then, one day, his sergeant, Ken Roberts, called him and told him that he had been transferred to Rome, New York. He wanted Brian to come and visit him and his wife, Pat. It was a blessing in disguise. Brian always felt close to Ken. He admired him and had made Ken his mentor from the first day they met. Brian was eager to visit them. After he returned home, I saw a change in him: he seemed less depressed. He decided to move up to Rome because he could use all the base facilities. Once there, Brian got a small apartment and entered the State

Brian, age eight, with an Indian, Black Elk, at Mount Rushmore, South Dakota, on our trip out West.

University of New York (SUNY) program. He came home to gather his belongings, and for the first time, we saw our son happy and excited about his new beginnings. From this move, he completed college and received his four-year diploma, majoring in psychology. I was very proud of him.

Brian in U.S. Air Force dress uniform.

Brian now lives in the Shalimar, Florida, area. Ken retired from the United States Air Force and moved near Eglin Air Force Base, where he became employed as a retiree. Ken suggested that Brian move near them because the weather was warmer and the necessary medical facilities Brian needed were nearby. Brian packed up and followed because he considered Ken and Pat his second family. I will always be most grateful to this couple for making him such an important part of their lives.

Because of Brian's declining disability, he only does volunteer work at the Emerald Coast Wildlife Refuge for injured and orphaned wildlife. Before that, however, Brian volunteered at a Veterans Administration office for several years, advising discharged military personnel about their many benefits after discharge. He enjoyed this a great deal because he met so many men, young and old, who needed his help. Many of these men participated in World War II, the Korean War, or Vietnam. Many were veterans who encountered multiple minor skirmishes in Third World countries. No matter where or when they served in the military, Brian found that many veterans needed to talk about their military experiences. Brian became their listener and quickly realized that many of these men deserved tremendous respect and should receive every government benefit available.

A cute story regarding Brian's fashion trademark, "Ol' Red," just occurred as I was putting the finishing touches on this book. For years, we never saw Brian without "Ol' Red," his very special red hat with the University of Georgia bulldog on it as an emblem of its football team.

As the years passed, "Ol' Red" began showing its age, deteriorating right on top of Brian's head. Many times I tried to get Brian to invest in a new hat, but I always received the same comment, "'Ol' Red' has become a part of me. I will not part with it nor do I want a new hat. It must completely disintegrate before I will ever consider getting another." No matter what I thought or said, it was an impossible situation. I finally got smart and decided it was better to say nothing. If he was happy with it, fine. I threw my arms in the air and stopped complaining. "Ol' Red" stayed put!

The other day, I received this little e-mail message from Brian. I would like to share this in hopes that all my readers will enjoy it as much as I do. However, one must imagine the condition of "Ol' Red" after twenty-three years of hard service.

Dear Friends and Family,

It is with sadness in my heart to announce the demise of my fashion trademark, "Ol' Red." This article of clothing held out for over twenty-three years. It finally succumbed to exhaustion. I tip my hat (if I still had one) to the person who worked tirelessly on its conception. It flew with me on all my Air Force movements, including a brief dip in the Union Valley Reservoir on one of our squadron fishing trips. It was rumored that when I would drink, the further back I wore it the drunker I was. Maybe so…. It accompanied me to the many whorehouses in the Reno, Nevada area (Mom, only kidding. Don't panic!) during my more rollicking and youthful days in the United States Air Force. It survived a treacherous header onto busy New Jersey Route 287 while Pat Dempsey was driving me to Newark Airport for my flight back to base. My admiration and gratitude to Pat for having the stones to backup on that extremely busy highway in order for me to retrieve it before it became a red blotch, embedded forever in the highway's asphalt. "Ol' Red" survived many spin cycles through the washer, and although this action helped to contribute to its demise, it did aid in fashioning its unique appearance. Perhaps these thoughts might make a good endorsement for those of you who may be contemplating some minor body enhancement. In closing, I'd like to put forth a thought that the next time you see a hat with a special uniqueness and style, try to imagine what it took for it to advance to such status. "Ol' Red" 02 JUN 80–22 JUL 03

My only thoughts as I read of "Ol' Red's" demise were, "At last, thank God! I'm not sure if I will recognize my dear son without it. Yes, it's true. 'Ol' Red' is gone, but it will never be forgotten. Three cheers for the 'Ol' Red', and may Brian never find another fashion trademark that will literally disintegrate off his head. Rest in peace, 'Ol' Red.' Perhaps, now, Brian and I will no longer need to argue over you."

TYPICAL HOLIDAY DINNER WITH THE FAMILY The entire family had been invited for Thanksgiving dinner at Aunt Affie and Uncle Bud's home in Bloomfield, New Jersey. It was a beautiful day. Everyone was speaking to each other for a change, and this was a rare treat. However, turmoil was always present whenever the family did get together. Someone was usually on the outs with some other member, each one refusing to give in to the other. However, today was going to be different. Ha! Wishful thinking.

We were in good spirits and ready for some much needed laughter. Aunt Affie always had a funny story or joke to tell. Uncle Bud was his usual conservative, penny-pinching self, never failing to remind his guests how much this dinner was costing him. Bud was a graduate of Princeton University. He had worked his entire way through Princeton and was extremely proud of his accomplishment. Pepper and I admired him for this. However, Uncle Bud used this as a reminder of our own lack of a higher education. He put up with us for Aunt Affie's sake, and we did the same. Whenever we were invited to dinner at Auntie's house, Bud would always serve the meat to each individual. We, quickly, learned *never* to ask for more than one slice. To ask for a second piece would only mean humiliation at the hands of this intelligent man. Of course, my dad was the exception to this rule. I often thought that Bud was afraid of him, since he never quarreled with him. Dad always asked Bud for the fork so he could pick out his own meat. Bud always meekly gave it to him as his facial expression changed from a disgusting smugness to total despair. Dad never knew when to quit when Bud tried to pull this kind of nonsense. His comments ran like this: "You better go slice some more meat, Bud; only this time, please put some meat on the platter." Pathetically, Bud would obey, all the time letting

his other guests know how good that meat would taste the next day, especially in a sandwich.

Uncle Bud never failed to check each of us out as we were leaving, just to make sure we were not taking any of the leftovers home. However, Aunt Affie would always send one of us out the backdoor with a bag of goodies while someone else would hold Uncle Bud's attention at the front door. Anyway, before I go any further, I'd better finish my story about the fish and the two boys.

We had just finished the main course. Everyone was complaining about how full they were. Aunt Affie decided to clean off the table, put the food away, and do dishes before we had dessert and coffee. The men were enjoying the break because it gave them a chance to watch some of the football game. We women were helping in the kitchen. Susan and Paul were outside playing while John and Kevin were in the basement. They were quiet, and I was happy. Everything was going so smoothly. Little did I know that, within minutes, all hell would break loose.

The two kids came up from the basement and immediately went outside. I thought it was strange, but didn't give it a second thought. However, an uneasiness began to creep over me. I tried to convince myself that all was going well. I saw Uncle Bud going down the cellar stairs. Suddenly, we heard him scream out, "Those damn kids, where are they? My fish, my fish are all dead!" Everyone looked at each other, speechless. Apparently, Uncle Bud had gone down to feed his fish and had come upon the disastrous sight. He kept all the fish in one of two water-filled tubs: one had fresh water and the other had salt water. Unfortunately, none of us knew this, nor did the kids. Goldfish and salt water do *not* go together.

Well, I'm sure you can imagine what happened. John and Kevin were fascinated by Uncle Bud's strange and beautiful collection. However, the more they watched these beauties swim about, the more the poor fish looked overcrowded. Apparently, the kids felt sorry for them and decided to put a few in the other tub. They began to net them and, one by one, dropped their catch into the empty tub until both tubs held some. According to them, they felt that they were helping Uncle Bud. They couldn't understand why everyone

was so upset. They also wondered why Uncle Bud raised the fish to be sold. I tried to explain that each fish was considered valuable, but they really didn't understand the damage and upset they had caused. By the time Bud went to feed his collection, the fish that were in the salt water, were now floating on top.

Oh, my God, what could we say? He ranted on and on about our delinquent and destructive kids. We dared not say a word. Pepper and Andy tried to calm Bud, but to no avail. His fortune and hard work were now floating on top of the water. All he kept repeating was, "They're gone; they're dead." God, we felt terrible, but what could we do? The kids should've never touched anything in the fish room, but they did, and we were frantically trying to calm the situation.

We offered to pay for or replace the dead ones, but Bud was much too angry to reason with. Well, at this point, Aunt Affie decided it was time to serve coffee and dessert. No one felt like eating anything more. We just wanted to go home, but the boys first had to apologize to Uncle Bud. They looked like they were about to meet the firing squad as they meekly whispered, "Where is *he*? We heard him all the way outside. We didn't know that they were dead. We thought they were just sleeping."

What could any of us say? Our lovely get-together had just gone down the drain, as had the many fish. Well, Pepper again offered to pay for the damage, but Bud refused to take any money. Instead of saying goodbye, he announced that it would be better if we not come back anytime soon, and he then disappeared upstairs. In the meantime, Aunt Affie was busy in the kitchen putting together a bag of goodies for each family. She had Susan and Paul as her co-conspirators. They were to take the packages out the backdoor and put them into each car. Her orders were, "Don't let Uncle Bud catch you!" So much for another holiday with the family! Unfortunately, during these special occasions there was always some incident that ruined the concept of family togetherness.

ON STRIKE Being taken for granted, day in and day out, is a situation no one should ever have to experience. During the first year of our marriage, I didn't know what the words "taken for granted" meant. I loved this man. I

loved making a home for him. I wanted to believe that he cared and truly loved me. However, feelings of confusion began to emerge within me as Pepper's attitude became more and more difficult to understand. I began to realize that he never expressed any compassion, sympathy, or love. His way of showing love was through sex. However, even then, he never spoke gentle and affectionate words. I missed this, but when I spoke about it, he refused to discuss it.

I refused to believe that I was being taken for granted because it was always easy to find an excuse for Pepper's lack of appreciation. I found myself living in an environment in which praise, appreciation, gentleness, kindness, and empathy did not exist. Whenever I complained, he let me know damn fast where he stood. He believed that those emotions turn a man into a wimp, and *he* was no wimp. He was his own man and needed no one else. What surprised me more than anything was how proud he always appeared after making such remarks. However, as days and months turned into one year after another, I knew that much was missing from our family. A hug, a sweet kiss out of the blue, a gentle word, and empathy when one was distraught were absent from our home.

I was failing my boys by allowing these perfectly normal, human emotions to be silenced. I tried to show them the importance of these feelings and the impact that they could have on a loved one, a friend, or even a foe. I wanted them to experience the joy that comes from healthy emotions, not those wrapped in anger. Guilt filled me. I felt I was a failure. I tried to convince myself that tomorrow was another day and that Pepper just might say, "I love you!" I was looking for the impossible. My emotional needs were a mess.

As the years passed, I began to notice how everything that I did meant little to Pepper. Whenever I complained about this, he always told me to grow up, adding, "You don't need praise to do what you're supposed to do." He was sounding more and more like my mother years before. I felt his coldness, and it hurt. He would *not* give me the satisfaction of feeling kindness, love, thoughtfulness, empathy, or appreciation. I knew I was alone, really *alone*. In many ways, I felt my marriage was traveling down the same path as my childhood.

Reality forced me to see that escape to a better life was impossible. I wanted to believe that he had no idea of what his meanness was doing to

Our three boys—my heart, my love (l–r): Brian, Kevin, and Paul.

me. Realistically, I knew, and the anger inside me was ready to burst. I was unable to help myself from having thoughts such as: "What has happened to me? How can he do this to me? Why am I allowing this?" These thoughts left me devastated.

Pepper had a way of making me feel like I had done something wrong. My sense of guilt about not being a good wife or mom left me crushed. The months passed, and nothing changed. I would tear the house apart. I scrubbed and shined until everything—floors, walls, windows, curtains, furniture—was spotless. I baked and cooked just to keep my mind off of my failures. Laundry day was every day. I even found myself ironing our underwear. When there was nothing more I could do in the house, I went outside. I cut the lawn, weeded my garden, and gave each flower a little TLC. Frustration was my buddy. Work was my salvation. I did all Pepper's office work, typing letters, paying bills, answering phones, ordering materials, etc. I could go on and on.

I remember the first time I revolted. I had worked hard all day. It was dinnertime. I was tired and wanted to get dinner behind me. Pepper and the kids hustled into the kitchen. I felt exhausted as I placed the chicken potpie on the table and began to serve it. I had worked all day making this meal, and I was happy to see how delicious it looked. Immediately, the kids started

eating. It made me feel good to see how much they were enjoying it. (And you can enjoy it, too: see Appendix D for my Chicken Potpie recipe.) I was surprised by my thoughts. The fresh, colorful tablecloth added to the beauty of the moment, making the meal even more enjoyable. It was a perfect scene that reminded me of a Norman Rockwell painting of a family enjoying dinner together. How proud and warm I felt. It was a rare moment of satisfaction for me, and that was a pleasant surprise.

However, time did not stand still to allow me to savor my moment of happiness. I sensed a disaster was in the making. I watched the expression on Pepper's face as I placed his dinner in front of him. He announced, "I'm not eating this mess. You know I like my meat and vegetables separated. I'm not eating this garbage!" I looked at him in disbelief. How could he say that to me? I had worked so hard making it. I felt my anger rising, and for the first time, I thought, "How dare he say that to me?"

I picked up the chicken potpie, dumped it in the garbage, and then took his plate and dumped it as well. The kids looked at me, dumbfounded and bewildered. The three of them sat frozen in their chairs looking at me, waiting to see what would happen next. I could tell that they dared not speak. Shocked by my actions, Pepper didn't know what to say. I spoke first. "Now, get your own dinner from now on. I'm though. I'm on strike. No more cooking and working so hard just to try to please you. It's impossible. No matter what I do, you only find fault." I was shocked by my own behavior. Pepper, enraged, left the table and went into the office, announcing how crazy I was becoming. I sat down, glad that the moment had passed. I couldn't look at my kids as one by one they filed out of the kitchen and quietly went to their bedrooms. God, I was ashamed.

A BUMP ON THE TRACKS During the 1950s and '60s, my life had become an emotional mess due to Pepper's "silent treatment" and his physical abuse. Whenever my life seemed completely chaotic and I felt totally lost, I would leave home, go to Pennsylvania Station in Newark, and catch the next southbound train, usually the Silver Meteor. I did this many times, trying to run away from my miserable life, but I never went any further than

Savannah, Georgia, before turning around and heading back home. I couldn't leave my boys behind. I had no choice. I carried all my pain with me, only to come home to more pain. They were my heart, my love. There was no escape. I would spend the day in Savannah and then catch the next train back to Newark. I knew that my leaving didn't bother Pepper at all. He had his boys, his home, his car, his business, and that was all that he needed. Pepper never asked or spoke about my leaving home for a couple of days. He knew that I had no place to go.

During one of these trips, I saw something very unusual. I was headed back home, and when we were about an hour into South Carolina, I decided to go to the club car, get a comfortable seat, and order a soft drink. It was going to be a long ride back to Newark. Across from me in the club car sat four giggly women who kept watching me as one man after another tried to hit on me. I gave them no encouragement, and, one by one, they moved on. One young man, however, sat down and began talking to me. The giggly ladies were still giggling and watching me with open mouths. I couldn't help but wonder what they were thinking. They reminded me of a bunch of high school girls giggling about sex. Suddenly, something happening outside drew my attention to the window.

It was dusk, but off in the distance, I saw an old truck racing down a dirt road in the same direction as the train. I was fascinated by its speed as it raised a huge cloud of dust that occasionally made it impossible to see the truck. As I stared, I heard myself say, "My God, that damned truck is going faster than hell. I hope they stop in time, or we might be in serious trouble." I knew something was going to happen.

Just then, we went around a bend, which allowed me to see both ends of our train. Up ahead, I saw that the truck had stopped by the tracks. Two men had gotten out, and they quickly removed a large bag from the bed of the truck and placed it on the tracks. The men then scrambled into their truck, turned it around, and raced back down the dirt road. I turned to the young man and said, "I hope I'm wrong, but I think something terrible is about to happen." Surprised, he looked at me and said, "Why do you say that?" Before I could answer, the train's brakes screeched deafeningly, but it was too

late—the club car had already passed over whatever was on the tracks. As it did, we felt a hard bump, a bump that told me that we had run over something or somebody.

For the first time, the women stopped giggling when I calmly announced, "I think we just ran over a body." The train finally stopped. The women could only say, "Oh, no! You must be mistaken." I replied, "I saw the whole thing. The minute I felt that bump, I knew what had happened." The previously giggling women looked shocked and uncomfortable.

All of the train's personnel sprang into action. The local police eventually arrived and, of course, had to investigate the entire scene before they would allow the train to continue on its way. A porter came through the club car and announced that there was going to be a delay due to a problem. Just as I had suspected, we had run over a body that had been dumped on the tracks. All the passengers were told to remain onboard during the delay, which turned out to be about two hours. When the conductor came through, I told him what I had seen. The young man excused himself and went back to his car. I really think that my reaction to what I had seen had scared him. I ordered another soft drink and decided to stay in the club car. The now no-longer giggly women also ordered another drink and asked me to join them.

OUR TRIPS TO BRUNSWICK, JACKSONVILLE, AND KINGSLEY LAKE
During the summers, I took my three children, and we traveled by train to visit my Aunt Lillie and Aunt Leonia for a two-week vacation. We stayed one week with Aunt Lillie in Brunswick and another week with Aunt Leonia in Jacksonville and Kingsley Lake, Florida. It was always interesting because my two aunts were so different and basically lived just as differently, but they shared a tremendous love for family. That was the most important value they left behind.

Aunt Lillie was a most gracious lady. She was loved by every one who knew her and by every member of our family. It was she who kept the family together. I believe Uncle Sam was her biggest disgrace. She showed her graciousness by holding her head high even though she knew every woman,

Aunt Lillie and Uncle Sam in front of their home in Brunswick.

either young or old, was subject to Uncle Sam's sexual harassment. He was a disgusting mess and a constant embarrassment to Aunt Lillie. Every woman in the family feared being caught in a room alone with him, especially when he was in the front sunroom, sitting in his big leather chair with its wide armrests. If you were in there with him, he would pat the armrests and say, "Come on over here, honey. Come over and sit by me." He would continue the same act and the same words until you just got up and left the room. Regardless of her age, each female family member learned, damn fast, what Uncle Sam's sneaky little act meant and what he really wanted.

One time, when I was in the garage, which was next to the sunroom, he came in and caught me by surprise. I told him to let go of me. He didn't. I turned around and stomped on his foot and gave him a kick in his shinbone. He let go damn fast. I knew that kick had hurt as he lamely headed for his favorite chair. I was really upset. I was embarrassed and angry. Here I was a guest in his home. How dare he? I noticed how he kept watching the doorway with those shifty eyes of his as if he were afraid Aunt Lillie might come in. I gathered my papers and left the room. He never tried to be cute with me again.

I couldn't help but wonder where the men in the family were. Why didn't one of them knock the shit out of him? Certainly, they knew about Uncle

Sam's revolting sexual advances on all of us females. Thinking back, I hope that he never messed around with the really young girls in the family. Somehow I can't help but think that even they were sexually fondled. If this bastard were alive today, he sure as hell wouldn't be sitting in that big brown leather chair. Uncle Sam would find himself in prison, being some tough dude's playmate for a change. That would have been justice. Revenge is sweet, so they say.

Physically, Uncle Sam was a very large man. Mentally, his expression, smirk, and those shifty eyes appeared threatening and evil, which always left me with uncomfortable feelings, not knowing what to expect. Somehow, I thought Aunt Lillie deserved better. He had little respect for anyone. He thought that his money allowed him pleasures that were definitely out-of-bounds for such a dog. As gracious as Aunt Lillie was, I think she shed many tears. I hate to think what went on behind their closed doors. They had a lovely home and lived extremely well, but I personally didn't think any of it was worth having to put up with him.

Aunt Lillie learned to be a wonderful hostess and entertained people from all types of backgrounds. She always had full-time maids, but Johnna Mae was the best. She was an excellent ol' cook, the one my kids remembered. Aunt Lillie was also an excellent cook herself. I believe that all the Whorton women have that special trait. It's in our genes, since our great-grandmother, Susan Lincoln, had been considered an outstanding cook. However, I heard she hated cleaning but loved cooking.

While staying with Aunt Lillie, we visited every member of the family or she would invite them to her home for dinner so I could enjoy them as well. The kids went swimming, boating, fishing, crabbing, and in general, had a great time. I loved just being with the family. My dear,

Wyman, my cousin, standing behind his parents, Aunt Jessie and Uncle Freddie.

Aunt Leonia, Uncle Elmo, Aunt Marguerite, and Aunt Affie (l–r).

sweet Aunt Lillie died of breast cancer in 1969. Her absence was and is painfully noticed, at least by the generation who knew her. Even now when I go back to Brunswick, I pass her home and can't help but think of her loving and gracious ways. She was my idea of a real true Southern lady.

Aunt Leonia and Uncle Gordon—Uncle Sam's brother, but nothing like him, thank God—were just the opposite. Aunt Leonia reminded me of Granny in the TV series *The Beverly Hillbillies.* It never mattered how many people came to their home, there was always room for one more. The table was always filled with an abundance of food. She had no maid and did everything herself. What a woman. They just don't make that breed anymore, unfortunately. She was kind, loving, and gentle, as was Uncle Gordon. He was a real gentleman, one who deserved a great deal of respect. On their shopping day, Uncle Gordon would drive Aunt Leonia to every store around Jacksonville if they could save on a special item. They were so funny. They spent all their savings on gas, but that made no difference. None of us could understand why they did it.

Those two dear people will always be in my heart, as will Aunt Lillie. They owned a home at Kingsley Lake, a little more than an hour southwest of Jacksonville. Aunt Leonia and Uncle Gordon would take us to the lake whenever we came to visit. My kids loved it. Besides us, they would also have

a half dozen of their grandchildren there as well. Aunt Leonia was famous for her lemon-meringue and coconut-custard pies. Oh, they were good! Ham, rump of beef, fried chicken, biscuits, collards, creamed corn, yams, and potatoes are just a few foods that would be on the dinner table. (To get an idea of Aunt Leonia's ability as a cook, try her recipe for Crab au Gratin; see Appendix E.) Besides the cooking, she did all the housework, washing, and ironing. In other words, she never stopped.

Aunt Leonia was an amazing woman. She had the stamina of an ox and a heart that was filled with love of God and family. Sharing and giving was a way of life for her and Uncle Gordon. The spirit of Christmas was her constant companion throughout the entire year, not just during the Christmas season. A funny little scene still sticks in my mind whenever I think of her and Uncle Gordon. Every evening, after all the day's work was completed, she would gather up her dogs and spend the entire evening picking, plucking, removing, and killing the dogs' fleas. God, hours would go by, but she never stopped till the dogs were free of those little pesky, bloodsucking insects. After that, Aunt Leonia would put the dogs down, ask everyone if they wanted some kind of snack, and if not, she would gather up her belongings and head for the bedroom with both animals trailing behind her. Between her conversations with those miserable mutts, she always managed to shout out, "Good night all. Sleep well. Love you. See you in the

morning." Aunt Leonia lived to be 102 years old. She and Uncle Gordon gave each of us a wonderful legacy of the importance of love and family. God bless both of them.

We always took the train out of Jacksonville to go back to Jersey. When it was time to pack up, Aunt Leonia would always have a bag of food for me to take home. One year, I had two whole country hams, an old fourteen-inch iron frying pan, a bag of corn meal

Aunt Clara (r). I have no picture of Uncle Julius, who passed away many years ago.

Aunt Affie, Mother, Aunt Mary, and Aunt Jessie (l–r).

(yellow and white), and God knows what else. It was always a surprise when I got home and opened my bag.

One year, Paul came home with a real honest-to-goodness rifle and a fishing rod. Neither was in a covered case. Everyone knew what we were carrying. Kevin had a glass jar full of little chameleons. We were waiting in line for the train to arrive when he dropped the jar and all the little slimy critters went running around the platform. Uncle Gordon turned out to be as fast as those chameleons. He caught most of them, but Kevin was still upset. Paul was laughing, grabbing one by its tail and hollering for Kevin to get something to put them in.

I was holding Brian because he was only about four years old. One of the passengers produced a jar with a lid. I'm sure we looked like a bunch of hillbillies, hollering, crying, shouting, and running all around. Oh, well, just another small incident in the lives of the Martin family. Ah, the joys of being a mother! Everyone getting on the train gave me a hand with my luggage, the kids, and all the other objects and living creatures we were trying to bring home. This is an example of the way most of our train trips turned out. Over the years, I became accustomed to all the confusion that can occur when traveling with kids. I stopped worrying about what people thought. We always came home with ten times more than what we had when we went away.

MOTHER'S FLIRTATIOUS MOMENTS   After my father died on August 2, 1974, Mother became more dependent on me. I drove her around so she could get all of her errands completed. I didn't mind, since it was the first time in my life when she actually asked me to help her and looked like she cared for me.

One day, she called and said that she had to go to Mr. Minter's office, so I went down and picked her up. I found a parking space directly across from his office. I told Mother that I would wait in the car while she went ahead and took care of her business. She seemed very excited about seeing him. He was a good-looking man who could turn the heads of many women. I looked at Mother and was surprised to see such a happy expression on her face.

She got out of the car, and I sat watching her cross the street. Suddenly, I realized that she was strutting across that road like a bitch in heat. I kept watching her. I never saw Mother walk like that. I began laughing, not quite sure if my eyes were playing tricks on me. She had me spellbound. What was she doing? This holier-than-thou Baptist—who, during all my teenage years, refused to let any of my dresses show an inch of skin—was on the make.

My God, my mother was on a flirtatious rendezvous with her insurance man. By the time she reached the office door, I had sat back, shaking my head, not quite believing what I saw. A terrible thought entered my mind. Christ, what was going on inside his office? God, I just hoped she wasn't making a fool of herself. Every time someone came out, I held my breath. Finally, she appeared with a smile from one ear to the other. She was radiant as she crossed the street. I figured he must have flattered the hell out of her. You know, flattering words go a long way with most women, single, married, widowed, or divorced. Knowing Mother and her proper ways, I was hoping that her flirtatious moments paid off. God bless her! Even after she moved to Brunswick, Mother always made an appointment to see him whenever she came back for a visit.

During 1975, Mother and I went to Hawaii. We flew to Las Vegas for a couple of days and then flew out to Hawaii. While in the city of sin, we both spent more money than we had expected. The morning we were leaving, I got up very early and went downstairs to play the slot machines in hopes that the

good Lord would be kind and let me win some of our money back. Well, I started playing and within five minutes, I hit a $350 pot. I was thrilled. The cashier was as excited as I. I tried again, and God, I hit another $350 pot.

Neither of us could believe it. I had won $700 in less than fifteen minutes, and it only cost me two dollars. I had the girl put all the coins in a huge bucket. I went upstairs and woke up Mother. When she saw me at the door with the bucket of coins, she was speechless. She got dressed, and we went downstairs and turned it all in for dollars. I split it down the middle with her and told her that God knew we needed some help and that He was there for us.

So, we went on to Hawaii with some spending money. We both felt better. It was going to be a nice vacation. The flight went well, and as soon as we stepped off the plane, we each received an orchid lei. We arrived amidst all the excitement Hawaii could offer. We went to our hotel and got settled in. Then I suggested that we go downstairs to the bar, listen to the lovely Hawaiian music, and enjoy a couple of Hawaiian drinks. It had been a long day. I had heard the music playing on our way into the hotel, and I wanted to listen to it over a drink.

The bar was empty except for a lone gentleman. We had our choice of sitting anywhere. I saw a table and suggested we sit there. Mother immediately said, "Oh, no, Teeny, let's sit at the bar." I said, "Okay." I followed her and, of all the places she had to pick, she sat right next to the gentleman. I

Mother and me in Hawaii: "You're as young as you feel!"

looked at her and wondered what she was up to. She began talking to the man. Her Southern accent got stronger. He was quite impressed. She was laughing and having the best time. She was flirting, once again. My God, she was good at it. I was amazed. She had more nerve than I did. I was suddenly feeling more like her mother rather than her daughter. The drinks were great. We enjoyed the music, our new acquaintance, and the lovely atmosphere. We had a great time. Mother said, "Relax, dear, nobody knows us." The gentleman sat with us the entire evening. My mother was the best flirt I had come across in a long time. She was a good sport, and I enjoyed being with her. It was nice to experience the closeness I always wanted from her, even if it did include an unexpected lesson in the flirting game.

A couple of days into our stay in Hawaii, we were beginning to enjoy all the activities available. I had read where there was going to be a pig roast and luau that evening on one of the nicest beaches on the island. The entertainment included fire dancers, sword swallowers, and of course, hula dancers. The transportation was also provided, and the bus would be right outside our hotel. It couldn't be better, so I signed us up. Mother was excited as well. I saw a gleam appear in her eyes and reminded Mother to behave. She came back with the remark, "Behaving could ruin a lot of fun". Now those few words and her mischievous smile caught me by surprise. What was she thinking? Behaving could ruin a lot of fun. I thought about her comment, shrugged my shoulders, and agreed. What the hell! Like Mother said, "No one knows us." I never saw my mother act as if she were on the make. God, could this behavior come from her breakdown? Again, I began to feel more like her mother. What's going on with her? Whatever it was, she was having a good time, no one was getting hurt, and I was constantly laughing at this sudden and unexpected new side of Mother. It felt too good to be true. I loved her, and we were laughing together and actually enjoying each other's company.

We noticed that our hotel had many extremely well-dressed Japanese guests who all smelled like *money*. I decided it most be one of the island's better hotels. When we went down to the lobby, the desk clerk mentioned that all the guests in the hotel were invited to a Japanese wedding that was going to take place later in the day. He said that the wedding was going to

be beautiful and that we shouldn't miss it. I realized that it was going to be impossible for us to attend, but we did go up to the floor where the wedding was going to take place.

We saw the bride and groom as they were entering the reception hall. They both were dressed in white. The bride's pearl-laden gown was lovely, but her black hair made her standout in a magnificent way. She looked like royalty. We learned later that the large corporations in Japan buy these hotels for their employees' use. It's one of their benefits. All employee vacations include the entire family, even grandma and granddad, and are paid by the corporation. Now, that's a *great* deal.

THE BELLY DANCERS We were well into the 1960s, and life had become a challenge to our way of thinking and living. I was ready to seek the unusual, even if it meant acting a little crazy, like the rest of the populace. There is a song by Bob Dylan containing words that describe it all: "The times, they are a-changin'." With this in mind, I felt I would attempt to do just that. It started as a dare and ended up as one of the most fun times in my life: belly dancing! Wow! It sounded stimulating, definitely daring, and better yet, almost forbidden. How very different! How very sexy and sensuous! I was almost afraid to say the words out loud, but I kept thinking, "Yes, let's go for it!"

After recuperating from my hysterectomy during the end of August 1969, I received the Morristown High School Adult Night Courses brochure. I had been thinking about taking a course, but none of those scheduled seemed to interest me except one, Belly Dancing. The brochure made the course sound like fun. I was tired of my life being just one job after another. I was still searching for the real me. Perhaps this type of dance might help me overcome my terrible shyness and sense of inadequacy.

One of my friends, Anne Miller, readily agreed her life was in the same rut as mine. Before signing up for this course, we spoke with several of our friends in hopes that they might also be interested, if only for the exercise. One by one, they decided it was not for them because they felt it was too risqué for them. Anne and I decided to sign up. We felt it was a daring

challenge, and it felt good. We took our first big step to do something so untypical of ourselves.

Little did we know how much fun and excitement was waiting for us. Many new friendships developed through our study of this creative and sensuous art. For the first time, we found a dance we could do without a partner. What a perfect idea! Our men weren't interested in taking us dancing anymore. "What the hell! Let's do it," were our thoughts.

Anne was in her late-thirties, and I was in my mid-forties. We were ready. We knew that if we had second thoughts about it, we could change our minds. We could hardly wait to begin. We arrived at the class a half-hour early to make sure we would be there on time. Another lady, Carolyn Smith, arrived shortly after us, and we immediately became friends. Carolyn was as excited about this course as we were. She was no spring chicken—she was about nine years older than me. Her determination and excitement encouraged Anne and me. The more Carolyn talked, the more we realized that she, too, needed a diversion, as well as the exercise.

More and more women entered the gym; their anxiety floated in with them. Many acted as if they wanted to forget the whole idea and just slip away before someone recognized them. We were all thinking, "What am I doing here?" Our eyes were searching the room, looking for the person who was going to be our instructor. Suddenly, the weirdest music began playing.

The only picture I have of a couple of us gals belly dancing at one of the local nursing homes.

Several of the girls said, "My God!". We looked at each other in total bewilderment. "What is that?" someone remarked. "I never heard that kind of music before!" We could also hear a sharp ringing and clicking sound (made by "zills," more commonly known as "finger cymbals"), a most unusual vibration to our ears. It was getting closer and louder, giving off a more metallic pitch. The sound seemed to linger outside the gymnasium doorway. The zills quieted, and the music became soft and gentle.

A single hand appeared on the inside doorframe and slowly inched its way upward. Then, gliding ever so gracefully and moving her body with sensuous and sexy motions, a belly dancer entered the room. Our mouths flew open as we sat, fascinated by this most unusual and unexpected introduction. A skimpy, colorful, and ornate outfit displayed her beautiful, curvaceous figure. Her arms, outstretched and swirling gently about her body, moved slowly as her hands created lovely ballet-like motions. Attached to her two middle fingers were zills, which made cymbal-like sounds as she clicked them together. Demurely, she allowed her long veil to flow about her, creating a submissive mood.

We watched her gentle movements as she danced about the room. When the music picked up speed, the dancer's style also changed. She began moving quickly. Faster and faster she danced. Her body was a continuum of motion. Her hips moved in a circular rotation. Her stomach appeared to roll in time to the music. We learned much later that this was called a belly roll. She was fantastic! We were spellbound by the beauty of her dancing. Then the music became almost wild. Once more, her style changed. The mood of the dance reflected the mood of the music. She appeared anchored to one spot, yet every part of her body was shaking, rolling, or shimmying. Even the zills seemed to release their own frenzied rhythm, as did the many decorative bangles that were wrapped around her ankles, waist, neck, and arms. By this time, we were completely intoxicated by the dance and the dancer. Harriet Zullo was her name; she was a whirling dervish of motion and sensuality.

Harriet's performance had definitely stimulated our appetite for learning. The more she danced, the less convinced we became of our own agility. Each of us was trying to refute these thoughts as Harriet began to take us through

the basic steps. We were to follow her movements and keep up with her as best we could. I found myself sneaking fast glances at the other girls to see if they were able to follow any better than I.

Wow! We were awkward, clumsy, and completely uncoordinated. We started to laugh at each other's inability to move sensuously. Our bodies were not in sync with our minds. We were convinced that it was not as easy as it looked, but it made us feel *great*. No matter how tired we were before our lessons, we found that the dancing revived us. They made us feel satisfied with our accomplishments and ourselves in such a sensuous art. Unbeknownst to us, our egos were on an upswing.

We wondered when and why Harriet got involved in belly dancing. Finally, during one of our breaks, she told us how she, too, needed to find a diversion from her everyday life as a wife and mother of ten children. She must have been desperate! We were surprised to learn that she had been doing belly dancing only for the past few years. Serena, the famous East Coast belly dancer who lived in New York City, was Harriet's mentor and instructor. Our group had a chance to meet her when we were invited to attend a party at her studio in the city. That is another story, which I shall go into later.

Our group consisted of nine other women who were also escaping from their home lives. By our second year, belly dancing had become a way of life for all of us. We began practicing at each other's homes once or twice a week. We were bonding into a real dancing troop. We could see our own progress by watching each other. We were slowly beginning to get it all together.

As agonizing and difficult as it was physically, we were becoming quite agile. We were able to do back bends, splits, slither on the floor and rise sensuously. Learning to use our veils properly was quite an ordeal. We had to learn to present an aura of sensuality with them as we danced. It sounds so easy, but it was difficult. We noticed when we used our veils, a look of intrigue spread across the faces of the observers. It was important that we had everything in sync, since that is the secret of the dance. Months passed by, and we were still very much involved.

During the following year, Harriet mentioned that she was going to teach belly dancing in Mendham at the Seniors Recreational Center. Well, we all

signed up, of course, and followed her to Mendham. By then, our husbands could not believe how much we were into our new form of exercise. Ladies who signed up as newcomers asked if they could join our practice sessions at our different homes. Our troop grew as four more women joined us. We decided that it was time to show our husbands what we had learned by having a belly-dancing party with a buffet supper. Once a month, we would take turns having the party at our different homes. Everyone came with her favorite covered dish. After our performance, the buffet became our husbands' favorite event. The hostess would make the dessert and provide the non-alcoholic beverages. We continued doing this for several years.

It was a lovely time in our lives as we looked forward to entertaining each other in such a fun way. The problems that drew us into belly dancing still existed, but we found it was easier to live with them because our lives now seemed to coincide with the crazy mood of the '70s. We were having a ball and didn't care what anyone thought. Like the times, we were "a-changin'" and loving every moment. During this second year we joined the Morris Plains Adult Class for more belly dancing. We were going twice a week, but within a short time, we found that was too much.

We went to the garment district in New York City and bought lovely, sheer materials—as well as unusual bangles, beads, bells—so we could make our own dancing outfits. We even invested in belly-button jewels. We were really into it. Some of us made very sheer pantaloons to dance in because they helped us feel more comfortable. Even the pantaloons made us look sexy and sensuous by the time we added all the little extra glitters.

When we performed in front of an audience, our favorite outfits were usually long, sheer, split skirts. We would decorate our bodices and bras with small, shiny, metallic-disk ornaments so that every move would create a jingling sound. We wore many bracelets and always had decorative belts, laden with bangles, that hung below our waists. We danced barefoot. We each had our own zills. It was extremely difficult to learn how to click them properly to the many different tempos of the music. Most of us never really mastered this part of the dance.

SELENA'S PARTY Two years into our dancing, Harriet informed us that Selena had invited all of us to a party at her Manhattan studio in New York City. We had seen Selena portray a belly dancer in many old movies, but at that time, her name meant nothing to any of us. However, now it was different! We were excited about the invitation and having an opportunity to actually watch her perform with her complete troop.

Pepper drove us into the city for the event. Selena's studio was on the second floor of a dingy old building, directly in back of the new and famous Americana Hotel. We were all expecting something entirely different and felt a little leery as we opened the door. Pepper took the lead because the stairway was narrow and dark. We could hear a great deal of noise, music, and laughter above us. As we approached the top of the stairway, Harriet appeared with Selena. We were impressed by her gracious manner, but surprised by how much older she appeared. We began mingling and found the crowd most unusual yet friendly. A lovely buffet of exotic Middle Eastern foods added to the atmosphere. We didn't know what we were eating, but it was delicious.

Pepper was one who always checked out the location of the nearest exit, no matter where we went. He became extremely uncomfortable when he realized the only way out of the building was the stairway we had come up. It was a firetrap in his mind, and he wanted us out of there as quickly as possible. I began checking the area for exit doors. There were none, only the narrow stairway we came up. The build-up of smoke from everyone smoking and the absence of air-conditioning was reason enough for our leaving. However, this observation made it even more so. Harriet came over and told us that Selena and her group wanted to see us dance. By this time, none of us was that interested in performing. We managed one dance and quickly thanked our hostess and departed. A feeling of relief came over us as we walked to our car. We never forgot that trip. During our third year of belly dancing, we went out as a dance troop to many of the local nursing homes, hospitals, senior citizen retirement homes, and civic organizations to entertain.

A group of the girls was asked to go down to the International Casino in Atlantic City to perform and entertain a group of ladies whose husbands were there for a conference. They danced for the women and then had a

session to teach them some of the sensuous movements. It was a big success. Anne and Carolyn were in charge of that tour. Anne did a beautiful dance that included a perfect back bend. She rose up with such ease and lovely motion, which is extremely hard to do, that she shocked herself. Many people complimented her on her performance. What a boost to her ego!

PAUL AND DEBBIE'S WEDDING   It was May 8, 1976, the day of Paul and Debbie's wedding. They were married in the Methodist Church in Morristown, and the reception was held at Debbie's parent's home. Betty and Don Vroom had a beautiful home and had everything attractive and lovely. The table was set up as a buffet. The food was delightfully tempting and deliciously prepared. We all stayed for several hours, and then many of our close friends and family came back to our home for a little more celebration.

Marty and Pat Flanagan and their wives came back with us, and the two boys, slightly intoxicated by now, sat in the kitchen and began singing. With their arms around each other, tears began running down their cheeks as they sang "Mother Machree" and "Danny Boy." The more Irish songs they sang, the heavier the tears flowed. It was the beginning of one of the most fun nights I ever had.

Mother and Affie had come up from Brunswick. Uncle Elmo and Aunt Marguerite had arrived from Florida. As a surprise for my guests, I invited my belly-dancing troop to join us, dressed to perform, and they danced magnificently. Elmo and Marguerite often remarked that they never laughed so hard as they did that night nor had they ever attended a wedding reception with such unusual guests and entertainment. With the belly dancing, the tearful singing of the Flanagan boys, and everyone's laughter, the evening became a treasured memory that stills makes me smile.

CRYSTAL PALACE, MY FIFTEEN MINUTES OF FAME   I also demonstrated my belly dancing talent during the summer of 1977 when Mother; Aunt Leonia; her daughter, Claire; my youngest son, Brian; and I went to Disney World in Florida. We rented a condo and stayed for several days. While in the park, we stopped at the Crystal Palace for something to eat. A

musician played his accordion, and many people danced with or without partners. I got the feel of the music and joined in the fun. I began doing a few belly-dancing steps, nothing too suggestive, when I suddenly found myself alone on the floor. Everyone had stopped dancing and was watching me.

Before I knew what had happened, Disney's cartoon-character dog, Goofy, had come into the Crystal Palace, announcing loudly that he wanted to dance with the belly dancer he had been watching. He came onto the dance floor, stood before me, bowed, and placed his large front paws into my hands and then, ever so gracefully waltzed me across the floor. I was embarrassed at first, but Goofy reassured me that I was doing great. I no longer felt awkward. I had to keep an eye on his tail because it was long and dragging, and I was afraid I would step on it. His big, floppy ears were almost touching the floor, as well, and his black, bulbous nose reminded me of my bicycle horn of years ago. I had all I could do not to press it with my hands just to hear if it would honk. He was adorable.

When the audience began clapping and shouting, "More! More!" Goofy gave me a big hug and whispered in my ear, "Let's belly dance, kid. Knock them dead!" Whoever the person was under that costume had to be fun loving because he portrayed Goofy so well while inspiring me to continue. I glanced at my family, hoping to see their approval. I felt great. A sense of pride came over me when I saw how much everyone was enjoying our dancing. My family appeared very impressed by Goofy's and my unrehearsed performance. They nodded their heads for us to keep going. My ego never felt like it did that day as Goofy and I performed at the Crystal Palace in the middle of Disney World. With Goofy at my side, it was my fifteen minutes of fame!

PILFERING PETALS   We left the Crystal Palace and walked in the direction of the famous Polynesian Hotel, which is located in the center of Disney World. By the time we arrived, Claire and I decided to go upstairs to the Hawaiian Cocktail Bar for a much needed, refreshing drink. Brian wanted to join us rather than stay in the lobby with Mother and Aunt Leonia. We left them sitting on the retaining wall, which was filled with many beautiful flowering plants.

As we were departing from the bar, I glanced over the balcony and couldn't believe what I saw; I quickly called Claire and Brian to come and look. There, below, were Mother and Aunt Leonia with their pocketbooks opened, stuffing individual plants into their bags. "God," we all gasped. What in the hell were those two thinking? They were stealing the Polynesian Hotel's beautiful flower display, right in the center of the lobby, and right under the nose of Disney security. Pilfering is the only word that came to my mind, but no matter how one puts it, it was downright stealing. Claire and I hoped that we would reach them before security spotted these two innocent-looking old ladies. Brian couldn't stop laughing. Even he knew what his grandmother was doing. He had seen his grandma and great aunt acting like modern-day "Ma" Barkers. He kept asking if he could pretend to be one of the Barker boys and give the old gals a helping hand in getting out of the hotel with their valuable loot.

Despite all his kidding, he mentioned something very important. How were we going to replace the plants? And what if they refused to put them back? Jesus, it must run in the family. Brian had more fun in those few minutes than he did the entire day in Disney World.

Mother and Aunt Leonia saw us coming and quickly got up and headed for the front door. We couldn't believe that they were scrambling to get away from us, but they were. We watched them flee. Claire and I were beside ourselves. They had no intention of replacing the plants. I am sure the security cameras watched the whole process and figured that they were just too old broads who weren't worth the time it would take to write them up or arrest them, so they just let them go, even though the evidence was sticking out of their bags in all directions. I was hoping that is what security was thinking. By the time we caught up to them, they were sitting and waiting for the next trolley to take them back to our quarters. They both took on the appearance of two totally innocent and naive little old ladies. How deceiving this picture really was; only the five of us knew the truth of their pilfering the lovely flowering plants.

Once we caught up to them, we asked one question, "Why?" Neither Mother nor Aunt Leonia answered. They totally ignored our question. Their

only words to us were, "How were your drinks? We waited and waited, but you all took so long we decided to leave and wait for you at the trolley stop. We've been waiting a long time for this damn trolley and you three. Now let's go home."

They had no intention of mentioning, much less giving back their pilferage nor did we bother to mention their shameful behavior. Thank God, they didn't get caught. Brian still talks about Mama as his very own "Ma" Barker. It was a day none of us ever forgot. Not only did those flowering plants survive the trip, but they also made a beautiful border along the entire length of Mother's walkway. They reproduced many times over throughout Mother's stay in Brunswick. These two old gals were determined to bring a little of Disney World back to Brunswick, and by golly, that's exactly what they did.

OUR PERFORMANCE ON THE AMTRAK TRAIN During the spring of 1978, Carolyn, Dotty, and I decided to visit my mother in Brunswick, Georgia. We took the Amtrak train out of Newark. About an hour into the trip, we went into the club car to enjoy a beverage. While there, Carolyn began talking to several young people, and we immediately became traveling companions. During the conversation, Carolyn told them about our belly dancing. She mentioned that we had our music and our outfits with us in our bags because we wanted to show the family in Brunswick how well we could dance. She also told them

Two belly dancers, Carolyn and me, and the professional singer, Dotty (l–r).

that Dotty was a professional singer and had a beautiful voice. Word spread quickly among the young college kids. It was spring vacation and that meant party time. They were all headed for the beaches in Florida.

The club car was filled with people. They wanted us to perform once they heard about our special talents. One of them brought out a guitar, and

Arriving in Brunswick: Aunt Lillie, Uncle Sam and my mother took us three gals to the Cloisters on Sea Island for dinner (l–r): me, Aunt Lillie, Uncle Sam, Carolyn, and Mother. Dotty took the picture.

Dotty began singing. That did it! Everyone in the club car joined in excitedly. The conductor came in and sat down, fascinated by her beautiful voice. He gave his permission for us to sing and dance as long as there were no complaints. Carolyn and I went back to our car, got into our belly-dancing outfits, and returned to the club car. On returning, we were amazed to find the car filled with even more people, all eager to enjoy our show. News spread quickly from one car to another. More and more people came in. It was a night of just fun. No one got out-of-hand.

The club car was packed and stayed that way most of the night. We all sang, laughed, and danced. It was a night I will never forget. Even the porters were finding excuses to come into the club car and stay long enough to join in a song or two. Young couples with their children came in to participate in the singing. The railroad had hired a detective named Mooney to travel aboard the train in case trouble broke out among the vacationing college crowd. He came over and asked if he could sit with us because his job called for him to stay in the club car. He was pleased because our entertaining kept everyone in good spirits, allowing him to enjoy the same fun with no problems. The more Dotty sang, the more people came. Her voice was beautiful. We belly danced well into the night. The crowd applauded excitedly after each performance. The conductor joined us many

times during that evening. He kept saying that he never had a trip where his passengers had so much fun.

That morning, when the train stopped in Jessup, Georgia, to let us off, all the young people came and said their goodbyes to us. They hugged and kissed us, all the time talking about how they would never forget their trip on Amtrak with such fun ladies. They wanted to know when we were going back to New Jersey so they would be sure to get on the same train. They wanted our addresses to keep in touch. Detective Mooney came out to say goodbye and, with a big smile, mentioned that the shenanigans of last evening would have to be written up in his report. With that he gave each of us a big hug and got back on the train. Many people waved goodbye from their car windows.

Mother and Affie stood looking in disbelief at the crowd surrounding us. When the conductor came to say goodbye and thank us for such a fun evening, they were speechless. For a brief moment, I saw a gleam in my mother's eyes that was not familiar to me. I hoped it was the long-awaited feeling of pride in her unsophisticated daughter. However, the gleam disappeared as she surveyed the crowd returning to the train.

MOTHER'S MOVE TO BRUNSWICK, GEORGIA   Around November 1974, Affie and Bud left to go down to Brunswick. It was, then, that Mother

A section of the front of Mother's home in Brunswick.

Mother and me in her home in Brunswick.

Mother and me visiting Cousin Gerald.

had a breakdown, and I had to put her in Morristown Memorial Hospital. During January of 1975, I asked Dr. Weissglass if he felt it would help Mother if she flew down to Brunswick to visit her brothers and sisters. He was all for it. "Great idea, Teeny! Will someone meet her at the airport?" "Absolutely," I said. So we got busy and made all the necessary arrangements. Mom seemed delighted. I felt that she was finally looking forward to something new.

Three days later, Mom called and told me that she had bought a house in Brunswick. A couple of weeks later, she flew home, excited about her decision and ready for a new life. We called a realtor and Mother began packing. The New Jersey house sold quickly. Pepper and our boys cleaned out the house. Mother told them what she wanted to keep, and everything else that had any value she either gave it away or sold it to whomever. Finally, she was ready to make arrangements for the moving van, and within a day, the van was heading south.

SAVANNAH'S BRIDGE   My friend, Anne Miller, and I drove Mother and her car south. We were anxious to see her new home and get her settled in. As we approached the South Carolina and Georgia border, I noticed an extremely high bridge. Now, I had *never* driven over anything as straight up and high as that bridge. This monstrosity kept getting closer and higher. I could feel myself shaking. "Anne, roll down your window. I need some air." As we approached the bridge, I heard Anne say, "Teeny, are you alright?

You're as white as a ghost." I replied, "Don't talk to me, right now. Oh, my God!" I accelerated the car, desperately wanting to get up and over that frightening bridge. I tightened my hands around the steering wheel. By now, my entire body had become rigid as sweat began to pour down my face. It seemed endless as we kept going up. I managed to open my window.

Mother began to add her comments. That was the last thing I needed. "Now, dear, what's wrong with you? You act scared to death. You're being ridiculous." I could feel my hands tightening even more. I felt lightheaded and strange. Suddenly, I heard myself say, "Shut up, Mother! Don't say another word."

I couldn't pull off to the side because there was no place to stop. It was too late to turn around because there were cars coming and cars behind me. I had no choice but to keep driving. What only took a couple of minutes seemed like it took forever. Before I knew it, we had reached the top and were on the way down. Slowly, color returned to my face. Anne handed me a tissue to wipe the sweat off my forehead, adding, "I think the worst is over, Teeny. Relax. I'm glad it was you driving instead of me." We were now off the bridge, headed down Route 17 for Brunswick.

THE BLESSING OF THE SHRIMP BOATS While we were in Brunswick, the blessing of the shrimp boats took place. Several of my cousins boarded their boats and asked us to join them. We did, and it was the most exciting event Anne and I ever attended. Our crew had brought all kinds of food and drink on board. We were on the lead boat. The entire scene was that of a parade of color as each boat proudly displayed its own flag and banners. The long-stretching armada seemed to glide out into the bay as the sounds of music, laughter, and the smells of down-home cooking lingered over each boat. The Black people on board our boat began playing their music as their women sang. Their young children, keeping time with the music, tap danced as they mesmerized their audience. They knew that we were strangers. For those few hours, we were all one. We danced, sang, ate, and enjoyed the rare and exciting moment. If only one of us had had a camera to capture the significance of the day. Both Anne and I experienced the beauty of the Black culture as it embraced the blessing of the shrimp boats.

When we reached the area where the bay and the ocean meet, the boats circled, and we watched as flowered wreaths were dropped, one by one, into the water. Then a local priest gave the blessing, the boats blew their horns, and shouts of joy floated upward to the heavens. Each boat lay idle, swaying gently, allowing the excitement to be devoured by all. With no warning, one by one the boats powered up, and the roar of engines churned the water into turbulent swells as each boat took its place in the procession. The parade of colors headed in the direction of home.

KEVIN, BRUNSWICK POLICE OFFICER   Kevin graduated from Bayley Ellard High School and went to County College for a year. He wanted to be a police officer. He took the local police tests, but found getting a job difficult because many area city police were being laid off at that time. They were applying and being hired by the local towns who were seeking officers.

That summer, Kevin drove to Florida to seek out police departments that were looking for men interested in becoming police officers. On the way back home, Kevin stopped and visited Mother. While there, he decided to see if the Brunswick Police Department was hiring. In the meantime,

Kevin in his Brunswick Police Department uniform.

Mother called Uncle Sam to see if he would make a phone call on behalf of Kevin. He contacted the deputy chief of police, whom he knew personally, and told him that Kevin was on his way down to headquarters to see if there were any openings. He was hired on the spot. To this day, I can still see him getting out of the car with a police uniform lying across his arms. He had a smile from one ear to the other ear. We were so happy for him. Of course, that meant that he had to come home and gather all his necessary belongings and then head back to Brunswick.

Mother was thrilled to have Kevin with her. She had plenty of room, and he was a good companion. Kevin was getting on-the-job training that no college course could ever give, and he was pleased. Brunswick was filled with

all types of people and situations. It was a great learning experience for him. However, the city of Brunswick paid their police officers very little, considering the danger that each one was exposed to while on duty.

Kevin also worked a second job, doing security work at the Brunswick Hospital. This not only gave him a little more money, but he also enjoyed it. After a couple of years, Kevin met Mindy, who also worked in the hospital, and they began dating. Several months later, Kevin was hired by the Morris Township Police Department and returned home. I could tell that something was bothering him. When I asked him what was wrong, he told me that he missed Mindy and that he was going to call her and ask her to marry him. He did, and she said, "Yes!"

ARRIVAL OF FAMILY AND FRIEND   Kevin and Mindy's wedding was an exciting time. Pepper and I drove south. Paul, Debbie, Kitty, and Ita (Kitty's cousin, whom we truly loved) flew down, and we met them in Jacksonville. Brian came from Texas, where he was stationed in the Air Force. His buddy, Pat Dempsey, flew down to be with him. Pepper, Kitty, Ita, and I stayed with Mother. We made arrangements for Paul, Debbie, Brian, and Pat to stay at a motel just down the street from Mother's home. Irene and Bob Morra arrived and stayed at the same motel. It worked out well, and everyone was comfortable. The weather was unbearably hot. The motel had a large swimming pool where our guests spent their spare time cooling off.

A MOONLIGHT CRUISE   I learned that it was the groom's parents who had to give a party the night before the wedding. I guess it is similar to the rehearsal parties we have up in the North. Because I seem to enjoy doing out-of-the-ordinary things, I asked my cousin if I could rent his ferryboat for that evening. I thought it would be fun and different to take a moonlight cruise up and down the bay. He said yes, and I was thrilled. The captain was my cousin's father-in-law. My Uncle Elmo was the regular captain, but he was my guest for the evening, and I wanted him to be able to join us. I also asked if he knew of a small band that I could hire for the evening. He recommended one, and after speaking with them, I engaged them right away.

I had a good-sized crowd coming, so I knew I had to have a variety of food, drink, and entertainment. My family in Brunswick helped me get it all together. Affie, Mother, and I made many different salads; roasted and cooked meats—such as ham, roast beef, and pork—plus BBQ pork and chicken were all part of the menu. (You'll find my recipe for BBQ with Sauce in Appendix F.) I hired a local caterer to prepare a nice shrimp salad, fried shrimp, crab au gratin, and deviled crab. He also brought all the paper products, the necessary equipment to keep things hot or cold, tables, and extra chairs. This young man helped to decorate the ferry, adding his own creativity in making a festive and romantic mood. We were all excited because the evening was coming together beautifully. Pepper was very proud of what I had managed to put together so quickly. He never complained about the cost. I had a great time using my imagination for such a very unusual, yet special event.

Mindy's family including her grandparents, aunts, uncles, and their kids, plus their many friends, were as excited as we. Her grandmother, Barbara Jacobs, had a horrible fear of boats and water, but no way was this moonlight cruise going to stop her. She had to cross a gangplank of two wobbly, thick boards placed next to each other. I feared for her safety and didn't want her to panic half way across. She did it and turned and flashed a big smile to those still waiting to come aboard. It even scared me as I crossed those wobbly boards. God bless that woman! Her fears were not going to ruin a night in which she could share and watch all the fun wrapped around her granddaughter, Mindy, and the love of her life, Kevin. I also invited the Brunswick Police Department, since Kevin was well liked by the entire staff, even if he was a Yankee.

Everyone was ready for a moonlight ride down the Brunswick River and into the bay. I had all the food set up inside the large cabin. There were plenty of seats for those who wanted to sit and enjoy eating under cover. I served drinks up on deck, as well as hot and cold drinks in the cabin. It worked out well. It was a warm evening. I was hoping that the night air would create a pleasant breeze. The ferry was rocking with the excitement of laughter, music, dancing, eating, and drinking.

The trip was going smoothly when, all of a sudden, I realized the ferry was no longer moving. Mindy's grandfather, Willard Jacobs, asked me if I thought we had a problem. Barbara was calm, thank God, and seemed not to notice anything unusual. I didn't want to frighten her, but Willard was right, something was wrong. I went to look for Pepper and found him and Brian leaning over the side of the ferry, sick as dogs. Pepper said, "I think we're on a sandbar. Look! All I see is sand. You better go see the captain." Yes, Pepper was right. The captain had grounded the boat on a sandbar in the middle of the bay, and we were going to be stuck until he was able to get us off.

I asked Leroy, Danny, Wyman, and William B., all my cousins, if they knew how to solve this unexpected problem. They began to laugh and assured me that they would work their magic. They found some long poles and began pushing them into the sandbar, knowing this method should loosen the craft. The captain reversed the engine, revving it as fast as he could, hoping that the boat would free itself. Nothing happened. We were stuck and going nowhere.

Brian felt better the minute the ferry stopped moving. He went up on deck to join the fun. I also went up on deck. Everyone was having too much fun to notice that we weren't moving. Brian began to dance. It was the first time I had ever seen him dance. He did the Texas hoedown. I couldn't believe it. Was he drunk or just overjoyed for his brother? No way was I going to stop his fun or his dancing. I was too excited for him. He was funny and thoroughly enjoying himself. Everyone was watching him. The musicians played while Brian danced the hoedown. We all asked him when he learned how to do it. He said, "When you're in Texas, you do as the Texans do, and they do the Texas hoe-down. My buddies taught me so there wouldn't be a problem the next time we went out on the town."

While we were stuck, Pepper began to feel better and joined the crowd. He enjoyed talking to Willard and Ken, Mindy's dad, but I knew he was concerned, as were the other two men. They decided to go down to where my cousins were trying to loosen the boat. They watched anxiously, wanting the problem resolved before anyone panicked. About an hour later, the boys finally got the ferry to move slightly. The captain revved up the engine, once

again, and the boat slid off the sandbar. Their so-called magic worked. Few of our guests knew of the problem. Most thought we stopped so everyone could enjoy the beautiful waterfront homes whose lights shimmered across the bay, adding to the romantic mood of the evening.

It was a beautiful night, perfect for lovers and this special event. It seemed as if the moon descended upon our party, spreading its light far beyond the sides of the ferry. It was almost like a guide for the captain as the craft slid in and out of the well-lit pathway. The evening was all that it should have been, a romantic and wonderful, fun-filled night, one, I never want to forget.

KEVIN AND MINDY'S WEDDING   Saturday, June 6, 1981, the day of Kevin and Mindy's wedding, was one of the hottest days of the summer. The temperature was well up in the high 90s. It was early morning and we all knew that it was going to be a blister-burning day as the temperature rose.

The small, beautiful interior of the Methodist Church was the setting for their marriage ceremony. Flowers were placed around the altar. The simplicity of the atmosphere in the church gave everyone a sense of comfort and intimacy as participants in this young couple's wedding. The ceremony took place at 3:00 P.M.

The bride and groom with Ken and Cindy Knapp (Mindy's parents).
Pepper and I are in back of Kevin.

The organ began to play and the congregation stood and turned toward the entrance area. Standing in the vestibule was Ken with his beautiful daughter at his side. Mindy's gown was of white satin with a lovely lace bodice. The lace extended down her arms as sleeves. It was a clever effect and added to the gown's appearance. Her beautiful train trailed behind her. Ken's expression was filled with pride as he took Mindy's arm, and they began to walk down the aisle. In those few moments, Ken represented the dignity and pride every man feels as he gives his daughter away in marriage. His appearance was stately. It was beautiful as the two of them approached Kevin at the altar. Mindy's bouquet was made with a mixture of pink and white rosebuds, adding a lovely finishing touch to the bride's gown. The maid of honor followed in an attractive off-the-shoulder pink gown. Paul stood by Kevin's side as his best man. Kevin's outfit was light blue with a hint of navy blue in the jacket and on one stripe down the side of the pant legs. Paul's jacket was the same as Kevin's, but his pants were navy blue.

As I looked at my two sons standing together as brothers and sharing such an important event, I felt proud. I knew and respected both of them for the fine, honest men they had become. At the same time, I couldn't help but think, "How in the world did our three sons turn out so well after living with such screwed-up parents for so many years? God only knows, cause I surely don't." I could feel my eyes filling with tears. I wanted to savor that moment as they stood together; a moment that made it all worthwhile. Well, enough of that; back to the wedding.

Naturally, pictures were taken. Cindy, Mindy's mother, wore a dark-blue sleeveless afternoon dress, and I wore a sleeveless white dress with a small floral design. We both looked charming. Neither of us tried to outshine the other. I guess that's why the wedding was so unique. The photographer captured Brian in his Air Force dress uniform. He looked sharp and appeared tall and very thin. My eyes filled with tears as I looked proudly on my youngest son. Before we were escorted to the reception room, more pictures were taken.

The wedding reception was held in the church's banquet hall. Several tables were decorated softly, displaying enticing finger foods, appetizers, cheese and crackers, and ambrosia (Southern style). Hot tea and coffee were

available on smaller tables. Several churchwomen were stationed at the different tables to assist the guests. Large punch bowls filled with several assorted Southern drinks disappeared as quickly as they were replenished. Their unusual flavors tempted each of our taste buds. The cold punch was most welcome as the terrible heat wave enveloped the entire area. The church had no air-conditioning at all, and everyone was feeling the discomfort from the dreadful heat.

Kevin and Mindy in 2002.

Beside the drinks, one of the tables held the groom's devil's-food cake, covered with a light chocolate icing. A small figurine on top of the cake showed a groom trying to run away from his bride, who was holding onto his coat tails. I had never heard of a groom's cake, but I was told it's a Southern tradition. I liked it, great idea! It is the groom who must make the first slice into his cake. I have a picture of Kevin cutting his groom's cake as Mindy stands by watching.

The bride's cake consisted of four layers, each layer smaller than the previous one. It was a most impressive sight because the design of the icing was exquisite. Naturally, the top of the cake held figurine of a bride and groom under a covering of white bells. An arrangement of magnolia flowers encircled the base of the cake. Mindy sliced her cake and nicely gave Kevin a bite of it, upon which he returned the same gesture.

It was now getting late in the afternoon. The excitement of the day was about to come to an end. As we exited the church, a threatening thunderstorm loomed overhead, ready to drench everything in its path. When Kevin and Mindy appeared, they found their car covered in shaving cream with a "Just Married" sign hanging from one of the many streamers. As the couple waved their goodbyes to everyone, a huge bunch of cans, attached to the rear bumper, bounced about loudly as the car disappeared from sight. Pepper and I often said, "It was one of the nicest weddings we ever attended."

CUMBERLAND ISLAND Once Mother got settled in Brunswick, I visited her a couple times a year. Of my three boys, Brian spent most of his summers with her. As I had mentioned earlier, my Uncle Elmo was the captain on my cousin's ferry that took visitors/tourists to and from Cumberland Island. We had to drive about fifty miles to the small town of St. Marys, where the ferry was docked. Every day it made two runs to the island: one in the morning, one in the early afternoon, as well as the two return runs.

Cumberland Island's history goes back to the 1500s, when Indians and the Spanish shared, fought, and died on its sandy soil. The island is off the coast of Georgia. Before the Civil War, there were several large plantations on this island. They raised sea-island cotton and sugar cane with the help of their many slaves. Fruit trees were planted and did well for years until a heavy frost killed them. After the Civil War, several millionaires of the late 1800s and early 1900s built huge homes there as their summer refuges.

Every time my boys, Pepper, and I went south, we loved going to Cumberland with my uncle. We had unforgettable times doing this. The island was beautiful and is still secluded from the rest of the world. There are no stores, grocery or retail, no concession stands, no gas stations or billboards: nothing but an unbeliev-able and untouched island. Wild hogs; wild horses; huge snakes including diamondback rattlers and cotton-mouth moccasins; alligators; and other unpleasant beasts hide in its massive undergrowth, swamp, and beach areas.

Me on Cumberland Island's beach, with ocean and palm trees in background.

Whenever we arrived, we always took the path that led to the beach. On this pathway, many oak trees overlap each other making an enormous, long canopy that extends right up to the dunes. Huge oak trees, draped with Spanish moss, are scattered about the island, added to its unique atmos-phere. It was never unusual to spot wild horses and wild hogs running up

Dotty and me up in one of many giant oak trees on the island.
My cousin, William B., is standing.

and down an empty beach. Deer, raccoons, mink, and otters are common, no matter where you go. For all its beauty, it is still a very dangerous island.

The water surrounding Cumberland is a breeding ground for sharks. Even my boys feared going for a swim. We found many shark teeth, some very large and extremely old, buried in the ground where they were washed ashore decades ago. High sand dunes separate the beach from the rest of the island. People are not allowed to climb up the dunes. However, two of my friends and I managed to take a snapshot of each of us on one of them.

Plum Orchard, owned by the Rockefeller family, is still standing. My Uncle Freddie was one of the caretakers after the home was closed up during the 1970s. He took me inside Plum Orchard, and I was able to walk around and see what a magnificent home it must have been when the family spent its summers there. The thought of ever tearing down that massive Georgian-revival structure would be terrible. The architecture is rare.

Another large home, Greyfield, is still standing and is operating as a luxurious inn. Mrs. Lucy Ferguson, a daughter of Thomas Carnegie, brother and silent partner of steel magnate Andrew Carnegie, owned Greyfield back in

the 1970s and 1980s when I was there. Mrs. Ferguson knew Elmo because she took the ferry across to the mainland every now and then and always went up to the bridge to talk to him. I had an opportunity to meet her during that time, and she took me through Greyfield. Years later, John Kennedy, Jr., and his bride, Caroline Bessette, honeymooned at the inn after they were married in the island's small church.

The kitchen fascinated me because it was located on the first level. All the food was carried up to the dining room in a dumb waiter. The rooms on the second floor were dark and seemed to have an air of mystery, almost scary, within their thick walls. I also had a chance to go to the few remaining small slave quarters. I believe the Ferguson family has since turned these slave quarters into private living quarters for visitors at the inn.

One other home, owned by Thomas Carnegie, was called Dungenese. This home caught fire back in 1959, and when I was there in the 1970s and 1980s, it lay in ruins. The only objects standing were several large chimneys. I have stood many times looking at the ruins and thought how fascinating it must have been when life ran through its massive structure. These homes represented the typical Southern plantation of the 1800s.

MY BANISHMENT FROM THE RITTER FAMILY   Florence and Pauline had not seen Mother at all since my dad died in August 1974. They became enraged the day Mother read his will. Florence insisted that Mother was reading the wrong will because this will left us three girls nothing until Mother died. Mother told her that Dad had made a new will, removing Florence from being the executor. Before the new will, Florence was apparently to have total control of his money and estate. Mother said that Dad became concerned and decided to change his will. He never told anyone what he had done. Upon hearing that news, the two girls left extremely upset and immediately stopped all communication and association with Mother. Pauline's attitude apparently was the same as Florence's. She thought she was getting money as well. I never gave it any thought. I expected nothing. I never knew anything about Daddy's will or thoughts concerning his money. I guess I was, one might say, not too smart! I was as shocked as Mother and Affie.

The Ritter Family (l–r): Florence, Dad, Pauline, Mother, and me.

Mother told me that she had put the deed to her Brunswick, Georgia, home into my name, but she had occupancy rights for the rest of her life. She also mentioned that the house would be deducted from my share of our inheritance. I asked Mother to tell Florence and Pauline what she had done so that they would understand that it was her decision and her decision alone. I didn't want them to think I had anything to do with this. Shortly after that, Mother called me and told me she was coming up for Easter.

I called Florence and asked if she and her family would come for Easter dinner because Mother was coming up. She and her two children came, and I thought everything went well. What I didn't know was that Mother told Florence that she had put my name on the deed to her home. Florence and her kids went home, but the next day, she came and took Mother up to her home. A few days later, Florence brought Mother back because she was leaving for Brunswick the following day. However, Mother seemed rather upset with me, and I couldn't understand why. She said very little about her visit with Florence, but I presumed it went well. Perhaps now we could all move on and enjoy each other in a more normal way.

Once Mother returned to Brunswick, her attitude toward me changed drastically. Florence and Pauline began visiting her every couple of months. Before I knew it, I received a letter from Mother's lawyer requesting that my signature be removed from her deed. Mother wanted the house back in her name because she no longer trusted me. The letter was terrible. Mother began

phoning me, cursing and hollering. I was shocked and hurt by the terrible accusations she was screaming at me. I really didn't know what was going on.

In the meantime, Florence had flown Mother back up to her home. She and Ray took Mother to the bank that was handling Dad's estate, and Mother withdrew all of her money. They took her back to Easton, Pennsylvania. Mr. Figurelli from the Morris County Trust Company, who had charge of Mother's accounts, called me in a terrible state of shock and asked me if I knew what my mother had done. It was hard for me to believe, but it was true.

A short time later, I got several letters from another lawyer informing me that Mother was going to sue me if I didn't return the deed to her. By this point, I couldn't understand any of my mother's or my sister's thinking. What was wrong? It was still her house. She had life rights to it. I couldn't do anything with her home, nor did I want to.

I took the letters to my lawyer, Mr. Sheldon (Shelly) Simon. He read them and said that he would handle everything and that I was, by no means, to return the deed. He said that he felt that the home would be sold immediately, and I would end up with nothing. Shelly told me that he remembered the day my father changed his will. He was an intern in Paul Bangiola's office at that time and had never forgotten my dad's determination to remove Florence's name as executor and trustee of his will.

My sister, Florence; Ray; and their two children, Michael and Pamela.

During the mid-1980s, I received a couple of letters from my Aunt Affie and Fred informing me that my mother and sisters considered me "dead," no longer a member of the Ritter family, and that I was also being disinherited. Throughout the years, I wrote one letter after another to Mother. I begged, pleaded, and cried. My heart was broken for both of us. I felt that I should have given the deed back, but I knew it would have done no good. As the years passed, mother's hatred for me and my family had become irreversible.

I didn't know how to deal with my feelings. I was lost. My grief and shock were tearing me apart. My boys were married and had no time to help me. My family had no idea how desperate I was. I had to try to deal with it in my own way.

It was more than I could handle. I was living with unanswered questions that were eating at my heart, my gut, my mind. I could feel myself falling apart. How could my mother and sisters banish me in such a way? How could Pepper and my boys not see my terrible despair?

My younger sister, Pauline, and her family. Little Paul had not been born yet.

One evening, Pepper and I had a terrible argument. He told me that he was tired of hearing about it and wanted me to get over it. I screamed, "I can't! Help me! Please!" I struck him, and then all hell broke loose. It wasn't a pretty sight, the two of us beating on each other. I was afraid, angry, and humiliated. I felt completely lost as Pepper's cold, empty eyes stared down on me. As I got up, he told me again that I'd better get over it. I hurt, physically and mentally. I went upstairs and took an overdose of sleeping pills. Pepper called 9-1-1. I was taken to the emergency room, where they pumped my stomach. Then I was taken up to the ICU, where I stayed for several days. After I recovered, I began seeing a psychiatrist. I went to him for about three months. Finally, I was discharged. I began to realize that only I could change my life and that

all the talking in the world was not going to change anything. It was up to me to take control of my life.

My life started to change. Pepper's remarks didn't bother me as much. It was as if I had closed my ears and never heard what he was saying. It felt good. A short time later, I returned to my job at AT&T. Work is truly good for the soul. I put my banishment behind me. I held no hate toward Mother or my sisters. I knew I had to live with the situation, but it no longer overwhelmed me. For the first time, I began to believe in me. I began to realize that I didn't need anyone's approval. I began to believe in me even though it left me emotionally empty. It felt good, but I knew I still had a long way to go.

I visited Mother several times during 1986 and 1987. Each time, I left her home in a state of disbelief because of her hatred. I will never forget the time I got on my knees and begged her to forgive me for whatever she thought I had done. She raised her foot and kicked me. I got up from the floor, got my suitcase, and left her home. The last time I ever saw Mother, when I arrived at her home, she immediately began shouting at me, and I had to leave before she had a heart attack.

One of Affie's letters told me that Florence had moved Mother into a small three-room apartment and that her home had been rented to strangers. Many of Mother's beautiful things were sold off at a house sale. Affie was shocked when she saw where Mother was living and told Florence she should be ashamed of herself. A short time later, Affie found that her relationship with Mother changed to the point that she never knew how her sister was thinking. By the time Mother moved out of Brunswick, their relationship had come to a terrible end. Affie was being treated the same way I was. It broke Affie's heart. She finally could feel and understand the depth of my pain.

Mother lived in the apartment nearly a year. After Ray died, Florence and Mother moved to Scottsdale, Arizona.

In 1991, Affie and I went to Phoenix, Arizona, to visit all the canyons, such as the Grand Canyon, Bryce Canyon, etc. We went to Scottsdale and stopped at their home, hoping that we could see Mother. There was no answer, so we left a note telling Mother where we were staying and our phone number. We waited anxiously, but we never heard anything from

either of them. Another time when I was visiting some friends who had retired in Fountain Hills, Arizona, they took me by Florence's home, and I left another note. Again, nothing. *I had been banished, buried because of the desire for a dollar, greed, revenge, power, and control.*

OUR FOUR GRANDCHILDREN   Both Pepper and I adored our grandchildren. When they were small, they gave us such joy. They were all the things that grandparents ever expect from their very own. We were fortunate to have had two little girls (Elizabeth and Kelsey) and two little boys (Ryan and Travis) as grandchildren.

Some of the happiest times were when we made cookies together. Of course, most of the time it wasn't worth all the trouble, but they were happy, and I felt it was important. Whenever the holidays were approaching, I would make a large assortment of cookies. This was something I always did for my own children, and they still love to come into the house and find some kind of goodie waiting for whoever wants something to nibble on. The kids loved to decorate every cookie. What a mess! The kitchen had at least one coat of icing, and so did everything else the kids touched. Today they still love my cookies, and I am happy.

I loved to take them up to the different farms to pick apples, peaches, or strawberries when they were in season. One year I was lucky and took all four kids strawberry picking. I have pictures of them with their baskets filled

Strawberry picking with Travis, Beth, and Ryan. "We never do anything in a small way!"

with the fruit. They ate as many as they picked. It was wonderful hearing them laughing and enjoying our time together. I have fond memories of those many times.

Beth and Ryan always called me by the traditional name, "Grandma," but Travis and Kelsey never called me Grandma. As a small child, when Travis came over to visit, I always stopped whatever I was doing and played with him until he went home. One day when he came to visit, I excitedly said, "Oh, Travis, you came to play with your buddy." From that moment on, Travis began calling me "Buddy," and I have been Buddy ever since. Kelsey never heard me called anything but "Buddy," so I became Buddy to her as well.

I loved to take them shopping. When I did, I was bombarded with a constant string of requests and "hints": "Oh, wait a minute, Grandma/Buddy." "Oh, look how pretty this is." "Please, please, Grandma/Buddy, I won't ask for anything else." I could almost read their little minds. I knew what to expect, but I loved just watching their excitement. It was worth every cent it was going to cost me.

One year we were able to take Beth and Ryan up to New York State to visit Brian. We stopped for breakfast during the five-hour drive. We were ready to eat. The kids ate a good breakfast, which included a couple of doughnuts. They devoured them quickly. Well, I'm sure you know what I had to do. Yes, I ended up buying a dozen to take with us. We ate doughnuts until they were coming out of our ears. They were really good. Pepper and I often spoke about that trip and wished we could have had more trips with Beth and Ryan. Brian lived east of Syracuse in a village about five miles from Rome, New York. He had bought a home, and we went up to see it. It was in the country and directly across the street was a large farm with all kinds of farm animals. The kids had a great time.

Beth has never had any trouble devouring her favorite cookie, Snickerdoodles. Ryan also has his preference when it comes to snacks: my butter cookies with butter-cream icing covering each one. I have also noticed that he never turns down my peanut-butter cookies. (My recipes for these three treats are in Appendix G.) My grandchildren give me the feeling that I am important to them, and that is worth more than anything I can think of.

Halloween with Travis, Beth, Kelsey, and Ryan.

I have seen much more of Travis and Kelsey. Their lives have been very different from those of Paul's children. Kelsey has always loved my brownies, sour-cream Belgian waffles, and pumpkin pie. The pumpkin pie has my secret ingredient, and *only* Kelsey knows what it is. My cheesecake and tropical pound cake are two of Travis' favorite desserts. Both Travis and Kelsey insist that I make the pound cake whenever they have a birthday. Kelsey does not like icing, so I leave half of the cake plain, with only confectionary sugar sprinkled on her half. Travis wants icing on his half, so I make it according to his likes. I would say that they have Buddy well trained, and I love it! (You'll also find my recipes for Sour-Cream Belgian Waffles, Pumpkin Pie, Cheesecake, and Tropical Pound Cake in Appendix G. My recipe for Buddy's Brownies is in Appendix I.)

Over the years, I was able to take my four grandchildren to see the Christmas show at Radio City Music Hall. We always stopped and had our lunch in the restaurant on the lower level of Rockefeller Center so my grandchildren could watch the skaters better. I couldn't help but notice how impressed they always seemed. After lunch, we would walk along Fifth Avenue to see the many stores with beautifully decorated Christmas window displays. Naturally, shopping became the next item on our agenda. They were good times that we shared together.

All my grandchildren have touched my heart in many ways. I am so proud of Beth and Ryan and their accomplishments throughout their young

years. Kelsey is my little sweetheart. She loves me a great deal. I can tell by how worried she gets if I am not feeling well. She will do anything for me and is always keeping an eye on me. It is a nice feeling, and I eat it up. Travis is my little soldier because he reminds me of Pepper and Brian in many ways. Whenever the family goes on vacation, I'm usually sitting in the front seat. We sing, laugh, eat, and have a great time together. I don't think either of these two children will ever forget us. When Pepper was ill, they were with us almost every day. Pepper loved to see them. They made him smile, something I couldn't do.

TRAVIS' STORY   The simple statement from the movie, *Forrest Gump*, "Life is like a box of chocolates. You never know what you'll get," is a clever remark, as well as a true one. No one knows what tomorrow will bring, and few people worry about it so long as today is sunny and bright. What foolish thinking. One's world can go to hell within a minute, a day, or it may begin in the mother's womb, long before birth. Such is the case for so many handicapped children who are born with devastating afflictions.

Every new parent awaits that one moment when their eyes look upon their tiny newborn with its perfect little fingers, toes, and beautifully shaped head and body, but this is not the way it is for many couples. They, too, gaze lovingly at their newborn, but something is wrong. Bewilderment takes over because their tiny newborn is different from other infants. This precious child has a deformity. Did something go wrong during the pregnancy? Is this defect in the genes, or is there no explanation for the handicap?

The couple waits for answers to their many questions. Unfortunately, we don't hear about these families often nor do we feel their pain. We only learn about their lives when they are exposed to the public through either the news media or charitable organizations soliciting financial contributions to help with a particular child's handicap. In most cases, physical conditions appear upon birth, but many neurological and psychological conditions stay hidden until the child begins developing.

One of the lesser-known neurological disabilities is Tourette syndrome. Many people have never heard of this condition. It affects young boys more

Travis Beau Martin: "Oops! Caught in the act!"

than girls, usually by the age of five. One of the first signs of Tourettes is a constant blinking of the eyes, and then motor and vocal tics, Obsessive-Compulsive Disorder (OCD), slight Attention Deficit Disorder (ADD), and mental "tics" start manifesting themselves.

My grandson, Travis, is a victim of this disability. It was the blinking of his eyes that caught our attention. Mindy called Travis' pediatrician, who referred her to a neurologist. This doctor said that he felt sure it was Tourette syndrome. As a family, we were all shocked because we had never seen or heard of this disability. We looked at both sides of our families and could find nothing that showed it was genetically related. (I knew that my family was horribly dysfunctional and had all kinds of psychological problems, but none of us had neurological problems, at least I don't think so, but it wouldn't be the first time I could be wrong.) How, why, and where did this Tourette syndrome come from? These questions have never been answered, and to this day, they leave us wondering about what went wrong. Was it just fate, an unfortunate and difficult disability, or was it similar to the saying, "Life is like a box of chocolates. You never know what you'll get"?

From the day Mindy talked with the neurologist, my grandson's life has been a constant bout of tics and the terrible frustration and fear that accompany each and every tic. These involuntary tics come in many forms, such as nose-wrinkling, facial grimaces, head or hand jerks, body shrugs, and

jumping. Tourettes causes the many muscles in the body to go out of control, sometimes causing the sudden thrust of an arm or a leg. At times, tics will affect the eyes, causing them to roll up into the Tourettes sufferer's head.

Tourettes vocal tics include barking noises, nonstop throat clearing, and the endless repetition of a word or sound, the so-called phonic tics. Some vocal tics cause the patient to suddenly begin shouting all kinds of filthy words. If this occurs in public, people usually turn away in disgust, never knowing that the person is unable to control the outburst. The humiliation must be horrifying for a Tourette syndrome victim who normally would never utter such foul language. Vocal tics, such as a loud squeal or even a scream, can be alarming, but again, Travis can't always control these either. When he is able to suppress them on occasion, they come back with a vengeance later.

Tourettes tics can last for hours. Travis is constantly apologizing. He is so afraid that the outside world will laugh at him or consider him a threat. Travis is an extremely kind and gentle young person. He would be horrified if anyone ever thought he was dangerous in any way. His home has been his only source of security. Schooling has been difficult because his tics can interfere with his thinking. For many years the local school system has provided a special-ed teacher to work with him one-on-one for a couple of hours each day. Many times, the teacher would come to the house; other times Travis would go to school, depending on his medical condition. Travis is now in the eighth grade. He will be with his peers for the first time during several different classes in the hope that he will be able to adjust by gaining more confidence in himself.

By the time many young patients have reached their mid-teens, their Tourettes symptoms subside, making life more bearable. They are the lucky ones. Hopefully, Travis will fall into this category. Anything would be an improvement in his lifestyle. Since he developed Tourettes, Travis has had almost no normal childhood. He missed the fun of doing all the things little boys love to do. Now that he is fourteen, I hope his Tourettes will begin to allow him the freedom, strength, and courage to enjoy other adolescents and the outside world. Unfortunately, many Tourette syndrome patients never

improve and can become even more disabled because of the ongoing, never-ending tics and the emotional strain of trying to control each one. This can be extremely difficult. No one knows the vengeance that these tics can wreak on a patient when he or she does try to control them. It is such an agonizing pain that the outside world cannot possibly imagine unless they are familiar with the symptoms or have a family member that has Tourettes.

Most people know little about Tourette syndrome, even though there is the Tourette Syndrome Association. Patients and families of Tourettes children can turn to this organization, but the help it can offer is limited. The entire family must learn how to adjust to the physical and emotional aspects of this disability and the difficulties it presents to those trying to maintain a normal family environment. I am a firm believer that there is a reason for everything. God only gives each of us as much pain as he feels we can stand. The rest is up to us. Each of us has a special gift, but unless we try to find it, we will go though life never knowing our true capabilities. I believe that we find it through our own hardships and our determination to overcome them.

Until the public is made more aware of this disheartening and difficult disability, these young, innocent Tourettes patients continue to live with unjustified and hurtful blame for behavior they cannot control. As Travis' grandmother, I have seen and felt the hardships, heartache, and pain that are always present. No one is excluded. Regardless how small or how severe a situation may present itself, love, patience, understanding, and the necessary intelligence and strength are the most powerful medicines for Tourettes victims.

KELSEY'S STORY My youngest granddaughter is a constant delight. I look at her and see a lovely child and a beautiful young woman down the road. She amazes me because at times she seems much more mature than her age. Kelsey is sensitive, caring, and very protective of her "little ol' Buddy."

Life is full of unexpected surprises, good and bad. Unfortunately, Mindy and Kevin learned that Kelsey had been diagnosed as dyslexic, which means that she has a great deal of trouble learning to read. My little granddaughter attended the Boro Grammar School since kindergarten. She is now in the fifth grade, but is no longer attending Boro School.

By the time Kelsey had reached second grade, Mindy noticed that her daughter was having difficulty reading. Mindy began attending each and every meeting with her teacher, hoping to hear something positive. She went along with the school's suggestion of putting Kelsey into a special reading group. However, she was still below average in reading. Something was definitely wrong and involved the school system, the child, and the parents.

Kelsey was beginning to realize that she was different from most of the kids in her classroom when it came time for her to read. She was losing confidence in herself and was beginning to pretend she didn't feel well in order to stay at home. Mindy was more alarmed than ever and knew that something more had to be done. Kelsey was living an emotional nightmare for a nine-year-old child.

Kelsey Brie Ann Martin, age four, at Cape May.

Because of Travis' Tourettes, Mindy knew about the child-study team at Rutgers University and made an appointment to have Kelsey tested. By January of her fourth year, the study team's reports all showed that Kelsey was dyslexic. Her reading skill was evaluated at a level just below that of an average first grader, even though the school was using the Wilson Reading approach.

Sometimes life just doesn't seem fair. Mindy and Kevin were angry and emotionally upset by Kelsey's problem. The Rutgers group had told them that, with proper training, Kelsey would learn to read. She was never considered retarded in any way nor did the testing show a more severe problem than dyslexia. Mindy kept all the reports and continued to take Kelsey to this child-study group. Today, Kelsey is attending the Banyan School in Fairfield. They also use the Wilson approach, but they apply it in her other subjects, as well. Hopefully, this will solve Kelsey's problem.

OUR TRIP TO IRELAND   On May 28, 1987, Pepper and I left for Ireland. I knew that a group tour would not please him, so I made arrangements to

have a car waiting for us when we arrived at Shannon Airport. This would allow us to go wherever we wanted with no reservations anywhere. We had an evening flight, which gave us a chance to sleep and ready for our first full day in southern Ireland, also known as the Free State. As we approached Shannon Airport, I looked out and saw the many different shades of green covering the open fields below. Once we got our car and a map, we decided to head for Cork, which is in the southern part of Ireland. Then we planned to head west to the Ring of Kerry, the Dingle Peninsula, Killarney, and the Tralee area.

We began to see the remains of one castle after another, once we left the Shannon area. King John's Castle was open to the public as a tourist attraction, but we decided that the Cork area would be more interesting. We passed through the towns of Limerick, Tipperary, and Fermay, arriving in Cork around noontime. It was a strange sight to see rows of houses, each with some type of fencing surrounding and separating it from the other homes. It was as if each family looked upon its small plot of land as its dynasty, off limits to the outside world.

We found a bed and breakfast tourist home that was located within walking distance of the city itself. The owners, Mr. and Mrs. Malloy, were eager to talk about the area and all that it offered. The River Lee separated the town into two sections, the old and the new. Our walking tour included the business sections of Cork, as well as the shops scattered about on many of the side streets. Shopping and sightseeing kept us much busier than we had planned. It was late, and we still had not had dinner. The restaurant we chose was located in old Cork. It was highly recommended by the Malloy's. On our way, we walked over an interesting arched stone bridge whose history goes back centuries. Our first day in Ireland proved to be fascinating but exhausting. We were surprised to find the sun still out when we left the restaurant around 11:00 P.M. The manager told us that the light was not from the sun but from the aurora borealis. Total darkness at that time of the year only lasted three to four hours. We stood looking up at this strange sight as streaks of colors spread throughout the heavens. It was beautiful.

We spent a couple of days in Cork and then continued our trip. The Lakes of Killarney had a mist that hung over them and presented an eerie

scene. Some of the surrounding mountains looked like they were made of stone, while others were covered with trees and greenery. The contrast between the lakes and the mountains was typical of the many myths that spread across Ireland. The Ring of Kerry and the Dingle Peninsula disclosed a rare beauty. Along the narrow roadways and open fields, sheep with differently colored markings roamed freely, as did the herds of cattle. The colored marks were "brands" that indicated each animal's owner. We learned that the animals had priority over other traffic on any roads that we traveled. It was like we had gone back in time. There were no major highways. Every turn of the road presented something unusual to our eyes as we passed through the many small coastal villages.

It was a painter's paradise. Both of us loved every moment. We walked about the villages, going into one shop after another, talking to the local people, going down on the docks where the fishermen were gathered. We saw their catch of the day and listened to their tales. Both of us hated to leave the rustic simplicity of the area.

On our way to Tralee, we spent the night at a working farmhouse. It was an experience I never forgot. The owners (I can't remember their names) had just opened their farmhouse as a B&B. We were their first guests, and the

Pepper showing the width of the mountain road at the end of our trip around the Ring of Kerry.

fact that we were Americans made it even more exciting for them, or so they said. The men took Pepper around the farm, showing him their animals and equipment and explaining everything they did. Little space separated the barns from the farmhouse, allowing the smells to seep into every corner of the house. They apologized for the odor, but reminded us that it is all part of living on a farm. They were right! Our room was lovely and we slept well.

The next morning, before we were out of bed, wonderful smells floated up from the kitchen. We came downstairs to a lovely scene. Our table was near a large window that looked out on the farm. It was set with a real country charm. Breakfast featured eggs, (fresh that morning), ham, Irish bread and rolls, plus hot Irish oatmeal and coffee with their own heavy cream. As we sat, enjoying every moment, we began to feel eyes on us. We turned and saw two cows looking in at us, their noses pressed against the window. It was funny. They watched us eat every morsel of food. I do believe that if we had opened the window, they would have joined us.

The next day, we traveled north to Tarbert, crossing the River Shannon by ferry. We saw many homes with thatched roofs, which naturally caught Pepper's attention. We decided to turn off at Ennis so we could go over by the Cliffs of Moher. I never knew that Ireland had such high cliffs. I managed to take pictures that show the height of those cliffs. Unbelievable! A detour well taken! Highways (nothing like ours) made the miles go by quickly as we traveled northeast to Dunguaire. From Galway, we detoured to the west to see the Connemara area, famous for its stones. I brought several pieces of jewelry made from these stones. It was an interesting area. Then Pepper drove north into Mayo County where Croagh Patrick Mountain was located. This is where St. Patrick brought Christianity to Ireland, or so the story goes. We circled back to Tuam, where we spent another night at a local hotel. It was nothing special. We were in no hurry as we drove north. There was much to see.

Pepper became interested in the many peat bogs. At one of the sites, he stopped so he could talk to the men. They told him that they would begin to dig a small area, using a special rectangular-shaped shovel. As they dug, they would slice the peat into many different sizes. Then, they would dry the

peat out, and it would be sold as peat moss. This was used in fireplaces in place of wood. Stone walls dividing the huge, open fields are another familiar sight throughout Ireland. They are everywhere. Many walls had broken down but their remains were still part of an existing one. To our surprise, we found that many children, most of whom were under ten years of age, hitchhiked. It was hard to believe that Ireland allows this.

We picked up a little girl about four years old and her brother, about seven years old. They were very talkative and had no fear of anyone harming them. They were on their way to meet their mother at their grandmother's home. I taped our entire conversation as we traveled in the direction of the four crosses where they wanted to go. It was, at least, a thirty-five-mile trip for these kids, and both of us just shook our heads as they climbed out of our car.

Small donkeys were another interesting sight. They are used to pull carts filled with sod and other brush. We would see an occasional one just walking along the side of the road. This would have looked so out-of-place in our world, but it was an everyday occurrence in Ireland. Gypsies are common throughout Ireland. We saw many with their small trailers parked along the highway. No matter how many campers we saw, each one would have its occupants' wash hanging over the railings of the highway. The gypsies do not have a good reputation among the Irish people. They are definitely put down on a lower level than the Irish.

We traveled through the towns of Ballyhaunis, Sligo, Bundoran, and Ballyshannon and finally stopped in Donegal for the night. All the homes are made of stone and concrete. We stopped at one shop after another as we headed north. The small towns were waiting for tourists like us. I bought two Claddagh rings, which should be worn with the crown towards the knuckle, if one is single. If one is married, one wears the crown towards the nail. Each shop had its own supply of Irish wool sweaters, hats, and pleated and plaid skirts. In the coastal village of Killybegs and Inver, west of Donegal, I bought Beth a lovely Irish plaid skirt, and Pepper bought himself an Irish tweed cap. He enjoyed wearing his souvenir until he could no longer go outside. Donegal tweed is world famous.

In Donegal we found a delightful B&B overlooking Donegal Bay. The owner couldn't do enough for us. His native wit and charm, as well as his constant advise about where we could get the best buys, kept us entertained. I remember my first breakfast at this quaint B&B. We sat on an enclosed porch, looking out at the bay. It was a picture-perfect scene. Irish oatmeal, eggs, fruit, Irish bread and lots of coffee with cream, were our breakfast. I taped a lot of our conversation with our host; he was a natural. I wanted to capture what he said and the wonderful sound of his voice. I still have those tapes, and I occasionally listen to them and relive some wonderful times.

I wanted to go to the Beleek china outlet, hoping to get some good buys on their fine china. Our host suggested we go back to Ballyshannon and pick up the road that would take us to Enniskillen, where the Celtic Weave China shop was located. It was operated by two couples whose family had worked for generations creating Beleek china. When Beleek decided to mass-produce its products, these couples opened their own shop. We decided to take our host's advice, since the shop was located just a short distance from a military guard post at the border with Northern Ireland.

It was a sad sight to see soldiers carrying weapons and checking each person waiting to go into Northern Ireland. The trip proved to be everything our host said it would be. I was able to purchase a beautiful small bowl with hand-painted floral sprays of many flowers. For our evening dinner, our host suggested we try what he considered to be the best local restaurant. Once again, he was right. While we waited to be seated, we were entertained by two Englishmen who insisted on buying us one drink after another. I think that by the time the four of us left, we were all pretty tipsy. It was an evening of funny stories, laughter, and song.

We spent three days in the Donegal area and then drove up to Derry, which is in Northern Ireland. However, just after we passed the military guard post outside the city limits of Derry, Pepper realized that we had never exchanged our money for English pounds and that there was no way for us to get any money because the banks were still closed. We turned around and went back into the Free State. Just a short distance from the guard post, we saw a hotel and decided to stop there for the night.

There were no cars in the parking lot, and I didn't think it was open. Nothing was nearby, only empty fields that stretched for miles. I wondered why such a location had been picked for this hotel. How could they make any money? It was strange. Pepper opened the door and went in. The desk clerk asked him to sign the registration book if we wanted a room for the night. When he opened it, we both noticed that they had not had a visitor since November 1986. I looked at him with concern. I was ready to leave. He went ahead and signed us in. The clerk told us to go into the recreation room, have a drink, and enjoy the fire she had started a short time ago. She also mentioned that she was going to turn on the heat so that our room would be warm and we would have hot water. That worried me even more as I thought, "My God, what have we walked into?" Well, we followed her advice, ordered a drink, and sat by the fire.

I noticed a group of men huddled together at a corner table in the back of the room. They appeared to be planning something. I whispered, "Oh, my God, I bet they're IRA men, Pepper! This place is their hangout!" One of the men got up. I watched him as he lumbered toward us. He was strange and creepy. "If they are all like him, we could be in big trouble, Pepper!"

I noticed that the men had immediately turned their attention in our direction. I felt uncomfortable and wanted to leave. The clerk came in with the dinner menu, informing us that no food had been prepared, but that she could defrost some shrimp and fish. I ordered fried shrimp, and Pepper ordered broiled fish. The dining room was huge and every table was set as if there were going to be a party. By this time, my imagination was out of control. I had convinced myself that it was a perfect setting for a murder. No one knew our whereabouts. The clerk and those strange men knew we were American tourists. They knew we probably had plenty of money on us. When our food came, I found I could not eat. I began thinking that they could have poisoned it. That did it! I dumped all my food into my pocketbook. Pepper couldn't believe it. Finally, the woman came in and told us that our room was ready. Thank God!

We went down a long, poorly lit hallway to our room. I took a chair and propped it under the doorknob as Pepper just sat, shaking his head in disbelief

as he watched me. By now, I was terrified of what could happen. There was no TV to watch nor anything else to do, so we went to bed. Pepper asked me if I was going to get undressed. I said, "No way. If any of them try to come into this room, I'm out that window!" All Pepper could say was, "You gotta be kidding."

Sleep was almost impossible for both of us. I slept in my clothes. At 6:00 A.M., Pepper woke me and said, "Let's go!" At that, I grabbed my bag and followed him to our car. I could not believe I had worked myself into such a terrified state. Even though Pepper acted like everything was fine, he seemed as anxious as me to get moving. We both needed some coffee, so we drove back to the small village of Bridgend and found an open coffee shop. As early as it was, the coffee tasted good. Afterwards, we headed for Northern Ireland and the city of Derry with its military guard posts and soldiers bearing guns as they patrolled the streets.

Upon arriving in Derry, we found a newspaper store open and thought that perhaps they would be able to make change. Pepper explained our money problem to the owner. He, in turn, called over another man, and began to explain our situation to him. They told us that the local bank would not open until 9:00 A.M., which left us with a two-hour wait. They suggested that we go around the corner where we would find a hotel. We were to go in and ask for Mike.

When we entered the hotel, Mike was standing there with a big smile. He told us that the two men were friends of his and that they had called him in hopes that he would help us with our problem. Mike told us that he loved Americans and that he was going to cook us a Northern Ireland breakfast that would beat any breakfast we had in the Free State. By that time, all the banks in Northern Ireland would be open. It was the best breakfast we had. We offered to pay with what money we had, but he insisted it was a gift from the country we were now in.

We left Derry and headed southeast, going through several small towns. Each town had soldiers walking back-to-back with guns aimed for immediate action. This was alarming to see because it showed us the reality of everyday life in Ireland. When we reached Dungannon, we stopped at the first bank we saw, parked the car, and both of us went in.

When we came out of the bank, a man was standing by our car. He asked us if we were Americans. He told us that one person must always stay in a parked car when in the business section of any village, town, or city. Otherwise it would be towed away, immediately. He explained that a parked car had blown up the previous week and had torn apart a building down the street. Several people had been killed. He advised us that this rule was strictly enforced throughout Northern Ireland. I took pictures of this area showing the soldiers and the police headquarters, which was well secured with barbed-wire fencing and observation cameras.

We headed south to Newry, where we detoured, passing through the villages of Rathfrilan and Kilcoo, in order to reach the coastal town of Newcastle, Northern Ireland, by the Irish Sea. We arrived in Newcastle in a rainstorm. We walked out on the beach, but the weather had turned bitter cold. Just off the beach was The Dog Head Inn, and we decided to go there for lunch. It was a good idea. At least we could get warm. I have pictures of the area that show the nasty weather, as well as the entrance to the inn.

After we ate, we decided to take the route on the ocean side of the Mourne Mountains and Silent Valley. Driving along the coastline was thrilling. We passed through small villages, such as Bloody Bridge, Glassdrummond, Annalong, and Ballymartin. The town of Kilkeel was as far south as we could go.

Then we headed back up to Warrenpoint, where we passed one of the prettiest gazebos I have ever seen. In this town I found my two Lladro jesters and two Lladro ballet girls. At that time, my little granddaughter, Beth, was taking ballet lessons. She was about eight years old when she was in her first dance recital. When I saw these two Lladro figurines, I knew I wanted to add them to my collection. I always prized them because they reminded me of our trip to Ireland (our last trip together). They also reminded me of how funny and cute my granddaughter looked in her little tutu, tights, ballet slippers, and the two small ribbons that tied her hair back when she was performing in one of her recitals. Lladro figurines are well known throughout the world. They are made in Tavernes Blanques, Spain, under the guidance of the three Lladro brothers, Jose, Vicente, and Juan. They mastered the fine art of creating extraordinary beautiful porcelain figurines.

I have been collecting Lladro figurines for over twenty years and have at least seventy-five interesting pieces.

We continued traveling until we arrived in the small town of Armagh, where Pepper was going to try to locate his cousin, Mary, and some other family members he had never met or known about. Military guard posts were at each entrance and exit to Armagh. Again, the reality of the times looked us in the eyes, and it was frightening. Soldiers were everywhere. We had a hard time finding where Mary lived. Out of desperation, we asked the guards if they knew her, and to our surprise, they did. She used to ride a small motorcycle into town, always stopping at their post. She was a novelty to them. They gave us directions to her home. When we arrived at her small cottage, she was surprised, having never thought that Uncle Joe's son would come to Ireland.

At first, Mary thought we were Jehovah's Witnesses and was about to run us off with her broom. After she learned who we were, we stayed with her for several days, going all around Armagh and the surrounding area. While we were there, we had the real English version of fish and chips for the first time. Each dinner was wrapped in a thick newspaper. We sat on one of the sidewalk benches and enjoyed our tasty meal. Mary took us over to another cousin's home about five miles away from Armagh. Pepper had never heard of this cousin and her family, but he was happy to meet them. We checked out the large food stores to see if they sold anything unusual compared to our groceries in the U.S. I believe we went into every shop in Armagh.

We continued south to the town of Drogheda, where we were going to visit Dessi and Anna Mathews and their sister Kitty and her husband, Tom. This particular area, the valley of the River Boyne, has prehistoric sites dating back to 5000 BC. Now that really impressed me! We girls were constantly shopping and sightseeing while Dessi and Pepper did their thing. One afternoon we drove up to Slane and walked around an eighteenth-century castle. Pepper noticed how straight the road had been, compared to all the other roads. Dessi told him that, centuries ago, a nobleman from Dublin had the road straightened so it wouldn't take him so long to get to his mistress, who lived in Slane.

Late that afternoon as we wondered about Slane, we decided to have dinner in a nearby restaurant, and then our hosts took us to their favorite Slane pub. It was a lifetime remembrance. The locals were drinking, singing, and telling stories and jokes, each one trying to outdo the others. Their songs brought laughter and tears to all of us. The more everyone drank, the more beautiful and sorrowful the songs became. We spent an exciting week with Anna and Dessi.

We toured the city of Dublin, including a ride on the double-decker bus. We toured Trinity College, the Civic Museum, St. Patrick's Cathedral, and the Mansion House. I know that Moran's pub in Drogheda was a favorite spot for Pepper and Dessi because it was well known for its Guinness beer and oysters. We hated to leave, but our trip was over. We said our goodbyes as tears filled all of our eyes. We knew that we would probably never see each other again.

We felt sad as we left the Drogheda area on the drive across the midlands that would take us to the Shannon Airport. We arrived in the area around noon, but decided to stop in a small village and have lunch. Our plane was not taking off until late afternoon. We never expected our last meal in Ireland to be of such high quality. The restaurant was small, similar to any Irish cottage. Once inside, we felt its simplicity, its warmth from the large stone fireplace, and the aromas of Ireland's favorite foods, which floated throughout. Our lunch consisted of baked Irish Salmon with a special sauce and vegetables. We have never had salmon that had been cooked or that tasted like that since we came home.

The young couple who owned the restaurant were Americans. He had been a chef in one of the big hotels in New York City. They told us that while they were vacationing in Ireland, they both fell in love with its simplicity. They went back to the States, sold everything, and moved to that area of Ireland. After our meal, we drove to the airport, where we returned our car, checked-in at our airline's counter, and went to our flight's waiting area. An hour later we were allowed to board the plane. Both of us sat reflecting on our unforgettable trip as we waited to take-off.

As the plane lifted into the sky, we saw the coastline of Ireland disappear. It was a sad moment because neither of us had ever enjoyed each other's company as much as we did on this trip. This was a rare treat, and it felt

good. Our silent thoughts were the same. We wished we had taken this trip many years ago. Perhaps we would have made the same move that the young couple in the restaurant made. Perhaps a move such as that would have made our love deeper, our relationship closer, and given us a better understanding of who we were.

PEPPER'S ILLNESS, FAIRLEIGH DICKINSON UNIVERSITY/EPOP GROUP By the end of 1987, Pepper's health forced him to make one of the hardest decisions of his life. Because he was finding it more and more difficult to climb ladders and handle heavy bundles of shingles, he knew that he had no choice but to retire. "Retire" was a word that had never been allowed to be mentioned or discussed. His life was no longer the way he had planned. It was the beginning of the end for him. He was in the early stages of losing control over his life and, eventually, my life as well. This was devastating for him.

For several decades, Pepper was convinced that his death would be the result of a roofing accident, never an illness. Thus, his attitude, from the day he quit roofing, was wrapped in anger, resentment, and torment. As the days turned into months and the months into years, Pepper came face to face with the fact that he had no control over his destiny. He was going to die of emphysema, of an illness. He could not believe that an illness was going to take him down. This was not the way he had it planned.

Most people look forward to their retirements, but Pepper was not like most people. His satisfaction and contentment were wrapped up in his work and his home. He loved his home. It was his castle. He loved his work. It gave him power, satisfaction, pride, and wealth that grew out of sweaty, grinding, backbreaking drudgery.

I had no idea what an impact this was going to have on my life. In the beginning of his illness, my daily schedule stayed the same. It had not affected my job at AT&T. I enjoyed the benefits of my weekly paychecks and the feeling of gaining more and more control of my own life. I felt comfortable on leaving him by going to work. It became my escape from his scrutiny and disapproval. I knew that he was still able to take walks, drive the car, talk to people, and do small jobs around the house. Even though Pepper turned

the business over to Paul, he continued to play a part in it by doing all the office work. This arrangement worked well for both of them.

As time passed, Pepper and I were learning to make the most out of what faced us both. In a way, the two of us found happiness and satisfaction in our everyday lives that seemed to mask our real concerns and problems. We still continued to argue and find fault with each other. Pepper held on to his desire to control every situation, but he knew that both of our lives were changing.

By 1989, Pepper began going upstairs as soon as I returned from work. He began the silent treatment again. He only came downstairs when family or friends came in, and then, once again, he talked around me. I had all I could do not to scream at him. I didn't need this, not with everything else that was going on. At mealtimes, he would come down and eat and then go right back upstairs, never saying a word to me. I tried to act like it didn't bother me, but it did. He continued in this manner for a period of six months. Nothing changed. It was terrible to live in a house under such conditions. I wanted to run away but didn't have the courage. My conscience would never allow me to do this. I had a lifetime to run out on him (if I had had the courage), but should I now when he really needed me? I may have been screwed up in many ways, but I knew the difference between what was right and what was wrong. I knew how terribly empty my life had become. So much was missing from our lives.

Over the years, I turned to God with one prayer after another. I kept on cooking, cleaning, washing, and managing to go to work. Nothing changed except that I was beginning to feel as if I were learning how to live around his difficult moods. I often thought, "How can people live like this?" I knew that many men like Pepper still held on to the old tradition: men are in complete charge over their families. Much to my surprise, I began to feel this was a whole lot of bull, and I was getting fed up with this type of view-point. I enjoyed that strange feeling. Working in the corporate world, as I was now, surrounded by younger people and listening to their views on the ways of the world, I began to feel that women no longer needed to stay under the control of their spouses. Pepper's actions no longer bothered me. I was beginning not to worry whether he loved me or not. As much as I

wanted his love, I knew he would never give me that satisfaction. He couldn't give it, and I was determined that it was not going to destroy me. I knew that he needed me more than I needed him at this point in our lives. I found that knowledge was very satisfying.

During 1991, I became ill and went out on sickness disability for one year. Pepper was surprised by this, as well as disappointed and angry at the thought of my being at home all day. By 1992, suffering constant bouts of pneumonia and chronic obstructive pulmonary disease (COPD), I was forced to go on long-term disability. Silently, we both knew that the future was going to be difficult. We were constantly adjusting our lives to accommodate unexpected everyday situations. However, I continued receiving disability checks every month from AT&T, which made my illness a little easier to accept. When the AT&T checks stopped, I went on Social Security disability. When I became sixty-five years old, I began receiving my social-security check plus my monthly pension check from AT&T. Life was good to me. It allowed me to keep my independence intact.

One day, it seemed as if nothing mattered anymore. I realized that Pepper was actually enjoying our hellish situation. My feelings were changing from anger to pity. I felt sorry for him. All the mental and physical abuse I had lived with throughout our fifty-one years together no longer tormented me. Right up to his death, I felt that nothing mattered except that I was going to survive any way I could. No way was I going to walk out and loose everything that I, too, had worked so hard for. I was determined to put up with anything and everything if I could just have a better life down the road.

The most painful thought that I have had to live with all these years was never hearing Pepper say, "I'm sorry." There were so many times when situations arose where those words should have been said, but his pride and stubbornness would not allow it. I knew that he was grateful for not being placed in a nursing home. I knew that long ago he cared, and I hopefully thought that perhaps he was sorry for the many unpleasant times as well. Underneath all of this, I knew that we did love each other a lifetime ago. I knew that I had managed to survive and that, in itself, was my greatest reward. However, it left me with an emptiness that will be with me for the rest of my life.

In 1995, I joined the Fairleigh Dickinson University senior group called the Educational Program for Older People (EPOP). One had to be over sixty-five years old to join. This program allowed me to take credited college courses for only one hundred dollars. I signed up for many different writing and computer courses. It became wonderful therapy for me. I had started to write these memoirs and felt I needed more training in writing. I enjoyed being with the young college kids, listening to their ideas and goals. To my surprise, they, in turn, loved to listen to my stories about things that happened long before any of them were born. We had very interesting debates. Various professors often remarked that I contributed a great deal to the class, making it refreshing and exciting for the younger people. I stayed with the EPOP credited courses for nearly four years and accumulated almost enough credits for two years of college. I was short by three credits. When Pepper's health took a turn for the worse, I had to stop.

It was during these years that I also began seeing many of my friends' own health beginning to decline. Life was becoming more and more frustrating and difficult for each of us. We were living with constant pain somewhere in our old bodies. Just walking sometimes hurt. Eyes were becoming blurry, indicating problems in the making. Some of us were getting more bent over. Our bones were more fragile and our breathing more difficult due to emphysema, asthma, or COPD. Many experienced severe stomach problems, as well as serious heart problems. More and more friends were developing some type of cancer.

Aging really hit home when my friend, Donna Osanna, died suddenly. Her death left everyone who knew her in a state of shock. Donna, Mildred Heffernan, and I, who all worked together in the emergency room for many years, always kept in contact with each other. Death, however, waits for no one. The three of us had planned to meet for dinner, but that morning I saw Donna's obituary in the paper. I called Mildred. Words could not describe our feelings. We were stunned, speechless at the loss of such a dear friend and companion.

Donna's death was just another example of life's unpredictability. Tomorrow is not guaranteed. It's a gift given to us by God. Pepper was slowly deteriorating, and I knew death was waiting for him as well. We were aging, and with that came tremendous medical expenses. We all are, or should be,

entitled to Medicare, but its coverage of medical expenses is limited. Secondary insurance is costly, and inflated medical charges were taking a toll on what little money many of my friends had. Because Mildred's health had deteriorated so badly, she had to leave the Morris County area. She and her husband had been separated for many years, but they both found that they needed each other in order to survive. It was easier to maintain one apartment rather than two. Monies were not keeping up with the constant increases in the cost of living. This has become a big problem for most seniors.

The classes I took at Fairleigh Dickinson University inspired me. Writing became a new source of therapy. I feel that it is similar to cooking, but instead of ingredients, it's a combination of words, which when finished, becomes a story. Pepper was slowly dying. He needed me. My life was wrapped around him except for the few hours each week I spent at Fairleigh. Pepper's illness gave me strength I never knew I had. Fairleigh Dickinson University provided the therapy. It was a great combination, certainly better and cheaper than bi-weekly visits to a local psychiatrist or joining a grieving-therapy group that seemed (at least to me) to immerse themselves in a never-ending cycle of misery, pain, and refusal to move on with their lives.

WRITING FICTION AND POETRY   Even though I was still writing my memoirs, I knew that I needed a different challenge, so I began writing about two old ladies, their afternoon outing, and the events that followed. I call the short story "Reflections." It is fiction, but it seemed different from my other writing because it had nothing to do with my life or with any of my family or friends. My fiction writing took me to the world outside, and I reveled in its creation. Writing had become my partner. It was as important to me as a security blanket is to a small child.

My classmates (kids still in their late teens) had to critique it, and both the professor and I were surprised by their comments. One girl said, "This story was very moving to me because I never thought elderly people lived with such fears and loneliness. I decided that whenever I see an elderly person sitting alone, I will be sure to say, "Good morning" or "Have a nice day." Apparently, my story touched each of them; they all felt tremendous

compassion for the main characters, two old women. It was as if I had opened a door that exposed them to another side of life that they had never seen or thought about. I was surprised to have seen such a positive response to something I wrote.

My mood swings are fairly evident in my short story but are even more noticeable in some of the poetry I wrote. I'm including these in my memoirs (see Appendix B) because they show my rocky emotional state during those few years. My poem "Generations" is a perfect example of my periodically depressed state of mind. The two other poems I've included in Appendix B are "Nature at Work" and "A Day on the Beach." Apparently my mood swings were on a high when I wrote those. They express an appreciation of God's gifts.

I feel sure that "Reflections" will never be published. I can't imagine magazines such as *Good Housekeeping, Ladies Home Journal,* or *Reader's Digest* publishing it because of the depth of the despair it reflects. I know that the AARP magazine would definitely frown on its subject matter and would probably consider it "R-rated" material, but I found that my writing awoke something in my young classmates and that made it all worthwhile.

The EPOP group had special non-credited classes of their own in which we all participated, each of us choosing to enroll in one or more. These classes included square dancing, video travelogues, computer training, scientific subjects, debates on present day problems, great books discussion, etc. They asked me to take over one of the classes that pertained to video travelogues. It sounded interesting, and I accepted their invitation. So, for four years, I presented "Armchair Travels." Once a week, I went to the library and got a movie on one particular country. I would take it home and watch it, then go back to the library and gather relevant information in case anyone had a question about the country. I would bake a little something that represented the area and serve it to my group.

I had about six very loyal ladies who never missed a session during those four years. I often wondered if they came for my delightful goodies or for the movie of the week. As I presented this course, I began to feel my self-confidence and self-image improve, and I felt an emerging pride that I was not used to. It was nice. I was beginning to see myself as a person for the first

time. I liked who I was becoming. I was not vicious, hateful, greedy, or a control freak. I was just a little old lady who found herself alone and was trying to make it on her own.

The EPOP group was my blessing in disguise. I met many interesting and helpful people. Geraldine Cucciniello, assistant to the EPOP director, was always ready to help answer any of our questions or help us solve a problem. She became a dear friend whom I will never forget. She was a true believer in education, no matter how old a person might be. One of our EPOP ladies, Jeannette Sleever, graduated cum laude with a four-year degree from Fairleigh Dickinson University two years ago. This amazing woman was ninety-five years old. Jeannette is still attending classes and has become an inspiration to many young adults, as well as us, who are still young at heart, and who have had the pleasure of knowing her and seeing her accomplishments and drive. Today, the EPOP is now called The Florham Institute for Lifelong Learning (FILL), but to me, it will always be the Educational Program for Older People (EPOP).

By the beginning of 1999, Pepper began showing signs of deterioration due to his illness. Our trips to the VA hospital became the big event of his day, even though they exhausted him. We stopped going out for an occasional lunch or dinner because the different smells bothered him. Occasionally, he would sit on the front porch or walk to the end of the driveway. I could see the illness was taking over. Our immediate family, Ron Mowder, Annie Miller, and my next-door neighbors, Marcia and Gary Windt, were the only people he seemed happy and comfortable around.

He had become completely dependent on me. I knew this was painful for a man who had never depended on anyone. I became his punching bag, his sounding board, and his only reason for living. His dying would have put me in control, and that was not what he wanted. I allowed him to think that he still had control over me. There was nothing else I could do. He needed me more than ever. I knew that, and that knowledge gave me a strength I had never known I had.

Pepper was finding it difficult to go to the VA hospital. I, too, felt the strain. Going to the VA Hospital meant loading the car with oxygen tanks and equipment and getting Pepper in and out of the car, not to mention

making sure his oxygen was working correctly. He panicked whenever he thought he was not getting oxygen.

Once we arrived at the VA hospital, I had to run around and find a wheelchair. Then I had to go back to the car, get him into the wheelchair, and push him to the building where his doctor was located. This was not easy for either of us. I tried to convince Pepper that it would be more convenient if I bought a wheelchair, but this idea was not received too well, and I never mentioned it again. Pepper had no idea the struggle, the stress, and the breathlessness I experienced while doing all of these things. However, I can't complain. Pepper got good care, and he liked his doctor. That, in itself, made the trip well worth any aggravations the two of us encountered and endured.

In May 1999, the doctor ordered hospice nurses to come to our house. Pepper's health was declining, and the trip to the hospital was becoming much too difficult. This was the beginning of his final demise. It turned out to be a very long, slow process. Time became endless for him. He was desperately afraid that I would put him in a nursing home. He wanted to die at home, in his own bed. I tried to assure him that I would carry out his wishes.

His emotional state had become a seesaw: up one minute and down the next. His highs brought pleasant moments for both of us. However, his down times were filled with terrible frustration, anger, and hurtful words to anyone and everyone who was in the room with him. It was almost impossible for me to help him through these down times. I never knew what to expect. Each month, the nurses were increasing his morphine and other drugs.

I had to start shaving and washing him. He was getting weaker as the months passed. I fixed nourishing meals every day, hoping each meal would give him the necessary strength to overcome the weakness he was living with. He ate little, and his strength kept dwindling away.

I remember the last day he went outside. It was mid-September. The day was exceptionally beautiful, warm and inviting. I opened the front door, hoping that the warmth of the day would flow throughout the house as well. To my surprise, my grandchildren were sitting on our front steps, laughing and talking to their grandfather. I couldn't believe it. Pepper was sitting out there, watching them, enjoying their laughter. He said not a word, but as I

watched him, I felt that he was cherishing this one beautiful moment God had given him. He looked exhausted, but strangely happy. Gary and Marcia saw him sitting there and came over to talk to him. They were excited to see him outside. (Gary was very fond of Pepper, and many times before Pepper became housebound, he took Pepper with him when he had to drive into the city to make a delivery.) Travis, Kelsey, and Baby Beau, my little Maltese, were sitting around him when, all of a sudden, Marcia said, "I've got to get a picture of this!" With that, she ran home and returned with her camera. That was the last picture taken of Pepper. It was the last time he went outside his home. It was his last wonderful breath of fresh air.

As I watched him approaching death, I prayed that he would at least say he cared for me. One day, he gently took my hand, squeezed it, and gave me the tenderest smile I ever saw. For one moment, a look of gentleness and compassion spread across his face. I wanted so badly to believe it all meant that he truly loved me. It was a moment filled with warmth, one that we had never experienced before with each other. It was strange. I felt, for the first time, that this was his one and only moment of showing me that he did care. I accepted it and now cherish that moment for what it was. Our life together over fifty years was hard, but we survived with our scars hidden deep within our hearts. We both needed to feel loved, he as much as I, but neither of us could show it or speak such gentle words as "I love you."

By early November, I began to feel that death was waiting to come in. Pepper was sleeping most of the day and night. When he was awake, he was too exhausted to talk. Life was draining from him. The heavy doses of morphine were numbing his pain. The hospice nurses told me that it was just a matter of time before he passed away. Pepper was going in and out of consciousness. I was exhausted.

I experienced the smells of death when Pepper's bodily functions became uncontrollable. It was a nightmare. I tried so hard to help him, but he was dead weight, unconscious, and my breathing had become difficult. The stress on me was unbearable. I was gasping for breath, pulling and tugging at him, trying to clean him, trying to give him a little dignity. I called Paul and Kevin to come and help me. I could no longer do this by myself. They took turns staying nights so I could get some sleep. The last three days were hard on the three of us.

It was difficult for me to stay in Pepper's room. I felt helpless as what little life was left in him began to seep away. I could feel the presence of death throughout the room. It seemed to slowly envelop Pepper's lifeless body. I didn't want to believe it was happening, but I knew that it really was, and that left me feeling cold and frightened.

PEPPER'S DEATH   On November 12th, at 6:00 P.M., I called Kevin to come over because Pepper had either died or was in the process of dying. I touched his forehead, hoping to see some sign of response from him. He did not move. His eyes were closed. I pulled the blanket off him and felt his feet. God, I will never forget that kind of cold. My heart began beating faster as I quickly felt his chest and arms. His body was no longer soft and warm. I knew something terrible was happening. I felt myself shiver as I looked at his motionless body wrapped in death. I kissed his forehead, whispered goodbye, and left the room. Kevin came right over, and shortly after 7:00 he came down and told me that Pepper was gone. I was thankful that his pain was over and that he could now rest in peace. I was thankful that it was over for me as well.

I had Pepper's casket closed, so there wasn't any public viewing of his body. It made everything so much easier. I was surprised, however, at the large crowd that came to pay their respects. Between all of my friends and my family's friends, I felt very proud. I cried very little. I believe I had done all my grieving a long time ago. I had one afternoon and evening viewing. I didn't think any of us needed to prolong the agony. Before we left the funeral home, I had Pepper's casket opened so my family and I could say our final goodbyes.

The next morning, we had a mass at St. Virgil's Church, and then we all went to our different cars. Paul, Debbie, Beth, and Ryan rode together as a family. Kevin and Brian went in Kevin's van. My cousin, Leroy, and his wife, Courtney, came up from Virginia Beach. They followed in their car. Behind them followed our many friends.

I had arranged a large black limo for Ann Miller, Mindy, Kelsey, and Travis, and me. When the two kids saw the limo, they got very excited. When I told them that we were going to ride in it, they were about to burst with excitement. They immediately forgot where we were going and the occasion. Watching them was a much-needed change. Kelsey was mesmerized by the

limo's beauty and comfort. After entering the limo, they began checking out everything. They found a bar with soda and other accoutrements, a small television, seats that were nothing like their car's seats, etc. Naturally, they wanted to try the soda, turn the TV on, and swirl about in their seats. What sadness they had inside the church quickly turned into amazement as our limo moved out onto the avenue. The police stopped all traffic, which allowed our procession to move forward without interruption. We had to laugh when Kelsey said, "I hope the driver doesn't loose us. He's so far away!"

The darkened windows fascinated them as well, once they realized that they could see out but no one could see in. The kids felt very important. It was funny! It was a welcomed break from the sadness we all were feeling. I couldn't help but think how much Pepper would have enjoyed such a delightful scene. He loved his four grandchildren. He was able to show them love and that was all that mattered. Silently, I hoped his spirit was traveling with us. The Morris Township police escorted the funeral procession over to the Gate of Heaven Cemetery. They did that out of respect for a fellow police officer, Kevin, and his family. Pepper would have been proud of such an honor.

A few words and prayers were spoken by Sister Mary at the graveside. A military salute was given in Pepper's honor as they presented me with the American flag. Ryan, my grandson, who was standing next to me, was surprised as I placed the flag in his hands. His eyes filled with tears. I knew that I had done the right thing. It made me feel happy to share this with him.

After the funeral, Mindy and I had made arrangements to have a buffet luncheon at the Bretton Woods Inn for family members and friends. The inn was located in Morris Plains, which made it convenient for everyone. We were pleased to see how nicely they had prepared everything. The buffet table held an assortment of hot and cold foods, as well as coffee, tea, and a nice selection of desserts. We all spoke of happier days and times we had shared with each other. It was a wonderful way to end such a sorrowful, yet thankful time. After the luncheon, we all went in different directions. I went home glad it was all over. For the first time in my entire life, I found myself alone. I had no one to answer to. I was about to become my own person.

My Life as a Widow

It was strange to suddenly find myself alone, yet I felt comfortable. I had been grieving for years, and now it just felt good to know that Pepper was at peace and I was ready to get on with my life as a widow. I felt I was well prepared because my past had shown me that I had the courage and the strength to survive.

It seemed like every time I went grocery shopping, I would run into one or two women who had lost their husbands several years ago. They would always give me a kiss, hold my hand, and of course, never fail to say, with the most pathetic voices, "How are you doing, dear? It's so hard. You must come and join our Mourners group. It's a way of grieving and sharing it with others who have lost a loved one. We're just trying to accept our husbands passing." These few words and their sympathetic voices made me shake my head in disbelief. I always left a little disgusted. I thought, "My God, get a life. Their husbands passed away several years ago, and they're still with a Mourners group. What in the hell is wrong with them? There are just as many men as women in this group. They must love to wallow in it. Boy, that's not for me!" I walked away with a smile on my face. Not out of disrespect to any of these women, but thankful I had learned the importance of moving on.

There was so much I wanted to do. First, I decided to get my house in shape. It had been terribly neglected over the many years. I did a complete overhaul, inside and out. It took me two years, but when I finished, my home looked lovely. Everything matched. Each item complimented another. New

windows, carpeting, furniture, drapes, shades, etc. added to the improvements. I began to work on the outside areas. I fenced off one side of my backyard. I had the patio replaced and created a rose garden with annuals— such as snapdragons, zinnias, marigolds, etc.—scattered among the roses.

I had the house painted a different color for the first time ever. I picked out a slightly darkened tan with dark red shutters and white window frames for the new windows. I had a concrete walkway installed that goes around to the back fence with a gate opening onto my patio, allowing me to water my flowers in the front of my house. I also had a new concrete floor poured in the garage. Everyone complimented me on my many changes and improvements. I felt good about what I accomplished and was thankful for having the money to make my home as charming and comfortable as possible.

MY TRIP TO ITALY   In May 2000, Fairleigh Dickinson University was putting together a trip to Italy for students studying Italian. At that time, only ten college kids had signed up, and the travel agency needed at least another ten people to make it worthwhile. Geraldine asked me if I would be interested in going. Even though I was doing a lot of costly renovations, I decided I was going to sign up. I asked my neighbor, Frances, and my long-time friend, Clementine, if they would like to join me. To my surprise, they signed up. Seven EPOP members signed up, and the trip was on.

We flew overnight to Milan, Italy, where we changed planes to fly to Venice. Our hotel was located on the mainland rather than the island itself, much to our disappointment. The next morning our guide suggested that we walk to the train station to take the express vaporetto across the Grand Canal. What she failed to tell us was it was over a mile walk, and some of us ol' cronies weren't use to that particular distance and gait. It was exhausting. We quickly forgot our pain the minute we arrived in view of St. Mark's Square. By the way, it is true that one definitely needs to wear a hat or head-scarf when visiting this famous spot because of the "danger" posed by flying pigeons to the tourists below.

It was like something out of the movies. I fell in love with Italy the moment I looked around at this very old and famous area. Naturally, we had

to take a ride in one of the famous gondolas. Our gondolier sang and another man played the guitar, which added a lovely touch as we rode up and down the many canals. We went to the Basilica, then to the Doges' Palace and the Bridge of Sighs. In the center of the Bridge of Sighs is one window where the prisoners could look out and see daylight for the last time. Then they continued crossing the bridge. They were taken down many narrow stairways into the dungeons where they were held until death relieved their hunger, punishment, and disease. This area made each of us shiver as we passed through the remains of such a hellhole.

We went to Murano, the famous glass factory, where I bought two unusual glass clowns and a lovely deep-red wine bottle with six matching small glasses. I also bought a dog, a mother elephant, and baby elephant brushed with gold leaf and molded of fused glass, which creates brilliant floral motifs in the classic millefiori style. I wish I had bought a couple of the other small animals with this particular design, such as the giraffe, which they had for sale.

That evening Clementine, Frances, and I went back over to see St. Mark's Square. The surrounding atmosphere was a delight. The square was lit up. Cafés were serving customers who were enjoying the night air while they sat drinking and watching the parade of people pass by. It was an electrifying evening, one I will never forget. The next day we boarded our bus and departed for Florence.

On our way, we stopped in Padua to visit the Basilica of St. Anthony and then continued on to Florence. When we arrived in Florence, our bus driver took us to the top of one of the seven hills that surround Florence. From Michelangelo Square, we looked out on a spectacular view of the city. Then we returned to our hotel and settled in for the night. The next day, we visited the leather factory, where I bought Mindy and me each a beautiful pocketbook made by Alviero Martini. To this day, both of us are still receiving compliments on our bags. We saw the River Arno and the Ponte Vecchio, a famous covered bridge. We also visited the many jewelry stores that specialize in gold. The three of us bought several lovely gold chains. We did very well in terms of price.

My traveling companion, Frances Scarano, and me standing near Rome's famous Coliseum.

We also toured the Accademia where the original of Michelangelo's famous sculpture, *David,* is displayed. Then we toured Signoria Palace and Square, as well as the Duomo. We also saw the Doors of Paradise and the Doors of the Holy Cross, which have been standing for centuries. That afternoon, most of us traveled to Pisa to see the leaning tower. We returned to Florence for the night. Our dinners were very good and, naturally, we enjoyed our many glasses of wine.

The medieval village of San Gimignano, surrounded by high walls, sits atop a mountain with views that look out on rows of vineyards as far as the eyes can see. The village fascinated me. It was the first time I had walked on centuries-old stone walkways. This place took my breath away. Inside this village, the huge fortress-like building has many little shops squeezed in small rooms that opened on the narrow street. In this village I found beautiful painted Italian pottery. It was in every shop. I had to buy several pieces because I found them attractive and colorful. Our trip was still in its early stages, so I had them shipped home. I could tell that this tour was going to include a lot of shopping.

On our way to Rome, we traveled through the evergreen Chianti countryside of Tuscany and made a stop in the medieval village of Siena. We

visited a winery as well as an olive grove. We bought wine and olive oil. In Siena, we had to go down steep, narrow streets to get to the Marketplace, which comprises the town square and the shopping area. There were many entrances to the Marketplace. It was exciting and fun. We had lunch at a highway restaurant called Auto Grille. We visited St. Mary of the Angels Church and continued on to Assisi, where we stopped to see the Basilica of St. Francis, patron saint of animals. We arrived in Rome that evening and had our dinner at the hotel. The next day was a day of leisure. The three of us walked miles as we visited the Coliseum and walked down del Fori Imperiali, which holds the old ruins of ancient Rome. We saw the Arco Di Costantino. Men dressed in ancient Roman costumes chased after the tourists to have pictures taken with them. We also walked around the Altar of the Nation building, which was also part of ancient Rome.

Then we moved on to find the Spanish Steps. I was amazed at how well I was doing when it came to my breathing. We stopped whenever I felt tired or began gasping and wheezing. Before we knew it, we were standing in front of the Spanish Steps. I knew that I could never climb to the top. Clem and Frances agreed. The steps were crowded with people who were either sitting on the steps and just talking or resting before trying to continue upward. I never heard anyone ever say the exact number of steps and was surprised to find that no one I asked knew how many there are. Their only remark was, "Oh, there's a lot!"

(After getting home from Italy, I called Geraldine at Fairleigh Dickinson University and asked her if she knew. Again, I heard, "Oh, there's a lot." I laughed and said, "That's the answer everyone gives." God bless her, she began calling many people until she finally found a person who knew. Excitedly, she called me with the answer. There are exactly 137 steps.)

To our surprise we spotted Jeannette Sleever walking up the Spanish Steps (I spoke of her earlier in my EPOP story). At that time, she was ninety-three years old. She put us to shame when she reached the top and waved to the multitude of people below.

After sitting for a while, we headed in the direction of the Trevi Fountain. It is a masterpiece of sculpture. We threw a few coins in this fountain for luck, and then we moved on to the Basilica of St. Pietro, which houses

Michelangelo's sculpture, "Moses between Rachel and Lesh." Also in this basilica, encased in glass, are the chains with which the apostle Peter was bound on Herod orders. I'll bet we walked ten miles that day, but it was fascinating. We did little shopping because we concentrated on sightseeing. One could never get bored in Rome. Italy was more than I ever expected.

Before the day was over, we heard that John Travolta, the American movie star, was going to be signing his new book in a bookshop around the corner from our hotel. When Frances heard this, we had to rush to the bookstore, and Frances was able to get in line with all the kids. Clem and I watched her parade across the stage to the table where John Travolta was sitting. He was surprised to see this little old lady standing in front of him. He held her hand, spoke to her for a few minutes, and then signed her book. She was excited. Frances turned and faced the crowd with a smile that seemed to spread from one ear to the other. Everyone clapped as she held up her book. She was like a big kid having a wonderful moment of fun, and then she walked off the stage. God bless her. Frances was a good sport.

The following day, we visited St. Peter's Basilica and its famous square, the pope's residence on the top floor of the Vatican, saw the changing of the guard, the Vatican Museum, and the fabulous Sistine Chapel. In St. Peter's Basilica we saw the statues of "The Pieta" and "Black Peter," as well as many others. We were fortunate to have been at the Basilica at that particular time because certain doors are opened only every twenty-five years, and we were allowed to enter through them. There was so much to see in Rome that it was impossible to see it all in two days, but I thought we did pretty well. We traveled to the catacombs, but I didn't go down in them because I still have a bit of claustrophobia and would have run out of that terrible darkness screaming like a crazy woman. That night we had our last dinner in Rome, and it was fantastic. We had no complaints about the meals we were served.

We headed south toward Tivoli, where we visited the Villa d'Este and its hundred fountains. I didn't go down the many stairs. I was afraid I wouldn't be able to climb back up. When the gang came back, they were exhausted. They said the fountains were gorgeous, especially the famous Organ Fountain. The Villa had many balconies with views of the landscape below.

We went to the Villa Adriana, which consisted of the ruins and remains of an ancient villa. One of the ruins contained many original beautiful tiles, still intact. Unbelievable! The grounds around these ruins are well preserved. Standing statues still surround the ruins of the Spar, where the inhabitants bathed.

After leaving this area, we traveled to the village of Pompeii, where we went to the cameo factory. I bought several lovely cameos for Mindy, Kelsey, and myself. I watched the cutter create a beautiful cameo pin from a huge piece of layered shell. It is extremely tedious work.

We continued south along the coastline by way of the Amalfi Drive. It turned out to be the most fascinating ride I have ever taken. Besides being beautiful, it's exciting, due to the narrowness and construction of this route. On one side of the roadway, the foot of sheer mountain cliffs seemed to rest on the road's asphalt. On the other side was nothing but an occasional small, one-rail fence that was supposed to prevent any car from going off the tremendous cliffs, which dropped straight into the Mediterranean Sea. It felt and looked as if we were traveling amongst the clouds.

The road was barely wide enough to allow two cars to pass, let alone any larger four-wheeled contraption like our bus. We passed through one little village after another. Each one proudly displayed its own beautiful beach. One shop after another was lined across this lovely scene. These villages were located at the base of each mountain, although houses were built straight up the mountainside.

God, it was awesome! In these little villages we saw laundry hanging over the balconies and railings of the many homes and hotels. I had seen pictures of such scenes, but had never viewed them in person. I fell in love with the entire route, its interesting pottery, and its craft-filled shops. We passed through the villages of Positano, Praiano, Furore, Conca dei Marini, Amalfi, Ravello, Minori, Maiori, Erchie, Cetara, and Vietri sul Mare. We stayed in Maiori overnight. That evening we went shopping and bought pottery and other souvenirs.

We encountered quite a problem on this mountainous drive. On the move again, everyone was in good spirits, excited by the constantly changing

scene that surrounded us. The road had once again become extremely narrow. Laughter reigned among the students. I looked out the window as we were approaching a very sharp curve and saw the nose of another bus coming around the bend. That part of the bus was grinding up against a stone wall due to the severity of the curve. "Oh, my God, one of us isn't going to make it" was my immediate thought. One must remember this entire episode took only seconds.

The kids began hollering at our driver. They were in hysterics as we older folks watched in disbelief. At least our bus was on the mountain side. Thank God for that! The back of the other bus had not reached the stone wall. It was positioned in such a way that it was impossible to back up. If its driver had even tried to do that, he possibly could have sent the bus over the edge, dropping it and its passengers into the Mediterranean Sea. This thought made me shudder. Foolishly, neither driver stopped. It was like these men were playing chicken. Who was going to stop first? Anyone with any common sense could see this was not good thinking. Well, at this point, our bus was grinding against the mountain. The other side became tightly lodged against the other vehicle. Neither bus could move.

I looked behind us, and to my surprise, the traffic was backed up all the way down to the village we had passed through on our ascent. It was rush hour, and no one was going any further. Both drivers had rolled down their windows and were screaming at each other. Neither man could get out of his bus nor could we, their passengers. I'm sure every word had to have been pretty vile. By then, we could see the other driver running up and down the aisle of his bus, arms moving in every direction, screaming and totally out of control.

The people in the cars behind us were out on the road surveying the problem. Many were just laughing at the ridiculous mess everyone was in. Others were cursing, shouting, and blowing their horns. Apparently, the same scene was taking place behind the other bus. I looked around, and, to my horror, realized that there was no way we could get out of this vehicle. I mentioned this to Josephine, our leader. She looked at me and her only remark was, "Oh, great!" We sat and waited, hoping someone on the outside would get help or come up with a solution to our problem.

Traffic backed up behind the stuck buses on the narrow mountain road.

Have you ever seen a bunch of Italian men in a heated dispute? Well, it had turned into a chaotic mess. Finally, someone went back down to the village and got the police, who arrived on small motorcycles. The scene resembled something from a Keystone Cops movie as they ran about screaming and shouting. One by one, they began sizing up the situation of each bus, measuring distances of anything and everything that looked to be part of the problem. Even these men began to lose control because they all had different ideas about how to untangle the intolerable situation. God, it was getting funnier by the minute. Several of us took pictures of this scene, and I can't look at mine without laughing.

A person riding a moped seemed to come out of nowhere and flew past our bus. Apparently, there was enough room between the buses for this motorbike to squeeze through. The Keystone Cops were directing our bus to move forward and the other to go backwards, very slowly. Few of us knew Italian, but by their actions, we knew exactly what they were saying. By now, we were glued to the windows, watching, waiting for something to happen, as were the folks in the other bus. Slowly, both buses were beginning to inch a part. There was movement and a scraping sound, as the buses released each other. Another moped flew by. It was a good sign. Words were no longer being shouted; instead, one of the cops began writing what liked like tickets.

Lo and behold, each driver received one. We moved forward. The problem had been solved.

The next day we took the ferry to the Isle of Capri. As we were approaching the bay, we saw the famous rocks of Capri and a lovely view of this city. The village is built on three levels on the side of a huge mountain. It held a bustling atmosphere with many shops and restaurants on each level. We took the tram, which rushed straight up to the second level. To get to the third level, one had to walk up a steep grade. I took one look at that hike and decided to stay put. I shopped while I waited for Clem and Frances to come back. The view was terrific.

We decided to walk down the mountain rather than take the tram. We got a little off track, however, and one might even say that we were lost. It proved to be most interesting because we saw much of the residential areas that were built into the mountain. The road was easy to walk on, so I had no trouble. We continued our descent, enjoying the lovely lawns, lemon trees, homes, and flowers. We had plenty of time, thank goodness.

By the time we reached the first level, we found ourselves a distance from where our ferry was docked. We meandered among the many shops for a few souvenirs as we headed toward our ferry. Time allowed us to stop for a cup of cappuccino. Our walk had made us thirsty. I had never tasted such wonderful cappuccino, nor have I since. The lemons grown on Capri are huge compared to our Florida and California lemons. I was happy that Capri was included in our tour. It was a delightful day's outing.

We returned to Maiori, where we spent the night. The next day we began to cross over a large range of mountains as we headed inland, north to Naples. The view was spectacular. I never realized how mountainous this terrain is. Once we had crossed over these mountains, we saw Mount Vesuvius. Our trip was in its final hours. At Naples, we took a plane to Milan and then departed for home.

As you can see, I fell in love with Italy. It was a complete surprise. I honestly don't know what I expected. I had nothing to compare it with because this was my first trip to any part of Europe. Ireland didn't have the ancient atmosphere or the varied terrain of Italy. I guess that is why I found it so fascinating.

MY TRIP TO SPAIN AND PORTUGAL   On April 28, 2001, I traveled to
Spain and Portugal with the Essex County Retired Educators. Clementine
belonged to this organization and asked me if I would like to be her companion. We had an overnight flight and arrived in Madrid, Spain, on Sunday
morning. We got settled in our rooms, and in the afternoon, we toured
Madrid. That evening we attended a welcoming dinner with flamenco
dancing as the entertainment. We spent two and a half days touring Madrid.
There was much to see.

The next day, we had a full day of touring, which included the city of
Toledo. When I saw how high up we had to go, I knew I was in trouble. Our
guide told me there was an escalator that would take us up to the Cathedral
Santo Tome. Thank God, I would not have made it otherwise. However, our
guide failed to tell me that once we got off the escalator, we had to walk *up*
the rest of the way. There would be no bus, no elevator, no escalator, no car,
nothing except each person's own two legs. I looked up, and my heart began
to sink. I didn't know what to do. How was I going to keep up with the
group? I felt frightened. However, I was not the only sufferer. There were
several other people in our group who found themselves struggling with
their own medical problems as we climbed.

The streets narrowed. Lots of little shops were squeezed together, all
selling fascinating merchandise. Most of us wanted to stop, rest, and look in
the different shops. However, our guide refused and kept ordering us to
follow. He never stayed with us. It seemed almost deliberate. By then, about
six of us were in bad shape and in desperate need of rest. I thought I was going
to die. The guide was extremely nasty as he once again announced that if we
didn't keep up with him, we were going to be left behind. I personally didn't
think the trip up the mountain to see that cathedral was worth the torture
that our damned guide "enjoyed" putting us though. It was so deliberate!

As we started the long descent down the mountain, we stopped at a small
restaurant called Palacio de Fuensalida and had lunch. It felt good to rest. It
was the best meal we had had so far. The view was magnificent as we ate on
the balcony overlooking the valley below.

The bus met us halfway down, and we were driven to the factory where
they make the famous Toledo scissors and other unusual items. The local

stone is extremely hard and is one of a kind, found only in the surrounding mountains. I bought Travis an armored knight on horseback, holding his spear. It was an artisan's delight. I knew Travis would like this because it was so unusual. I had it shipped home. He loved it. It was a good choice. I got Mindy a lovely Toledo bracelet and a pair of Toledo scissors. I bought several pairs for myself as well. It was a hard day on all of us. After dinner, everyone just wanted to take it easy.

The next day, we traveled to Caceres, a historical Spanish town with its old Moorish walls and watchtowers still intact. After lunch, we continued on to Lisbon, Portugal. That evening, we went to dinner at a local restaurant and were entertained with "fado" music.

Upon arriving in Lisbon, we toured the city, stopping at such famous places as the Monastery of Los Jeronimos, the Carriages Museum, Monsanto, and Castle St. Jorge and Rossio. Everything was old, and it was fascinating to me to think it had all stayed intact hundreds of years. We departed Lisbon the next morning and traveled to Sintra, a beautiful town, as well as one of the oldest in Portugal. The Atlantic Ocean was always in view as we went to Cabo da Roca, the most western point of Europe, and visited Casks and Estoril, which were close by. Casks has a beautiful bay and is rich in fishing. Estoril has the largest casino in Europe.

My traveling companions (l–r): Lucille, Clementine, Judy, me, Jeanette, and Mary Ann.

The next morning, we headed for Obidos, Nazare, and Datalha. We had lunch in Nazare at a little restaurant called Mar de Sol. For the first time, we were served the favorite food of Portugal: "Sardines with their heads on and eyes bulging as if ready to pop out of their sockets." Just to look at them turned my stomach. I couldn't eat them. I ate bread. It was wonderful. I would have starved without it. These towns all had a medieval atmosphere, especially Obidos because it was once an old Moorish city. In Batalha a fourteenth-century monastery is still standing. It was built to commemorate victory over the Spanish. Later, we traveled back to our hotel for dinner and relaxation.

I was not fond of the food. I was beginning to long for a hamburger; a hot dog would have been a treat. A steak would have made me feel like I had died and gone to heaven. I couldn't get excited about this trip. I saw nothing but filth. I didn't like the people. I thought many were rude. However, when we stopped at several sightseeing areas, many local women had stands where they sat crocheting lovely table spreads. They were similar to my mother's crochet handwork of years ago. I bought several different items. I admired their artistic abilities.

We traveled south along the coastline to Vilamoura and on to Algarve, the southernmost province of Portugal. We made a stop at the Jose Maria de Fonseca Winery, where I bought several hot plates with designs depicting the winery. By the time we reached our hotel, we were able to do a little shopping, since the day was rather quiet.

The next day, we toured areas where high cliffs held back the ocean. It was fascinating. For millions of years, these cliffs have been ripped apart by the force of the ocean, creating unbelievable formations. Again we came across women who had set up stands where they sold their handmade creations to tourists. I bought several items from them as well. Their crocheted pieces had an interesting and unusual design. No way would I find this type of handwork in the states. We visited Portimao, Lagos, and Sagres. We had lunch on our own, which was a nice change. The following day, we traveled to Sevilla, Spain.

The ladies that Clementine and I traveled with were a pleasure. Thank God, we all got along together. It was a difficult tour. None of us expected it to be so hard on us physically. We traveled from the Atlantic Ocean over to

the Costa del Sol on the Mediterranean Sea. We drank sangaree and ate lots of bread. I noticed that crème brûlée is one of the most popular desserts throughout Europe. We spent two nights in the Sevilla area, touring more cathedrals, Plaza de Espana, Giralda Plaza, the Casa depilaros. Again, we were allowed to have lunch on our own and free time. It felt good, but I was getting tired.

We departed for Marbella, Spain, via Ronda. This city is located at the foot of the Sierra Blanca mountains. On our way to Marbella, we stopped at a leather factory, and I bought a beautiful leather coat. It was cold, and the coat felt good. We spent the night in this city, and the next morning we moved on to Granada, which was founded in the eighth century by the Moors. We toured the Alhambra, which was built in the thirteenth century and has its own fortress, towers, palace, and lovely gardens.

After breakfast, we traveled back to Madrid; our trip was nearing its end. We were given free time to do as we wanted. We went shopping and had dinner out. Once back at the hotel, I packed my things because I would be leaving to fly to Brussels early the next morning.

76TH INFANTRY DIVISION'S LAST TOUR On May 11, I left Clementine and the group and flew from Madrid, Spain, to Brussels, Belgium to join the 76th Infantry Division's last tour, which covered the route Pepper traveled through Europe during World War II. I decided that since I was already in Europe, I might as well do and see as much as possible. I had finished putting together Pepper's own war story and thought it would be interesting to see for myself all the places he mentions.

Upon arriving in Brussels, I found that my tour group had already left for a tour of the city. I had the hotel get me a taxi with a driver who spoke English and was willing to take me on a private tour of the area. He was great. The city is cut into two parts, the old and the new. He took me to the old section first because he thought it would be more fascinating than the newer area. I saw and walked on the cobbled streets, saw sidewalk musicians playing their different instruments, small cafés with people sipping drinks at the small tables on the sidewalks. Stone buildings that had existed for hundreds of years surrounded us as we moved slowly, allowing me to inhale its ancient aroma. I loved it.

That evening, I met my roommate. As soon as she came into the room, I could almost read her mind. It was the way she looked at me. She immediately told me that I should not expect to travel around with her because she had already hooked up with someone. "Oh," I said, "that's fine. The last thing I want is to be tied down with a stranger and having to waste time doing what they want. I like traveling alone and doing what I enjoy. I'm glad we understand each other. No problem. I think I'll go down and have some supper in the dining room. See you later." With that I left the room.

I went downstairs and found the dining room. I saw a couple that was on our tour and went over and introduced myself. Out of the clear blue, the gentleman told me that they preferred to sit by themselves. I was beginning to feel a little uncomfortable. Jesus, was it me? Did I forget to put something on? I looked down quickly to make sure I was dressed properly. Well, whatever was wrong, there wasn't much I could do about it, so I found a table and sat down. My waiter suggested that I order their white asparagus, which they served with a special sauce. I wish I had asked for that recipe. Oh, it was good! I ordered the crème brûlée for dessert because, as I've said, it seemed to be the most popular dessert throughout Europe. When I returned to my room, I was glad to find my roommate had gone out. It had been a long day after flying up from Madrid, so I went to bed hoping that tomorrow would be better as far as my traveling companions went.

I met the rest of the tour group the next morning, and we began our trip to Luxembourg. On the way, we stopped and saw the monument where the Battle of the Bulge took place and continued on to Luxembourg for the next three days. We made a stop in the village of Clervaux and met burgomaster Jean Nickels, who honored the eight veterans who were traveling with us and had taken part in the horrific Sauer River crossing by the American soldiers. The village had a beautiful bronze statue honoring the GIs. Mr. Nickels gave each of the eight men a bouquet of flowers to lay at the base of the statue. It was a very touching moment; each man was crying as he laid the flowers around the statue.

The villagers also opened up the castle and served our group wine, cheese, crackers, and other goodies. In appreciation, the villagers had special medals made honoring these men for their bravery. Again, tears flowed like

76 TH INFANTRY DIVISION RETURN TO EUROPE

A "NOSTALGIC JOURNEY"

Responding to requests to arrange another 'ONAWAY' tour to Europe, a truly "Nostalgic Journey" and "Heritage Tour" has been scheduled to depart on May 15, 2001. Customized to follow the routes and visit the special areas where the 76th served, this is a trip designed especially for veterans of our division, their families and even friends who would be interested. Plan to join us! Bring your grandchildren also. It will be a great experience for them (and you) as you retrace places which are part of their heritage.

This is truly a "Nostalgic Journey" designed to enable you to again see your special places combined with popular tourist attractions - a great blend of features which include the little "out-of-the-way" rural areas that most tourists do not see.

A leisurely pace is being scheduled in recogniztion of the advancing years of WWII veterans with a minimum of walking.

THIS WILL BE THE LAST TIME around - so JOIN US - and share in some of the most pleasurable moments of your life as you retrace the historic sites of our wartime service with the added pleasure of sharing them with families, friends, and wartime buddies.

Register with deposits on or before December 15, 2000, and receive a FREE Travel & Cancellation Insurance Policy.

ITINERARY

2001

Wednesday, May 9 - USA/ALOFT. Depart the US this evening via trans-Atlantic jetliner. Meal service aloft.

Thursday, May 10 - BRUSSELS. Arrive Brussels this morning. After forming our group transfer to our Brussels hotel. Balance of the day is free to rest and adjust to time change. Tonight a Welcome Reception and Tour Director's briefing will highlight the exciting days to come. WR

Brochure for this fascinating trip.

the wine. Mr. Nickels came over and talked to me and asked if he could drive me down the mountain to the center of the village. He had been told by the veterans that I had Pepper's story with me. He asked me if I would be kind enough to send a copy to him to put it in their small museum of World War II memorabilia. When I arrived home, I sent him one. We have been writing to each other ever since.

While traveling from one place to another, I began to notice every field was just a mass of brilliant yellow plants. I asked our guide, Peter, about them; he told me that these were canola plants, which are used to make canola oil. He said that we had come at the height of their beauty. By the following week, these plants would have turned a nasty brown. Peter lived in England and had been a travel guide for many years. He was an excellent guide, very pleasant, and one of the few who spoke to me.

At the village of Echternach, we crossed the Sauer River. It was just a small stream of water, nothing like I expected. It was hard to believe that this small stream had been a raging torrent of melted snow when our soldiers were trying to build a bridge so that the GIs and their equipment could cross into Germany. The construction engineers were being picked off, one by one, by the Germans on the other side of the river. I saw the banks where Pepper and the other men were ordered to stay until they got the word to

Typical old cobblestone street in the old section of Brussels, Belgium.

move out. While there, we toured other areas, including nearby parts of Germany, including Katzenkopf, Irrel, Niederweis, Eisenach, Welschbillig, Arenrath, Wittlich, Trier, and other villages. The town of Trier had the same antique atmosphere as the old section of Brussels. It fascinated me.

Well, I must get back to my traveling companions. I don't believe I ever meet a stranger group of people in my whole life. Thank God, Bob Sherman and his grandson, Kevin, were traveling with us. He was most kind and had me sit with them whenever we ate as a group. I pretty much traveled by myself, but as I said before, that didn't bother me at all. Whenever I wanted to walk around with this kind man, he was only too happy to have me join them.

Several times when we had dinner on our own, my roommate asked me if she could join me. Her friends had gone elsewhere, and she had no one to eat with. I'm sure she must have been embarrassed. However, I will never ask for a roommate again. I will pay the extra money and get a single room.

Our route also took us across the Rhine River. It is a well-traveled river because it leads to the ocean. This river flowed between two mountain ranges, and our drive along it was the most scenic of the entire trip. Huge grape vines, leading up to the top of the smaller hills, were everywhere. One village after another, rested at the foot of a mountain range. On the tops of many of the mountains were unimaginable castles. They took my breath away. How did the people, centuries ago, build such monstrosities as these

Festung Königstein

The Konigstein castle, which dates back to 1200 and was used by the Germans in WWII.]

castles? How did they get all the necessary equipment and material up to the top of these mountains?

These villages had many shops that I would have loved to gone into, but this was, unfortunately, not a shopping tour. The further I got into this trip, the more I began to realize that this was definitely a man's tour, not a lovely shopping trip! Oh, well! We went on to what was formerly East Germany and headed into Jena, Gera, Zeitz, Zwickau, and Chemnitz, where we spent the night. We spent two days in the Chemnitz area. I found it just as interesting as the other old cities in which we stayed.

We were free to do some shopping in Chemnitz. I stayed pretty much in the old section with its cobblestone walkways and very old stone buildings. I enjoyed my walk; the old section fascinated me. I went into a few unique shops where I bought several interesting small wind-up musical boxes. I had a nice day. It felt good to be free and out from under the people I was traveling with. After this, we traveled to Dresden. It, too, had all the flavor of the old and the new. Some of us visited the Koenigstein Fortress rather than visit the famous porcelain factory outside of Dresden. I decided to visit the fortress.

One other area that completely stunned me was our visit to the site of the Buchenwald concentration camp, not far from the town of Weimar. As I walked around the grounds of this camp, I saw one building after another representing death in some form or fashion. It was hard to believe the inhumanity with which man can treat his fellow man.

We spent two days in Berlin, touring such places as the Berlin Wall, the Brandenburg Gate, the Reichstag, and the Tempelhof Airport that was used during the Berlin Airlift. We were given an entire afternoon to shop and venture freely around the city. I walked down the famous Kurfürstendamm (or "Ku-Damm," as the Germans call it) and went shopping in one of the most famous and magnificent stores in Europe, the KaDeWe. It had every thing I wanted except the beautiful beer steins I saw in the small villages along the Rhine River. I wanted to get my three boys each one as a little memento from me.

Every village we stopped at and were allowed to shop for an hour or less, I looked for a Kathy Kruse doll. I wanted to buy Kelsey one. When we stopped in Weimar, I found a lovely Kathy Kruse doll, but the shopkeeper would not

accept my Traveler's Check. She was going to hold the doll until I could go to the bank and cash it in for German money. Unfortunately, by the time I found the bank, it was too late for me to go back to the shop and pick it up. The bus was waiting for me. My friend, Clementine, has several of them. She loved the child-like expression that these German dolls have. One cannot buy them in the United States. I found one in Berlin at the KaDeWe department store and had it shipped home to Kelsey. On May 20th, we flew from Berlin to the Zurich Airport in Switzerland to catch our return flight to the U.S.

SEPTEMBER 11, 2001   It was early Tuesday morning. I watched the sun announce the beginning of another lovely September day. Nothing appeared unusual as I sipped my coffee and read the local newspaper. Nine-eleven seemed no different from any other morning. Unbeknownst to all but a few, however, events that would lead to unimaginable horrors had already been set into motion.

At 8:55 A.M., Mindy called me and quickly said, "Mom, turn your TV on. A plane has struck the upper floors of one of the World Trade Center towers!" I gasped, knowing by the sound of her voice that something terrible had just happened. I turned on my TV and found myself looking at an unimaginable, frightening scene. No words can express the horror that was unfolding before my very eyes.

The entire area looked like a war zone. The panic of the masses resembled the attack on Pearl Harbor, but these were civilians, not military personnel. Bewilderment, fear, torment, and pain are just a few adjectives that reminded me of the similarities of these two horrific times. People who were able to run began to fill the streets, trying to escape from the terror that engulfed this section of New York City. I watched as the air became filled with all kind of debris, wrapped in a huge thick, white fog-like coating of soot, smoke, and waste that had been part of the tower's structure. It seemed to grow larger, spreading its debris over everything until it overpowered those running to safety. It was a scene of terrible death and unbelievable destruction.

Fire trucks, police cars, ambulances, and EMT personnel surrounded the entire area, helping those who managed to get out of the building. Firemen

and police officers could be seen running into the tower, now a burning inferno. I watched as many of these men passed through doors to the stairwells that would lead them upward in hopes of saving those people still alive and needing help. Many of these men were never seen again, but they showed us all a perfect example of what the word "hero" really means.

Suddenly, around 9:05 A.M., the camera turned to the North Tower as another plane appeared out of nowhere and plunged into the upper section of this tower as well. Again the world watched as another hellish and terrifying event became a part of our TV viewing. The people on the scene reacted as they had less than a half and hour ago. It was obvious that these two planes crashing into the towers were not terrible accidents but a calculated attack by some terrorist group. Terror and shock entered Americans' living rooms, our workplaces, and any other area that had a TV or a radio receiving the broadcasts that described this horrific scene.

It is said that every generation has its own day of infamy, and looking back, I must agree. For my generation, it was December 7, 1941, with its early morning sneak attack on Pearl Harbor by the Japanese. Nine-eleven suddenly revived the terrible anguish and pain of nearly sixty years before. Then, through radio bulletins and reports, our imaginations had recreated the entire chaotic scene of the December 7th attack. When we entered World War II, most information came either by radio, the local newspaper, or newsreels at local movie theaters. As a result, news was always at least a day old. Newsmen's photos from the front lines were sometimes as much as a week or two old, but that was the way it was back then. Nine-eleven was much different in that respect, but in many ways, it was very similar.

Within fifteen minutes of the second plane hitting the WTC, another terrifying event unfolded in Washington, D.C. A hijacked American Airlines plane, carrying sixty-some people, slammed into the Pentagon, causing massive explosions and fires. TV again showed us the devastation of the attack. A number of people who worked in the area where the plane crashed were killed and many more were injured. It was as if we were watching a horror movie.

Around 10 A.M., a special bulletin announced the crash of a United Airlines plane near Shanksville, Pennsylvania. This plane had taken off from

Newark Airport, headed for San Francisco, and had approximately forty-five people on board. Everyone was killed. Before it crashed, however, one of the passengers had a cell phone and called his wife. He told her that the plane was being hijacked. Then, she heard a man say, "Let's roll," and their conversation ended. Apparently, the plane was being diverted from its regular course by terrorists, and some of the passengers were attempting to retake control of it. Many have speculated about events aboard that plane, but we will never know exactly what happened.

Within three hours, the American people had experienced four airliner crashes, watched the collapse of the World Trade Center towers, and knew that more than 3,800 lives had been lost. This was by no means what one would call a normal day. We realized that we were vulnerable, no longer safe from the dangers of the outside world. Attempts to rescue those trapped in and under the debris and recover the bodies of the dead began immediately. The public watched as TV showed the cleanup of the towers, as well as the hardship of recovering bodies from the gigantic pile of debris. It took more than a year to clear the site, but those few hours of terrifying horror will always remain a part of our lives. It is truly a day of infamy that none of us will ever be able to forget.

It always surprises me when I notice the Twin Towers in old movies or in old commercials. Prior to nine-eleven, I probably wouldn't have even realized that they had just flashed by on the screen. On a hill just a short distance from my home, we could always catch site of them. I drove there just before the North Tower collapsed. I saw thick, black smoke drifting upward into the sky. As more and more people arrived to watch the disturbing sight, I stood there feeling stunned and wondering why this was happening. The thought that the towers are gone still bothers me. The thought that so many innocent people died inside the Twin Towers' crumbling walls reminded me of two lines from a poem by Robert Burns: "Man's inhumanity to man / Makes countless thousands mourn!"

Just a short distance from my home, near the spot were we could always see the top of the Twin Towers, sits a section of steel that was once part of the huge structural beams of one of the towers. It was salvaged to create a memorial for

those who had lived in our area and were killed that day. Many of these casualties were young people between the ages of twenty and fifty. There were many living victims, as well: parents, brothers, sisters, a lovely fiancée or a fun-loving fiancé, friends, neighbors, and many others. The saddest living victims, however, were the young children and teenagers who had a parent or parents working in the towers that day. It took months before all of the bodies were recovered and identified, or failing that, merely listed as "missing."

In the wake of those events, patriotism suddenly exploded throughout America. The American flag was displayed everywhere: on cars, buildings, homes, clothing, etc. There was no more talk of burning "Old Glory" or denouncing and spitting on our veterans who had protected our rights and fought for our freedom. It brought back "American pride," if only for a short while. I see signs that, once again, "American pride" is loosing the strength it had during and after nine-eleven. How quickly the nation forgets. Both political parties backed President Bush for taking immediate action to secure the entire country the moment he was told of the attacks on the World Trade Center. It was a very brief, shining moment for President Bush. The political game was being played by every politician. It was a most unusual moment, a moment that quickly dissolved in time.

My generation had watched the changes of the last four decades turn our society into a group of self-serving people who took our liberties for granted and gave nothing back in return until nine-eleven. We lived through many wars, long before that horrific day. I hope that nine-eleven has given the younger generations a better understanding of what my generation felt when we heard that Pearl Harbor had been attacked and more than 2,400 American military men had been killed in less than two hours. Each war sent home those who made the greatest sacrifice. Freedom comes at a very high price!

Life has been good to our children and their children. They know little about the Great Depression and the terrible struggle most families experienced just to survive. My generation knew what hunger felt like. We remembered the long bread lines and the awful squalor people were forced to live in. After World War II, our lives began to improve because the economy turned around. For decades, our society grew in wealth and job

opportunities became available, as did homes, cars, better living conditions, including the long-promised "chicken in every pot." My generation, however, began to see and feel the lack of patriotism among our children. Decades passed as their ideas continued to shock us. It took nine-eleven to open their eyes and make them realize how easy our beliefs and lifestyle could be taken away. Freedom, the flag, our civil rights, our security as a nation suddenly revived their sense of togetherness and patriotism. The old saying, "The more things change, the more they stay the same," is very true. Nine-eleven proved that. We all live in an illusion that we have "control" of our own lives, but actually, we have very little control. At any moment, our lives, our beliefs, and our way of living can be turned upside-down. Nine-eleven is the perfect example of that.

A Visit to Brian's House   During the summer of 2002, Mindy, my grandchildren, and I decided to visit Brian in Fort Walton Beach, Florida. (Try my recipes for Buddy's Brownies and Blueberry Muffins, which make great "road food"; you'll find them in Appendix I.) We drove south down Interstate 81 and made an overnight stop in Cherokee, North Carolina. In the evening, we attended a performance called "The Trail of Tears." It was a very powerful play about the terrible struggle the Cherokee had when the U.S. Army drove them west on foot. We visited the Cherokee Museum and then took a tour that showed the different types of Indian crafts and how they had been made. We noticed a sign along the highway that mentioned Indian dancing. It sounded interesting, so we stopped.

A couple of Indians were sitting by a wooden platform, and we asked when the show was going to begin. They said, "Immediately." So we sat down, ready for the dance of fire, war dance, wedding dance and any other dance that they were going to do. They passed the hat around for our donations, so Mindy put twenty dollars in the hat. The Indian went back over to the other Indian and put on his beautiful headpiece and did a dance. We clapped and sat, waiting for the next dance. The Indian stepped off the platform and walked away. The other Indian joined him. Mindy and I looked at each other with surprised and quizzical expressions. We realized we had just been taken, but good.

The next day, we arrived at Brian's around 5:00 P.M. He suggested we go out to dinner because the kids were hungry, and he doesn't cook. That was fine with us, so he took everyone to the Hightide Restaurant, where we had oysters and fried shrimp. Oh, God, they were wonderful! By the time we had finished dinner, it was time to go back to the house and get ourselves settled in for the next few days. The kids were tired of riding, and it had been a long day. The next day, Brian took us over to the Air Force base, and we saw many different planes and got a feel for life on a military base. For lunch, we went to Guiseppi's Wharf, where we had oysters, hushpuppies, cream corn and crab soup. Again, I can only say, "Wonderful."

For dinner, Brian took us to McGuire's Eatery, where the walls were covered with dollar bills. Over the years, people left one-dollar bills to be tacked on the walls of the restaurant. It was amazing. Bills were everywhere, including the ceiling. The kids, naturally, had to tack a couple of dollars on an empty spot. The next day, we did some more sightseeing and went to Buffalo Reef's Restaurant for chicken and Buffalo wings. Brian said these were the best in the area. He sure knew the good places to eat. Our trip had turned into an eating adventure, but no one was complaining, not even the kids. The night before we left, Brian took us to Pocono Joe's Restaurant, which was located in Destin. It was situated on the beach and had wide, wooden window shutters that were opened. The beach, sand, and ocean gave the place a tropical atmosphere. We could hear the ocean rolling in and out. The moon was full, beaming downward to create a romantic and beautiful setting.

Once we were seated, we ordered a coconut-cream and rum drink that I will never forget. I believe both Mindy and I would go back just for that drink. God, it was good! Again, we all enjoyed another seafood dinner. The next day, Brian took us over to meet the people he works with. He volunteers several days a week, helping them with injured animals, birds, and other local critters. He took us over to the local aquarium, where dolphins and seals perform for the public. The kids loved the show.

We went down to a lower level and were able to see the dolphins underwater, speeding up and down the tank. One of the dolphins came by the window I was looking through, and he stopped and stared at me. Then he

took off rapidly and turned and came back and stared at me again. I became fascinated by his actions. He came back again and stopped and looked directly at me and just stayed there. Mindy began noticing this dolphin and his reaction to me. It was the coolest thing. I was stunned, yet couldn't leave. He just kept coming back and checking me out. I almost felt like we were bonding. Even the kids got excited about the dolphin's fascination with me. Jesus, I must be getting damn old if that's the best I can do. On the other hand, not everyone can fascinate a mammal like I apparently did! Yeah, that's okay. I'm nuts, but the dolphin liked me. I was glad to see my son happy with his life. I was glad we had made this visit. I feel guilty because I don't visit more often, but knowing Brian, I don't think it makes him feel less loved.

Well, it was time for us to head east to Brunswick, Georgia, for a short visit with two of my cousins, and Mindy and the kids were going to stay with her family. Again, my visit had turned into constant dining. We drove up to Darien and had dinner at a restaurant called Magnolia Tea Room, where they served delicious seafood. The following day, we decided to go to a small restaurant on Route 17 just on the outskirts of Brunswick. I think it was a two-way fish camp. Don't ask me what that is. I don't know. It was called Mudcat Charley and was occupied by a gang of young tough-looking rednecks. Their motorcycles were all lined up near the outside steps. That should have told us something. I could see a big ruckus in the making as they had one drink after another. The food was good, but we left as soon as we finished.

SEVEN LAYERS OF LOVE AND HOW IT CONTINUED TO GROW
Throughout my younger years, I remembered being told by my auntie that we were related to Abraham Lincoln. This theory apparently started with my great-grandmother's name being Susan Lincoln. Proudly I passed this information on to my children and, eventually, on to their children. My two oldest grandchildren, Beth and Ryan, often mentioned this fact to several teachers throughout their school years. One day, a teacher questioned Ryan's declaration. When Ryan asked me how I knew that we were related to Abraham Lincoln, I began to realize that Auntie never went into any details, only that Susan's last name had been Lincoln. No one in the family ever

really questioned Auntie about our lineage. The more I thought about it, the more I thought how strange it was that we didn't know more. I knew it was time for me to try to uncover the truth. Either we weren't related or we were and if so, how? I didn't want my grandchildren embarrassed if this family lore proved to be false.

The week of August 25, 2002, my daughter-in-law, Mindy; my two younger grandchildren, Travis and Kelsey; and I traveled to Oriental, North Carolina, to try to clarify our possible relationship to Abraham Lincoln. Our journey into the past was just beginning. I was filled with the excitement of not knowing what we would uncover.

Once we approached Route 55, just outside of New Bern, North Carolina, I knew our long ride would soon be coming to an end. Oriental was just down the road. Bayboro, Merritt, and Florence were familiar town names that began appearing on the many road signs. I could feel my excitement growing as each sign turned my thoughts to my yesteryears. It was almost like I was coming home after being away so long. It was a strange feeling. I didn't want to lose it, not yet, anyway. I hoped it would stay with me until we finished our genealogical search of great-grandmother Martin's roots. This exploration was considered top priority. Anything else that we might find interesting would be "icing on the cake." My eyes stayed glued to the window. I didn't want to miss anything.

To my surprise, however, each bend in the road revealed a landscape that I barely recognized. Much was new. The twenty-first century had arrived in Pamlico County. The things and places that I remembered no longer existed. Pamlico's growth had brought prosperity. It made me sad, even though I knew that change was necessary and that progress was even better. The dirt roads were now paved roadways. Cars had replaced the mules and carts. Farmlands and wooded areas had been covered by malls, condos, and housing developments. Electricity and indoor plumbing had made the oil lanterns, hand pumps unnecessary until a hurricane tears up the area. A TV antenna or satellite dish was anchored on the roof of every home. To my disappointment, the most joked-about necessity, the outhouse, has become extinct. I remembered my childhood walks down a small oyster-shell path to the

outhouse, always fearful of seeing a snake or some animal on the way. To make matters worse, a disgusting smell always hung in the air. It surrounded the entire area, forcing one to never linger any longer than necessary. I'm sure it was a surprise to many when the Sears catalog was no longer needed for any other purpose than reading. Ah, the rewards that come from progress!

Our trip to Oriental had another purpose. It was to introduce Travis and Kelsey to this small, rural community and the area that captured my heart as a youngster. The villagers whom I had known were either dead or had moved elsewhere. A few family members were still living throughout the county, but I only vaguely remembered them. I'm not sure if they would know me after all these years, but I do have their addresses and plan to visit them. I want my grandchildren to be able to envision my playground in the South. More than anything, I want them to be able to say, "We were there!"

We arrived at the Oriental Marina Motel around 5:30 P.M. I knew it was going to be a twelve-hour ride, no matter which route we took. Mindy was surprised. She thought the map was deceptive. When the kids saw the pool, they wanted to go swimming, but hunger took us to the dining room instead. By the time we had finished our dinner and walked back to our room, swimming was no longer important. We were too exhausted to do anything more.

The next morning, I was the first one awake. I was eager to get started but decided to get a much-needed cup of coffee before venturing any further

Oriental's small harbor as it appears today.

than I had to. The idea of walking changed once I entered a small café called The Bean. It served all types of hot and cold beverages, bagels, buns, etc. As I sipped my coffee, my attention was drawn to a scene that was meant for an artist's brush. The inlet was busy with many different boats entering and leaving their berths. One moment the bay seemed calm, and then it began churning until it appeared uncontrollable as the roar of the engines forced the boats into motion. Yachts, sailboats, and fishing boats filled the small harbor. The Bean was a meeting place for those folks who spent nights on their yachts and sailboats and needed a good cup of coffee to get them moving the next morning. An early morning shrimper hurried in for another refill, as did a local businessman. It definitely was the early risers' hangout.

By 6:45 A.M., the small café was ready for business. I heard that Oriental is now considered the sailing capital of the East Coast. That was interesting. Once again, progress in the making. Looking about, I could see that money was definitely coming into the community. I had every good intention of walking around the area, hoping to see something recognizable. However, between the coffee and the people I was meeting, I decided to enjoy the moment and wait until Mindy could drive me around.

No one was a stranger. Conversation took care of that. It was a nice feeling. On our second morning, Kelsey awoke in time to accompany me over to The Bean. A gentleman by the name of Ben Casey, who was standing right behind us as we were being waited on, began chatting with another customer. I heard Mr. Casey mention that he had written a book called *Mama Always Said*. My immediate thought was, "Wow, a writer." I had to meet him. Perhaps he could give me information or advice about writing, editing, publishing, or anything else pertaining to writing.

As soon as the other customer left, I turned and said, "Excuse me, are you a writer?" That was all it took, a simple question. Mr. Casey nodded. I quickly told him about Pepper recording his service years from 1943 to 1946, including his experiences in the European theater during World War II; how I put it all together; and where it is today (in the Library of Congress). Because I had recently received the Certificate of Registration from the United States Copyright Office, located in and associated with the

Library of Congress, I was now considered a published author. Mr. Casey's eyes lit up. He was all ears. I sighed with relief. I knew I had captured his attention! He said, "Call me Ben, please."

Ben gave me good advice as well as the name and address of his publisher. He told me that he was writing another book and hoped to have it published soon. I was impressed and said, "Your foot is definitely in the door! Unfortunately, I am still trying! Maybe, someday!"

I wasn't aware that Kelsey had memorized our short introduction until we returned to our motel room. To my surprise, she began to describe our chitchat, leading up to Ben and my introduction. None of us was prepared for Kelsey's rendition. To get the full humor of her performance, one must imagine this nine-year-old child acting out the meeting of two adults, both eager to talk about a subject in which they shared an interest—writing!

She began her version by using a prissy, high-pitched voice. I guess that was supposed to be me speaking. Her arms and head moved in all directions, trying to compliment the voice. "Buddy" (my grandchildren's nickname for me) speaking, "Excuse me, are you a writer?" With a deep voice, "Ben" said, in a very casual manner, "No! I'm a want-to-be writer." Again, "Buddy's" high-pitched voice exclaimed, "Me, too!"

While in Oriental, we experienced a rather freakish series of events. Each revolved around my love of my grandmother's "seven-layer" cake. Grandmother often said, "Teeny, dearest, I know how much you love this cake, but there is something even nicer about it." I looked at Grandmother with a puzzled expression. I never forgot her words, "I know whenever you think of this cake, you will be thinking of me as well." God bless her! Her words were so true. Throughout the decades, I looked for a recipe similar to the one she used. I often wondered if she even wrote it down. I never saw her use anything that looked like a recipe when she was making her specialty. I'm sure that she had made it so many times that she didn't need one. My hopes faded with the passing of time. I had to settle for our local bakery's seven-layer cake. Grandmother died in 1965. I was convinced the recipe went with her. My search was over. I often regret not asking her for the recipe.

The second day, we drove up to New Bern. We went to the Hall of Records to try to locate a document that would show the lineage of my

great-grandmother, Susan Lincoln. While we were in the records room, one of the employee's was in the process of having a birthday party. A table with all kinds of goodies, veggies with dips, and small sandwiches and drinks were available for everyone in the room. Finally, the birthday cake was brought out, and we all sang "Happy Birthday." I was surprised to see how high the cake appeared. The strangest feeling came over me. I had to check it out. My jaw must have dropped down to my feet as I heard one of the ladies say it was a fifteen-layer cake. "Oh, God, could this be similar to grandmother's, only higher?" I thought. Well, one of the girls handed me a slice. Much to my surprise, it was almost as good. I asked the gal who made it if she would share her recipe. She promised to send it to me, but I never received it.

During the morning of the third day, we drove up to Bayboro and visited my cousin, Sybil Whorton Gatlin. Because of her age, ninety-three, I was hoping that she either had met Susan Lincoln or had information or stories about her. Sybil was not very helpful. She was unable to answer most of my questions but did mention that she heard Susan was petite and loved to cook. Sybil added, "Susan's name was never mentioned and nobody ever asked about her." How strange!

Mindy and I began to feel that there was a lot more to this story than anyone knew. This intrigued both of us. We had to keep looking for some answers. I asked Sybil if anyone in the family ever talked about our relationship to Abraham Lincoln. She was surprised and told us that she had never heard that before. Mark, her grandson, had just come in when he heard my question about Lincoln. This good-ol' boy, or should I say, this real redneck got rather excited. "Please, don't tell me we're related to a man who ruined the South and its way of life. I'm trying to get into the Sons of the Confederacy! Christ, I'll never get in if this is true."

At first, we thought he was only kidding until Mindy gave me a nudge and a look that immediately told me to be quiet and not say a word. She started talking to him, mentioning that she had been born and raised in Georgia and had come north after she married Kevin. "Oh," Mark added, "you know exactly what I mean!" "Oh, yeah!" was her reply. She was good! She knew how to work this guy. Calm, once again, returned to the room. We decided it was time to leave before Mark became unhinged again or began

delivering another sermon on the evils of Lincoln. Some are still fighting the Civil War. Has no one told him that the war is long over? "Ol' Abe" was no longer mentioned, at least, not while we were in their company.

That evening, we decided to have dinner at the Oriental Steamer Restaurant because we heard they serve great seafood. We were told that their fried oysters were considered the best in the area. A very tasty baked sweet potato, zucchini, salad, and iced tea were included. We were not disappointed. The chef introduced himself and then asked if we had enjoyed the dinner. He suggested we try his favorite dessert, which he makes himself. His favorite turned out to be a seventeen-layer cake. "What did you say?" I asked. "Did you say a seventeen-layer cake?" Yesterday, it was a fifteen-layer cake. Today, it's a seventeen-layer cake. My God, what are you doing to me? All of a sudden, I'm seeing and eating nothing but layer cakes. I had to see his creation.

Chef Jeff took me over to a case that held salads, sliced fruit, and several different types of desserts. There it was, his beautiful masterpiece. I couldn't believe it. It looked exactly like Grandmother's, only much higher. Excitedly, I said, "Pinch me, quick, Mindy. I must be dreaming." We ordered a slice without any hesitation. It was sumptuous. I complimented Chef Jeff and then asked to have a couple of slices to take back to the motel. Well, I thought I had died and gone to heaven. The cake was growing by leaps and bounds, one layer on top of another. I wanted to ask the chef if he would share his recipe, but I knew the answer before he even said it. "No," was his reply.

The third day, we visited the villages of Florence, Merritt, Vandemere, and Whortonsville. These villages played a part in the Whortons' and the Lincolns' roots. In Merritt, we visited Florence Martin Sanders (daughter of Edward and Rosa Martin, great-granddaughter of James G. Martin, who was the brother of Timothy M. Martin, my great-grandfather). I was hoping that Florence would have stories or information on the Martin family. She knew little except the location where Susan was supposed to be buried and the site of Susan and Timothy's home, where my grandmother was raised. She showed us a very thickly wooded area, filled with heavy undergrowth, and said, "Somewhere in there is the grave of Susan Lincoln. Many stones are placed over the gravesite with some of the stones having initials scraped in them. There are several other

graves as well." She added that her boys had been in there many times and knew exactly where the gravesite was. I eyed the area once more and decided, "No way in hell are we going to enter those woods."

I could picture lots of mosquitoes, snakes, and even a bear or a wildcat. Mindy agreed, so we left the only possible clue for another time. Next, Florence took us to Whortonsville and showed us the site where Grandmother and Granddaddy Whorton had their home. I vaguely remembered the old homestead. Mindy took several pictures of the area, hoping they would help us find the site again if we ever returned. Before our visit ended, we had a chance to meet Florence's son, Jim. He told us that he would go back to the gravesite sometime during winter, once the area was free of its wild summer inhabitants, take pictures for us, and even try to get pictures of the stones that have markings on them. That was good enough for me! Again, our travel for that day was rather disappointing. We still knew little about Susan.

Upon our return to Oriental, I invited Edna Whorton, a family member by marriage, to join us for dinner. I told her about our unusual and tasty experiences over the past few days. Edna was quite amused and suggested that we have dinner at the Oriental Steamer, in hopes that the chef's favorite dessert would be on tonight's menu. It was on the menu, only this time, the chef had made a *twenty*-layer cake that was better than the one we had the day before. Again, it freaked me out. My thoughts were becoming a little scary. By then, I was convinced that this cake thing was way out of control! However, I was determined to enjoy the moment, no matter how high the cakes got or how much I ate.

Edna seemed surprised when I told her that I had never seen this type of cake in the North. I knew that none of my friends would ever make it. It had to be time consuming. Edna told us that this is the most popular cake in the Pamlico area and has been for decades. As we were leaving the restaurant, she mentioned that her friend had a recipe for a fifteen- to seventeen-layer cake and she would get it for me if I wanted it. I immediately said, "Yes!" Edna mentioned that she remembered Grandmother's cake and assured me that her friend's recipe was just as good, but it had more layers. (Edna's friend's recipe for the Fifteen- to Seventeen-Layer Cake can be found in Appendix J.)

On the fourth day, we had lunch at the M & M Café and found that they had, without a doubt, the best crab cakes and fried onion rings we have ever tasted. However, this eatery did not have any layer cake for dessert, so that evening we went back to Steamer's and enjoyed another slice of the now *twenty*-layer cake. This was turning into a great game! Just what is the limit of layers one can put on a cake? Chef Jeff came by our table and mentioned that he would be making a *twenty-five*-layer cake the following day and suggested that we come by and try it.

How could we say no? However, time did not allow us to sample this delightful and unimaginable cake the next evening because we went elsewhere for dinner. We still had one more day left before leaving for home. We knew that our last meal would be at the Steamer, allowing our taste buds the enjoyment of Chef Jeff's cooking and baking. By now, we considered ourselves connoisseurs of the foods and desserts of Oriental.

Saturday was our last day in the Oriental area. It was a very busy day. We still had many things to do. We were trying to tie all our genealogical information together. We said our goodbyes to Sybil, Florence, and Edna. There was only one place that we had not visited, Minnesott Beach. Back in the early 1940s, this was one small, bustling playground for the Marines who were stationed at Cherry Point Marine Base. Minnesott Beach and the Marine base are separated by the Neuse River. Every Saturday night, Ray Whorton would drive us kids down there. I have already described those Saturday nights in the story of my childhood in North Carolina.

Within minutes of arriving at Minnesott Beach, I knew that everything I remembered was now only a memory. Nothing was familiar. We sat, watching the free ferry unload its passengers and their cars. All of a sudden, Mindy said, "Shall we take a ferry ride?" "Yes, let's do it!" was my reply. So, we took the twenty-minute ride across the Neuse River. It turned out to be a very good idea. It was refreshing. It woke us up. Once on the other side, we drove just a short distance and then decided to catch the ferry on its return to Minnesott. We were lucky. We just made it. Mindy and the kids went up on the second deck.

I stood looking out over the water and thought about my great-grandmother, Susan, and the information we had uncovered on the Whorton and

the Martin families. Although Susan had apparently been well thought of, little was known about her. I still felt that there was something mysterious about her existence. There is a story hidden somewhere, and she is the main player. She was not buried with her second husband, Timothy Mydyette Martin. He was much younger than his wife, approximately nineteen years younger. He was born on March 18, 1853.

When you compare the date Timothy was born and the date Susan married Wiley R. Whorton, it appears she robbed the cradle. Timothy's father's name was Joseph Martin, birthplace unknown. His mother's maiden name was Elisabeth Calhoon, born in Craven County before it became Pamlico County. Timothy spent his life farming, died on February 9, 1925, at the age of seventy-three, and is buried in the Bethel Freewill Baptist Church Yard Cemetery, located in Whortonsville.

My grandmother came from this marriage. Her name was Louvenia Ernestine Martin. My name, after I married Frank Martin, became Lavenia Ernestine Martin. The only difference in the two names is the spelling. Many people back then only had a limited education. They spelled by the way the word sounded. During our research, we found a half-dozen ways they spelled Lavenia. We found that Whorton had also been spelled "Wharton." Who is correct? It left us wondering who belonged to whom. It can be very confusing!

It's complicated. We are related to Wiley R. Whorton through my grand-father Whorton's family. Susan became a Whorton through her marriage to Wiley. Her name became Susan Lincoln Whorton. This is how we're related to Sybil and Florence. Susan had four children with Wiley. The 1870 census for the area lists information on Wiley Whorton's household. Susan's age is given as thirty-two. When the 1900 census was taken, Susan was listed as being sixty-five years old at her last birthday. There are no records, to date, showing where Wiley or Susan is buried. They were married on October 12, 1855, in Craven County.

I left Oriental feeling as if I were leaving behind a tragic and unfinished story about my great-grandmother, Susan Lincoln Whorton Martin. Her secrets were buried with her. I knew I had to return to the area. I wanted to

locate her resting place and, perhaps, find the answers to my many questions concerning her roots, existence, and death. As we approached the highway that would take us back North, mixed emotions seemed to bubble within me. I knew that my life had been built on tears and laughter, but it was here where my laughter prevailed. I turned and watched the village disappear. Tears began to roll down my cheeks as pangs of sadness bounced against my heart.

We left Oriental early in the morning, 4:30 A.M. to be exact. When we were going through New Bern, we stopped for gas. As Mindy was filling the car, the clerk came running out of the store. He appeared very excited. I guess I should say "over exuberant." I thought he was going to help her. Instead, he seemed elated to meet her. Mindy continued pumping as he spoke.

When she got back into the car, she asked if we had heard the conversation between the two of them. I said, "No. What was wrong with him?" She began laughing. "Oh, my God, Mom, he saw our license plate, 'ZOC666,' come up on the screen and he wanted to meet the 'devil's handmaiden.'"

"What was even scarier was his continued 'enthusiasm' when I tried to explain that I wasn't. He refused to believe it. He kept repeating how honored he was to meet someone who carried the 'devil's numbers' so boldly and openly for the world to see." For several miles down the road, we kept checking the rear-view mirror just in case he made a few calls to the rest of the local devil worshipers. Oh, the people we met! The places we've seen! The things we learned.

I knew that our trip had turned into an unbelievable adventure. After thinking about how we had been tracing family roots, enjoying lavish foods, eating cake that grew higher by the day, receiving a recipe that could have come from the grave, and meeting a writer and the local devil worshiper, my sadness quickly disappeared. It was a most unusual and rewarding adventure. The next thing I knew, as silly as this might sound, General MacArthur's well-known quote (as he was leaving Corregidor at the beginning of World War II) popped into my head, "I shall return!" I heard myself quietly say, "So shall I, someday."

CAPE MAY WITH KEVIN AND MINDY Every summer after Pepper died, I went to Cape May, New Jersey, with Kevin and his family for five or

six days. It is a three-hour drive and that made it even nicer. We always stayed at the Camelot Motel, which had efficiency apartments, perfect for the five of us. The beach and the small amusement area are directly across the street from our motel. There is also a miniature-golf course in front of the motel. The motel has a swimming pool, which the kids enjoy as much as the ocean.

The kids and I slept in one room because it had two queen-size beds. Mindy and Kevin had the other bedroom. We had a small kitchen, large enough for us to fix a nice breakfast and lunch. In the evenings, we went out and had luscious seafood dinners. After a few visits, we knew which restaurants were the best. (And you don't have to go to a restaurant to enjoy Cape May's wonderful seafood; see the recipe for Deviled Crab in Appendix K.) The Washington Street Mall had everything we needed: lots of interesting shops with unusual merchandise. I loved walking around this area. It is where I found bread made in the shapes of lobsters, crabs, and shrimp. I had to buy two of these loaves because Kelsey was intrigued by them. She and Travis love lobster, so, naturally, that made the bread taste even better. We have become so familiar with the area that there is never any question about where we are going.

Mindy, Kelsey, and I always try to save one day for a trip to Lewes, Delaware, which calls for a ferry ride across the Delaware River. This is a quaint old town with lots of small shops. We usually enjoy having our lunch on the bayside of the town. It is a special day as it's considered the girls' day out. For some unknown reason, I have been having a problem of falling unexpectedly, and this happened on one of our trips to Lewes. Mindy and Kelsey were walking ahead of me, and the next thing I knew, I was falling. I tried to catch myself and accidentally hit Kelsey's back. She turned around and saw me going down. I looked up and saw two concerned and surprised faces looking down at me. "Mom, are you alright?" I sat there for a minute. "Yes, I think so."

I got up and saw that my knee was bleeding and needed some immediate attention. Several people came over, and a gentleman ran to the drugstore and came back with a couple of large Band-aids. He also had a wet paper towel to clean the wound. After my unexpected spill, we continued our shopping and

then took the bus back to the ferry. I came home with an unexpected souvenir, a bandaged and sore knee. Regardless, a good time was had by all!

The Cape May Courthouse Zoo is a great adventure, not just for children, but for adults as well. Unfortunately, few people know it exists. It has every animal imaginable and is just as interesting as the popular Bronx Zoo in New York City. If I ever won the lottery, I would buy a home in Cape May. I love the area.

PAULINE'S DEATH   On July 2, 2003, I received a call from my cousin, Danny Whorton, who told me that he had some bad news to tell me. I said, "My God, has your mother died?" "No," he said, "Your sister, Pauline, passed away." I gasped. I heard myself saying, "Pauline's dead? Oh, my God, what happened?" Quietly, Danny spoke, "Teeny, she died last November or December 2002." I was stunned by his words, but after a moment, I was finally able to speak: "What? She died seven months ago? Who told you?" Danny continued, "Uncle Elmo and Marguerite were staying with Diana because they had an appointment at the Mayo Clinic in Jacksonville. While in Brunswick, they decided to visit us." There was a pause, then Danny said, "Mom asked Marguerite how your mother was and if anyone had heard how Pauline was doing. Out of the clear blue, Marguerite announced, 'She's dead. She died either in November or December of last year.' Then, she quickly added, 'Oh, God, I just made a slip of the tongue. I wasn't supposed to tell anyone.'"

Danny had quickly asked her, "Marguerite, you did call Teeny, didn't you?" She said, "No." He had looked at her in disbelief and added, "'You mean to tell me that you never called her? That's her sister. Jesus, Marguerite, what in the hell is wrong with you? You weren't going to tell the rest of the family either, were you?' Teeny, none of us were suppose to know, if that is any comfort to you. Mom and I are so sorry, but we had to call you."

Between my sobs, I managed to thank him, and then I hung up the phone. I sat down and cried because I knew that death had just finalized our relationship as sisters.

Still upset, I went into the Internet, located the *Billings Gazette* site, and found Pauline's obituary. She had died in the evening of December 30 at the

Deaconess Billings Clinic. I called Pauline's husband, Andy, saying, "Please don't hang up on me. It's Teeny. I just heard about Pauline." I couldn't control my grief anymore. I cried. I couldn't speak. Thank God, Andy was compassionate and felt my pain. He cried, and we cried together. Andy told me that Pauline had developed diabetes four years ago and that she had become blind over the past year. She could no longer work or drive and life at home had become difficult for her. He said that on the evening of December 30, Pauline began having trouble breathing, and he took her to the clinic. Upon arriving, he went in, found a wheelchair, and then returned to the car where he found Pauline had gotten out and apparently wandered off. He found her lying in the road, headed in the direction of their home. She died shortly after the ambulance brought her back to the clinic.

I was furious with Marguerite and Diana. I considered them special family members because we always kept in touch. I visited Diana around Easter 2003 and was shocked to learn that she had known of Pauline's death shortly after my sister died and had never told me about it during my visit. She and Marguerite came up with three pathetic excuses for their behavior, but I could find no justification in any of them. So much for family! Their deceit left me in a state of shock. The joke was really on me, only I didn't find it funny. My sister had died, and now I'm having trouble trying to understand why two family members, whom I have always loved for fifty-some years, used such poor judgment in hiding news of my sister's death from me and the other family members, regardless what the situation might be. I felt that I had been betrayed and lied to.

The one thing I have learned from all of this is that the word "love" is only a word and that it is overused in today's society. It sounds beautiful but can mean so little. Talk is cheap. Actions speak louder than words when it comes to the true meaning of love. I get a sick, cynical feeling when I hear the word "love" spoken so freely by everyone anymore.

MY MOTHER'S DEATH Around 9:00 P.M. on July 30, 2003, Marguerite called me. I would have been completely crushed if she hadn't. Once was enough! Marguerite told me that Mother had passed away early that

morning. Florence had called her with the news shortly after Mother's passing, and by that evening Marguerite decided to call me.

Mother had turned ninety-seven on July 16. I felt sad, yet I found myself unable to grieve. I loved her, but I felt a terrible numbness. I cried, but it wasn't for Mother. I knew she had lived many years and was at peace now. She was no longer that screaming, cursing stranger who had invaded her mind twenty-some years ago. I was grieving for the loss of "my mother" and for the demise of the entire Ritter family.

To this day, my only living sister has not called me regarding Pauline's or our mother's deaths.

Isn't life funny? Dad changed his original will because he became terrified when he realized that he had put Florence in control of his entire estate, including complete charge of Mother. Florence never forgave him when she learned, just after he died in 1974, that he had changed his will. Once she got her hands on Mother, nothing stopped her.

Even though Dad died thirty-some years ago, Florence's revenge was not meant only for the living, but for the dead as well. In my opinion, everything that Dad had taken away from her, Florence managed to get back, plus more because she buried Mother in Sun City, Arizona, rather than have her buried in the family plot next to Dad in the Morristown Evergreen Cemetery.

Will it be Florence or me when death comes calling for one of us? How will the Grim Reaper arrive? Will our dying come quickly and quietly, or will death stall, allowing us to linger for months, even years, burdening our loved ones? We are no longer young. It is our time to get ready to meet our God. I feel that one of us might be going to "hell" and the other one may be lucky enough to make it to "heaven." Which one of us might be that lucky one? Oh, God, please let it be me, or at least, show me the way!

Florence can't do anything more to me. I hope that her revenge has given her the satisfaction she has sought all these years, but what did she really gain? Money! Property! I don't need either of them, thank God.

Today, I am happy I kept my home in Morris Plains. I have had a long and hard road to travel, but I managed to survive. What regrets I have had are no longer important. I did the best I could. I made a lot of mistakes and

a lot of bad choices. I just pray that I didn't instill any hate or disfavor in too many people who walked alongside me as we traveled down the path of life. I can live with myself, accept myself as I was and as I am now, and that, to me, is one of the secrets of life.

GOING FORWARD Everyone wants a drink from the Fountain of Youth in hopes that its mythical powers might work. I even went to St. Augustine where this wonderful spring is located, just to drink its miraculous agents. Ah, the Fountain of Youth! All these many years, I waited for its magic to kick in. Well, I awoke one day and found that something had gone wrong. I had become a "senior citizen." Wow! Am I supposed to be old? I looked in the mirror and couldn't believe what I saw. Yes, lots of winkles, lines, and dentures (no wonder I'm constantly drooling). But hold on: I'm not finished yet. I saw a double chin with a very noticeable jowl (that's the term for loose flesh below the jaw), partially gray hair, and to my horror, the beginning of what looked like a moustache. Another surprising jolt occurred when I discovered that I'm getting shorter! What a whammy! This little secret was kept under lock and key, that's for sure. I just hope my peers realize that this could and probably will happen to them. My Aunt Love became shorter as she got older, but she was the only one I ever knew who actually shrunk. So much for surprises. God, I have to look up to see my family anymore. What really shocked me is the delight my grandchildren take in my plight. They laugh themselves silly. What can I say except laugh while you can because "aging isn't for sissies"? God, what happened?

Even my cabinet over the bathroom sink holds a whole new line of products, familiar only to the "senior citizen." I won't go into great detail about these specialties, but it should be helpful to the next generation to know what they can expect. It's not all fun and games. That cabinet contains items such as tubes of depilatory cream, Efferdent®, multiple pill bottles, and an assortment of small wee-wee pads, not the "big boy" undies known as Depends. Those big boys are stored well out of sight, even from the family. After all, we "senior citizens" still have our dignity, no matter what we have to use.

Thank God for hair coloring. I have never seen so many blonds at the age of eighty as I have since I became one of those "senior citizens." Quit trying

to be an "old" Marilyn Monroe. You can only cover up so much. It's too time consuming. Be yourself. We're all in the same boat. Look upon every winkle as a success story. Most aging folk could use a good face lift, tummy and backside tucks, and the many other tucks that would help firm all the sagging parts of our ol' bodies, but why go to that trouble and pain. Besides, most of us, can't afford such luxuries.

Our lives change in many ways, and the best way to deal with aging is to laugh. Laugh at yourself when you realize you did something silly, said something usual, or forgot why you went upstairs. Laugh when you can't remember why you went to the refrigerator and end up staring at its contents. Laugh when you forgot where you put something that, naturally, was always very important. Laugh when you find that you don't have the strength in your hands to remove the lids from modern-day jars, including those darn little pill-bottle lids, no matter what the directions say. Laugh when you're driving and find yourself lost. Laugh when you now need to keep a daily supply of Depends on hand for nighttime use only, at least in the early stages. That eventually becomes a twenty-four-hour necessity. If you don't know what Depends are, believe me, you will, soon enough.

These are just a few examples of some of the things that are part of an ordinary day for an older person. Every day, a senior citizen comes up against another problem with more frustrations. Believe me, it can become very aggravating. Don't get mad! Laugh. It's good for the soul. Unfortunately, the joke is on us. There is no Fountain of Youth. It is a myth. Face it: we are old!

Most of us, thank God, are still young at heart and want to think that way as long as we can, but life, especially for aging citizens, is unpredictable. Bad health is always lurking around the next corner. Don't get bitter—just be glad you can get out of bed in the morning and get back in it that evening. Just remember, we've lived a lifetime and survived.

The younger generation can't imagine us ever having been like them, young, beautiful, and with gorgeous, firm bodies—bodies to die for. But we were. Many look upon us as unusual novelties with little common sense. Gather 'round, my peers: we know that we traveled down long, hard roads, and we're not as dumb as those youngsters think.

Most of us find that our minds haven't caught up with the face that's in the mirror. What happened? We're still thinking young! Wow, yes! Keep that thought going so that when you see your reflection, you can say, "Stranger, stay your distance, because I still have much to learn, things to do, and places to see." We have a lifetime of stories to tell and experiences the young have not yet encountered and probably never will. We leave behind our heritage built on values, principals, and morals, all entangled with good common sense.

UNTIL NEXT TIME . . . It's hard to believe that I have managed to write this much of my life story. What surprises me are the many untold stories that are a part of my life. However, knowing that, I must finish with the old teaser, "To be continued . . .." I want to believe that my tomorrows will help me fulfill a few more dreams that occasionally flare up within me. I felt a wonderful sense of satisfaction, discovered much about myself, and gained so much from my source of therapy as I traveled back in time in order to put my life down on paper. Hopefully, the events surrounding more of my past, my today, and my tomorrows will continue through my writings about Saturday's Child and her remaining years. So, until next time . . ..

Appendix A

KNOLLCROFT KENNELS CHAMPIONS   Carl Sillman, historian of the English Setter Association of America, Inc., also found some genealogical information on my dad's dogs Bess and Prince because their father was the famous Rummey Stagboro. He was the top-producing sire of English setter champions in his day. He lived from 1929 to 1942 and sired thirty-three champions. This dog is still famous, if not legendary, to this day. He had a huge impact on the breed. Some of Dad's dogs figure in the pedigrees of many champion English setters. Nancy Lou was bred to Rummey Stagboro several times, and she produced five champions. Stagboro, End O'Maine, and Haon were all fairly famous kennels at that time as well, particularly Stagboro. White Flash and Chief were sired by a dog named Ch. Sturdy Max, who was a son of Rummey Stagboro. Sturdy Max was also a very famous English setter show dog and a top sire as well. I couldn't help but feel proud when I realized that Dad's dogs were connected with some famous English setters.

Knollcroft Bess—breeder/owner: Paul M. Ritter
   Date of birth 6/9/1935—Orange Belton
   Rummey Stagboro was Bess' father
   Queen of Stagboro was the mother
Knollcroft Prince (birth date, sire, and dam same as his littermate, Bess)
   He produced one Champion offspring (Champion Knollcroft Nancy Lou) and five Champion grandkids:

Ch. Knollcroft Nancy Lou (Top Producing Dam) TPD
Borne: 1/15/1937
Published 9/1937
Champion: 9/1943—TPD
Champion Nellie of Stagboro was Nancy's mother
Breeder: Paul M. Ritter 1/15/1937—Blue
Sb 9/37 owner Oswald Love
Nancy Lou's children:
>   Lady Juliet of Seafren—By Rummey Stagboro
>   Born: 12/3/1938
>   Published: 3/1940
>   Champion: 8/1943

>   *Ch. Modern Gil of Stagboro—By Rummey Stagboro
>   Born: 12/3/1938
>   Published: 4/1941
>   Champion: 8/1943

>   Nancy Girl of Stagboro—By Rummey Stagboro,
>   Top Producing Stud (TPS)
>   Born: 4/24/1940
>   Published: 8/1940

>   *Ch. Buzz of Haon—By Rummey Stagboro, TPS
>   Born: 4/24/1940
>   Published: 5/1941
>   Champion: 6/1943

>   *Ch. Rusty of Haon – By Rummey Stagboro, TPS
>   Born: 4/24/1940
>   Published: 10/1940
>   Champion: 5/1944

*Ch. End O'Maine Wampum—By Ch. Cedrick of Delwed, TPS
   Born: 9/6/1944
   Published: 8/1945
   Champion: 6/1949
*Ch. End O'Maine Comment—
By Ch. End O'Maine Weather Vane
   Born: 1/10/1947
   Published: 9/1947
   Champion: 6/1949

The names that have an asterisk are the five champion kids by Knollcroft Nancy Lou, which made this bitch a top producing dam (TPD)
   Knollcroft Chief—sb 8/36—Breeder/Owner: Paul M. Ritter
      DOB: 3/9/1936 – Orange
      Ch. Sturdy Max was the father
      Ch. Nellie of Stagboro was the mother
   Knollcroft White Flash—same as Knollcroft Chief
      One champion offspring:
      Ch. Rockwood Royal Rouge—By Ch. Alan-a-Dale of Marional
      Born: 1/8/1940
      Published: 5/1941

Appendix B

"The Martians Are Coming!"—Recipe   When Orson Welles'
radio production of *The War of the Worlds* came on the air, Mother was in
the kitchen making the bread for the next day. It was her bread and dinner
rolls that I remember so clearly. I found her recipes for the bread and rolls
many years ago and still make them for special occasions and the many holidays throughout the year. I decided that between the creating, baking, and
eating Mother's wonderful homemade bread and small cloverleaf-shaped
rolls were and still are as exciting as the night we heard *The War of the Worlds*.

Cloverleaf Dinner Rolls
4-½ cups all-purpose Flour
⅓ cup Sugar
2 packages Fleischmann's® Active Dry Yeast
1 tsp. Salt
2 Eggs
¾ cup Milk
½ cup Water
⅓ cup (⅔ stick) Butter/Margarine (I prefer Butter.)

1. In large bowl, combine 1-½ cups flour, sugar, undissolved yeast, and salt.
2. Heat milk, water, and butter until warm (105–115 degrees F). Butter
   does not need to melt.

3. Gradually add to dry ingredients. Beat 2 minutes in electric mixer at medium speed, scraping bowl occasionally.
4. Add eggs and ½ cup flour, beat 2 minutes at high speed, scraping bowl occasionally. Stir in remaining flour (2-½ cups) to make soft dough. Knead dough until dough looks and feels comfortable as you knead it.
5. Lightly oil top, cover bowl tightly, and refrigerate for two hours or up to two days before shaping. Dough should double in size.

To Shape: Divide dough into 18 equal pieces. Divide each again into 3 equal pieces. Roll into balls. Place 3 balls in each section of 18 greased 2-½" muffin pan cups.

To Rise: Let rise in warm, draft-free place until doubled in size. Brush tops with melted butter or lightly beaten egg. Optionally top with poppy or sesame seeds. (I leave mine plain or may dust the tops with flour.)

To Bake: Bake at 375 degrees for 15 to 20 minutes or until golden brown. Remove from pans and cool on wire racks.

Appendix C

VISITING FAMILY IN BRUNSWICK, GEORGIA—RECIPE   Cooking has been one of the important traits in every woman who carries the Whorton genes. I know that my generation has benefited from and enjoyed this trait because we all were and still are good cooks. We learned much more than just cooking from Aunt Lillie and the other Whorton women in our family. We learned how to present a beautiful table; not only how to serve every dish properly, but also how to make it tempting and appealing to those waiting to be served; and the importance of entertaining in a gracious manner. Sybil Whorton Gatlin of Stonewall, North Carolina, said that our love of cooking can be attributed to our great-grandmother, Susan Lincoln Whorton Martin. Susan's granddaughter, Florence Martin Sanders, who lives in Merritt, North Carolina, remembered her vaguely and agreed Sybil.

This was one of Aunt Lillie's favorite recipes.

SHRIMP CREOLE WITH RICE

Remove shells, and de-vein 2 lbs. fresh shrimp. Bring water to boil in large pot, add shrimp. Cook 3 minutes or until shrimp turn pink. Drain well and rinse with cold water.

1 medium-size sweet Red Pepper, seeded and chopped
1 medium-size Green Pepper, seeded and chopped
2 cloves Garlic, minced
½ cup chopped Onion

2 Tbsp. Olive Oil or Butter (whichever you prefer)

2 cans (14-½ ounces) Cajun-style Stewed Tomatoes, undrained. (You can
use plain stewed tomatoes, undrained, with ¼ tsp. Tabasco® Red Pepper
Sauce or Frank's® Red Hot® Pepper Sauce.)

Hot cooked Rice

Stirring constantly, sauté red and green peppers, garlic, and onions in olive
oil until tender. Add stewed (Cajun-style) tomatoes and bring to boil.
Reduce heat and simmer for ten minutes. Add shrimp and cook until thoroughly heated. Serve over rice.

Serves: 4–6

Appendix D

ON STRIKE—RECIPE Ah, yes, a dinner I will never forget. My delicious, wonderful, tempting, satisfying, and long awaited meal turned out to be a disaster in the making. I can look back on that evening and "now" laugh but it meant something more to me than dinner itself, way back then. It was the first time I ever did something like that and walked away both humiliated and gratified all at the same time. It seemed to be the story of my life; I worked hard for my living, nothing came easy. However, this recipe is still one of my favorites. When I make it, I make a large pot full and divide it into many small casserole dishes and freeze them. It's time consuming but worth it.

CHICKEN POTPIE
Make piecrust and set aside.
Stock:
1 Chicken (about 6 lbs.)
2 cups chopped Celery, Onions, Carrots, and Parsley

Place chicken and chopped vegetables/herbs in stockpot and cover with water. Simmer for 2 hours. Strain stock. If necessary, add chicken broth to make 6 cups of stock. You can't hurt the stock. When chicken is cooked, take it out of the pot, cut the chicken into medium-size diced pieces, and set it aside.

Filling for Potpie:

Bring 6 cups of chicken stock to a boil in large pot. Add:

5 large Carrots, sliced in small pieces

15 quartered Mushrooms

½ lb. String Beans cut in small lengths

15 white Boiling Onions

5 or 6 Potatoes cut in quarters, not too large

½ bag of Okra (frozen is fine)

½ bag frozen or 1 can of Yellow Corn

½ bag of frozen Sweet Peas

You have to judge the amount of vegetables you would like in your potpie. I like it thick, so I always use spices that would add to the flavor as well. You can use your own imagination. Cover and simmer for 15 minutes until vegetables are tender. Remove vegetables with slotted spoon and set aside. Return pot to heat.

Melt 4oz. of unsalted butter, then add ⅔ cup flour.

Cook and stir until all is well mixed. Add stock and bring to a boil, stirring constantly. Reduce heat, add ⅔ cup of heavy cream, and simmer for a couple of minutes. Stir in diced, cooked chicken and the cooked vegetables. Add more flour and cream if stock is not thick enough. Add ¼ cup of chopped fresh parsley and season with salt and pepper. Fill casserole dishes, then lay pastry over filling, cut vents in top. Bake 20–25 minutes in preheated oven at 400 degrees until crust is nicely brown. (You can also put piecrust on bottom of dish as well as on top.)

Appendix E

OUR TRIPS TO BRUNSWICK, JACKSONVILLE, AND KINGSLEY LAKE— RECIPE These were the times when we headed south by train. Every summer, the kids and I would take off for the sunny South. We left looking like ordinary travelers. However, on our return to Jersey, we looked more like a bunch of gypsies on the move. Our suitcases were packed with souvenirs, old iron frying pans (10- to 14-inch ones that I still use), hams, yellow corn meal, and much more. Aunt Leonia always took me grocery shopping just before we had to leave. She insisted that I take half the South home with me, and I did. It was always a big surprise when I opened our suitcases after getting home. I don't know how I managed the collection of mess that we carried home. Paul had his fishing pole and BB gun. Kevin always found his yearly supply of slimy little creatures that we *had* to bring home. Year after year, we traveled the rails between New Jersey and Florida. The good times we had made it all worthwhile.

AUNT LEONIA'S CRAB AU GRATIN
4 Tbsp. Butter or Margarine
2 Tbsp. Flour
1-¼ cups Milk
¼ tsp. Salt, a touch of Pepper
1 small Onion, minced

½ cup Celery, chopped in small pieces
2 tsp. Parsley, chopped fine
¼ cup Sherry or White Wine (optional)
¾ cup Cheddar Cheese, grated
1 lb. lump Crabmeat, picked through
Paprika
Cheese-and-garlic flavored Croutons, mashed into fine pieces

1. Melt butter or margarine in small saucepan. Add flour, salt, and pepper, and stir until well blended and smooth, free of lumps.
2. Pour in milk gradually, while stirring constantly until mixture starts to thicken. Stir in sherry or wine and ¼ cup of cheese. Remove from heat. Cheese need not melt.
3. Stir in crabmeat, onion, celery, and parsley and pour mixture into deep casserole dish. Top with remaining cheese, croutons, and paprika.
4. Bake at 350 degrees for 15–20 minutes until hot and cheese melts.

Serves: 4–6

Appendix F

A MOONLIGHT CRUISE—RECIPE I am a person who doesn't always follow the crowd or go with the "norm." I love the unusual, the unexpected, yet pleasant things, and lean mostly to original thoughts and actions. The groom's family was expected to put on a party the night before the wedding. A thought came to me: a moonlight cruise. Who else would ever come up with such an idea? I rented my cousin's ferry and was about to burst with excitement. I had a lot of work to do in order to get this plan into motion. It turned out to be a delightful evening. We ate continuously, danced under the moon as the band played music that each generation could enjoy, and drank in the mystical and magical sounds and sights that swept over the ferry. Yes, we even got stuck on a sandbar for over an hour, and, yes, a few guests including Pepper and Brian found themselves leaning over the rail, but I believe a good time was had by all, regardless of the few distractions.

This is an excellent recipe for BBQ. I make it every time our neighborhood holds its annual "block party." The neighbors always request it.

BBQ WITH SAUCE
2 large Onions, chopped
2 Tbsp. Bacon Fat
2 Tbsp. Vinegar
2 Tbsp. Brown Sugar

4 Tbsp. Lemon Juice

1-⅔ cups Tomato Catsup

1 bottle of Heinz® Chili Sauce

3 Tbsp. Worcestershire Sauce

½ tsp. Dijon Mustard

½ cup of KC Masterpiece® original BBQ sauce

1 cup Water

Salt (to taste)

1 cup Celery, chopped in small pieces

4 or 5 drops of Tabasco® Red Pepper Sauce

Brown onions in bacon fat until yellow and tender. In the meantime, combine all the other ingredients in a separate bowl. When onions are cooked, add other ingredients to the onions and simmer for 30 minutes. Makes about 2-½ cups of sauce. Add cooked, diced pork, beef, or chicken to the sauce and put in refrigerator overnight to get the wonderful flavor of meat or poultry with the sauce.

Serve with semi-hard rolls.

Appendix G

OUR FOUR GRANDCHILDREN—RECIPES At Christmas time, these cookies are my four grandchildren's favorite, especially Ryan. Even though he is in college, he still looks forward to a TLC package, filled with his very special cookies. When he was little, I always enjoyed watching him decorate each one. I have been making these for fifty-some years. My three boys never knew what it was not to have homemade goodies waiting for them when they needed a snack. I have carried this over to my grandchildren in hopes that they will do the same for their children. It all began with my great-grandmother Susan Lincoln Whorton Martin, who is known to have been a fabulous cook.

BUTTER COOKIES
Mix together thoroughly:
1 cup soft Butter
½ cup Sugar
1 Egg
Stir in 3 tsp. Vanilla or Almond Extract.
Sift together and stir in:
3 cups sifted all-purpose Flour
½ tsp. Baking Power

Chill dough. Roll very thin (⅛ inch). Cut into desired shapes and place on ungreased pan. (If desired, press an almond or pecan half into top of each cookie.) Bake at 425 degrees for 5 to 7 minutes until they are a delicate brown. Cool, then decorate with colored icing.

Confectionary Icing:
½ box Confectioner's Sugar
1 tsp. Vanilla or Almond Extract
3 Tbsp. melted Butter
Enough milk/cream to thin down mixture enough to spread on cookies.

—

PEANUT BUTTER COOKIES
Mix together thoroughly:
1 cup half Butter, half Crisco®
1 cup Peanut Butter
1 cup Sugar
1 cup Brown Sugar
2 Eggs
Sift together and stir in:
2-½ cups all-purpose Flour
1 tsp. Baking Powder
1-½ tsp. Baking Soda
½ tsp. Salt

Chill dough. Roll into balls the size of large walnuts. Place 3 inches apart on lightly greased baking sheet. Flatten with fork dipped in flour. Bake at 375 degrees for 10 to 12 minutes until set, but not hard.
Yield: 7 dozen

—

My oldest granddaughter, Elizabeth (Beth), just adores my Snickerdoodles. For those who may not know what Snickerdoodles are, well they just happen to be a great treat and will only tease your taste buds for more. One can become "addictive."

SNICKERDOODLES
Mix together thoroughly:
1 cup soft Shortening

1-½ cups Sugar
2 Eggs
Sift together and stir in:
2-¼ cups sifted all-purpose Flour
2 tsp. Cream of Tartar
1 tsp. Baking Soda
½ tsp. Salt

Chill dough. Roll into balls the size of small walnuts. Roll in mixture of 2 Tbsp. Sugar and 2 Tbsp. Cinnamon. Place about 2 inches apart on ungreased baking sheet. Bake at 400 degrees (moderately hot oven) for 6 to 8 minutes until they are light brown but still soft. (These cookies puff up at first, then flatten out with crinkled tops.)
Yield: about 5 dozen cookies

—

There is nothing more gratifying to me than watching my family enjoy the many different foods and desserts that I have prepared over all these many years. Travis is my connoisseur, especially when it comes to some of his favorite desserts. My cheesecake is one of those.

CHEESECAKE
Crust:
1 cup Flour
¼ cup Sugar
1 tsp. grated Lemon Rind (optional)
1 Egg Yolk
¼ tsp. Vanilla Extract
½ cup soft Butter

Combine the ingredients in a large mixer and blend to form a soft dough. Chill for one hour. Press on bottom and up the sides of a 3 x 9" round, spring-form pan. Preheat oven to 500 degrees.

Filling:
Five 8-oz. pkgs. Cream Cheese
2-¼ cups Sugar
3 Tbsp. Flour
¼ tsp. Salt
6 Eggs (add one at a time)
1 tsp. Vanilla Extract
1 tsp. Almond Extract
1 cup Sour Cream

Filling: Combine ingredients. Blend until smooth. Pour into crust. Bake at 500 degrees for seven minutes. Turn oven down to 200 degrees and bake for one hour and 15 minutes. (If you use a 3 x 10" spring-form pan, same as above, but bake one hour and a half.) Cool away from drafts. Chill. Do not remove sides of pan until completely cool. DO NOT OPEN THE OVEN DOOR ONCE YOU PUT THE CAKE IN. HAVE FAITH AND BE PATIENT. IT'S WORTH IT!

—

Now here is the pie that has priority over any other food that I could put in front of Kelsey. She will eat it morning, noon, and night. With each slice, Kelsey always says, "Nobody makes pumpkin pie as good as Buddy's." I have made Kelsey my little taster. If she likes it, then it has to be good. One day, Kelsey watched me make the filling and when I brought out my secret ingredient, Kelsey was excited and said, "No, Buddy, this is 'our' secret 'cause I know it now, too." Since that time, she tells everyone that she is the only one who knows the secret ingredient in her first love, Buddy's pumpkin pie.

PUMPKIN PIE
3 Eggs, well beaten
1 can Libby® Pumpkin
¾ cup Sugar
½ tsp. Salt
1 tsp. Cinnamon

½ tsp. Ginger

¼ tsp. Cloves

1 can Carnation® Evaporated Milk or Light Cream

Mix the above ingredients together and beat well. Then, just before you pour ingredients into pie pan, Then …

Stir in 3–4 tbsp. Secret Ingredient (only Kelsey knows the secret).

Bake at 425 degrees for 15 minutes, then reduce temperature to 350 degrees for 45 minutes or until knife inserted in center comes out clean.

—

Whenever my two grandchildren spent the night, I always had to make my sour-cream Belgian waffles for their breakfast. It became a ritual. One evening, Kelsey asked me to make my waffles for the morning meal. Unfortunately, I didn't make the batter that night, and I found myself very tired the next morning. I decided to use one of the packaged waffle mixes. I didn't think Kelsey would notice the difference. I acted like nothing was unusual and proudly began to bake them. When the waffle iron's bell rang to announce that the waffles were ready, Travis and Kelsey came running, ready to put a dent into this wonderful treat. With each bite they took, I watched as their faces began to change from delight to puzzlement. Suddenly, Kelsey said, "Buddy, these aren't your waffles. Why didn't you make yours? I can't eat this." It seemed as if they both realized these weren't the real thing. Well, I learned right then and there, I couldn't fake it. Their taste buds knew the difference. I smiled. It was then that I realized that my grandchildren had just created a legend of their own with my sour-cream waffle batter. Hopefully, in time, it may be passed down to their children.

SOUR-CREAM BELGIAN WAFFLES

3 Eggs, separated

1 tsp. Vanilla Extract

¾ cup Milk

¾ cup Sour Cream

½ cup Melted Butter or Margarine

½ tsp. Baking Soda

½ tsp. Salt

2 tsp. Baking Powder

1-½ cups Flour

1. Beat egg yolks in a large bowl
2. Beat in milk, melted butter, vanilla extract, and sour cream.
3. Combine flour, salt and other dry ingredients.
4. Sift into egg mixture and beat well
5. Beat egg whites until stiff, then, carefully fold into batter.

Bake and serve with pure Vermont Maple Syrup or other fruit toppings.
Yield: 12 servings

—

This cake is a must whenever one of us has a birthday. No store-bought birthday cake for Travis and Kelsey. I have strict orders to make this cake and this cake "only." I can put icing on only half of the cake because Travis likes icing on his. Kelsey's half must not have any icing at all, only confectionary sugar sprinkled over her half. This cake also travels with us whenever we go on vacation. It holds up beautifully. The older it gets, the better it tastes. As you can see, we pack well and I am not just talking about suitcases. I love this cake because it goes great with a cup of coffee or a cup of tea.

TROPICAL POUND CAKE

2-¼ cups all-purpose Flour

½ tsp. Salt

½ tsp. Baking Soda

1 tsp. Nutmeg

1 cup Butter

2 cups Sugar

3 Eggs, beaten well

1 cup Sour Cream
1 tsp. Vanilla Extract
1 tsp. Almond Extract

Grease and flour a 10" tube pan. Cream butter and sugar together. Add eggs and beat well, then add vanilla and almond extracts. Sift flour and dry ingredients and add to mixture alternately with sour cream. Beat until smooth, then pour batter into greased and floured 10-inch tube pan. Bake at 325 degrees for 1 hour, then raise oven temperature to 350 degrees and bake another 15 minutes. Cool cake, make icing or glaze.

Glaze:
1 cup Powdered Sugar
2 Tbsp. Lemon Juice

Beat until smooth, then drizzle over top of completely cooled cake and let it run down sides.

Appendix A

FICTION AND POETRY

REFLECTIONS BY ERNESTINE L. MARTIN   Nellie's foot pressed down on the accelerator as she watched the speedometer exceed the local speed limit. "Christ, what am I doing?" Her voice sounded strange. She knew that these weekly trips to see Annie were becoming more and more difficult.

Shaking her head, she bitterly thought of their problem. "Well *politics* did it again. God, how could they have moved the nursing home into this ugly monstrosity? Greyfield is a mental hospital, not a nursing home! *Politics*! *Politics*!" She continued venting. "It's insulting. Annie's poor because the state and the county took her home, her money, and now they have the nerve to consider her indigent. How dare they! What more do they want? The only thing left is her dignity. They're already maneuvering in that direction. I can see it coming. What will become of us, Annie?"

Unconsciously, Nellie had slammed her fist down on the shifter for the automatic transmission. It interrupted her anger. A burning sensation crept over the entire hand. "Damn it, that hurts!" She pulled off the road and stopped. She tried to get feeling back into her hand. "Well, thank God, that's all the damage I've done, today. I better get moving. Annie's waiting." Again, her thoughts turned to Greyfield. "Jesus, a shelter for the homeless, a drug rehabilitation center; both, right next to Annie's ward; I don't believe it! What's next?" Concerns for Annie's safety and care had, once again, presented itself.

"How I wish I could turn around and go home," she thought, "but, I can't. I can't do that to Annie." Nellie began to wail, "Damn you, Annie, damn you for getting sick. I never wanted to admit you. What in the hell could I have done? Oh, I miss you!" Tears slid down her cheeks. Vehemently, Nellie continued to moan as she felt her foot pressing on the pedal. The car again accelerated, as did her anger.

"It's been five years, Annie. Five years in this hellhole! Your funds ran out during your stay at Sunrise Nursing Home. Even if we pooled everything we had, I still had no choice. You'll never know how devastated I felt the day I walked away from you. Leaving you in that cold, miserable ward was the hardest thing I ever did. Every minute, I wonder what kind of care they are really giving you. I know it's just a job to them. The aides and nurses don't give a damn anymore. They've seen it all. Life has left them numb." Her body trembled, her heart pounded, and her anger vented throughout the small car. "Oh, God, this isn't living. Nobody cares!" Nellie moaned as she felt pangs of guilt race through her entire body.

The outburst ended. A calm spread through her body. It felt good. She slowly lifted her foot off the accelerator. Off in the distance, Nellie saw the outline of Greyfield. She gave a deep sigh and wiped the tears from her eyes. At this point, life came in the form of weekly visits. There was nothing else for either of them.

Nellie approached the main driveway of Greyfield. This large, cold-looking building frightened her. She prayed that she would never be one of its occupants. She had seen many of her friends disappear behind its walls, never again to be as they once were.

The strange world within Greyfield was only known by those who visited its inhabitants and the sufferers themselves. Unfortunately, death was usually their only visitor. It came as a welcome caller, ending their pain and suffering. Nellie was amazed at how quickly the outside world forgot these sick and lonely people. Each one waited, day after day, month after month, to see a familiar face, a family member. Terrifying as it was, Nellie faced the realities that existed among many of her peers. Loneliness, physical and mental illnesses, and death were all partners in the game of life. Time no longer

existed for many. Slowly, one by one, they faded away, allowing new patients to take their place. The process would start all over again. It was these thoughts that haunted Nellie.

Nellie felt compelled to make these weekly trips because Annie was family. Childhood brought them together, and their relationship grew throughout the years. They attended the same schools and, later, the same college. They found jobs with the same company. They became engaged at the same time and, once married, their bond became even stronger. The two families became one. They grieved and supported each other as their parents and siblings passed on. Together, they shared a lifetime filled with happiness, hardships, and tragedies. Age made them inseparable.

Alzheimer's disease was destroying Annie as she drifted in and out of reality. Confusion became her partner as well. Nellie could no longer take care of her on a day-to-day basis. She had no other choice but to place Annie in Greyfield. Guilt invaded Nellie's every thought. Their families and friends were deceased or miles away, unable to care for either of them. How could she abandon Annie at this point in their lives? She feared the day when Annie would no longer remember her or need her.

Spotting a parking space near the main entrance, Nellie parked the car and walked toward the oversized front door. She entered the foyer area slowly. An eerie and unwelcome apprehension spread through her body. The door banged shut. She could not retreat. She knew if she did, she would never return.

As Nellie entered a larger room, she gasped. The area was filled with badly deteriorated furniture. "How depressing. Nothing like home," she thought as she glanced around. "Why are the shades drawn? Christ, it's cold in here!" The tiled floor echoed her every step. The walls were bare except for one small sign that showed the direction of the waiting room. It seemed as if life did not exist within the room. No nurse, attendant, or patient was anywhere in sight. A tomb-like, clammy coldness pervaded the entire structure.

Nervously, Nellie continued on. Shivers made the hairs on her arms stand straight up as goose bumps roughened her skin. She began rubbing her hands over her arms. "This is ridiculous," she thought. Again, Nellie's heels echoed and re-echoed with each step, sounding as if she were being followed. She quickened her pace until the waiting room came into full view.

Tall, slender, and fashionably dressed, Nellie appeared younger than her eighty-two years. Her short, bluish-gray hair fell neatly around her gentle face. As small beads of sweat made her conscious of her anxiety, she felt her facial muscles tighten, masking its softness. She wiped her brow. Her face felt hot and flushed.

She approached the receptionist's desk. Annie's doctor had approved Nellie's request to take Annie out for the day. However, if the supervisor on Annie's ward had not received the permission notice, the outing would be cancelled. This problem had occurred many times in the past. She wanted no delays, no questions, and certainly no misunderstandings.

The receptionist, Miss Hefferon, recognized Nellie and immediately called Annie's supervisor to have her brought down. She turned toward Nellie, nodded, and beckoned her to have a seat. The wait seemed endless.

An unexpected commotion of angry voices interrupted the quietness of the room. A door flew open, exposing a scuffle between an attendant and a young patient. Another aide was trying to block the doorway as the young man plunged forward with clenched fists. He began screaming that he wanted to get out. His fist struck the aide, knocking him down. Within seconds, the patient and the attendant were on the floor as well. The struggle continued as shouted profanities echoed throughout the area. This was not what Nellie had expected. An ashen color quickly supplanted the redness in her face. She felt her hands shaking as she tightened her grip on her purse.

Another attendant hurried over to help subdue the young man. Nellie sat frozen, unable to move. Her eyes were fixed upon the struggle until someone was able to close the door, sealing the men within. For a brief moment, Nellie had seen life behind that thick, steel door. It unnerved her. The only escapee was the venting of the patient's anger and then a sickening yet welcoming silence.

Nellie became aware that Miss Hefferon was talking to her, "Are you alright, Nellie? I hope it didn't upset you. That kid is here for drug rehabilitation. They've been renovating this particular ward as a new drug rehabilitation unit. I'm sorry you had to see the incident. Try to relax. Annie should be coming any moment now."

Nellie's voice turned into a whisper, "Yes, I'm alright. God, what's taking so long? They should've had her ready." She began to feel an anger rise within her. She waited. Off in the distance, Nellie heard the familiar sounds of another ward door slamming shut, flaunting its strength to incarcerate patients. Her anger began to diminish as she once again breathed a sigh of relief for not being "*one of them*." She heard voices and footsteps as the steel door across the room opened. "Thank goodness," she thought as Annie and her supervisor appeared. Nellie stood up with arms outstretched, ready to embrace her dear friend.

Annie fell into Nellie's beckoning arms. Then, ever so gently, Nellie moved Annie away from her as she realized that something was different about her friend. "Oh, my God," Nellie heard herself saying. "You're so unkempt! Why didn't someone help wash and dress you?"

Annie's use of cosmetics reminded Nellie of a small child who had just gotten into her mother's makeup. Her lipstick was much too thick, the rouge too dark, and the face powder overdone. Nellie chuckled as she gazed at Annie's funny face. Her chuckle seemed to relax the mood of the moment. Annie threw her arms around Nellie, holding her tightly as if she feared Nellie might disappear. Then Annie gave her several loving kisses on each cheek, stepped away from Nellie, and began laughing. Surprised by this sudden burst of unexpected laughter, Nellie blurted out, "What are you laughing at?"

Still chuckling, Annie said, "My lips are stamped on your cheeks. You look so funny. Now, you're the messy one!" Nellie realized that it had been a long time since she had heard such laughter coming from her friend. "Annie seems more like herself, thank God," she thought as she threw her arms around Annie and hugged her tightly. Annie's body stiffened, no longer relaxed by the moment.

Nellie slowly released her hold, and as she stepped back, she watched a sad expression emerge, destroying Annie's lovely smile. Annie's voice was pathetic and pleading, "I've been waiting so long. Please, take me home."

Guilt began to build within Nellie as she turned away from Annie. Eye contact was impossible at this moment. Nellie knew she had to get control of herself or Annie would be even more devastated than she already appeared. She sat down and began fumbling in her purse. Gaining her composure,

Nellie quietly added, "Perhaps, I should come more often. I'm sorry, Annie. You mean a great deal to me. We're as close as two sisters could ever be. I love you, Annie."

Nellie sensed a queasy feeling in the pit of her stomach. It seemed as if she just noticed how badly Annie's health and appearance were declining. Signs of neglect hovered around her. Annie's wavy, gray hair had turned to a sickening yellow color and hung down to her shoulders. Nellie managed to hide her angry thoughts from Annie: "How could they let her deteriorate like this? I must get her hair washed and cut. It reeks with nicotine. Christ, she needs a damn bath. How dare they! Jesus, she looks like hell."

Nellie continued staring at her dear friend, shocked at how discolored her teeth had become from the constant smoking, as well as the lack of any recent dental care. For the first time, Nellie noticed that Annie seemed to be losing weight. Her clothing hung loosely from her body. Empathy began to fill Nellie, leaving her with thoughts of running away with her friend.

Nellie's thoughts turned to Annie's ward. She remembered the terrible urine odor, as well as the other smells that came with old age, that pervaded every corner of the room. Her nostrils would burn long after she left the nursing home. "Oh, God! Don't let me end up like them. Please," she thought. She felt herself tremble. She felt herself sniff the air, deeply, inhaling as if she were taking her last breath. This gesture angered her. "Christ, I can still smell it." This unexpected motion had, indeed, awakened the stench of death. It seemed to never leave the room; it blanketed each patient, descending and spreading its strong fetor over its next fatality. Nellie gasped, shivering as she looked at Annie. Many times she prayed that Annie would defy death's stench. The doomed seemed to welcome its presence, patiently, almost peacefully. Nellie felt her body tremble. Her eyes searched the large room for an open window. There was none. Her chest tightened, longing for fresh air. Nellie felt empty as she thought how long both of them had suffered the affects of this type of living.

Still boggled by Annie's physical condition and frightened by the realization of Annie's failing health, Nellie's thoughts turned inward, "It seems as if it happened overnight. Why haven't I noticed this before? My God! I'll be all

alone when Annie passes. There will be no one to come to my aid, visit me, or take me out."

Reality began to play its tricks of tomorrow in Nellie's mind. Again her thoughts took over: "Oh, my God! No one will care if I am alive or dead! I'll be totally alone!" Startled by these thoughts, Nellie heard herself mutter, "Never!" She felt her eyes filling with tears. Desperately she tried to mask her pain with a pathetic cough as she struggled not to cry aloud. Nellie turned away from Annie and quickly reached for her handkerchief to dry the tears from her high cheekbones. Suddenly, she realized that Annie was looking at her strangely and then heard her whisper, "Are you talking to me, Nellie? Is something wrong?"

"No, Annie, it's nothing. I guess I just got carried away with my own thoughts and didn't realize that I was talking aloud. I'm sorry." With a deep sigh, she gathered their belongings and stood up.

Nellie took Annie by the arm and hustled her toward the front door, eager for the freedom just beyond it. Nellie pushed the heavy door with all her force. It opened wide, struck the outside railing, and came to a halt. Nellie and Annie gasped as brisk, fresh air permeated their windpipes.

Each one took another deep breath and released it slowly, enjoying the effects of refreshing air and the cool breeze that played about them. It felt good! Nellie lifted her face toward the heavens. Annie's lips parted as if she were saying a silent prayer of thanks for the revitalizing of her body. Freedom seemed to surround both of them as they stood briefly on the small landing, scanning the countryside.

Nellie felt Annie tug at her arm. They moved down the steps and headed toward Nellie's car. After they both got comfortably seated, Nellie started the engine. She turned to Annie, and with a nonchalant gesture said, "We have a lovely afternoon waiting for us, Annie. Shall we see what kind of trouble we can get ourselves into?" With that, she slowly drove the car away from the curb and into the moving traffic.

"Let's go shopping!" Annie responded with such enthusiasm that she surprised Nellie. "I want a red dress." Nellie chuckled at Annie's excitement. They were wrapped in camaraderie. When the town came into view, Nellie stopped talking in order to concentrate on her driving. Annie continued

with her nonsensical chatter. She was totally oblivious to the traffic and Nellie's silence. Suddenly Annie squealed, "Nellie, stop the car! Look at all those shops. Stop the car! Oh, we've passed them. It's too late."

"Don't worry, Annie, we're going to a different mall. We'll have lunch before we start shopping. We're almost there. I think it might be best if we get your hair cut on our way home." Nellie proceeded down the main street until she found a parking space and maneuvered the car into the empty spot. "We're lucky to have gotten a space so close to the entrance of the mall, Annie."

"Yes. Will you help me look for a frilly, red dress for tonight's dance? I want lots of frills 'cause Bob expects me to look my best. Do you think we'll have enough time?" Annie remarked in a more subdued voice.

Surprised by Annie's unexpected comment, Nellie felt an uneasiness. Her friend was beginning to drift in and out of reality: her husband, Bob, had been dead for years. "We will," Nellie reassured her. The two ladies got out of the car and began walking. "Let's go into this restaurant for lunch. It looks cozy and quiet. Are you ready to eat?" With a nod of her head, Annie agreed.

After lunch, they went in several shops, just as they had done many times in the past. However, Nellie began to sense that Annie was showing signs of tiredness. Annie was no longer interested in shopping. She appeared moody, her cheeriness had disappeared, and she seemed annoyed. "I'm tired of shopping, Nellie. Let's go home. It's getting late, and I have to fix dinner. Bob will be home soon." Nellie was beginning to feel the stress of the day as well. "Oh, God, not again!" thought Nellie.

"We'll make this our last stop. I just want to run in and pick up a package. Why don't you sit on that bench opposite the store and wait for me? I'll only be a minute. Don't forget, we must get your haircut before we leave town." Guilt walked away with Nellie.

With a slightly irritated voice, Annie replied, "All right. Please, hurry!" She moved toward the bench. Nellie disappeared into the store. "At least I can sit down and rest," Annie thought. "It will feel good to get off my feet."

Annie settled herself on the bench. She began to feel her body relaxing from the fatigue that had crept throughout her. She watched as the shoppers moved hurriedly down the street, only to disappear into the many shops. She felt envious of the young men and women, their children, the middle-aged

couples, arm-in-arm, as they walked in front of her. Their bodies were strong and healthy, not like the old people that were a part of her everyday existence. She was totally engrossed in her private passing parade. The hot sun beamed down on her. It felt good. It was warm.

Without warning, the scene before her came to a halt. Her parade had to catch up with itself. Annie smiled at a woman sitting across from her, and the lady returned the smile. Annie called over to her, "What a lovely day, so warm and sunny." No reply came as the lady continued to sit very still, just like her. Annie began to feel uncomfortable. She thought that perhaps she knew her from somewhere! But where? The woman continued to stare at her, mimic her; yet said not a word.

Annie cupped her hands over her eyes in order to watched the stranger more closely and asked, "Why are you looking at me like that? Do I know you?" Again, no reply came from across the way. Several people walked by and looked strangely at Annie. The old lady became distorted as they interfered with Annie's view of her. Annie's parade no longer held her attention. She wanted to focus on the stranger across from her. "Who is she? Do I know her?" The uncertainty irritated her.

A small child asked her mother as they passed by, "What's wrong with that old lady, Mama?" Again, another lull in the parade. Annie was thinking the same thing. "God, she does look old." She tried to force another smile along with a slight wave of her hand. The old lady said nothing as she continued to mimic Annie's every move. Annie felt intimidated. It had been a lovely day until now.

"Why is this old lady doing this to me?" Her cheeks turned red from the anger that was building within her. She wanted to leave. "Where is Nellie? What's taking her so long?" She stood up and said loudly, "Nellie, please hurry! I'm so tired." The stranger was now also standing and appeared to be talking to her, but Annie could not hear a word she was saying.

Agitated, Annie shrieked, "If you are talking to me, lady, you'll have to talk louder. I can't hear you." She sat down, and the old lady did the same. "Stop mocking me!" Annie cried out.

Hearing the commotion, a police officer walked over and began to talk to Annie. "Are you alone, ma'am?" Quickly, Annie told him she was waiting

for Nellie. The passers-by had developed into a crowd, nearly surrounding her. Annie began to cry, blurting out that the old lady on that other bench was frightening her.

By now, Annie was in a terrible state of confusion. She turned to the officer, saying, "Where did the old lady go? I can't see her. I never saw her walk away! Oh, where is Nellie? She was only going to be a minute." The officer dispersed the crowd. Once again, the old lady became visible.

Excitedly, Annie cried out, "There she is! Do you see her?" Annie's body began trembling. The officer looked in the direction of the old lady. Ever so gently, he patted Annie's hand, assuring her that there was nothing to fear. He would stay with her until her friend returned.

Annie looked at the old lady and was surprised to see an officer with her, as well. Then she spotted something familiar lying on the stranger's bench. Annie jumped up, screaming, hysterically, "Give that back! You have my purse! Give that back!" The officer picked up Annie's handbag from the bench and placed it into her hand and then suggested that they both sit down and wait for Nellie.

Nellie came running from the store, "My God, Annie, what's wrong? What happened to you? Why is this officer here?" Annie's agitation seemed to lessen as tears rolled down her cheeks. She looked in the direction of the old lady as Nellie tried to comfort her with a hug and reassuring words. The officer kept the shoppers moving as Annie continued to mumble.

"Nellie, look at that old lady. She's making fun of me, and she had my purse. Do you know her? Please, go and see who she is." Nellie moved away from Annie. She turned in the direction of the old lady. It was then that she realized her friend saw a reflection of herself in the huge plate-glass window. Nellie put her arms around Annie, pulled her close, and explained what she had seen.

Angrily, Annie pushed away, "I don't like you, Nellie; you're mean. I don't look like that. I'm not that old lady! Take me home, right now. I'm going to tell Bob on you. You're not nice at all." Annie began to cry.

Nellie thanked the officer for being so kind and staying with Annie until she returned. He wished them well and went about his policing. After a few moments, Nellie gently took Annie's hand and led her away, hoping that her

explanation of the incident would be forgotten. However, both ladies were visibly upset by the scene. Such a hideous reflection, an old lady. "That's not me! I'm not an ugly old lady. Please, God, just let me die," sobbed Annie.

Nellie found herself shaking as well. The thought "What if it were me?" sent shivers down her spine. She felt chilled as she wrapped her arms across her chest to get some warmth back into her trembling body. The remembrance of the hospital's stench seemed to fill Nellie's nostrils. Once, again, she felt the same burning sensation. Guilt, fear, and panic began to take over within her.

"Oh, God, please, not me!" She knew those frightening walls were closing in on her. It was just a matter of time before she became another Annie.

The ladies walked toward the car. The haircut was no longer important. An occasional child would run past them, bringing a slight smile to their strained faces. Neither woman could remove the depression that had invaded their day.

Nellie hustled Annie across the street. Silently they walked until they arrived at the car. Nellie opened the car door for Annie and said firmly, "I'm taking you home. I'm not taking you back to that hospital." Then she got in, switched the car radio on, and turned the tuning dial until she found soothing music. It relaxed both of them. Nellie reassured Annie that everything was going to be fine. She felt serene in her decision to keep Annie with her. For the first time, she knew what she had to do.

During the drive home, Nellie was surprised as Annie suddenly talked about their youth, their wedding days, and how beautiful they both were. She spoke of their husbands. How manly their young men looked as they walked down the aisle to join them. Nellie found herself enjoying Annie's remembrance of past years, since she had not heard her speak of their past in a long time. Nellie breathed easier; Annie seemed like herself, like the Annie she knew long ago.

A slight clearing of the throat indicated that Annie was on the verge of crying. Nellie took Annie's hand in her own and gave it a gentle squeeze. She found it necessary to wipe away her own tears. Again, Annie surprised Nellie as she changed the subject to the birth of Nellie's first child. "I was excited

as you, Nellie, remember? Many people thought I was Elizabeth's mother. I loved that thought. She was like my own, wasn't she? I prayed so many times to have had a child of my own. I guess the good Lord figured Elizabeth needed two mothers. Looking back, I believe He was right. She was a handful."

"Heavens! Annie, stop talking for a minute. Give me a chance to say a word or two." Childlike, Annie stopped, turned toward Nellie and waited. Nellie smiled and continued, "You were always there for us, Annie. When Elizabeth died in that car wreck, it was you who got us back on our feet. I wanted to die with her when we heard the news. Even though you were as devastated as we, you knew our family had to accept her death and get on with our lives. It took a long time, Annie. Without you, our family was not complete, but time has changed our lives, my dear. Everyone that we loved has gone. We are the only ones left." Annie rested her head against the back of the seat and nodded in agreement. Again, Nellie patted Annie's hand. Words were no longer necessary.

In the driveway, Nellie pressed the automatic garage door opener and pulled into the garage. Annie had fallen asleep. Nellie did not wake her. She rolled up all the windows except one and left the engine running as she pressed the button to close the garage door. She walked toward the back of the car and picked up her garden hose lying on the floor. She stood staring at the tailpipe a few moments, deep in thought. Then she took the hose and stuffed it into the tailpipe, tying it on with the scarf from her dress. She took the other end and squeezed it in the nearly closed back window.

She got back into the driver's seat. Resting her head against the back of her seat and glancing over at Annie, Nellie found her thoughts drifting back in time. "We go back a long ways, dear. We shared so many things: the high school dances, our weddings, our terrible grief over the loss of our husbands and Elizabeth."

Nellie felt a sudden coldness pass over her. She shivered, releasing an agonizing moan. Her life passed before her, taking her back to their youth. Softly, she uttered, "Ah, yes, we were so happy, so young." Nellie paused in her thoughts. "We had no idea what life was all about, did we? I remember your mother always giving orders to our dates to have us home at a decent

hour." Nellie continued to reminisce. "God, every time mother would tell them to be gentlemen, we wanted to run and hide! Remember, how it took what seemed like hours before we could talk to them?" Tears filled Nellie's eyes as the moment revealed their beautiful and innocent youth, so short-lived, so long ago. "Oh, those precious years, gone, long gone, never to be again."

Drowsiness began to interfere with her thoughts and words. She looked at Annie and slowly whispered, "Forgive me, Annie." At that moment, a smile crept across Annie's face as if she understood and was giving her consent. Nellie's eyes became heavy. A lethargic sensation took over her body. She gently placed Annie's hand in hers and slowly drifted off.

The engine kept running, and the radio continued playing.

—

GENERATIONS • WALKING DOWN THE PATH OF LIFE

When I was a child, the water was clear. It sparkled and glowed as its taste overflowed. It filled our good earth as we drank in its worth. No dirt was found in our water so pure. No poison made us fear to drink the gift God made so clear.

The air smelled fresh, and it tasted the same as each breath we inhaled gave us no pain. We could not see it nor feel it at all. It was part of God's plan for everyone to enjoy.

Purity reigned in the souls God made until we decided to throw it away. We took our souls out of His Grace and destroyed the spirit that He so embraced. We failed to follow His rules of life, causing the pain we suffer each night. Is this His way to show us His anger by making life's road so difficult to handle?

Do our souls lie buried forevermore beneath the filth we now adore? We failed to preserve the good things in life, ready to settle for drugs, sex, and a world full of strife.

We live with excuses to satisfy our needs, but God will make us fall on our knees, to explain our decline in our worldly ways, to explain our downfall to His dismay. Never to be the way it was, for purity came from God

whom we should love and adore. Today is different. Something is gone.
Please, God, forgive us, for we have strayed far from your home.

There is no return. We have gone too far. His works, His world is torn apart.
A sadder world we have made as we watch it dissolve into decay, removing the good we once had, leaving behind so much bad.

The Golden Years are upon me now as I wander back in time. Searching for the things I lost which I will never find, for they probably never existed, only in my mind.

There are no good old days and never will there be. It is just a fantasy made up to help us think we're free. Each generation is the same but none of us want to take the blame. Free of the terrible things we did to God's land and our fellow man.

How much have times really changed? Again, each generation is to blame. We failed our God who stands above, looking down with tears of love. Yesterday's memories are all the same. Each generation will feel the pain as their memories, slowly, melt away. Memories twisted, more false than true, that can slowly disappear and never again be reviewed.

We want to believe that we caused no harm as we walked down life's path, arm in arm. We want to remember only the good things that passed. Yet, we cover our face when we see the truth, our sins, the damage we did in our youth.

We close our eyes. None of us are free. We owe each other a chance at life, a life filled only with love and decency. Perhaps, then God's tears will cease to flow when he sees how much we love the gifts he spread among the young and the old.

—ERNESTINE L. MARTIN

—

Nature at Work

As I strolled down the quiet country road,
    my mind drifted back to other days
        when youth filled my heart in every way.

I ran through the fields, which were many back then,
        enjoying their fragrance and sounds within.
The smell of the fresh cut hay hung thick
        as the beauty of the wild flowers
            sought to be picked.
The small and fragile buttercup waited to be found
        as the softness of its yellow reflected on the ground.

The bluebells were scattered in groups of their own,
        creating a fragrance that lingered and flowed
            over the fields that I freely roamed.
Each tiny bell was as blue as the sky
        as it swayed, slowly, side to side.

The black-eyed Susans waved gently in the breeze,
        resembling drunken soldiers out on a spree.
They held a special beauty, all of their own,
        deep yellow to orange rays with a dark black cone.
The white daisies looked beautiful
        as their purity reigned high.
Each stood looking straight up at the sky.
Their small fluffy petals
        blended with the color of the clouds,
Tempting every intruder before their beauty died.

Perched on the head of a thistledown
        a bright colored goldfinch released a mellow sound,
            per-chick-o-ree, per-chick-o-ree,
                a song as sweet as it could be.
The seeds that came from the thistle head,
        filled its feathered belly for the rest of the day.

The fields came alive as flocks swooped by,
        descending, searching for a special surprise

that laid hidden, scattered,
Unseen by the human eye.
This was their paradise. This was their home,
provided by God so long ago.

Silence overtook the noisy field
as the birds settled down to a tasty meal
of seeds from flowers that swayed above
and insects that scurried deep down in the mud,
sharing God's gifts of beauty and love.
The bumblebees buzzed, and the butterflies fluttered
over the tops of most of the flowers.
They helped to create nature's harmony and balance
as each added their special God-given talent.

The beautiful colors that nature displayed
made a trip to the country a worthwhile day.
For the eyes to gaze on, for the heart to feel,
the excitement of nature in its wonderful field.
No matter whether one is young or old,
nature is fascinating and good for the soul.

—ERNESTINE L. MARTIN

—

A DAY ON THE BEACH

I walked along the edge of the shore,
listening to the sea's mighty roar.
The frothy white foam twixt my toes
reminded me of the first winter snow.

The waves beat the sand with all their might.
I stopped and stared at the turbulent sight.

I felt the power of each swell so near,
as it forced the water into the atmosphere.
The spray of the ocean upon my face
gave me a thrill I still embrace.
Refreshingly, soothing in its own way,
it left me thankful for a lovely day.

It made me feel warm, contented within,
helped by the spray upon my skin.
A feeling of connection slowly began,
as the endless waves crept o'er the sand.

Slowly, I maneuvered through the shifting land,
as the tides of the seas altered the sand.
The crestless waves no longer spanned,
the area where the jetties began.

The sandpipers scuttered to the edge of the surf,
picking and searching about their wet turf.
The need to eat in order to survive,
created these hardships in keeping alive.

Their long, thin legs scurried the watery sand,
each piper followed a chain of command.
I watched in amusement at this playful scene,
unfolding before me with a quiet serene.

The sand crabs sprinted in and out of their holes,
slithering on the slippery sand, out of control.
They feared the seagulls might plummet and fall,
to snatch up their dinner, regardless how small.

My eyes searched the sand, the tide moved out,
seashells became plentiful as they tumbled about.

Their colors, like rainbows, as the sea and sun met,
glittered upon the shells, a beauty I'll ne'er forget.
I looked for something special
        that might wash upon the shore.
Like a brilliant gem, a silver piece,
        a coin I could restore.
A treasure from yesterday
        would be a wondrous find.
Something from another time
        before I was designed.

The sea had become calm, not a wave in sight,
as the beach became quiet, as quiet as night.
I gathered my treasures and finds of the day,
and, slowly, began to walk away.

The sky was ablaze as the sun went down,
the evening darkness wore its crown.
Filled with sparkling stars that showed the way,
for the moon to travel into another day.

It was time to leave the beach behind,
only in spirit but, not in my mind.
I tucked it away for another day,
when I may want to go and play.

—ERNESTINE L. MARTIN

Appendix I

A VISIT TO BRIAN'S HOUSE—RECIPES There are special desserts that we travel with whenever we are going on vacation. This is one of them. I pack them in my favorite tin box and we munch on them from the time we leave home until the tin is empty. I'm sure we must look like a bunch of gypsies as we roll along the highway, singing, laughing, and eating ourselves silly with all the goodies I make for such an important event.

BUDDY'S BROWNIES
1 cup Crisco®
4 oz. Hershey's® unsweetened Chocolate
1-½ cups sifted all-purpose Flour
1 tsp. Baking Powder
1-½ tsp. Salt
4 Eggs, beaten until light yet thick (about 5 minutes)
2 cups Sugar
2 tsp. Vanilla Extract
2 cups Pecans/Walnuts, chopped coarsely

Preheat oven to 350 degrees.

In double boiler, melt Crisco® and chocolate together, then let cool.

Sift dry ingredients together.

Beat eggs until thick. Add sugar, chocolate mixture, and vanilla extract to beaten eggs, and blend well.

Add dry ingredients and nuts into mixture. Mix well, then pour into greased and floured oblong baking pan (13 x 9 x 2"). Bake for 30 to 35 minutes. Let cool, then cut into squares.

Yield: approximately 25–30 brownies.

—

Another wonderful treat that we always carry with us whenever we travel the open road is my Blueberry Muffins. Oh, my, they are good and easy to handle. This recipe makes at least twenty muffins. They have been on Interstate Highways 95, 81, 10 along Florida's panhandle area; Route 70 in North Carolina; and the entire length of the Garden State Parkway. I firmly believe in the statement, "Don't leave home without them." They are moist and not crumbly at all. As soon as the Jersey blueberries are ready to be picked, I'm shopping for all the necessary ingredients. Time waits for no one, and neither do Jersey blueberries. I buy many quarts. What I don't use right away, I freeze so I will have that flavor long after their season is over. Pepper always said that he hated to tell me how much he liked something I would make because he would then get it every other day for the next year. I do believe he was right, as much as I hate to admit it. Oh, well, cooking and baking were and still are two of my loves. Thanks, Great-Grandmother Martin: Your legacy sure has had a positive impact on me and my family. May it continue through the many generations to come.

BLUEBERRY MUFFINS

½ tsp. Baking Powder

2-⅔ cups self-rising Flour

1 tsp. Nutmeg

1 cup Buttermilk

2 Eggs, beaten

1 stick of Butter, melted

2-½ cups of Blueberries

1-¼ cups Sugar (Depends on how sweet the berries are. Add more, if necessary.)

Thoroughly mix 2-½ cups of flour with baking powder, sugar, eggs, and buttermilk. Add melted butter and blend together. Mix berries with remaining flour (2 Tbsp.). Fold berries into batter and spoon into greased muffin pans or paper cups (make each ⅔ full). Bake at 400 degrees for 20 to 25 minutes (until tops are golden brown).

Yield: 20–24 Muffins

Appendix J

SEVEN LAYERS OF LOVE AND HOW IT CONTINUED TO GROW—
RECIPE This recipe is the same cake my grandmother always made for me when I visited her during my youth. My story describes the continuous growth of this layer cake and why it meant so much to me. I hope that anyone who makes this cake will keep my story in mind and will enjoy it as much as I. It truly is a cake that grew with an unforgettable love and nostalgia that will last forever. I believe that is why it is so magically tasty.

15-TO-17 LAYER CAKE (FROM ORIENTAL, NORTH CAROLINA)
Cake:
2 cups Sugar
2 sticks Margarine
3 cups self-rising Flour
1 cup Milk (judge on amount)
5 eggs, separated
Dash of Vanilla Extract

Cream sugar and margarine. Add egg yolks and flour. Use milk as needed and add vanilla extract. Beat egg whites and fold into batter. Add more milk to make batter thinner than normal (similar to pancake batter).

Spray 9" cake pans with Pam® Cooking Spray. Pour in just enough batter to cover bottom of pans. Bake at 300 degrees for a very short time, until

cake appears done. (Each layer will look like a large pancake when it is taken from the pan.)

Rotate 6 pans for speed, be sure and spray pans each time with Pam® Cooking Spray. Stack on wire racks until all are done and icing is cooked.

Icing:
1 cup Hershey's® Cocoa
Dash of Salt
6 Tbsp. Margarine
4-½ cups Sugar
2-¼ cups Milk
1-½ tsp. Vanilla Extract

Combine coca, sugar and salt in large saucepan, add milk gradually and mix well. Bring to a boil on high heat, stirring continuously. Reduce heat to medium, but continue to boil mixture, without stirring, until a small amount of mixture, dropped in cold water first, forms a soft ball. Remove from heat, add vanilla extract and margarine to mixture. DO NOT STIR. Allow to cool slightly, then ice layers quickly to prevent icing from becoming hard. If it seems to be too hard, add small amount of milk to keep the needed consistency.

Appendix K

CAPE MAY WITH KEVIN AND MINDY—RECIPE My cousin, Diana, shared this recipe with me. It was originally my Aunt Jessie's recipe and is the best deviled crab I have ever eaten. Whenever we are leaving Cape May, we always stop at the Lobster House Fish Market to fill my large cooler with a taste of the seashore. Because they have such fresh seafood, I have them pack my shrimp and crabmeat on ice to keep it cold until we get home.

DEVILED CRAB
White Sauce:
¼ cup Butter
¼ cup Flour
2 cups Milk
Melt butter, add flour, and whisk-in milk; cook until thickened.

Crabmeat:
1 lb. Lump
1 lb. Claw
Spices:
2 Tbsp. Worcestershire Sauce
1 Tbsp. prepared Mustard
2 Tbsp. Tomato Catsup
¼ tsp. Salt

¼ tsp. Pepper

1 ½ tsp. Hot Sauce (either Tabasco® Red Pepper Sauce or Cayenne
    Pepper)—I prefer the Tabasco® Red Pepper Sauce.

½ cup Saltines, crumbled, add to Crabmeat, then mix all together.

Mix spices together and add to cooled white sauce. Taste spice sauce before
you add the crabmeat. Also you must pick through the crabmeat and remove
any pieces of shell. Add crumbled Saltines to the crabmeat and mix it with
the spice sauce. Then put mixture into crab shells, sprinkle paprika on top
of crab, and bake at 350 degrees for 35 to 45 minutes.